S0-BJI-427

THE RANDOM HOUSE

PERSONAL COMPUTER DICTIONARY

PHILIP E. MARGOLIS

RANDOM HOUSE
NEW YORK

Library of Congress Cataloging-in-Publication Data

Margolis, Philip E.
    The Random House personal computer dictionary / Philip Margolis.—1st ed.
        p.   cm.
    ISBN 0–679–73480–5
    1. Microcomputers—Dictionaries.   I. Title.
II. Title: Personal computer dictionary.
QA76.15.M37   1991
004.16′03—dc20   91-15419
                                                                CIP

Book design by M 'N O Production Services, Inc.
Illustrations by Jared Schneidman Design Inc.

Manufactured in the United States of America
98765432

PREFACE

I often get the same two-part response from people when I reveal that I'm a technical writer by profession. The first reaction is puzzlement; the second, after I explain by confessing that I write computer manuals, is a torrent of complaints about the low quality of these books.

Naturally, I assumed that these people were referring to manuals written by other writers. I would commiserate, agreeing that it was a shame that not all technical writers could write lucid prose like me.

Over the years, however, I have come to realize that the problem is not necessarily that technical writers don't know how to write clearly—at least, that's not the primary problem. The main problem is that in an effort to be precise, technical writers are forced to use a highly specialized language.

This point crystallized in my mind as more and more friends and relatives bought computers, mainly for word processing. Frequently they would call me with a problem. "What does the manual say?" I would ask. They would reply that the manual might as well be written in Greek—it was incomprehensible. But when I read the same maligned manuals, I usually understood them without any problem. And once I defined all the terms for my friends, they too could understand them.

That "computerese" is so cryptic is not entirely accidental. One of its purposes is to serve as a password into the inner circle, instantly tagging an individual as a computer expert or novice. Anyone who has ever purchased a computer knows how salespeople like to fling the jargon around. If you blink, you mark yourself as a potential sucker. Even computer professionals often rank each other based on computerese proficiency.

Every complex discipline, whether it be law, medicine, or automobile mechanics, has its own specialized vocabulary, but two factors make computerese special. First, computers have become ubiquitous; many non-experts use computers every day. This certainly isn't true in other fields; you normally hire a lawyer, for example, when you need someone to translate a piece of "legalese." Imagine hiring a computer consultant every time you came across an incomprehensible passage in a computer manual!

The other factor that makes computer jargon special is that computers are still difficult to use. With cars, you just turn the key and go. Most people don't know the difference between a carburetor and a distributor, but that doesn't stop them from driving their car—at least until it breaks down. With computers, on the other hand, even the simplest programs require a basic understanding of how computers work and which parts are which.

There's not much hope that computerese will go away; the precision allowed by technical terms cannot be reproduced with parochial words. People who use computers (by choice or by necessity) must bite the bullet and learn the terminology. This dictionary is designed to help people do this as painlessly as possible.

One of the main goals of this dictionary is to demystify computers. Any reasonably intelligent person can understand how computers work. Once you understand the language, you realize that most of the concepts are relatively simple.

This dictionary differs from other computer dictionaries in that it is directed at laypeople rather than computer professionals. Consequently, I've made a special effort to define terms in the simplest language possible without sacrificing accuracy. I have not included every term in existence. Instead, I have focused on the types of terms that users of personal computers are likely to encounter. This means that I have left out many programming and engineering terms. In addition, I have concentrated on particular types of computer applications that are widespread, such as word processing, desktop publishing, and communications.

In writing each definition, I imagined a nonexpert coming across the term in an advertisement or instruction manual. I have tried to provide enough information to enable the reader to go forward and get beyond the jargon barrier. Many of the definitions, therefore, are longer than one might expect in a dictionary. The book is really a cross between a dictionary and an encyclopedia.

There are few things more frustrating than looking up a word and finding that the definition contains ten new mysterious terms that you need to look up. I have tried to avoid these circular definitions as much as possible, although sometimes they're unavoidable. I have at least refrained from using terms that are not included in this dictionary. In addition, most of the definitions include cross references to lead you to more information about a particular topic.

Like all languages, computerese is constantly evolving. Different companies use the same terms in different ways, and as the technology advances, new terms are coined to express the never-before-expressed. Even as I write, technical writers and editors are huddled together around the globe arguing about the differences between "option" and "switch." I have tried to reflect this shiftiness in the language, although I'm sure that some of my definitions will be dated by the time this book goes to print. Alas, obsolescence comes with the territory.

Many people have helped me to produce this book. In particular, I want to thank my three technical reviewers—Peter Darnell, Paul Hayslett, and Doug McGlathery—who made innumerable and invaluable suggestions. Obviously, any flaws that remain are my own. Finally, I want to thank my editor, Enid Pearsons, for her sage counsel and unflagging enthusiasm for the project.

Philip E. Margolis
Zürich, 1991

INTRODUCTION

"Computerese" is a tightly integrated language. To some extent, you don't know anything until you know everything. Most of the definitions in this dictionary include extensive cross references to help you overcome the circularity of the language. By jumping from one term to another, you can learn about an entire subject.

The following list organizes selected terms into broad categories. If you are interested in learning about a particular area of computer science, you might start by looking up the terms in the appropriate category. You can start with any term and the cross references will lead you to related terms.

ARTIFICIAL INTELLIGENCE

artificial intelligence	robotics
expert system	voice recognition
neural network	

COMMUNICATIONS

acoustic coupler	check sum
answer-only modem	communications
asynchronous	communications protocols
auto-answer	communications software
auto-redial	direct-connect modem
bandwidth	even parity
baseband transmission	external modem
baud rate	FAX machine
Bell 103	FAX modem
Bell 212A	full duplex
binary file transfer	Group 3 protocol
bps	Group 4 protocol
CCITT	half duplex
channel	handshaking

DATA STORAGE

volume   worm
Winchester disk drive   write-protect

DISPLAY MONITORS

active-matrix LCD	multifrequency monitor
analog monitor	multiscanning monitor
autosizing	non-interlaced
backlighting	NTSC
composite video	page-white display
convergence	paper-white display
CRT	pixel
digital monitor	plasma display
display screen	reverse video
dot pitch	RGB monitor
electroluminescent display	screen flicker
fixed-frequency monitor	screen saver
flat-panel display	scroll
flat technology monitor	smart terminal
gas-plasma display	Supertwist
genlock	terminal
intelligent terminal	TFT
interlacing	touch screen
LCD	TTL monitor
monitor	VDT radiation
monochrome	

GRAPHICS

aliasing	GEM
antialiasing	graphics-based
autotracing	graphics file formats
Bézier curves	gray scaling
bit map	handle
block graphics	HPGL
CAD	IGES
CAD/CAM	jaggies
CADD	paint program
CAE	palette
CGM	PCX
character mode	PIC
dithering	PICT file format
draw program	plot
DVI	plotter
DXF	presentation graphics
EPS	quickdraw

INTERFACES

alert box	insertion point
box	menu
button	menu bar
character based	menu driven
click	Microsoft Windows
command driven	moving-bar menu
cursor	overlaid windows
cursor position	pointer
desktop	pop-up window
dialog box	radio button
double click	scroll bar
drag	shift clicking
graphical interface	tear-off menu
GUI	tiled windows
hot key	title bar
I-beam pointer	window
icon	

MEMORY

DRAM	PROM
dynamic RAM	RAM
EEPROM	RAM cache
EPROM	ROM
flash memory	SIMM
main memory	SRAM
memory	static RAM
nonvolatile memory	virtual memory
page mode memory	volatile memory
parameter RAM	VRAM

NETWORKS

AppleTalk	Ethernet
ARCnet	FDDI
ARPANET	fiber optics
BITNET	gateway
broadband transmission	groupware
broadband ISDN	heterogeneous network
broadcast	ISDN
bulletin board service	local-area network
client/server architecture	local-area wireless network
connectivity	(LAWN)
diskless workstation	LocalTalk
electronic mail	NetBIOS

NetWare
network
network interface card
node
NFSnet
peer-to-peer
public carrier
server

token ring network
topology
TOPS
Tymnet
USENET
voice mail
wide-area network
workgroup computing

OPERATING SYSTEMS AND ENVIRONMENTS

ANSI.SYS
autoexec.bat
background
batch file
batch processing
BIOS
boot
clipboard
COM file
command language
command processor
CONFIG.SYS
configuration file
Control Panel
control program
CP/M
demand paging
desk accessory
directory
distributed processing
DOS
environment
EXE file
executable file
execute
expanded memory
extended memory
external command
file
file allocation table
file management
filename
Finder
folder

hidden file
high memory
internal command
launch
LIM memory
load
loader
memory resident
MS-DOS
Multifinder
multiprocessing
multitasking
multi-user
operating environment
operating system
OS/2
paging
parallel processing
parent directory
path
pathname
pipe
pop-up utility
Presentation Manager
process
realtime
redirection
root directory
segment
swap
system folder
systems software
task switching
time sharing

transaction processing
TSR
Unix
utility

virtual memory
working directory
Xenix

PRINTERS

Adobe PostScript
carriage
cartridge
cps
daisy-wheel printer
dot-matrix printer
draft mode
draft quality
font card
font cartridge
form feed
friction feed
HP-compatible printer
ImageWriter
impact printer
ink-jet printer
laser printer
LaserWriter
letter quality
line printer

liquid crystal shutter printer
LPT
near letter-quality
non-impact printer
page description language
paper feed
PCL
pin
PostScript
ppm
printer
resident font
sheet feeder
smoothing
soft font
spooler
thermal printer
toner
tractor feed

PROGRAMMING CONCEPTS

absolute address
address
address space
algorithm
AND operator
API
argument
arithmetic expression
arithmetic operator
array
assign
base address
beta test
binary
binary file
bind
bomb

Boolean expression
Boolean logic
Boolean operator
bug
call
character string
code
compiler
constant
copy protection
data structure
data type
debug
debugger
declare
double precision
dynamic variable

exclusive OR
expression
filter
floating-point number
function
hacker
hexadecimal
inclusive OR operator
invoke
iteration
kludge
library
link
linker
listing
loop
macro
module
NOR operator
NOT operator
object code
object oriented
octal
offset

operand
operator
OR operator
procedure
program
relational operator
relative address
reserved word
routine
run-time error
scientific notation
script
semantics
software
source code
stack
statement
static variable
subscript
system call
systems analyst
tree structure
variable
XOR operator

PROGRAMMING LANGUAGES

Ada
assembler
assembly language
authoring tool
BASIC
COBOL
C
C++
FORTRAN

GW-BASIC
high-level language
interpreter
LISP
low-level language
machine language
Modula-2
Pascal
programming language

SPREADSHEETS AND DATABASE MANAGEMENT

aggregate function
audit trail
browse
cell
column
database

database management
   system
data dictionary
data processing
dBASE
distributed database

Types of Computers

Excel
export
field
fixed length
flat-file database
formula
fourth-generation language
hypercard
Hypertext
import
join
Lotus 1-2-3
on-line service
query

query by example
query language
range
recalculate
record
relational database
report writer
spreadsheet
SQL
table
three-dimensional spreadsheet
variable length
variable-length record

TYPES OF COMPUTERS

Amiga
AT
clone
computer
diskless workstation
IBM PC
laptop computer
Macintosh computer
mainframe
minicomputer

notebook computer
palmtop
PC
personal computer
portable
PS/2
slate PC
supercomputer
workstation

VIDEO

CGA
EGA
graphics mode
Hercules graphics
MCGA
MDA
SVGA
Texas Instruments Graphics Architecture

text mode
TI 34010
VESA
VGA
video adapter
video mode
video standards
XGA

WORD PROCESSING AND DESKTOP PUBLISHING

boldface
clip art
continuous tone

Courier font
cut
desktop publishing

dingbat
editor
embedded command
even header
feathering
fixed pitch
flush
font
font family
footer
greeking
gutter
half tone
hanging paragraph
hard return
header
hyphenation
insert mode
justification
justify
kerning
landscape
layout
leading
left justify
line editor
mail merge
margins
microspacing
microjustification
monospacing

odd header
orphan
outline font
page break
page layout program
pagination
pica
pitch
portrait
preview
proportional font
proportional pitch
ragged
redlining
rule
ruler
sans serif
scalable font
search and replace
serif
soft return
spelling checker
style sheet
text wrap
thumbnail
typeface
vertical justification
widow
word processing
word wrap
WYSIWYG

PERSONAL
COMPUTER
DICTIONARY

abort: To end a program or function before it has finished naturally. The term *abort* refers to both requested and unexpected terminations. For example, many applications let you abort a search or a print job by pressing a specified *abort key*. On the other hand, programs can abort unexpectedly for any of the following reasons:

- bugs in the software
- unexpected input that the program cannot handle
- hardware malfunction

When a program aborts, you are usually returned to the operating system shell level. Contrast *abort* with *crash,* which makes the entire system, including the operating system, unusable.

➡ See also *bomb; crash; hang; shell.*

absolute address: A fixed address in memory. The term *absolute* distinguishes it from a *relative address*, which indicates a location by specifying a distance from another location (see Figure 1 at *address*). Absolute addresses are also called *real addresses* and *machine addresses*.

➡ See also *address; relative address.*

accelerator board: A type of *expansion board* that makes a computer faster by adding a faster CPU or FPU. Accelerator boards provide a relatively inexpensive way to increase the performance of a computer.

There are many accelerator boards for IBM PCs and compatibles. For example, a *286 accelerator board* contains an Intel 80286 microprocessor and will effectively give an IBM PC/XT the same computing power as an IBM PC/AT. Similarly, a *386 accelerator board* contains an Intel 80386 microprocessor. Accelerator boards are also available for the Apple Macintosh.

Note that adding an accelerator board to a computer affects only the speed of the CPU (and sometimes main memory). This may not have a large effect on your applications if the limiting factors are the speed of the disk drive or the bus.

Another way to upgrade a computer to a faster model is to replace the motherboard.

➡ See also *bus; coprocessor; CPU; expansion board; floating-point number; FPU; IBM PC; Intel microprocessors; main memory; microprocessor; motherboard; RAM.*

access: (v) (1) To use. For example, programs can *access memory,* which means they read data from or write data to main memory. A user can access files, directories, computers, or peripheral devices.

(2) More specifically, *access* often means to read data from or write data to a mass storage device. The time it takes to locate a single byte of information on a mass storage device is called the *access time.*

➡ See also *access time; byte; mass storage; memory; random access; read; write.*

(n) (1) The act of reading data from or writing data to a storage device.

(2) A privilege to use computer information in some manner. For example, a user might be granted *read access* to a file, meaning that the user can read the file but cannot modify or delete it. Most operating systems have several different types of access privileges that can be granted or denied to specific users or groups of users.

accessory slot: Same as *expansion slot.*

access time: The time a program or device takes to
locate a single piece of information and make it
available to the computer for processing (Table 1).
DRAM (dynamic random-access memory) chips for
personal computers have access times of 50 to 150
nanoseconds (billionths of a second). *Static RAM
(SRAM)* has access times as low as 15 nanoseconds.
The access time of memory should be fast enough to
keep up with the CPU. If not, the CPU will waste a
certain number of clock cycles, which makes it
slower.

Note, however, that reported access times can
be misleading because most memory chips, especially DRAM chips, require a pause between back-
to-back accesses. This is one reason why SRAM is
so much faster than DRAM, even when the reported
access times are equivalent; SRAM requires fewer
refreshes, so the pause between back-to-back accesses is smaller.

Access time is also frequently used to describe
the speed of disk drives. A fast hard disk drive for
a personal computer will support access times of
about 9 to 28 milliseconds (thousandths of a second). This means that the drive can make about 500

**Table 1: Typical Access Times for Different
Computer Devices**

DEVICE	TYPICAL ACCESS TIMES
SRAM	15–50 nanoseconds
DRAM	50–120 nanoseconds
EPROM	55–250 nanoseconds
ROM	55–250 nanoseconds
Hard Disk Drive	9–100 milliseconds
Erasable Optical	20–200 milliseconds
CD-ROM	300–800 milliseconds
DAT Drive	about 20 seconds
QIC Drive	about 40 seconds
8 mm Tape Drive	40–500 seconds

data accesses per second. Note that this is about 200 times slower than average DRAM.

The access time for disk drives (also called the *seek time*) refers to the time it actually takes for the *read/write head* to locate a sector on the disk. This is an average time since it depends on how far away the head is from the desired data. The performance of disk drives can be improved through special techniques such as *caching* and *interleaving*.

➧ See also *access; clock speed; CPU; disk cache; disk drive; dynamic RAM; head; interleaving; nanosecond; RAM; static RAM; wait state.*

accounting software: A class of computer programs that perform accounting operations. The simplest accounting programs, sometimes called *personal finance managers,* are single-entry systems that automate check writing and record keeping.

Double-entry systems include functions for general ledger, accounts receivable, and accounts payable. More sophisticated systems also support functions for payroll, inventory, invoicing, and fixed assets. Some high-end systems even support sales analysis and time billing.

acoustic coupler: A device onto which a telephone handset is placed to connect a computer with a network. The acoustic coupler might also contain a modem, or the modem could be a separate device.

Popular in the 1970s, acoustic couplers are no longer widely used. Nowadays, telephones connect directly to a modem via modular telephone connectors. This produces better connections than acoustic couplers and avoids the problems produced by irregularly shaped telephones. Still, acoustic coupler modems are useful in some situations such as in hotel rooms where the telephone cable is anchored to the wall. Modems that do not use an acoustic coupler are sometimes called *direct-connect* modems.

➧ See also *modem; network.*

active: Refers to objects currently being displayed or
used. For example, in graphical user interfaces, the
active window is the window currently receiving
mouse and keyboard input. In spreadsheet applications, the *active cell* is the cell, usually highlighted,
in which data can be entered or modified. The *active
program* is the program currently running.

➮ See also *cell; graphical user interface; spreadsheet; window.*

active-matrix LCD: A type of *LCD* in which the
screen is refreshed much more frequently than in
conventional LCDs. The most common type of active-matrix LCD is based on a technology known as
TFT (**t**hin **f**ilm **t**ransistor). The two terms, *active
matrix* and *TFT*, are often used interchangeably.

➮ See also *TFT.*

Ada: A high-level programming language developed in
the late 1970s and early 1980s for the United States
Defense Department. Ada was designed to be a do-
everything language, from business applications to
rocket guidance systems. One of its principal features is that it supports *real-time* applications. In
addition, Ada incorporates modular techniques
that make it easier to build and maintain large systems. Since 1986, Ada has been the mandatory development language for most U.S. military
applications.

Ada is named after Augusta Ada Byron (1815–
52), daughter of Lord Byron, and Countess of Love-
lace. She helped Charles Babbage to develop
programs for the *analytic engine,* the first mechanical computer. She is considered by many to be the
world's first programmer.

➮ See also *high-level programming language;
modular architecture; real time.*

adapter: (1) Any expansion board that is required to
support a particular device. For example, *video*

adapters enable the computer to support graphics monitors, and *network adapters* enable a computer to be attached to a network.

➡ See also *expansion board; video adapter.*

(2) Short for *video adapter.*

ADB: Abbreviation of *Apple Desktop bus,* a type of interface built into all versions of the Apple Macintosh computer since the SE. It is used to connect input devices such as the keyboard and mouse. A single ADB port can support as many as 16 simultaneous input devices.

➡ See also *bus; interface; Macintosh computer; port.*

add-in: (1) A component you can add to a computer or other device to increase its capabilities. Add-ins can increase memory or add graphics or communications capabilities to a computer. They can come in the form of expansion boards, cartridges, or chips. The term *add-in* is often used instead of *add-on* for chips you add to a board that is already installed in a computer. In contrast, *add-on* almost always refers to an entire circuit board.

(2) A software program that extends the capabilities of larger programs. For example, there are many dBASE add-ins designed to complement the dBASE database management system.

➡ See also *add-on; cartridge; chip; dBASE; expansion board.*

add-on: Refers to a product designed to complement another product. For example, there are numerous *add-on boards* available that you can plug into a personal computer to give it additional capabilities. Another term for *add-on board* is *expansion board.*

Add-on products are also available for software

applications. For example, there are add-on report generation programs that attach to popular database products such as dBASE and Lotus, giving them additional report generation and graphics capabilities.

The terms *add-on* and *add-in* are often, but not always, used synonymously. The term *add-in* can refer to individual chips you can insert into boards that are already installed in your computer. *Add-on,* on the other hand, almost always refers to an entire circuit board, cartridge, or program.

➩ See also *add-in; cartridge; expansion board; expansion slot; printed circuit board.*

address: A location, usually in main memory or on a disk. You can think of computer memory as an array of storage boxes, each of which is one byte in length (Figure 1). Each box has an address (a unique number) assigned to it. By specifying a memory address, programmers can access a particular byte of data. Disks are divided into *tracks* and *sectors,* each of which has a unique address.

There are several different types of addresses, as shown:

absolute address: A fixed location in main memory. Absolute memory addresses are also called *real addresses* and *machine addresses.*

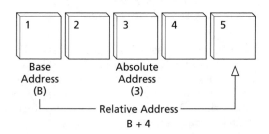

Figure 1
Memory Addresses

base address: The beginning address for a section of code or data.

machine address: A fixed location in main memory. Same as *absolute address*.

physical address: An actual address physically assigned on a circuit board.

relative address: A location indicated by specifying the distance from some other location called the *base address*. That is, the address is relative to another address. The distance between the two addresses is called the *offset*.

virtual address: A memory address in software that is mapped to a physical address. Most programs that run in a multiprocessing environment use virtual addresses.

Usually, you do not need to worry about addresses unless you are a programmer. However, if the program you are running contains bugs, you may see the term *address* used in an error message. For example, the message ILLEGAL ADDRESS means the program is attempting to access a part of memory that is not accessible. This error usually means that you have entered very unusual data for which the program was not prepared.

➧ See also *absolute address; base address; disk; machine address; main memory; memory; offset; relative address; sector; track.*

address space: The set of all legal addresses in memory for a given application. The address space represents the amount of memory available to a program. Interestingly, the address space can be larger than physical memory through a technique called *virtual memory*.

➧ See also *address; main memory; memory; virtual memory.*

Adobe PostScript: See *PostScript.*

aggregate function: A function that performs a computation on a set of values rather than on a single value. For example, finding the average or mean of a list of numbers is an aggregate function.

All database management systems support a set of aggregate functions that can operate on a set of selected records.

➧ See also *database management system, function.*

AI: Abbreviation of ***a****rtificial* ***i****ntelligence.*

alert box: A small box that appears on the display screen to give you information or to warn you about a potentially damaging operation. For example, it might warn you that the system is deleting one or more files. Unlike *dialog boxes,* alert boxes do not require any user input. However, you may need to acknowledge the alert box by pressing the Enter key or clicking a mouse button to make it go away.

Alert boxes are also called *message boxes.*

➧ See also *box; dialog box; graphical user interface; window.*

algorithm: A formula or set of steps for solving a particular problem. To be an algorithm, a set of rules must be unambiguous and have a clear stopping point. Algorithms can be expressed in any language, from natural languages like English or French to programming languages like FORTRAN (Figure 2).

We use algorithms every day. For example, a recipe for baking a cake is an algorithm. Most computer programs, with the exception of some artificial intelligence applications, consist of algorithms. Inventing elegant algorithms—algorithms that are simple and require the fewest steps possible—is one of the principal challenges in programming.

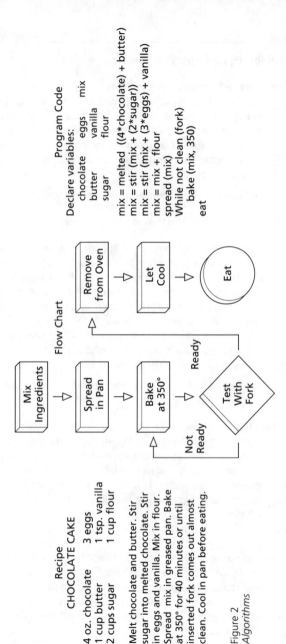

Recipe
CHOCOLATE CAKE

4 oz. chocolate   3 eggs
1 cup butter   1 tsp. vanilla
2 cups sugar   1 cup flour

Melt chocolate and butter. Stir
sugar into melted chocolate. Stir
in eggs and vanilla. Mix in flour.
Spread mix in greased pan. Bake
at 350° for 40 minutes or until
inserted fork comes out almost
clean. Cool in pan before eating.

Flow Chart

Mix Ingredients → Spread in Pan → Bake at 350° → Test With Fork

Test With Fork → Not Ready → Bake at 350°

Test With Fork → Ready → Remove from Oven → Let Cool → Eat

Program Code

Declare variables:
   chocolate   eggs   mix
   butter   vanilla
   sugar   flour

mix = melted ((4*chocolate) + butter)
mix = stir (mix + (2*sugar))
mix = stir (mix + (3*eggs) + vanilla)
mix = mix + flour
spread (mix)
While not clean (fork)
   bake (mix, 350)
eat

Figure 2
Algorithms

➡ See also *artificial intelligence; program; programming language.*

alias: (1) An alternative name for an object, such as a variable, file, or device.

(2) A UNIX shell command that enables you to assign an alternate pathname to a file.

➡ See also *device; file; name; variable.*

aliasing: The process by which smooth curves become jagged because of a change in resolution.

➡ See also *antialiasing; jaggies; resolution.*

alphanumeric: Describes the combined set of all letters in the alphabet and the numbers 0 through 9 (Table 2). It is useful to group letters and numbers together because many programs treat them identically, and differently from punctuation characters. For example, most operating systems allow you to use any letters or numbers in filenames but prohibit many punctuation characters. Your computer manual would express this rule by stating: "Filenames may be composed of alphanumeric characters."

Sometimes additional characters are considered alphanumeric. For example, on IBM mainframes the characters @, #, and $ are considered alphanumeric characters.

➡ See also *special character.*

Alt key: Short for *Alternate key,* the Alt key is like a second Control key. Not all computer keyboards have an Alt key, but it is standard on all IBM PCs and compatibles. You use it in the same fashion as the Control key—holding it down while you press another key. For example, an instruction to use the Alt-P combination means that you should hold down the Alt key while pressing and then releasing the P key. The meaning of any Alt key combination depends on which application is running.

➡ See also *ASCII; control character; keyboard.*

Table 2: Alphanumeric, Punctuation, and Special Characters

ALPHANUMERIC CHARACTERS

a – z
A – Z
0 – 9

PUNCTUATION CHARACTERS

;	semicolon
:	colon
,	comma
"	double quote
'	single quote
#	number sign or pound sign
/	slash
\	backslash
*	asterisk or star
^	caret
.	period, point, or dot
@	at sign
&	ampersand
~	tilde
!	bang or exclamation mark
-	dash
=	equal sign

SPECIAL CHARACTERS

Tab
Esc

ALU: Abbreviation of *arithmetic logic unit*, the part of a computer that performs all arithmetic computations, such as addition and multiplication, and all comparison operations. The ALU is one component of the *CPU* (**c**entral **p**rocessing **u**nit).

➠ See also *CPU*.

American National Standards Institute: See *ANSI*.

American Standard Code for Information Interchange: See *ASCII*.

Amiga: A family of personal computers produced by Commodore Business Machines. Amigas are powerful personal computers that have extra microprocessors to handle graphics and sound generation. They also have built-in MIDI interfaces for connecting to synthesizers and other electronic musical devices. Like Apple Macintosh computers, the Amiga line of computers is built around the Motorola 680x0 line of microprocessors. Amiga computers, however, are not compatible with Macintoshes because they use different operating systems. The less powerful Amiga models (the 500 and 1000) are not compatible with IBM PCs. With the higher models (the 2000, 2500, and 3000), IBM compatibility is an option.

➧ See also *graphics; microprocessor; MIDI; personal computer*.

analog: Almost everything in the world can be described or represented in one of two forms: *analog* or *digital*. The principal feature of analog representations is that they are continuous. In contrast, digital representations consist of values measured at discrete intervals (Figure 3).

Digital watches are called digital because they go from one value to the next without displaying all intermediate values. Consequently, they can display only a finite number of times of the day. In contrast, watches with hands are analog, because the hands move continuously around the clock face. As the minute hand goes around, it not only touches the numbers 1 through 12, but also the infinite number of points in between.

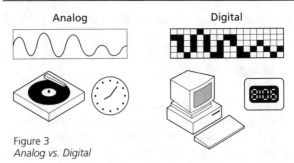

Figure 3
Analog vs. Digital

Early attempts at building computers used ana-log techniques, but accuracy and reliability were not good enough. Today, almost all computers are digital.

➡ See also *digital*.

analog monitor: The traditional type of color display screen that has been used for years in televisions. In reality, all monitors based on *CRT* technology (that is, all monitors except *flat-panel displays*) are ana-log. Some monitors, however, are called *digital monitors* because they accept digital signals from the video adapter. EGA monitors, for example, must be digital because the EGA standard specifies digi-tal signals. Digital monitors must nevertheless translate the signals into an analog form before displaying images. Some monitors can accept both digital and analog signals.

Most analog monitors are designed to accept signals at a precise frequency. They are therefore called *fixed-frequency monitors*. However, a special type of monitor, called a *multiscanning monitor,* au-tomatically adjusts itself to the frequency of the signals being sent to it. A third type of monitor, called a *multifrequency monitor*, is designed to ac-cept signals at two or more preset frequency levels.

➡ See also *analog; CRT; digital; digital monitor; display screen; fixed-frequency monitor; monitor;*

multifrequency monitor; multiscanning monitor; multisync monitor; video adapter.

AND operator: A *Boolean operator* that returns a value of TRUE if both its operands are TRUE, and FALSE otherwise.

➡ See also *Boolean operator; operand; operator.*

ANSI: Acronym for the *American National Standards Institute.* Founded in 1918, ANSI is a voluntary organization composed of over 1,300 members (including all the large computer companies) that creates standards for the computer industry. For example, ANSI FORTRAN is a version of the FORTRAN language that has been approved by the ANSI committee. To a large degree, all ANSI FORTRAN compilers, regardless of which company produces them, should behave similarly.

In addition to computer languages, ANSI sets standards for a wide range of technical areas, from electrical specifications to communications protocols. For example, FDDI, the main set of protocols for sending data over fiber optic cables, is an ANSI standard.

➡ See also *FDDI; portable; standards.*

ANSI.SYS: In DOS- and OS/2-based systems, ANSI.-SYS is the name of a device *driver* that makes a monitor conform to the ANSI standard. The ANSI standard specifies a series of *escape sequences* that cause the monitor to behave in various ways. For example, one escape sequence clears the screen while another causes all subsequent characters to be inverted.

In general, DOS and OS/2 programs do not use the ANSI codes because these codes are slower than the built-in BIOS codes. DOS programs that do use ANSI codes for compatibility with other devices require that you load the ANSI.SYS device driver in the configuration file, CONFIG.SYS.

➠ See also *ANSI; BIOS; CONFIG.SYS; device driver; DOS; escape sequence; monitor.*

answer-only modem: A modem that can receive messages but cannot send them. Only the most inexpensive modems are answer-only.

➠ See also *modem.*

antialiasing: In computer graphics, *antialiasing* is a software technique for diminishing *jaggies*—stairsteplike lines that should be smooth (Figure 4). Jaggies occur because the output device, the monitor or printer, doesn't have a high enough resolution to represent a smooth line. Antialiasing reduces the prominence of jaggies by surrounding the stairsteps with intermediate shades of gray (for gray-scaling devices) or color (for color devices). Although this reduces the jagged appearance of the lines, it also makes them fuzzier.

Another method for reducing jaggies is called *smoothing*, in which the printer changes the size and horizontal alignment of dots to make curves smoother.

➠ See also *graphics; gray scaling; jaggies; resolution; smoothing.*

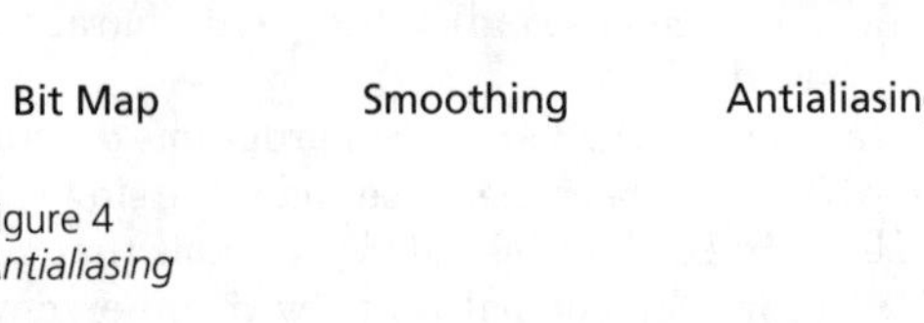

Bit Map   Smoothing   Antialiasing

Figure 4
Antialiasing

API: Abbreviation of *application program interface*, a set of routines, protocols, and tools for building software applications. A good API makes it easier to develop a program by providing all the building blocks. A programmer then puts the blocks together.

Most operating environments, such as MS-Windows and DESQview, provide an API so that programmers can write applications consistent with the operating environment. Although APIs are designed for programmers, they are ultimately good for users because they guarantee that all programs using a common API will have similar interfaces. This makes it easier for users to learn new programs.

➡ See also *application; DESQview; interface; MS-Windows; operating environment; routine.*

app: Abbreviation of *app*lication.

append: (1) To add something at the end. For example, you can append one file to another or you can append a field to a record. Do not confuse *append* with *insert*. *Append* always means to add at the end. *Insert* means to add in between.

➡ See also *insert.*

(2) A DOS command that enables you to specify directories in which programs should look for data files.

➡ See also *command; directory; file; DOS.*

Apple Desktop bus: See *ADB.*

Apple Macintosh computer: See *Macintosh computer.*

AppleTalk: A proprietary local-area network (LAN) architecture built into all Apple Macintosh computers and laser printers. AppleTalk is based on a *bus topology*. The original version can connect up to 32 devices within a distance of about 1,000 feet. An updated version, known as *Phase 2*, can support 16 million devices.

Although AppleTalk is relatively slow compared with other networks such as Ethernet and the IBM Token Ring, it is popular because it is inexpensive and simple. It can connect Macintosh computers and printers, and even IBM PCs.

The cabling scheme for AppleTalk networks is known as *LocalTalk*. However, AppleTalk can be used with other cabling schemes as well.

➡ See also *architecture; bus; local-area network; LocalTalk; Macintosh computer; protocol; topology; TOPS.*

application: A program or group of programs designed for end users. Software can be divided into two general classes: *systems software* and *applications software* (Figure 5). Systems software consists of

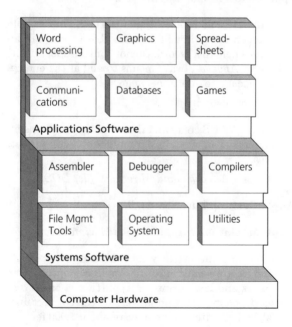

Figure 5
Applications Software and Systems Software

low-level programs that interact with the computer at a very basic level. This includes operating systems, compilers, and utilities for managing computer resources.

In contrast, applications software (also called *end-user programs*) includes database programs, word processors, and spreadsheets. Figuratively speaking, applications software sits on top of systems software because it is unable to run without the operating system and system utilities.

➡ See also *database management system; end user; operating system; software; spreadsheet; systems software; utility; word processor.*

Application Program Interface: See *API.*

ARC: To compress a file using the ARC format. The ARC data compression format, created by Systems Enhancement Associates, is particularly popular among bulletin board systems (BBSs). Another common format is *ZIP*. While ARC and ZIP are popular data compression formats for IBM PCs, *Stuffit* is a popular utility for Macintoshes.

Files that have been compressed with an ARC utility end with an .ARC extension. To decompress them, you need a utility called *ARC-E* (stands for *ARC-extract*).

➡ See also *bulletin board system; data compression; ZIP.*

architecture: A design. The term *architecture* can refer to either hardware or software, or to a combination of hardware and software. The architecture of a system always defines its broad outlines, and may define precise mechanisms as well.

An *open architecture* allows the system to easily be connected to devices and programs made by other manufacturers. Open architectures use off-the-shelf components and conform to approved standards. A system with a *closed architecture,* on the other hand, is one whose design is *proprietary,* making it difficult to connect the system to other systems.

➡ See also *open architecture; proprietary; standards.*

archival backup: A type of backup in which only files modified since the last backup are copied. Archival backups are much faster than full backups because fewer files are copied. Typically, users make a full backup of all data once a week and an archival backup each day between the full backups.

Archival backups are also called *incremental backups.*

➡ See also *archive; backup.*

archive: (v) (1) To copy files to a long-term storage medium for backup. Large computer systems often have two layers of backup, the first of which is a disk drive. Periodically, the computer operator will archive files on the disk to a second storage device, usually a tape drive.

On smaller systems, archiving is synonymous with *backing-up.*

➡ See also *archival backup; backup.*

(2) To compress a file.

➡ See also *ARC.*

(n) (1) A disk, tape, or directory that contains files that have been backed up.

(2) A file that contains one or more files in a compressed format.

(adj) In DOS systems, the *archive attribute* marks files that have been modified since the last backup.

➡ See also *attribute.*

ARCnet: One of the oldest, simplest, and least expensive types of local-area network. ARCnet was introduced by Datapoint Corporation in 1968. It uses a token-ring architecture, supports data rates of 2.5 megabits per second, and connects up to 255 computers. A special advantage of ARCnet is that it permits various types of transmission media—twisted-pair wire, coaxial cable, and fiber optic cable—to be mixed on the same network.

Although it has less capacity than other networks such as Ethernet and IBM Token Ring, it is nevertheless extremely popular because of its simplicity. A new specification, called ARCnet Plus, will support data rates of 20 megabits per second.

➡ See also *Ethernet; local-area network; token-ring network.*

argument: In programming, a value that you pass to a *routine*. For example, if SQRT is a routine that returns the square root of a value, then SQRT(25) would return the value 5. The value 25 is the argument.

Argument is often used synonymously with *parameter*, although *parameter* can also mean any value that can be changed. In addition, some programming languages make a distinction between arguments, which are passed in only one direction, and parameters, which can be passed back and forth, but this distinction is by no means universal.

An argument can also be an option to a command, in which case it is often called a *command-line argument.*

➡ See also *option; parameter; routine.*

arithmetic expression: An expression that represents a numeric value. Other types of expressions can represent character or *Boolean* values.

➡ See also *expression.*

arithmetic operator: See under *operator*.

ARPANET: A large wide-area network created by the United States Defense Advanced Research Project Agency (ARPA). Established in 1969, ARPANET has served as a testbed for new networking technologies, and it links many universities and research centers. However, it is currently being phased out and replaced with a more modern network called *NSFnet*.

➡ See also *NSFnet; wide-area network*.

array: A series of objects all of which are the same size and type. Each object in an array is called an *array element*. For example, you could have an array of integers or an array of characters or an array of anything that has a defined *data type*. The important characteristics of an array are:

- Each element has the same *data type* (although they may have different values).
- The entire array is stored *contiguously* in memory (that is, there are no gaps between elements).

Arrays can have more than one dimension. A one-dimensional array is called a *vector* and a two-dimensional array is called a *matrix*. To access a particular element in an array, you need to specify the array's name with one or more *subscripts*. For example:

$$A[5]$$

specifies the fifth element in a one-dimensional array named *A*.

➡ See also *data structure; data type; matrix; subscript; vector*.

arrow keys: Most computer keyboards contain four arrow keys for moving the cursor or insertion point right, left, up, or down. When combined with the Shift, Function, Control, or Alt keys (on IBM PCs), the arrow keys can have different meanings. For example, pressing Shift-Up-arrow might move the cursor or pointer up an entire page. On Macintoshes, the arrow keys can be combined with the Shift, Option, and Commands keys. The exact manner in which the arrow keys function depends on which program is running. Some programs ignore them.

The arrow keys are also called *cursor control keys.*

➡ See also *cursor; insertion point; keyboard.*

artificial intelligence: The branch of computer science concerned with making computers behave like humans. The term was coined in 1956 by John McCarthy at the Massachusetts Institute of Technology. Artificial intelligence includes:

games playing: programming computers to play games such as chess and checkers

expert systems: programming computers to make decisions in real-life situations (for example, some expert systems help doctors diagnose diseases based on symptoms)

natural language: programming computers to understand natural human languages

neural networks: Systems that simulate intelligence by attempting to reproduce the types of physical connections that occur in animal brains

robotics: programming computers to *see* and *hear* and react to other sensory stimuli

Currently, no computers exhibit full artificial intelligence (that is, are able to simulate human behavior). The greatest advances have occurred in the field of games playing. The best computer chess programs are now capable of beating most humans, although they still lose to grand masters.

In the area of robotics, computers are now widely used in assembly plants, but they are capable only of very limited tasks. Robots have great difficulty identifying objects based on appearance or feel, and they still move and handle objects clumsily.

Natural-language processing offers the greatest potential rewards because it would allow people to interact with computers without needing any specialized knowledge. You could simply walk up to a computer and talk to it. Unfortunately, programming computers to understand natural languages has proved to be more difficult than originally thought. Some rudimentary translation systems that translate from one human language to another are in existence, but they are not nearly as good as human translators. There are also voice recognition systems that can convert spoken sounds into written words, but they do not *understand* what they are writing; they simply take dictation. Even these systems are quite limited—you must speak slowly and distinctly.

In the early 1980s, expert systems were believed to represent the future of artificial intelligence and of computers in general. To date, however, they have not lived up to expectations. Many expert systems help human experts in such fields as medicine and engineering, but they are very expensive to produce and are helpful only in special situations.

Today, the hottest area of artificial intelligence is neural networks, which are proving successful in a number of disciplines such as voice recognition and natural-language processing.

There are several programming languages known as AI languages because they are used almost exclusively for AI applications. The two most common are *LISP* and *PROLOG*.

➡ See also *expert system; LISP; natural language; neural networks; PROLOG; robotics; voice recognition.*

ASCII: Acronym for the *American Standard Code for Information Interchange*. Pronounced *ask-ee*, ASCII is a code for representing English characters as numbers, with each letter assigned a number from 0 to 127 (Table 3). For example, the ASCII code for uppercase *M* is 77. Most computers use ASCII codes to represent text, which makes it possible to transfer data from one computer to another.

Text files stored in ASCII format are sometimes called *ASCII files*. Text editors and word processors are usually capable of storing data in ASCII format, although ASCII format is not always the default storage format. Most data files, particularly if they contain numeric data, are not stored in ASCII format. Executable programs are never stored in ASCII format.

The standard ASCII character set uses just 7 bits for each character. A larger character set, known as *extended ASCII,* uses 8 bits, which gives it 128 additional characters (Table 4). The extra characters are used to represent non-English characters, graphics symbols, and mathematical symbols. The extended characters and their ASCII codes have been defined by IBM. They have not been officially standardized, but most PC compatibles recognize them.

Another set of codes that is used on large IBM computers is EBCDIC.

➡ See also *EBCDIC; extended ASCII; text file.*

assembler: A program that translates programs from assembly language to machine language.

➡ See also *assembly language; machine language.*

assembly language: A programming language that is once removed from a computer's machine language (see Figure 57 at *programming language*). Machine languages consist entirely of numbers and are almost impossible to read and write. Assembly lan-

Table 3a. Standard ASCII
(Control Codes and Space Characters)

Decimal Value	Abbreviation	Description	Decimal Value	Abbreviation	Description
0	NUL	Null	17	DC1	Device control 1
1	SOH	Start of Heading	18	DC2	Device control 2
2	STX	Start of text	19	DC3	Device control 3
3	ETX	End of text	20	DC4	Device control 4
4	EOT	End of transmit	21	NAK	Negative acknowledge
5	ENQ	Enquiry	22	SYN	Synchronous idle
6	ACK	Acknowledge	23	ETB	End transmit block
7	BEL	Audible bell	24	CAN	Cancel
8	BS	Backspace	25	EM	End of Medium
9	HT	Horizontal tab	26	SUB	Substitution
10	LF	Line feed	27	ESC	Escape
11	VT	Vertical tab	28	FS	Figures shift
12	FF	Form feed	29	GS	Group separator
13	CR	Carriage return	30	RS	Record separator
14	SO	Shift out	31	US	Unit separator
15	SI	Shift in	32	SP	Blank space character
16	DLE	Data link escape			(Space Bar)

Table 3b. Standard ASCII
(Alphanumeric Characters)

Decimal Value	Character	Decimal Value	Character	Decimal Value	Character
33	!	65	A	97	a
34	ô	66	B	98	b
35	#	67	C	99	c
36	$	68	D	100	d
37	%	69	E	101	e
38	&	70	F	102	f
39	æ	71	G	103	g
40	(	72	H	104	h
41	)	73	I	105	i
42	*	74	J	106	j
43	+	75	K	107	k
44	,	76	L	108	l
45	-	77	M	109	m
46	.	78	N	110	n
47	/	79	O	111	o
48	0	80	P	112	p
49	1	81	Q	113	q
50	2	82	R	114	r
51	3	83	S	115	s
52	4	84	T	116	t
53	5	85	U	117	u
54	6	86	V	118	v
55	7	87	W	119	w
56	8	88	X	120	x
57	9	89	Y	121	y
58	:	90	Z	122	z
59	;	91	[	123	{
50	<	92		124		
61	=	93	]	125	}
62	>	94	^	126	~
63	?	95	_	127	⌂
64	@	96	'		

Table 4. Extended ASCII
(De Facto Standard for IBM PCs and Compatibles)

Decimal Value	Character	Decimal Value	Character	Decimal Value	Character	Decimal Value	Character
128	Ç	160	á	192	└	224	α
129	ü	161	í	193	┴	225	β
130	é	162	ó	194	┬	226	Γ
131	â	163	ú	195	├	227	π
132	ä	164	ñ	196	─	228	Σ
133	à	165	Ñ	197	┼	229	σ
134	å	166	ª	198	╞	230	μ
135	ç	167	º	199	╟	231	τ
136	ê	168	¿	200	╚	232	Φ
137	ë	169	⌐	201	╔	233	Θ
138	è	170	¬	202	╩	234	Ω
139	ï	171	½	203	╦	235	δ
140	î	172	¼	204	╠	236	∞
141	ì	173	¡	205	═	237	φ
142	Ä	174	«	206	╬	238	ε
143	Å	175	»	207	╧	239	∩
144	É	176	░	208	╨	240	≡
145	æ	177	▒	209	╤	241	±
146	Æ	178	▓	210	╥	242	≥
147	ô	179	│	211	╙	243	≤
148	ö	180	┤	212	╘	244	⌠
149	ò	181	╡	213	╒	245	⌡
150	û	182	╢	214	╓	246	÷
151	ù	183	╖	215	╫	247	≈
152	ÿ	184	╕	216	╪	248	°
153	Ö	185	╣	217	┘	249	·
154	Ü	186	║	218	┌	250	·
155	¢	187	╗	219	█	251	√
156	£	188	╝	220	▄	252	ⁿ
157	¥	189	╜	221	▌	253	²
158	₧	190	╛	222	▐	254	■
159	ƒ	191	┐	223	▀	255	

guages have the same structure and set of commands as machine languages, but they enable a programmer to use names instead of numbers.

Each type of CPU has its own machine language and assembly language. In the early days of programming, all programs were written in assembly language. Now, most programs are written in a high-level language such as FORTRAN or C. Assembly language is still used when speed is essential or when a programmer needs to perform an operation that isn't possible in a high-level language.

➡ See also *compile; machine language; programming language.*

assign: To give a value to a variable. In programming, you assign a value to a variable with a special symbol called an *assignment operator*. In many languages, the assignment operator is the equal sign (=). For example, the following C language statement assigns the value 5 to the variable x:

$$x = 5;$$

Such a statement is called an *assignment statement.*

➡ See also *operator; statement; variable.*

async: Short for *asynchronous.*

asynchronous: Not synchronized, that is, not occurring at predetermined or regular intervals. The term *asynchronous* is usually used to describe communications in which data can be transmitted intermittently rather than in a steady stream. For example, a telephone conversation is asynchronous because both parties can talk whenever they like. If the communication were synchronous, each party would be required to wait a specified interval before speaking.

The difficulty with asynchronous communications is that the receiver must have a way to distinguish between valid data and noise. In computer communications, this is usually accomplished through a special *start bit* and *stop bit* at the beginning and end of each piece of data. For this reason, asynchronous communication is sometimes called *start-stop* transmission (Figure 6).

Most communications between computers and devices are asynchronous.

➡ See also *communications; noise; start bit; stop bit.*

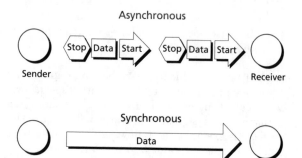

Figure 6
Asynchronous vs. Synchronous Communication

AT: Short for *advanced technology,* the AT is an IBM personal computer model introduced in 1984. It includes an Intel 80286 microprocessor, a 1.2MB floppy drive, and an 84-key AT keyboard.

➡ See also *floppy disk; IBM PC; Intel microprocessors; keyboard.*

AT bus: The expansion bus on the IBM PC/AT and compatible computers. The bus is the collection of wires and electronic components that connect all device controllers and add-in cards. The controllers are the components that attach to peripheral devices. The bus, therefore, is the main highway for all data moving in and out of the computer.

The AT bus, which runs at 8MHz and has a 16-bit data path, is the de facto standard for older IBM PCs and compatibles. Because all IBM PCs (until the high-end PS/2 models) had an AT bus, it has been possible for manufacturers to produce expansion boards that will work with any PC.

In 1987, however, IBM introduced a new 32-bit bus called the Micro Channel architecture (MCA). MCA is considerably faster and more sophisticated than the AT bus. Unfortunately, MCA is incompatible with the AT bus, which means that expansion boards designed for the AT bus will not work with MCA.

An alternative to MCA is the *Extended Industry Standard Architecture (EISA),* a high-speed 32-bit bus architecture designed by IBM's largest competitors. Unlike MCA, EISA is *backward compatible* with the AT bus.

The AT bus is sometimes referred to as the *ISA bus,* which stands for *Industry Standard Architecture.* However, ISA also includes the XT bus, which is an 8-bit version of the AT bus.

➠ See also *backward compatible; bus; EISA; expansion board; IBM PC; ISA bus; MCA.*

attribute: (1) A characteristic. In a word-processing application, an underlined word would be said to have the *underline attribute.* In database systems, a field can have various attributes. For example, if it contains numeric data, it has the *numeric attribute.*

(2) In database management systems, the term *attribute* is sometimes used as a synonym for *field.*

➠ See also *field.*

(3) In DOS systems, every file has a *file attribute* that indicates several properties of the file. For example, the file attribute indicates whether the file is read-only, whether it needs to be backed up, and whether it is visible or hidden.

➠ See also *DOS; file; hidden file.*

audit trail: A record showing who has accessed a computer system and what operations they have performed during a given period of time. Audit trails are useful both for maintaining security and for recovering lost transactions. Most accounting systems and database management systems include an audit trail component. In addition, there are separate audit trail software products that enable network administrators to monitor use of network resources.

➡ See also *security*.

authoring tool: A program that helps you write *hypertext* or *multimedia* applications. Authoring tools usually enable you to create a final application merely by linking together objects, such as a paragraph of text, an illustration, or a song. By defining the objects' relationships to each other, and by sequencing them in an appropriate order, authors (those who use authoring tools) can produce attractive and useful graphics applications. Most authoring systems also support a scripting language for more sophisticated applications.

The distinction between authoring tools and programming tools is not clear-cut. Typically, though, authoring tools require less technical knowledge to master and are used exclusively for applications that present a mixture of textual, graphical, and audio data.

➡ See also *Hypertext; multimedia; programming language; script.*

auto-answer: A feature supported by many modems that enables your computer to accept incoming calls even if you are not present. In *auto-answer mode,* a modem attempts to establish a connection whenever the telephone rings. This is an important feature if you are offering a service to which others can subscribe.

Auto-answer is also a critical feature for FAX modems because it enables you to receive FAX documents while you are away. All FAX machines are auto-answer.

➡ See also *FAX machine; FAX modem; modem.*

autoexec.bat: Stands for *automatic execute batch file*, the file that DOS automatically executes when a computer *boots up*. This is a convenient place to put commands you always want to execute at the beginning of a computing session. For example, you can set system parameters such as the date and time, and install *memory-resident* programs.

In the OS/2 operating system, the equivalent file is called *STARTUP.CMD*.

➡ See also *batch file; boot; memory resident; DOS; OS/2.*

auto-redial: A feature supported by many modems that causes the modem to continue redialing a number until it makes a connection. This is a useful feature if you subscribe to an on-line service that is frequently busy.

➡ See also *modem.*

auto-repeat: A feature of some keys on computer keyboards that causes them to repeat as long as they are held down. Most keys are auto-repeat.

➡ See also *keyboard.*

automatic acceleration: See under *dynamic acceleration.*

autosave: A feature supported by many applications in which the program automatically saves data files at predetermined intervals. This is an important feature because it reduces the amount of work you would lose if your system crashed. Usually, you can specify how often you want the application to save data.

➡ See also *crash; save; word processing.*

autosizing: (1) In graphics hardware, autosizing refers to a monitor's ability to accept signals at one resolution and display the image at a different resolution. For example, a VGA video card outputs images at a resolution of 640 by 480. An EGA monitor, however, can display images at a resolution of only 640 by 350. If the monitor supports autosizing, it will automatically adjust the size of the image so that the proportions are correct. Without autosizing, you will need to adjust an image manually so that it fills the screen properly.

➡ See also *EGA; monitor; resolution; VGA; video adapter.*

autotracing: The process of converting a bit-mapped image (or *raster* image) into a *vector* image (Figure 7). In a bit-mapped image, each object is represented by a pattern of dots, while in a vector image every object is defined geometrically.

Most autotracing packages read files in a variety of bit-mapped formats (PCX and TIFF are the most common) and produce a file in a vector format such as *Encapsulated PostScript (EPS)*. The conver-

Bit Map Image

Vector Image

Figure 7
Autotracing

sion techniques used, and the accuracy of the conversion process, differ from one package to another.

Autotracing is particularly useful for manipulating images produced by an optical scanner. Scanners produce bit-mapped images that cannot be manipulated by sophisticated tools until they have been converted into a vector format through autotracing.

➡ See also *bit map; Encapsulated PostScript; optical scanner; PCX; PostScript; raster graphics; TIFF; vector graphics.*

B

back end: See under *front end.*

backbone: Another term for *bus,* the main wire that connects nodes.

➡ See also *bus; network; node.*

background: (1) Multitasking computers are capable of executing several tasks, or programs, at the same time. In some multiprocessing systems, one of the processes is called the *foreground process*, and the others are called *background processes.*

The foreground process is the one that accepts input from the keyboard, mouse, or other input device. Background processes cannot accept interactive input from a user, but they can access data stored on a disk and write data to the video display. For example, most word processors print files in the background, enabling you to continue editing while files are being printed. This is called *print spooling.* In addition, many communications programs are designed to run in the background. Background processes generally have a lower priority than foreground processes so that they do not interfere with interactive applications.

Even though DOS is not a multitasking operating system, it can perform some specialized tasks, such as printing, in the background. Operating environments, such as Microsoft Windows and the Macintosh MultiFinder, provide a more general multitasking environment.

➧ See also *Microsoft Windows; MultiFinder; multitasking; process; spooling; task.*

(2) The area of a display screen not covered by characters and graphics. The background is like a canvas on top of which characters and graphics are placed. Some monitors allow you to control the color or shading of the background.

➧ See also *display screen; monitor.*

backlighting: A technique used to make flat-panel displays easier to read. A backlit display is illuminated so that the foreground appears sharper in contrast with the background.

➧ See also *background; flat-panel display; foreground; laptop computer; supertwist.*

backslash: The backslash character is \; a simple slash or *forward slash* is /. In DOS systems, the backslash represents the *root directory* and is also used to separate directory names and filenames in a *pathname.*

➧ See also *pathname; root directory.*

backspace: A character that causes the cursor to move backward one character space, possibly deleting the preceding character. The backspace character has an ASCII value of 8. Most keyboards have a Backspace key that invokes this character. When inserted in a file, the character causes a printer or other device to move backward one space.

➡ See also *ASCII; Backspace key; cursor; keyboard; pointer.*

Backspace key: A key that moves the cursor or insertion point backward one character space. In addition to moving the cursor backward, the Backspace key usually deletes the character to the left of the cursor or insertion point. It is particularly useful, therefore, for correcting typos. Note that the Backspace key differs from the Delete key, which deletes the character under the cursor (or to the right of the insertion point). To move the cursor or insertion point backward without deleting characters, use the arrow keys.

➡ See also *arrow keys; backspace; cursor; Delete key; insertion point; keyboard.*

backup: (v) To copy files to a second medium (a disk or tape) as a precaution in case the first medium fails. One of the cardinal rules in using computers is: *Backup your files regularly.* Even the most reliable computer is apt to break down eventually. Many professionals recommend that you make two, or even three, backups of all your files. To be especially safe, you should keep one backup in a different location from the others.

You can backup files using operating system commands, or you can buy a special-purpose backup utility. In general, backup programs are much faster than operating system shell commands because they use a DMA channel. In addition, the backup programs often compress the data so that backups require fewer disks.

➡ See also *archive; data compression; DMA.*

(n) (1) The act of backing up.
(2) A substitute or alternative. The term *backup*

usually refers to a disk or tape that contains a copy of data.

backward compatible: Compatible with earlier models or versions of the same product. A new version of a program is said to be backward compatible if you can use the same data that you used for the older version. For example, dBASE IV is backward compatible with dBASE III because you can use the same data files with both programs.

A computer is said to be backward compatible if it can run the same software as the previous model of the computer. For example, the IBM PC/AT computer is backward compatible with the IBM PC/XT, and the Mac II is backward compatible with the Mac Plus.

Backward compatibility is important because it eliminates the need to start over when you upgrade to a newer product. In general, manufacturers try to keep all their products backward compatible. Sometimes, however, it is necessary to sacrifice backward compatibility to take advantage of a new technology.

The flip side of backward compatibility is *upward compatibility*. Upward compatible is the same as backward compatible, except that it is from the point of view of the older model. For example, dBASE III is upward compatible with dBASE IV, just as dBASE IV is backward compatible with dBASE III.

Another term for *backward compatible* is *downward compatible*.

➡ See also *compatible; upward compatible*.

bad sector: A portion of a disk that cannot be used because it is flawed. When you format a disk, the operating system identifies any bad sectors on the disk and marks them so they will not be used. If a sector that already contains data becomes damaged, you will need special software to recover the data.

Almost all hard disks come with bad sectors (sectors damaged during the manufacturing process), so do not be alarmed if a utility reports that your hard disk has bad sectors. However, additional bad sectors should occur only infrequently if your drive is functioning properly. Floppy disks should not have any bad sectors.

➭ See also *disk; format; sector.*

ballistic tracking: See under *dynamic acceleration.*

bandwidth: The amount of data that can be transmitted in a fixed amount of time. For digital devices, the bandwidth is usually expressed in bits or bytes per second (bps). For analog devices, the bandwidth is expressed in cycles per second, or Hertz (Hz).

The bandwidth is particularly important for I/O devices. For example, a fast disk drive can be hampered by a bus with a low bandwidth. This is the main reason that new buses (MCA and EISA) have been developed for the IBM PC.

➭ See also *analog; digital; EISA; I/O; MCA.*

base address: An address that serves as a reference point for other addresses (see Figure 1 at *address*). For example, a base address could indicate the beginning of a program. The address of every instruction in the program could then be specified by adding an offset to the base address. For example, the address of the fifth instruction would be the base address plus 5.

➭ See also *address; offset; relative address.*

baseband transmission: A type of data transmission in which each medium (wire) carries only one signal, or channel, at a time. In contrast, *broadband* transmission enables a single wire to carry multiple signals simultaneously.

Most communications involving computers uses baseband transmission. This includes communications from the computer to devices (printers, monitors, and so on), communications via modems, and the majority of networks. An exception is B-ISDN networks, which use broadband transmission.

➥ See also *broadband ISDN; broadband transmission; channel; communications; ISDN; local-area network; network.*

BASIC: Acronym for *Beginner's All-purpose Symbolic Instruction Code.* Developed by John Kemeny and Thomas Kurtz in the mid 1960s at Dartmouth College, BASIC is one of the earliest and simplest high-level programming languages. During the 1970s, it was the principal programming language taught to students, and continues to be a popular choice among educators.

Despite its simplicity, BASIC is used for a wide variety of business applications. There is an ANSI standard for the BASIC language, but most versions of BASIC include many proprietary extensions.

➥ See also *ANSI; extension; programming language.*

basic input/output system: See *BIOS.*

batch file: A file that contains a sequence, or batch, of commands. Batch files are useful for storing sets of commands that are always executed together because you can simply enter the name of the batch file instead of entering each command individually.

In DOS systems, batch files end with a .BAT extension. For example, the following DOS batch file prints the date and time and sets the prompt to *GO>*:

```
date
time
prompt [GO>]
```

Whenever you boot a DOS-based computer, the system automatically executes the batch file named *AUTOEXEC.BAT,* if it exists.

Many operating systems use the terms *command file* or *shell script* in place of *batch file.*

➡ See also *AUTOEXEC.BAT; batch processing; DOS.*

batch processing: Executing a series of noninteractive jobs all at one time. The term originated in the days when users entered programs on punch cards. They would give a batch of these programmed cards to the system operator, who would then feed them into the computer.

Usually, batch jobs are stored up during working hours and then executed during the evening or whenever the computer is idle. Batch processing is particularly useful for operations that require the computer or a peripheral device for an extended period of time. Once a batch job begins, it continues until it is done or until an error occurs. Note that batch processing implies that there is no interaction with the user while the program is being executed.

The opposite of batch processing is *transaction processing* or *interactive processing.* In interactive processing, the application responds to commands as soon as you enter them.

➡ See also *interactive; transaction processing.*

BAT file: In DOS systems, *batch files* are often called *BAT files* because their filenames must end with a *.BAT* extension.

➡ See also *batch file; extension; filename; DOS.*

baud rate: The number of electrical oscillations that occur each second. The term is named after J.M.E. Baudot, the inventor of the Baudot telegraph code.

At slow speeds, only one bit of information is

encoded in each electrical change. The baud rate, therefore, indicates the number of bits per second that are transmitted. For example, a baud rate of 300 means that 300 bits are transmitted each second (abbreviated *300 bps*). Assuming asynchronous communications, which requires 10 bits per character, this translates to 30 characters per second (cps). For slow rates (below 1,200 baud), you can divide the baud rate by 10 to see how many characters per second are sent.

At higher baud rates, it is possible to encode more than one bit in each electrical change. For example, a baud rate of 4,800 may allow 9,600 bits to be sent each second. At high baud levels, therefore, data transmission rates are usually expressed in bits per second (bps) rather than in baud rates. For example, a 9,600 bps modem may operate at only 2,400 baud.

➭ See also *bps; modem.*

bay: Short for *drive bay,* this refers to a site in a personal computer where a hard or floppy disk drive or tape drive can be installed. Thus, the number of drive bays in a computer determines how many mass storage devices can be internally installed.

For IBM PCs and compatibles, bays can be *full height, half height, one-third height,* or *3.5 inch.* In addition, bays are described as either *internal* or *exposed.* An internal bay cannot be used for removable media, such as floppy drives. Some manufacturers use the terms *hidden* and *accessible* in place of *internal* and *exposed.*

Do not confuse bays with *slots,* which are openings in the computer where *expansion boards* can be installed.

➭ See also *disk drive; expansion board; mass storage; slot.*

BBS: Abbreviation of *bulletin board system.*

Bell 103: The standard protocol in the United States for transmitting data over telephone lines at transmission rates of 300 baud. The Bell 103A standard defines asynchronous, full-duplex communication. Europe and Japan use the CCITT V.21 protocol.

➡ See also *asynchronous; baud; CCITT; communications protocols; full duplex; protocol.*

Bell 212A: The standard protocol in the United States for transmitting data over telephone lines at transmission rates of 1,200 bps. The Bell 212A standard defines asynchronous, full-duplex communications. Europe and Japan use the CCITT V.22 protocol.

➡ See also *asynchronous; baud; CCITT; communications protocols; full duplex; protocol.*

Bernoulli disk drive: Named after a Swiss scientist who discovered the principle of aerodynamic lift, the Bernoulli disk drive is a special type of floppy disk drive from Iomega Corporation that is faster and has greater storage capacity than traditional floppy drives. Bernoulli drives come in a variety of sizes and capacities, from 10MB to 44MB.

A Bernoulli drive is really a cross between a hard disk drive and floppy drive. Like the platters in hard disk drives, Bernoulli disks float between the read/write heads, so there is no actual contact between the disk and the heads. But the disk itself is flexible and removable like a floppy disk. Because the disk is flexible, it is less susceptible than a hard disk to head crashes. Bernoulli disk drives, however, are not as fast as hard disk drives.

➡ See also *disk; floppy disk; hard disk drive; head crash; mass storage.*

beta test: A test for a computer product prior to commercial release. Beta testing is the last stage of testing, and normally involves sending the product to *beta test sites* outside the company for real-world exposure.

Bézier curves: Curved lines defined by mathematical formulas. Named after the French mathematician Pierre Bézier, Bézier curves employ four control points to define a curve (Figure 8). The two endpoints of the curve are called *anchor points*. The other two points, which define the shape of the curve, are called *tangent points* or *handles*. Typically, you can move the handles, shown as boxes on the display screen, to manipulate a curve. Nearly all illustration programs support Bézier curves.

➠ See also *graphics; vector graphics.*

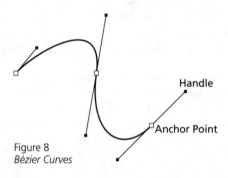

Handle

Anchor Point

Figure 8
Bézier Curves

BFT: See *Binary File Transfer.*

Big Blue: A slang name for International Business Machines Corporation (IBM). Blue is IBM's corporate color.

binary: Pertaining to a number system that has just two unique digits. For most purposes, we use the decimal number system, which has ten unique digits, 0 through 9. All other numbers are then formed by combining these ten digits. Computers are based on the binary numbering system, which consists of just two unique numbers, 0 and 1. All operations that are possible in the decimal system (addition, subtraction, multiplication, division) are equally possible in the binary system.

We use the decimal system in everyday life because it seems more natural (we have ten fingers and ten toes). For the computer, the binary system is more natural because of its electrical nature (charged versus uncharged).

In the decimal system, each digit position represents a value of 10 to the position's power. For example, the number 345 means:

3   three 100s (10^2) plus

4   four 10s (10^1) plus

5   five 1s (10^0)

In the binary system, each digit position represents a power of 2. For example, the binary number 1011 equals:

1   one 8 (2^3) plus

0   zero 4s (2^2) plus

1   one 2 (2^1) plus

1   one 1 (2^0)

So a binary 1011 equals a decimal 11. (See Table 5 for binary and decimal equivalents.)

Table 5: Decimal and Binary Equivalents

DECIMAL	BINARY
1	1
2	10
3	11
4	100
5	101
6	110
7	111
8	1000
9	1001
10	1010
100	1100100
1000	1111101000

Because computers use the binary number system, powers of 2 play an important role. This is why everything in computers seems to come in 8s (2^3), 64s (2^6), and 128s (2^7).

Programmers also use the octal (8 numbers) and hexadecimal (16 numbers) number systems because they map nicely onto the binary system. Each octal digit represents exactly three binary digits, and each hexadecimal digit represents four binary digits.

➡ See also *decimal; hexadecimal; octal.*

binary file: A file stored in binary format. A binary file is computer-readable but not human-readable. All executable programs are stored in binary files, as are most numeric data files. In contrast, text files are stored in a form (usually ASCII) that is human-readable.

➡ See also *ASCII; binary format; executable file; text file.*

Binary File Transfer (BFT): A proposed standard for transmitting data files using FAX modems. It is currently being reviewed by the CCITT and is not expected to become official until 1992.

➡ See also *CCITT; FAX modem; standards.*

binary format: A format for representing data used by some applications. The other main formats for storing data are *text formats* (such as ASCII and EBC-DIC), in which each character of data is assigned a specific code number.

Binary formats are used for executable programs and numeric data whereas text formats are used for textual data. Many files contain a combination of binary and text formats. Such files are usually considered to be binary files even though they contain some data in a text format.

➠ See also *ASCII; binary; binary file; EBCDIC; executable file; text file.*

bind: To assign a value to a symbolic placeholder. During compilation, for example, the compiler assigns symbolic addresses to some variables and instructions. When the program is bound, or *linked,* the binder replaces the symbolic addresses with real machine addresses. The moment at which binding occurs is called *bind time* or *link time.*

➠ See also *address; compile; link.*

binder: Same as *linker.*

BIOS: Acronym for *basic input/output system,* the BIOS is built-in software that determines what a computer can do without accessing programs from a disk. On IBM PCs, the BIOS contains all the code required to control the keyboard, display screen, disk drives, serial communications, and a number of miscellaneous functions.

The BIOS is typically placed on a ROM chip that comes with the computer (it is often called a *ROM BIOS*). This ensures that the BIOS will always be available and will not be damaged by disk failures. It also makes it possible for a computer to boot itself. Because RAM is faster than ROM, though, many computer manufacturers design systems so that the BIOS is copied from ROM to RAM each time the computer is booted. This is known as *shadowing.*

The IBM PC BIOS is standardized, so all IBM PCs and compatibles are alike at this level (although there are different BIOS versions). Additional DOS functions are usually added through software modules. This means you can upgrade to a newer version of DOS without changing the BIOS.

➠ See also *boot; I/O; DOS; operating system; Phoenix BIOS; RAM; ROM; shadowing.*

B-ISDN: See *broadband ISDN*.

bit: Acronym for *binary digit*, the smallest unit of information on a machine. The term was first used in 1946 by John Tukey, a leading statistician and adviser to five presidents. A single bit can hold only one of two values: 0 or 1. More meaningful information is obtained by combining consecutive bits into larger units. For example, a *byte* is composed of 8 consecutive bits.

Computers are sometimes classified by the number of bits they can process at one time or by the number of bits they use to represent addresses. These two values are not always the same, which leads to confusion. For example, classifying a computer as a *32-bit machine* might mean that its data registers are 32 bits wide or that it uses 32 bits to identify each address in memory. Whereas larger registers make a computer faster, using more bits for addresses enables a machine to support larger programs.

➡ See also *address; address space; register*.

bit map: A representation, consisting of rows and columns of dots, of a graphics image in computer memory (Figure 9). The value of each dot (whether it is filled in or not) is stored in one or more bits of data. For simple monochromatic images, one bit is sufficient to represent each dot, but for colors and shades of gray, each dot requires more than one bit of data. The more bits used to represent a dot, the more colors and shades of gray that can be represented.

The density of the dots, known as the *resolution,* determines how sharply the image is represented. This is often expressed in *dots per inch (dpi)* or simply by the number of rows and columns, such as 640 by 480.

To display a bit-mapped image on a monitor or to print it on a printer, the computer translates the

Figure 9
Bit Map

bit map into pixels (for display screens) or ink dots (for printers). Optical scanners and FAX machines work by transforming text or pictures on paper into bit maps.

Bit-mapped graphics are often referred to as *raster graphics.* The other method for representing images is known as either *vector graphics* or *object-oriented graphics.* With vector graphics, images are represented as mathematical formulas that define all the shapes in the image. Vector graphics are more flexible than bit-mapped graphics because they look the same even when you scale them to different sizes. In contrast, bit-mapped graphics become ragged when you shrink or enlarge them.

Fonts represented with vector graphics are called *scalable fonts, outline fonts,* or *vector fonts.* The best-known example of a vector font system is PostScript. Bit-mapped fonts, also called *raster fonts,* must be designed for a specific device and a specific size and resolution.

➡ See also *FAX machine; graphics; map; optical scanner; pixel; PostScript; raster graphics; resolution; scalable font; vector graphics.*

bit-mapped graphics: See under *raster graphics.*

BITNET: One of the largest wide-area networks, used extensively by universities. BITNET has gateways to many other networks, including USENET and ARPANET.

➡ See also *ARPANET; network; USENET; wide-area network.*

bits per second: See *bps.*

blank character: Also called a *space character.* A blank character is produced when you press the space bar.

block: (n) (1) In word processing, a block is a group of characters that you have marked to perform some action on them. For example, to move a section of text, you must first block it. This is sometimes called a *block move.*

To specify a block of text, you press special function keys (or click with a mouse) at the beginning and end of the block. The function keys differ from one word processor to another. Word processors usually display blocks by highlighting them on the screen.

➡ See also *word processing.*

(2) In data management, a block is a group of records on a storage device. Blocks are manipulated as units. For example, disk drives often read and write data in 512-byte blocks.

(3) In communications, a block is a fixed-size chunk of data that is transferred together. For example, the Xmodem protocol transfers blocks of 128 bytes. In general, the larger the block size, the faster the data transfer rate.

➡ See also *communications; Xmodem.*

(v) In word processing, to specify a section of text. See definition (1) above.

block graphics: Graphical images created in character mode.

➡ See also *character mode.*

board: See under *printed circuit board* and *expansion board.*

boldface: A font that is darker than the regular face. For example:

    normal font   **boldface font**

Most word processors allow you to mark text as boldface.

bomb: To fail. The term *bomb* usually refers to a program hanging or ending prematurely. Note that bombing is usually less serious than crashing, because bombing refers to a single program, whereas crashing refers to the entire system. The two terms, however, are not always used consistently.

    The Apple Macintosh computer actually has a bomb message (a picture of a bomb) that sometimes appears just before the system crashes.

➦ See also *crash; hang; Macintosh computer.*

Boolean expression: An expression that results in a value of either TRUE or FALSE. For example, the expression

    2 < 5 (2 is less than 5)

is a Boolean expression because the result is TRUE. All expressions that contain *relational operators*, such as the *less than* sign (<), are Boolean. The operators—AND, OR, XOR, NOR, and NOT—are *Boolean operators.*

    Boolean expressions are also called *comparison expressions, conditional expressions,* and *relational expressions.*

➦ See also *Boolean operator; expression; relational operator.*

Boolean logic: Named after the nineteenth-century mathematician, George Boole, Boolean logic is a form of algebra in which all values are reduced to either TRUE or FALSE. Boolean logic is especially important for computer science because it fits nicely with the binary numbering system, in which each bit has a value of either 1 or 0. Another way of looking at it is that each bit has a value of either TRUE or FALSE.

➧ See also *binary; Boolean expression.*

Boolean operator: There are four Boolean operators that can be used to manipulate TRUE/FALSE values. These operators have the following meanings, where x and y represent values of TRUE or FALSE (Table 6).

The OR operator is often called an *inclusive OR,* whereas XOR is an *exclusive OR.*

Boolean operators are used widely in programming and also in forming database queries. For example, the query

```
SELECT ALL WHERE LAST_NAME =
"Smith" AND FIRST_NAME = "John"
```

finds all records with the name John Smith. But the query

Table 6: Boolean Operators

OPERATOR	RESULT
x AND y	Result is *TRUE* if both x and y are *TRUE.* Otherwise the result is *FALSE.*
x OR y	Result is *TRUE* if either x or y is *TRUE.* Otherwise the result is *FALSE.*
x XOR y	Result is *TRUE* only if x and y have different values. Otherwise the result is FALSE.
NOT x	Result is *TRUE* if x is *FALSE.* Result is *FALSE* if x is *TRUE.*

```
SELECT ALL WHERE LAST_NAME =
"Smith" OR FIRST_NAME = "John"
```

finds all records with the last name "Smith" *or* the first name "John."

➡ See also *Boolean expression; Boolean logic; operator; query.*

boot: (v) To load the first piece of software that starts a computer. Because the operating system is essential for running all other programs, it is usually the first piece of software loaded during the boot process.

Boot is short for *bootstrap,* which in olden days was a strap attached to the top of your boot that you could pull to help get your boot on. Hence, the expression "pull oneself up by the bootstraps." Similarly, *bootstrap utilities* help the computer get started.

(n) Short for *bootstrap,* the starting-up of a computer, which involves loading the operating system and other basic software. A *cold boot* is when you turn the computer on from an off position. A *warm boot* is when you reset a computer that is already on.

➡ See also *cold boot; load; operating system; warm boot.*

box: (1) In graphical user interfaces, a box is an enclosed area, resembling a window, on the screen. Unlike windows, however, you generally cannot move or resize boxes.

There are many different types of boxes. For example, *dialog boxes* are boxes that request some type of information from you. *Alert boxes* are boxes that suddenly appear on the screen to give you information. Boxes can also be small rectangular icons that control windows. *Zoom boxes,* for example, enable you to make a window larger or smaller.

➡ See also *alert box; button; dialog box; graphical user interface; icon; window; zoom.*

(2) Slang for *personal computer* or *workstation.*

bps: Abbreviation of *bits per second*, the standard measure of data transmission speeds. Standard telephone lines are capable of transmitting data at a maximum speed of about 9,600 bps. However, the old metal telephone wires are steadily being replaced by fiber optic cables, which are capable of transmitting data at much faster rates. Specialized cables for transmitting data between devices support rates of over 500,000 bps.

A number of standards define the format for sending data at various rates.

➡ See also *asynchronous; Bell 103; Bell 212A; bit; CCITT; communications; communications protocols; fiber optic; MNP; modem.*

Break key: A special key on computer keyboards that temporarily interrupts the computer's communications line. This usually terminates an established modem connection. Not all keyboards have a Break key, and not all programs respond to it.

➡ See also *keyboard.*

broadband ISDN (B-ISDN): A proposed standard for transmitting voice, video, and data at the same time over fiber optic telephone lines. Broadband ISDN will support data rates of 1,500,000 bps.

➡ See also *bps; fiber optics; ISDN.*

broadband transmission: A type of data transmission in which a single medium (wire) can carry several channels at once. Cable TV, for example, uses broadband transmission. In contrast, *baseband* transmission allows only one signal at a time.

Most communications between computers, including the majority of local-area networks, use baseband communications. An exception is *B-ISDN* networks, which employ broadband transmission.

➡ See also *broadband ISDN; channel; communications; local-area network; network.*

broadcast: To simultaneously send the same message to more than one receiver. Broadcasting is a useful feature in electronic mail systems. It is also supported by some FAX systems.

➡ See also *electronic mail; FAX.*

browse: (1) In database systems, *browse* means to view data. Many database systems support a special *browse mode,* in which you can flip through fields and records quickly. Usually, you cannot modify data while you are in browse mode.

➡ See also *database management system; field; record.*

(2) In object-oriented programming languages, *browse* means to examine data structures.

➡ See also *data structure; object oriented.*

buffer: (n) A temporary storage area, usually in RAM. The purpose of most buffers is to act as a holding area, enabling the CPU to manipulate data before transferring it to a device.

Because the process of reading and writing data to a disk is relatively slow, many programs keep track of data changes in a buffer and then copy the buffer to a disk. For example, most text editors employ a buffer to keep track of changes to text files. Then, at the end of your editing session, the word processor updates the disk file with the contents of the buffer. This is much more efficient than accessing the file on the disk each time you make a change to the file.

Note that because your changes are initially stored in a buffer, not on the disk, all of them will be lost if the computer fails during an editing session. For this reason, it is a good idea to save your file periodically. Saving your file forces the word processor to copy the buffer to the disk. Some word processors automatically save files at regular intervals.

Another common use of buffers is for printing documents. When you enter a PRINT command, the operating system copies your document to a print buffer (a free area in memory or on a disk) from which the printer can draw characters at its own pace. This frees the computer to perform other tasks while the printer is running in the background. Print buffering is called *spooling*.

Most keyboard drivers also contain a buffer so that you can edit typing mistakes before sending your command to a program. Many operating systems, including DOS, also use a *disk buffer* to temporarily hold data that they have read from a disk. The disk buffer is really a cache.

DOS systems allow you to specify the amount of space to be reserved for disk buffers with the BUFFER command. Each DOS buffer is 528 bytes, so the command

BUFFERS = 20

reserves about 10K of main memory for buffers. Normally, the BUFFER command is placed in the CONFIG.SYS file, where it will be executed each time the computer is turned on.

On Macintoshes, the disk buffer is called a *cache*, and its size can be set on the Control Panel.

➡ See also *background; cache; CONFIG.SYS; Control Panel; DOS; save; spooling; word processing.*

(v) To move data into a temporary storage area.

bug: An error or defect in software or hardware that causes a program to malfunction. According to the folklore, the term originated when a moth trapped in the electrical workings of the first digital computer, the ENIAC, was discovered by Lieutenant Grace Hopper.

➡ See also *bomb; crash; hang.*

built-in font: Same as *resident font.*

bulletin board system (BBS): An electronic message center. Most bulletin boards serve specific interest groups. They allow you to dial in with a modem, review messages left by others, and leave your own message if you want. Bulletin boards are a particularly good place to find free or inexpensive software products. In the United States alone, there are thousands of BBSs (some estimates go as high as 15,000).

➡ See also *electronic mail; modem; network; SIG; SYSOP.*

bus: (1) A collection of wires through which data is transmitted from one part of a computer to another. You can think of a bus as a highway on which data travels within a computer. When used in reference to personal computers, the term *bus* usually refers to the *expansion bus.* This is a bus that connects all the various computer components—expansion boards and external devices such as disk drives and printers—to the CPU. Personal computers also have an *address bus* and *data bus* that connect the CPU with RAM.

The size of a bus, known as its *width,* is important because it determines how much data can be transmitted at one time. For example, a 16-bit bus can transmit 16 bits of data, whereas a 32-bit bus can transmit 32 bits of data. The bus is rarely larger than the CPU's address capability, and is often smaller. For example, the Intel 80386 microprocessor has 32-bit address capability, but is often combined with the AT bus, which is only 16 bits wide.

Like microprocessors, every bus has a clock speed measured in MHz. If the bus speed is much slower than the microprocessor, and you have memory on expansion boards, the expansion bus will create a bottleneck that slows down execution of programs. This is why it is usually better to add memory chips directly to the motherboard (which does not use the bus) rather than insert a memory expansion board.

The component responsible for connecting a particular device to a bus is called a *controller*. The controller must know how to transmit information on and off the bus. Each controller, therefore, is designed to connect to a particular type of device and a particular type of bus.

There are three types of expansion buses for IBM PCs and compatibles. Each type defines different *protocols* for regulating data traffic. The three bus standards are:

Industry Standard Architecture (ISA) bus: The bus used on PC/XT and PC/AT computers. The XT bus is 8 bits wide. The *AT bus,* which has become a de facto industry standard, is 16 bits wide. ISA buses run at a clock speed of 8MHz.

Micro Channel architecture (MCA) bus: A 32-bit, 10MHz bus used in the high-end PS/2 computers. MCA requires an Intel 80386 or 80486 microprocessor. It is incompatible with the AT bus, which means that it requires special MCA expansion boards.

Extended Industry Standard Architecture (EISA) bus: A 32-bit, 8MHz bus designed by a group of IBM competitors. EISA is similar to MCA, but it is *backward compatible* with the ISA bus, so that it can accept old expansion boards as well as new ones.

Several different types of buses are used on

Apple Macintosh computers. The fastest and most sophisticated is called the *NuBus* expansion bus.

➡ See also *ADB; AT bus; clock speed; communications; controller; CPU; EISA; IBM PC; Industry Standard Architecture (ISA) bus; main memory; Micro Channel architecture; microprocessor; NuBus.*

(2) In networking, a bus is a central cable that connects all devices on a local-area network (LAN). It is also called the *backbone.*

➡ See also *Ethernet; network; topology.*

business graphics: Same as *presentation graphics.*

bus mouse: A mouse that connects to a computer via an expansion board. Another type of mouse is a *serial mouse,* which connects to a serial port. Serial mice are easier to install, but the advantage of bus mice is that they do not use up the serial port, so you can use the port for a different device (a modem, for example).

➡ See also *bus; mouse; serial port.*

bus topology: See under *topology* (see Figure 68 at *topology*).

button: (1) In graphical user interfaces, a button is a small outlined area in a dialog box that you can *click* to select a command.

➡ See also *click; dialog box; graphical user interface; radio buttons.*

(2) In Hypertext databases, a button is an icon that when selected lets you view an associated object.

➡ See also *Hypertext; icon.*

(3) A *mouse button* is a button on a mouse that you click to perform various functions, such as selecting an object.

➡ See also *click; mouse.*

byte: A unit of storage capable of holding a single character. On almost all modern computers, a byte is equal to 8 bits. Large amounts of memory are indicated in terms of *kilobytes* (1,024 bytes), *megabytes* (1,048,576 bytes), and *gigabytes* (approximately 1 billion bytes). A disk that can hold 512K bytes, for example, is capable of storing approximately 512,-000 characters, or about 1,000 pages of information.

➡ See also *gigabyte; kilobyte; megabyte.*

— C —

C: A high-level programming language developed by Dennis Ritchie and Brian Kernighan at Bell Labs in the mid 1970s. Although originally designed as a systems programming language, C has proved to be a powerful and flexible language that can be used for a variety of applications, from business programs to engineering. C is a particularly popular language for personal computer programmers because it is relatively small—it requires less memory than other languages.

The first major program written in C was the UNIX operating system, and for many years C was considered to be inextricably linked with UNIX. Now, however, C is an important language independent of UNIX.

Although it is a high-level language, C is much closer to assembly language than are most other high-level languages. This closeness to the underlying machine language allows C programmers to write very efficient code. The low-level nature of C, however, can make the language difficult to use for some types of applications.

➡ See also *assembly language; high-level programming language; machine language; programming language; UNIX.*

C++: A high-level programming language developed by Bjarne Stroustrup at Bell Labs. C++ adds object-oriented features to its predecessor, C.

➡ See also *C; object oriented; programming language.*

cache: Pronounced *cash*, a cache is a special high-speed storage mechanism. It can be either a reserved section of main memory or an independent high-speed storage device. Two types of caching are commonly used in personal computers: *memory caching* and *disk caching* (Figure 10).

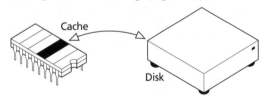

Figure 10
Disk Caching

A memory cache, sometimes called a *cache store* or *RAM cache,* is a portion of memory made of high-speed static RAM (SRAM) rather than the slower and cheaper dynamic RAM (DRAM) used for main memory. Memory caching is effective because most programs access the same data or instructions over and over again. By keeping this information in SRAM, the computer avoids accessing the slower DRAM.

When data is found in the cache, it is called a *hit,* and the effectiveness of a cache is judged by its *hit rate.* Many cache systems use a technique known as *smart caching,* in which the system can recognize certain types of frequently used data. The strategies for determining which information should be kept in the cache constitute some of the more interesting problems in computer science.

Some memory caches are built into the architecture of microprocessors. The Intel 80486 microprocessor, for example, contains an 8K memory cache.

Disk caching works under the same principle as memory caching, but instead of using high-speed SRAM, a disk cache uses conventional main memory. The most recently accessed data from the disk (as well as adjacent sectors) is stored in a memory buffer. When a program needs to access data from the disk, it first checks the disk cache to see if the data is there. Disk caching can dramatically improve the performance of applications, because accessing a byte of data in RAM can be thousands of times faster than accessing a byte on a hard disk.

➡ See also *buffer; disk cache; disk drive; dynamic RAM; main memory; RAM disk; static RAM; storage device.*

cache memory: See under *cache.*

CAD: Acronym for *computer-aided design.* A CAD system is a combination of hardware and software that enables engineers and architects to design everything from furniture to airplanes (Figure 11). In addition to the software, CAD systems require a high-quality graphics monitor; a mouse, light pen, or digitizer for drawing; and a special printer or plotter for printing design specifications.

CAD systems allow an engineer to view a design from any angle with the push of a button and to zoom in or out for close-ups and long-distance views. In addition, the computer keeps track of design dependencies so that when the engineer changes one value, all other values that depend on it are automatically changed accordingly.

Until the mid 1980s, all CAD systems were specially constructed computers. Now, you can buy CAD software that runs on general-purpose workstations and powerful personal computers.

➧ See also *CAD/CAM; CAE; digitizer; graphics; light pen; monitor; mouse; plotter; workstation.*

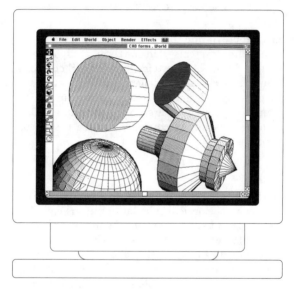

Figure 11
CAD Application

CAD/CAM: Acronym for *computer-aided design/computer-aided manufacturing,* computer systems used to design and manufacture products. The term *CAD/CAM* implies that an engineer can use the system both for designing a product and for controlling manufacturing processes. For example, once a

65

design has been produced with the CAD component, the design itself can control the machines
that construct the part.

➠ See also *CAD; CAM*.

CADD: Acronym for *computer-aided design and drafting*. CADD systems are CAD systems with additional drafting features. For example, CADD
systems enable an engineer or architect to insert
size annotations and other notes into a design.

➠ See also *CAD; CAD/CAM*.

CAE: Abbreviation of *computer-aided engineering*,
computer systems that analyze engineering designs. Most CAD systems have a CAE component,
but there are also independent CAE systems that
can analyze designs produced by various CAD systems. CAE systems are able to simulate a design
under a variety of conditions to see if it actually
works.

➠ See also *CAD*.

calculator: (1) A small hand-held computer that performs mathematical calculations. Some calculators
even permit simple text editing and programming.
   (2) A program on a computer that simulates a
hand-held calculator. Calculator programs let you
perform simple math calculations without leaving
the computer. The Apple Macintosh comes with a
calculator desk accessory. Likewise, Microsoft
Windows includes a calculator accessory.

➠ See also *desk accessory; Microsoft Windows;
program*.

calendar: A program that enables you to record events
and appointments on an electronic calendar. Computer calendars act like datebooks, but they have
several advantages over traditional datebooks:

> **automatic entries for regular events:** You can specify, for example, that the first Thursday of every month is bridge night, and the calendar program will automatically fill in the appropriate days.

> **signaling of upcoming events:** Most calendars will let you know that an event is approaching by issuing beeps.

> **clean deletion:** With an electronic calendar, you can erase an appointment without leaving a trace.

Calendar software is part of a more general category of software known as *PIMs* (personal information managers). A special type of calendar, called a *scheduler,* enables groups of users connected to a network to coordinate their schedules.

➡ See also *PIM; scheduler; utility.*

call: (v) To invoke a routine in a programming language. Calling a routine consists of specifying the routine name and, optionally, parameters. For example, the following is a *function call* in the C programming language:

```
printf("Hello")
```

The name of the function is *printf* and "Hello" is the parameter. This function call causes the computer to display the word *Hello* on the display screen.

A routine that invokes another routine is sometimes referred to as the *calling routine.* The routine that is invoked is referred to as the *called routine.*

(n) An invocation of a routine.

➡ See also *function; routine.*

CAM: Acronym for *computer-aided manufacturing,* a type of computer application that helps automate a factory. For example, the following are types of CAM systems:

- real-time control
- robotics
- materials requirements

All these systems are concerned with automatically directing the manufacture and inventory of parts.

➡ See also *CAD; CAD/CAM; robotics.*

Caps Lock key: A *toggle key* on computer keyboards that, when activated, causes all subsequent alphabetic characters to be uppercase, but has no effect on other keys.

➡ See also *keyboard; toggle; uppercase.*

capture: To save a particular state of a program. The term *capture* often refers to saving the information currently displayed on a display screen. You can capture the screen to a printer or to a file. The act of saving a display screen is called a *screen capture.*

The term *capture* is also used to describe the recording of keystrokes during the definition of a *macro.*

➡ See also *learn mode; keystroke; macro; screen capture.*

card: Same as *printed circuit board.*

carriage: The mechanism on a printer that feeds paper. A *wide-carriage printer* is a printer that can accept very wide paper. A *narrow-carriage printer* is a printer that accepts only standard-sized paper.

➡ See also *paper feed; printer.*

carriage return: Often abbreviated *CR,* a carriage return is a special code that moves the cursor (or print head) to the beginning of the current line. In the ASCII character set, a carriage return has a decimal value of 13.

Most word processors represent a hard return with a combination of line feed and carriage return codes.

➡ See also *ASCII; hard return; line feed; return; soft return.*

cartridge: (1) A removable storage medium (tape, disk, or memory chip). Some printers have slots in which you can insert cartridges to load different fonts. A font loaded from a cartridge is called a *font cartridge* or *cartridge font*.

Some computers (such as the Commodore Ataris) have slots in which you can insert cartridges to load programs. These *ROM cartridges* contain data and programs on read-only memory chips. They are convenient because they are durable, cannot be erased, and, unlike disks, are soundless.

The term *removable cartridge* usually refers to a type of hard disk that you can remove. Removable cartridges offer the speed of hard disks along with the portability of floppy disks.

➡ See also *Bernoulli disk drive; font cartridge; font; printer; removable cartridge; slot.*

(2) For laser printers, a *toner cartridge* is a metal container that holds the *toner*.

➡ See also *laser printer; toner.*

cartridge font: Same as *font cartridge.*

cascading windows: An arrangement of windows such that they overlap one another. Typically, the title bar remains visible so that you can always see which windows are open. Cascading windows are also called *overlaid* windows. An alternative arrangement of windows, in which every window is completely visible, is called *tiled windows* (see Figure 52 at *overlaid windows*).

➡ See also *overlaid windows; tiled windows; window.*

case sensitivity: A program's ability to distinguish between uppercase (capital) and lowercase (small) letters. Programs that distinguish between uppercase and lowercase are said to be *case sensitive.*

A case-sensitive program that expects you to enter all commands in uppercase will not respond correctly if you enter one or more characters in lowercase. It will treat the command *RUN* differently from *run.* Programs that do not distinguish between uppercase and lowercase are said to be *case insensitive.*

➡ See also *lowercase; uppercase.*

cathode-ray tube: See *CRT.*

CCITT: Abbreviation of ***Comité Consultatif International Téléphonique et Télégraphique***, an organization that sets international communications standards. CCITT has defined many important standards for data communications, including the following:

Group 3: The universal protocol for sending FAX documents across telephone lines. The Group 3 protocol specifies CCITT T.4 data compression and a maximum transmission rate of 9,600 bps. There are two levels of resolution: 203 by 98 and 203 by 196.

Group 4: A protocol for sending FAX documents over ISDN networks.

V.21: The standard for full-duplex communication at 300 baud in Japan and Europe. In the United States, Bell 103 is used in place of V.21.

V.22: The standard for half-duplex communication at 1,200 bps in Japan and Europe. In the United States, the protocol defined by Bell 212A is more common.

V.22*bis*: The worldwide standard for full-duplex modems sending and receiving data across telephone lines at 1,200 or 2,400 bps.

V.29: The standard for half-duplex modems sending and receiving data across telephone lines at 1,200, 2,400, 4,800, or 9,600 bps. This is the protocol used by FAX modems.

V.32: The standard for full-duplex modems sending and receiving data across phone lines at 4,800 or 9,600 bps. V.32 modems automatically adjust their transmission speeds based on the quality of the lines.

V.32*bis*: The V.32 protocol extended to speeds of 7,200, 12,000, and 14,400 bps.

V.42: An error-detection standard for high-speed modems. V.42 can be used with digital telephone networks. See *MNP* for a competing standard.

V.42bis: A data compression protocol that can enable modems to achieve a data transfer rate of 34,000 bps.

X.25: The most popular packet-switching protocol for LANs. Ethernet, for example, is based on the X.25 standard.

X.400: The universal protocol for electronic mail. X.400 defines the envelope for E-mail messages so all messages conform to a standard format.

X.500: An extension to X.400 that defines addressing formats so all E-mail systems can be linked together.

➧ See also *baud rate; bps; communications protocol; data compression; electronic mail; FAX machine; FAX modem; full duplex; half duplex; ISDN; MNP; modem; protocol; standard.*

cdev: Pronounced *see-dev*, a cdev is a special type of Macintosh utility program whose icon appears in the *Control Panel*. Cdevs must be placed in the system folder to work.

➧ See also *Control Panel; icon; Macintosh computer; utility.*

CD-I (Compact Disc-Interactive): A standard format developed by Philips International for storing video, audio, and binary data on compact optical disks. It supports 552MB of binary data and specifies several different types of video and audio encoding formats. Unlike conventional CD-ROMS, CD-I drives have a built-in microprocessor to handle many of the computing functions.

A competing standard, developed by Intel Corporation, is known as DVI (Digital Video Interactive).

➡ See also *CD-ROM; DVI; optical disk.*

CD-ROM: Abbreviation of ***C**ompact **D**isc–**R**ead-**O**nly **M**emory.* A type of optical disk capable of storing large amounts of data—up to 1GB, although the most common size is 550MB. A single CD-ROM has the storage capacity of 1,000 floppy disks, enough memory to store about 250,000 text pages.

CD-ROMs require a special machine to record the data, and once recorded, they cannot be erased and filled with new data. To read a CD, you need a CD-ROM player. Almost all CD-ROMs conform to a standard size and format, so it is usually possible to load any type of CD into any ROM player. In addition, many CD-ROM players are capable of playing audio CDs, which share the same technology.

Because CD-ROMs are expensive, read-only, and relatively slow, they have limited applications. Currently, they are used to store large amounts of information, such as encyclopedias. A more promising technology is erasable optical (EO) disks, on which data can be recorded and deleted as with magnetic disks.

➡ See also *disk; erasable optical disk; mass storage; optical disk.*

cell: In spreadsheet applications, a cell is a box in which you can enter a single piece of data. The data is usually text, a numeric value, or a formula. The entire spreadsheet is composed of rows and columns of cells. A spreadsheet cell is analogous to a *field* in database management systems.

Individual cells are usually identified by a column letter and a row number. For example, *D12* specifies the cell in column D and row 12.

➡ See also *field; formula; spreadsheet.*

central processing unit: See *CPU.*

Centronics interface: A standard interface for connecting printers and other parallel devices (see Figure 17 at *connector*). For personal computers, almost all parallel ports conform to the Centronics standard.

Although Centronics Corporation designed the original standard, the Centronics interface used by modern computers was designed by Epson Corporation.

➡ See also *interface; parallel interface; standard.*

CGA: Abbreviation of *color/graphics adapter*, a graphics system for IBM PCs and compatibles. Introduced by IBM in 1981, CGA was the first color graphics system for IBM PCs. Designed primarily for computer games, CGA does not produce sharp enough characters for extended editing sessions. CGA's highest-resolution text mode is 16 colors at a resolution of 640 by 200. Its highest graphics mode is 2 colors at a resolution of 640 by 200. CGA also supports graphics modes that provide more colors at lower resolutions.

CGA has been superseded by EGA and VGA systems, which are backward compatible with CGA.

➡ See also *backward compatible; EGA; graphics mode; IBM PC; palette; resolution; SVGA; text mode; VGA; video adapter; XGA.*

CGM: Abbreviation of *Computer Graphics Metafile*, a

file format designed by several standards organizations and formally ratified by ANSI. It is designed to be the standard vector graphics file format and is supported by a wide variety of software and hardware products.

➡ See also *ANSI; graphics; graphics file formats; standard; vector graphics.*

channel: (1) For IBM PS/2 computers, a channel is the same as an expansion bus.

➡ See also *bus.*

(2) In communications, the term *channel* refers to a communications path between two computers or devices. It can refer to the physical medium (the wires) or to a set of properties that distinguishes one channel from another. For example, *TV channels* refer to particular frequencies at which radio waves are transmitted.

➡ See also *communications.*

character: In computer software, a character is any symbol that requires one byte of storage. This includes all the ASCII and extended ASCII characters. In character-based software, everything that appears on the screen, including graphics symbols, is considered to be a character. In graphics-based applications, the term *character* is generally reserved for letters, numbers, and punctuation.

➡ See also *alphanumeric; ASCII; byte; character based; extended ASCII; graphics based.*

character based: Describes programs capable of displaying only ASCII (and extended ASCII) characters. Character-based programs treat a display screen as an array of boxes, each of which can hold one character. Display screens for IBM PCs and compatibles, for example, are typically divided into 25 rows and 80 columns. In contrast, *graphics-based* programs treat the display screen as an array of millions of pixels. Characters and other objects are formed by illuminating patterns of pixels.

Because the IBM *extended ASCII* character set includes shapes for drawing pictures, character-based programs are capable of simulating some graphics objects. For example, character-based programs can display windows and menus, bar charts, and other shapes that consist primarily of straight lines (Figure 12). However, they cannot represent more complicated objects that contain curves.

Character-based Program   Graphics-based Program

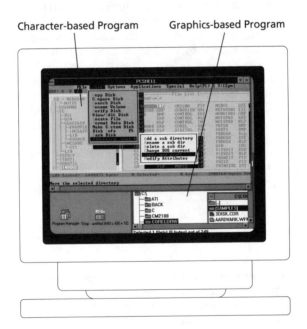

Figure 12
Character-based vs. Graphics-based Programs

Unlike IBM PCs and compatibles, the Macintosh computer is a graphics-based machine. All programs that run on a Macintosh computer are graphics based.

➡ See also *ASCII; backward compatible; character mode; DESQview; extended ASCII; graphical user interface; graphics; IBM PC; Macintosh computer; Microsoft Windows; pixel; text mode.*

character mode: Many video adapters support several different modes of resolution. All such modes are divided into two general categories: *character mode* (also called *text mode*) and *graphics mode*. In character mode, the display screen is treated as an array of blocks, each of which can hold one ASCII character. In graphics mode, the display screen is treated as an array of pixels, with characters and other shapes formed by turning on combinations of pixels.

Of the two modes, character mode is much simpler. Programs that run in character mode generally run much faster than those that run in graphics mode, but they are limited in the variety of fonts and shapes they can display. Programs that run entirely in character mode are called *character-based* programs.

➡ See also *ASCII; character based; pixel; video adapter.*

character recognition: See *optical character recognition.*

character set: A defined list of characters recognized by the computer hardware and software. Each character is represented by a number. The ASCII character set, for example, uses the numbers 0 through 127 to represent all English characters as well as special control characters. European ISO character sets are similar to ASCII, but they contain additional characters for European languages.

➡ See also *ASCII; character; control character.*

characters per second: See *cps.*

character string: A series of characters manipulated as a group. A character string differs from a name in that it does not represent anything—a name stands for some other object.

A character string is often specified by enclosing the characters in single or double quotes. For example, WASHINGTON would be a name, but 'WASHINGTON' and "WASHINGTON" would be character strings.

The length of a character string is usually the number of characters in it. For example, the character string "WASHINGTON" has a length of 10 (the quote marks are not included). Some programs, however, mark the beginning or end of a character string with an invisible character, so the length might actually be one greater than the number of characters.

➡ See also *character; name.*

chassis: A metal frame that serves as the structural support for electronic components. Every computer system requires at least one chassis to house the circuit boards and wiring. The chassis also contains slots for expansion boards. If you want to insert more boards than there are slots, you will need an *expansion chassis,* which provides additional slots.

➡ See also *circuit board; expansion board; slot.*

checksum: In communications, a simple error-detection scheme in which each transmitted message is accompanied by a numerical value based on the number of set bits in the message. The receiving station then applies the same formula to the message and checks to make sure the accompanying numerical value is the same. If not, the receiver knows that the message has been garbled.

➡ See also *communications; CRC; error detection.*

chip: A small piece of semiconducting material (usu-

ally silicon) on which an integrated circuit is embedded (Figure 13). A typical chip is less than
¼-square inches and can contain millions of electronic components. Computers consist of many
chips placed on electronic boards called *printed circuit boards*.

There are different types of chips. For example,
CPU chips (also called *microprocessors*) contain an
entire processing unit, whereas memory chips contain blank memory.

Chips come in a variety of forms. The three most
common are

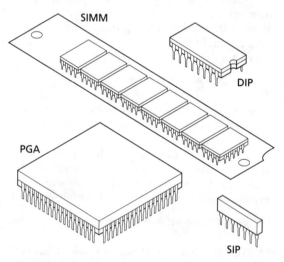

Figure 13
Chips

DIPs: Dual in-line packages are the traditional
buglike chips that have anywhere from 8 to 40
legs, evenly divided in two rows.

PGAs: Pin-grid arrays are square chips in which
the pins are arranged in concentric squares.

SIPs: Single in-line packages are chips that have
just one row of legs in a straight line like a
comb.

In addition to these types of chips, there are also single in-line memory modules (SIMMs), which consist of up to nine chips packaged as a single unit.

➡ See also *CPU; integrated circuit; memory; microprocessor; printed circuit board; semiconductor; SIMM.*

circuit board: Short for *printed circuit board.*

CISC: Pronounced *sisk,* CISC stands for *complex instruction set computer.* Most computers, especially personal computers, use a CISC architecture, in which the CPU supports as many as two hundred instructions. The opposite of a CISC architecture is a *RISC* (reduced instruction set computer) architecture, which supports far fewer instructions.

➡ See also *architecture; CPU; machine language; RISC.*

clear: To erase. *Clear the screen,* for example, means to erase everything on the display screen. *Clear a variable* means to remove whatever data is currently stored in the variable. *Clear memory* means to erase all data currently stored in memory.

➡ See also *display screen; memory; variable.*

click: (v) To press down and then immediately release a button on a mouse. Note that *clicking* a mouse button is different from *pressing* (or *dragging*) a mouse button, which implies that you hold the button down without releasing it. The phrase *to click on* means to select (a screen object) by moving the mouse cursor to the object's position and clicking a mouse button.

Some programs support a *double click,* meaning that you must click a mouse button twice in rapid succession. *Shift clicking* refers to clicking the mouse button while holding the Shift key down.

➡ See also *double click; drag; graphical user interface; mouse; shift clicking.*

(n) The pressing down and rapid release of a mouse button.

client/server architecture: A network architecture in which each computer or process on the network is either a *client* or a *server*. Servers are powerful computers or processes dedicated to managing disk drives (*file servers*), printers (*print servers*), or network traffic (*network servers*). Clients are less powerful PCs or workstations on which users run applications.

Another type of network architecture is known as a *peer-to-peer* architecture because each *node* has equivalent responsibilities. Both client/server and peer-to-peer architectures are widely used, and each has unique advantages and disadvantages.

➠ See also *architecture; local-area network; network; node; peer-to-peer architecture; process; server.*

clip art: In word processing and desktop publishing, clip art refers to illustrations that can be inserted into a document (Figure 14). Many clip-art pack-

Figure 14
Clip Art

ages are available, some general and others specialized for a particular field. Most clip-art packages provide the illustrations in several file formats so that you can insert them into various word-processing systems.

➡ See also *desktop publishing; word processing.*

clipboard: A special file or memory area (*buffer*) where data is stored temporarily before being copied to another location. Many word processors, for example, use a clipboard for cutting and pasting. When you cut a block of text, the word processor copies the block to the clipboard; when you paste the block, the word processor copies it from the clipboard to its final destination.

In Microsoft Windows and on the Apple Macintosh computer, the clipboard can be used to copy data from one application to another. The Macintosh uses two types of clipboards. The one it calls the *Clipboard* can hold only one item at a time and is flushed when you turn the computer off. The other, called the *Scrapbook,* can hold several items at once and retains its contents from one working session to another.

➡ See also *buffer; copy; cut; Macintosh computer; Microsoft Windows; paste; word processing.*

clock speed: Also called *clock rate,* the speed at which a microprocessor executes instructions. Every computer contains an internal clock that regulates the rate at which instructions are executed and synchronizes all the various computer components. The CPU requires a fixed number of clock ticks (or *clock cycles*) to execute each instruction. For example, an Intel 80286 microprocessor needs about 20 clock cycles to multiply two numbers together. The faster the clock, the more instructions the CPU can execute per second.

Clock speeds are expressed in megahertz (MHz), 1MHz being equal to 1 million cycles per second. Personal computers have clock speeds of anywhere from 4MHz to 50MHz.

Usually, the clock rate is a fixed characteristic of the microprocessor. Some computers, however, have a switch that lets you choose between two or more different clock speeds. This is useful because programs written to run on a machine with a high clock rate may not work properly on a machine with a slower clock rate, and vice versa. In addition, some add-on components may not be able to run at high clock speeds.

Some CPUs utilize *wait states*, idle clock ticks during which a CPU waits for slower memory to catch up. For example, a CPU running at 10MHz with no wait states is faster than a 12MHz CPU with one wait state.

Like CPUs, *expansion buses* also have clock speeds. Ideally, the CPU clock speed and the bus clock speed should be the same so that neither component slows down the other. In practice, the bus clock speed is often slower than the CPU clock speed. Many computers have a special fast bus that serves memory and a slower standard bus for I/O devices.

➡ See also *bus; CPU; instruction; microprocessor; wait state.*

clone: A computer, software product, or device that functions exactly like another, better-known product. For example, IBM PC clones are personal computers that offer the same functionality as an IBM PC but are produced by other companies. If the clone is good, you should be unable to tell the difference between it and the real product.

The term *clone* implies that the product is an exact duplicate. Note that the term *clone* is a bit stronger than the term *compatible*. For example, an IBM PC clone is a computer that has most, if not all, the same components as a real IBM PC. The term *IBM-compatible*, on the other hand, implies only that the computer is capable of running any program that an IBM PC can run. This does not mean that it is the same internally.

➡ See also *compatible; IBM PC.*

close: (1) To finish work on a data file and save it.

➡ See also *open; save.*

(2) In graphical user interfaces, to close a window means to exit an application or file, thereby removing the window from the screen.

➡ See also *graphical user interface; window.*

CMOS: Abbreviation of *complementary metal oxide semiconductor.* Pronounced *see-moss,* CMOS is a widely used type of semiconductor. CMOS semiconductors require less power than NMOS transistors, making them particularly attractive for use in battery-powered devices, such as portable computers. Many personal computers contain a small amount of battery-powered CMOS memory to hold the date, time, and system setup parameters.

➡ See also *semiconductor.*

COBOL: Acronym for *common business oriented language.* Developed in the late 1950s and early 1960s, COBOL is the second-oldest high-level programming language (FORTRAN is the oldest). It is particularly popular for business applications that run on large computers.

COBOL is a wordy language; programs written in COBOL tend to be much longer than the same programs written in other languages. This can be annoying when you program in COBOL, but the wordiness makes it easy to understand programs because everything is spelled out. Although disparaged by many programmers for being outdated, COBOL is still the most widely used programming language in the world.

➡ See also *programming language*.

code: (n) (1) A set of symbols for representing something. For example, most computers use ASCII codes to represent characters.

➡ See also *ASCII*.

(2) Written computer instructions. The term *code* is somewhat colloquial. For example, a programmer might say: "I wrote a lot of code this morning" or "There's one piece of code that doesn't work."

Code can appear in a variety of forms. The code that a programmer writes is called *source code*. After it has been compiled, it is called *object code*. Code that is ready to run is called *executable code* or *machine code*.

➡ See also *executable file; machine language; object code; source code*.

(v) Colloquial for *to program* (that is, to write *source code*).

➡ See also *compile; program*.

cold boot: The start-up of a computer from a powered-down state.

➡ See also *boot*.

color/graphics adapter: See *CGA*.

column: (1) On a display screen in character mode, a column is a vertical line of characters extending from the top to the bottom of the screen. The size of a text display is usually measured in rows and columns.

➡ See also *character mode; display screen*.

(2) In spreadsheets, a column is a vertical row of

cells. Spreadsheet columns are usually identified by letters.

➡ See also *cell; spreadsheet*.

(3) In database management systems, *column* is another name for *field*.

➡ See also *database management system; field*.

COM file: In DOS environments, a *COM file* is an executable command file with a .COM filename extension. COM files can be directly executed and are usually slightly smaller than equivalent EXE files. However, COM files cannot exceed 64K, so large programs are usually stored in EXE files.

➡ See also *executable file; EXE file; extension; file; DOS*.

command: An instruction to a computer or device to perform a specific task. Commands come in different forms. They can be:

- special words (keywords) that a program understands
- function keys
- choices in a menu

Every program that interacts with people responds to a specific set of commands. The set of commands and the syntax for entering them is called the *user interface* and varies from one program to another.

The DOS operating system makes a distinction between *internal* and *external* commands. Internal commands are commands, such as COPY and DIR, that can be handled by the COMMAND.COM program. External commands include the names of all other COM files as well as EXE and BAT files.

Another word for *command* is *directive*.

➡ See also *BAT file; COM file; EXE file; external command; function keys; internal command; keyword; menu; DOS; user interface*.

command buffer: A temporary storage area where commands are kept. (In DOS environments, the command buffer is called a *template*.) DOS and UNIX support several operations for manipulating the command buffer. For example, you can use the F3 function key in DOS to copy the template's contents to the display screen. This is useful for repeating a command, or for correcting a mistake.

Command buffers also make it possible for programs to *undo* commands.

➡ See also *buffer; command; undo.*

COMMAND.COM: The DOS file that contains all the DOS internal commands.

➡ See also *internal command; DOS.*

command driven: Refers to programs that accept commands in the form of special words or letters. In contrast, programs that allow you to choose from a list of options in a menu are said to be *menu driven.* Command-driven software is generally more flexible than menu-driven software, but it is more difficult to learn.

➡ See also *command; menu driven; user interface.*

command key: Macintosh computers have a special command key marked by a four-leaf clover or an apple. The command key is similar to a Control key—you hold it down while pressing another key to execute some operation. Typically, command-key combinations are shorthands for menu choices. For example, on the desktop, pressing COMMAND-O is equivalent to selecting the *open* option from the *file* menu.

➡ See also *control key; icon; keyboard; window.*

command language: The programming language through which a user communicates with the operating system or an application. For example, the

DOS command language includes the commands DIR, COPY, and DEL, to name a few. The part of an operating system that responds to operating system commands is called the *command processor*.

With graphical user interfaces, the command language consists of operations you perform with a mouse or similar input device.

➡ See also *command; command processor; graphical user interface; operating system; shell*.

command line: The line on the display screen where a command is expected. Generally, the command line is the line that contains the most recently displayed command prompt.

➡ See also *command; prompt*.

command line interpreter: Same as *command processor*.

command processor: The part of the operating system that receives and executes operating system commands. Every operating system has a command processor. When the command prompt is displayed, the command processor is waiting for a command. After you enter a command, the command processor analyzes the syntax to make sure the command is valid, and then either executes the command or issues an error warning. For operating systems with a graphical user interface, the command processor interprets mouse operations and executes the appropriate command.

Another term for command processor is *command line interpreter*.

➡ See also *command language; graphical user interface; operating system; prompt; syntax*.

Commodore Amiga: See *Amiga*.

common carrier: Same as *public carrier*.

communications: The transmission of data from one computer to another, or from one device to another. A *communications device,* therefore, is any machine that assists data transmission. For example, modems, cables, and ports are all communications devices. *Communications software* refers to programs that make it possible to transmit data.

➡ See also *cable; communications protocol; communications software; modem; network; port.*

communications protocol: All communications between devices require that the devices agree on the format of the data. The set of rules defining a format is called a *protocol.* At the very least, a communications protocol must define the following:

- rate of transmission (in *baud* or *bps*)
- whether transmission is to be *synchronous* or *asynchronous*
- whether data is to be transmitted in *half-duplex* or *full-duplex* mode

In addition, protocols can include sophisticated techniques for detecting and recovering from transmission errors, and for encoding and decoding data.

Table 7 lists the most commonly used protocols for communications via modems. These protocols

Table 7: Communications Protocols

PROTOCOL	MAXIMUM TRANSMISSION RATE	DUPLEX MODE
Bell 103	300 bps	Full
CCITT V.21	300 bps	Full
Bell 212A	1,200 bps	Full
CCITT V.22	1,200 bps	Half
CCITT V.22*bis*	2,400 bps	Full
CCITT V.29	9,600 bps	Half
CCITT V.32	9,600 bps	Full
CCITT V.32*bis*	14,400 bps	Full

are almost always implemented in the hardware; that is, they are built into modems.

In addition to the standard protocols listed in the table, there are a number of protocols that complement these standards by adding additional functions such as file transfer capability, error detection and recovery, and data compression. The best known are *Xmodem, Kermit, MNP*, and *CCITT V.42*. These protocols can be implemented either in hardware or software.

➡ See also *asynchronous; baud rate; Bell 103; Bell 212A; bps; CCITT; full duplex; half duplex; Kermit; MNP; protocol; synchronous; Xmodem; Ymodem; Zmodem.*

communications software: Software that makes it possible to send and receive data over telephone lines through modems. The following features differentiate various communications software packages:

maximum bps rate: The software package should be able to transmit data as fast as your modem. Maximum bps rates for communications packages vary between 9,600 and 57,600 bps.

automatic queue and redial: This is a useful feature if you use your modem to access a service that is frequently busy, such as a bulletin board system (BBS). When you enter the telephone number in a queue, the communications software will keep redialing the number until it gets through. This feature can also be implemented by the modem itself rather than by the software.

text editor: Most packages come with a text editor so that you can edit documents and messages you send and receive. The power of the text editor varies considerably from one package to another. Many editors, for example, do not perform word wrap.

macros: The ability to create macros is very important because you often go through the same steps every time you make a connection. By storing the connection sequence in a macro, you can perform the entire process with a single keystroke.

file transfer protocols: File transfer protocols enable you to transmit ASCII or binary files over a telephone line. The more protocols the package supports, the better. At the very least, it should support *Xmodem* and *Kermit*. For high-speed communication, you may require additional protocols, such as *MNP*.

script language: A script is like a program or batch file. It is a file of commands that can be executed without your interaction. The ability to write scripts is useful if you need to log on to services and transfer files while away from your computer.

remote: Packages that support a remote option enable your computer to accept calls while you are not there. This feature is also called *auto-answer*.

spooling: Packages that support spooling enable you to run another program while files are being transferred in the background. This is sometimes called *background processing*.

terminal emulation drivers: This is important if you plan to log onto a mainframe from your PC. Most mainframes require that the PC emulate a particular type of terminal. The more terminal emulation drivers a package has, the more mainframes you can log onto. Most packages support TTY emulation and emulate one or more DEC terminals (such as the VT52, VT100/102, or VT220).

In addition, some communications packages offer advanced programming capabilities that enable you to customize the interface using windows.

➡ See also *auto-answer; batch file; bulletin board system; communications protocol; editor; emula-*

tion; Kermit; log on; macro; mainframe; modem; multitasking; queue; script; spooling; terminal; window; word wrap; Xmodem; Ymodem; Zmodem.

comparison operator: Same as *relational operator.*

compatibility: The ability of one device or program to work with another device or program. The term *compatibility* can imply different degrees of partnership. For example, a printer and a computer are said to be compatible if they can be connected together. An *IBM compatible PC,* on the other hand, is a computer that can run the same software as an IBM PC. (Note, however, that many manufacturers claim IBM compatibility even though their computers cannot run 100 percent of the software made for IBM PCs.)

Compatibility of two devices, such as printers, usually means that they react to software commands in the same way. Some printers achieve compatibility by tricking the software into believing that the printer is a different machine. This is called *emulation.*

Be aware, however, that hardware compatibility does not always extend to expansion slots. For example, two compatible printers may not accept the same font cartridges. Complete hardware compatibility is denoted by the term *plug compatible.*

Software products are compatible if they use the same data formats. For example, many programs are compatible with dBASE. This means that the files they produce can easily be transformed into a dBASE database or that they can *import* dBASE files.

➡ See also *backward compatible; clone; dBASE; emulation; font cartridge; IBM PC; plug compatible; standard; upward compatible.*

compatible: (n) Indicates that a product can work with or is equivalent to another, better-known product.

The term is often used as a shorthand for *IBM-compatible PC*, a computer that is compatible with an IBM PC. Another term for a compatible is *clone*.

➡ See also *clone; compatibility*.

(adj) See under *compatibility*.

compile: To transform a program written in a high-level programming language from source code into object code. Programmers write programs in a form called *source code*. Source code must go through several steps before it becomes an executable program (Figure 15). The first step is to pass the source code through a *compiler*, which translates the high-level language instructions into *object code*.

The final step in producing an executable program—after the compiler has produced object code—is to pass the object code through a *linker*. The linker combines modules and gives real values to all symbolic addresses.

➡ See also *assembly language; compiler; interpreter; link; object code; programming language; source code*.

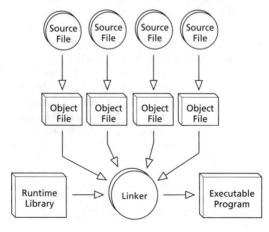

Figure 15
Compilation Process

compiler: A program that translates *source code* into *object code*. The compiler derives its name from the way it works, looking at the entire piece of source code and collecting and reorganizing the instructions. Thus, a compiler differs from an *interpreter*, which analyzes and executes each line of source code in succession, without looking at the entire program. The advantage of interpreters is that they can execute a program immediately. Compilers require some time before an executable program emerges. However, programs produced by compilers run much faster than the same programs executed by an interpreter.

Every high-level programming language (except strictly interpretive languages) comes with a compiler. In effect, the compiler is the language, defining which instructions are acceptable.

Because compilers translate source code into object code, which is unique for each type of computer, many compilers are available for the same language. For example, there is a FORTRAN compiler for IBM PCs and another for Apple Macintosh computers. In addition, the compiler industry is quite competitive, so there are actually many compilers for each language on each type of computer. More than a dozen companies develop and sell C compilers for the IBM PC.

If you intend to program in a high-level language, choosing a compiler is an important decision. You should investigate all the areas listed here before making your decision:

compilation speed: The time it takes to compile a program can vary widely from one compiler to another.

execution speed: How fast the resulting program runs is often the most important criterion for evaluating compilers.

error handling: Some compilers simply abort when they encounter an error in a program.

Others provide sophisticated messages that indicate exactly what the problem is.

language features: Although most high-level languages are standardized to a degree, every compiler supports unique additions to the language.

reliability: Some compilers are poor-quality products that fail often.

customer service: Compilers are complex products that require responsive customer service.

➧ See also *assembly language; interpreter; link; object code; programming language; source code.*

complementary metal oxide semiconductor: See *CMOS.*

complex instruction set computer: See *CISC.*

composite video: A type of video signal in which the red, blue, and green signals (and sometimes audio signals as well) are mixed together. This is the type of signal used by televisions in the United States (see *NTSC*).

In contrast, most computers use *RGB video,* which consists of three separate signals for red, green, and blue. In general, RGB video produces sharper images than composite video does.

➧ See also *NTSC; RGB monitor.*

compression: See *data compression.*

CompuServe: One of the first and largest public on-line data services. CompuServe supports a wide array of *special interest groups (SIGS)* and provides many types of electronic-mail services. In addition, it is connected to hundreds of different database systems.

➧ See also *electronic mail; online service; SIG.*

computer: A programmable machine. The two principal characteristics of a computer are:

- It responds to a specific set of instructions in a well-defined manner.
- It can execute a prerecorded list of instructions (a program).

Modern computers (Figure 16) are electronic and digital. The actual machinery—wires, transistors, and circuits—is called *hardware*; the instructions and data are called *software*.

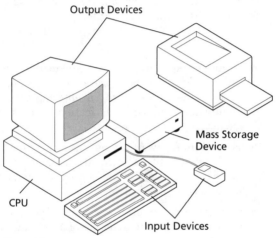

Figure 16
Computers

All general-purpose computers require the following hardware components:

memory: Enables a computer to store, at least temporarily, data and programs.

mass storage device: Allows a computer to permanently retain large amounts of data. Common mass storage devices include disk drives and tape drives.

input device: Usually a keyboard or mouse, the input device is the conduit through which data and instructions enter a computer.

output device: A display screen, printer, or other device that lets you see what the computer has accomplished.

central processing unit (CPU): The heart of the computer, this is the component that actually executes instructions.

Additional components enable the basic components to work together efficiently. For example, every computer requires a bus that transmits data from one part of the computer to another.

Computers can be classified by size and power as follows:

personal computer: A small, single-user computer based on a microprocessor. A personal computer has a keyboard for entering data, a monitor for displaying information, and a storage device for saving data.

workstation: A powerful, single-user computer. A workstation is like a personal computer, but it has a more powerful microprocessor and a higher-quality monitor.

minicomputer: A multi-user computer capable of supporting from 10 to hundreds of users simultaneously.

mainframe: A powerful multi-user computer capable of supporting many hundreds of users simultaneously.

supercomputer: An extremely fast computer that can perform hundreds of millions of instructions per second.

➡ See also *bus; CPU; digital; display screen; hardware; I/O; keyboard; mainframe; mass storage; memory; microprocessor; minicomputer; personal computer; printer; program; software; supercomputer; workstation.*

computer-aided design: See *CAD.*

computer-aided engineering: See *CAE*.

computer-aided manufacturing: See *CAM*.

Computer Graphics Metafile: See *CGM*.

concatenate: To link together or join. For example, concatenating the three words *in*, *as*, and *much* yields the single word *inasmuch*. Computer manuals often refer to the process of *concatenating strings*, a string being any series of characters. You can also concatenate files by appending one to another.

➻ See also *append; character string*.

concatenation: The act of linking together two or more objects.

➻ See also *concatenate*.

CONFIG.SYS: The *configuration file* for DOS and OS/2 systems. Whenever a DOS or OS/2-based computer boots up, it reads the CONFIG.SYS file (if it exists) and executes any commands in it. The two most common commands are *BUFFERS=* and *FILES=*, which enable you to specify the buffer size and the number of files that can be open simultaneously. In addition, you can enter commands that install drivers for devices and you can establish RAM disks.

➻ See also *boot; buffer; configuration; driver; DOS; RAM disk*.

configuration: The way a system is set up or the assortment of components that make up the system. Configuration can refer to either hardware or software, or the combination of both. For instance, a typical configuration for an IBM PC consists of 1MB main memory, a floppy drive, a hard disk, a VGA monitor, and the DOS operating system.

Many software products require that the computer have a certain *minimum configuration*. For example, the software might require a graphics display monitor and a video adapter, a particular microprocessor, and a minimum amount of main memory.

When you install a new device or program, you often need to *configure* it, which means to set various switches and jumpers (for hardware) and to define values of parameters (for software). For example, the device or program may need to know what type of video adapter you have and what type of printer is connected to the computer.

In DOS systems, you can configure the operating environment by placing commands in a file called *CONFIG.SYS*. These commands can specify the buffer size and install drivers for various devices. On Macintoshes, you configure the system with the Control Panel desk accessory.

➧ See also *CONFIG.SYS; Control Panel; DIP switch; jumper; parameter.*

configuration file: A file that contains configuration information for a particular program. When the program is executed, it consults the configuration file to see what parameters are in effect. The configuration file for DOS is called *CONFIG.SYS*.

➧ See also *CONFIG.SYS; configuration.*

configure: To set up a program or computer system for a particular application.

➧ See also *configuration.*

connectivity: A popular computer buzzword that refers to a program or device's ability to link with other programs and devices. For example, a program that can *import* data from a wide variety of other programs and can *export* data in many different formats is said to have *good connectivity*. On the other hand, computers that have difficulty linking into a network (many laptop computers, for example) have *poor connectivity*.

➠ See also *export; import*.

connector: The part of a cable that plugs into a port or interface to connect one device to another. There are many types of connectors, some of the more common of which are shown in Figure 17.

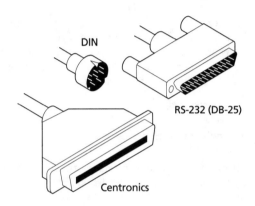

Figure 17
Connectors

➠ See also *interface; port*.

console: (1) The combination of display monitor and keyboard (or other device that allows input). Another term for console is *terminal*.

➠ See also *display screen; keyboard; terminal*.

(2) Another term for *monitor* or *display screen*.
(3) A bank of meters and lights indicating a computer's status, and switches that allow an operator to control the computer in some way.

constant: In programming, a constant is a value that never changes. The other type of values that programs use is variables, symbols that can represent different values throughout the course of a program.

99

A constant can be:

- a number, like 25 or 3.6
- a character, like *a* or *$*
- a character string, like "this is a string"

➧ See also *character string; variable.*

context sensitive: Refers to a program feature that changes depending on what you are doing in the program. For example, *context-sensitive help* provides documentation for the particular feature that you are in the process of using.

➧ See also *help.*

context switching: Same as *task switching.*

continuous tone: Refers to images that have a virtually unlimited range of gray levels. Black-and-white photos, for example, are continuous-tone images. In contrast, computer hardware and software can represent only a limited number of gray levels, typically 16 to 256. Converting a continuous-tone image into a computer image is known as *gray scaling.*

➧ See also *gray scaling.*

control character: Any character pressed in conjunction with the Control key. Manuals usually represent control characters with the prefix *CTRL-* or *CNTL-*. For example, CTRL-N means the Control key and *N* pressed at the same time. Sometimes a control character is represented by a caret (for example, ^N is the same as CTRL-N).

The ASCII character set defines 32 control characters, as shown in Table 8. Originally, these codes were designed to control teletype machines. Now, however, they are often used to control display monitors, printers, and other modern devices. In addition, many applications define control characters as shorthands for commands. For example,

Table 8: ASCII Control Characters

OCT	DEC	HEX	CHAR	SYMBOL	MEANING
0	0	0	^@	NUL	Null
1	1	1	^A	SOH	Start of Heading
2	2	2	^B	STX	Start of Text
3	3	3	^C	ETX	End of Text
4	4	4	^D	EQT	End of Transmit
5	5	5	^E	ENQ	Enquiry
6	6	6	^F	ACK	Acknowledge
7	7	7	^G	BEL	Bell
10	8	8	^H	BS	Backspace
11	9	9	^I	HT	Horizontal Tab
12	10	A	^J	LF	Line Feed
13	11	B	^K	VT	Vertical Tab
14	12	C	^L	FF	Form Feed
15	13	D	^M	CR	Carriage Return
16	14	E	^N	SO	Shift Out
17	15	F	^O	SI	Shift In
20	16	10	^P	DLE	Data Link Escape
21	17	11	^Q	DC1	Device Control 1
22	18	12	^R	DC2	Device Control 2
23	19	13	^S	DC3	Device Control 3
24	20	14	^T	DC4	Device Control 4
25	21	15	^U	NAK	Negative Acknowledge
26	22	16	^V	SYN	Synchronous Idle
27	23	17	^W	ETB	End Transmit Block
30	24	18	^X	CAN	Cancel
31	25	19	^Y	EM	End of Medium
32	26	1A	^Z	SUB	Substitution
33	27	1B	^[	ESC	Escape
34	28	1C	^|	FS	Figures Shift
35	29	1D	^]	GS	Group Separator
36	30	1E	^^	RS	Record Separator
37	31	1F	^	US	Unit Separator

CTRL-D in a word-processing application might delete a line.

Certain control characters are semistandardized. For example, CTRL-C often has the same effect as the Break key—it interrupts a program.

➡ See also *ASCII; Break key; Control key; keyboard.*

Control key: IBM PC keyboards contain a key called the Control key (labeled *Ctrl*). You use the Control key in the same way that you use the Shift key—keeping it pressed down while pressing another character. The result is a *control character,* which can have different meanings depending on which program is running.

➡ See also *control character.*

controller: A device that controls the transfer of data from a computer to a peripheral device; and vice versa. For example, disk drives, display screens, keyboards, and printers all require controllers.

In personal computers, the controllers are often single chips. When you purchase a computer, it comes with all the necessary controllers for standard components such as the display screen, keyboard, and disk drives. If you attach additional devices, however, you may need to insert new controllers that come on expansion boards.

Controllers must be designed to communicate with the computer's expansion bus. There are three standard bus architectures for IBM PCs—the *AT bus, Micro Channel architecture (MCA),* and *Extended Industry Standard Architecture (EISA).* When you purchase a controller, therefore, you must ensure that it conforms to the bus architecture that your computer uses.

➡ See also *AT bus; bus; chip; circuit board; CPU; driver; EISA; expansion board; Micro Channel architecture; peripheral device.*

Control Panel: A Macintosh *desk accessory* that permits you to set many of the system parameters. For example, you can control the type of beeps the Mac makes and the sensitivity of the mouse.

➡ See also *desk accessory; Macintosh computer.*

control program: (1) A program that enhances an operating system by creating an environment in which you can run other programs. Control programs generally provide a graphical interface and enable you to run several programs at once in different windows. Popular control programs for DOS-based machines include DESQview and Microsoft Windows.

Control programs are also called *operating environments.*

➡ See also *DESQview; graphical interface; Microsoft Windows; operating environment; operating system.*

(2) Another term for *operating system.*

conventional memory: On DOS systems, conventional memory refers to the portion of memory that is available to normal programs. DOS systems have an *address space* of 1MB, but the top 384K is reserved for system use. This leaves 640K of conventional memory. Everything above 1MB is either *extended* or *expanded* memory.

➡ See also *expanded memory; extended memory; main memory; DOS; user memory.*

convergence: In graphics, convergence refers to how sharply an individual color pixel on a monitor appears. Each pixel is composed of three dots—a red, blue, and green one. If the dots are badly misconverged, the pixel will appear blurry. All monitors have some convergence errors, but they differ in degree.

➥ See also *graphics; monitor; pixel.*

coprocessor: (1) A special-purpose processing unit that assists the CPU in performing certain types of operations. For example, a *math coprocessor* performs mathematical computations, particularly floating-point operations. Math coprocessors are also called *numeric* and *floating-point* coprocessors.

Some computers come with coprocessors built in. For others, you can add a coprocessor. A math coprocessor can increase a computer's speed and power dramatically, particularly if you are running programs that perform a lot of floating-point arithmetic (engineering and scientific applications, statistical analysis, and graphics). Note, however, that the program itself must be written to take advantage of the coprocessor. If the program contains no coprocessor instructions, the coprocessor will never be utilized.

In addition to math coprocessors, there are also graphics coprocessors for manipulating graphic images.

➥ See also *CPU; floating-point number; math coprocessor.*

(2) A *coprocessor board* is an *accelerator board* with RAM.

➥ See also *accelerator board; RAM.*

copy: (1) In word processing, *copying* refers to duplicating a section of a document and placing it in a buffer (sometimes called a *clipboard*). The term *copy* differs from *cut*, which refers to actually removing a section of a document and placing it in a buffer. After cutting or copying, you can move the contents of the buffer by *pasting* it somewhere else.

➥ See also *buffer; clipboard; cut; paste; word processing.*

(2) In file management, the term *copy* refers to making a duplicate of a file. In DOS environments, to move a file from one directory to another, you first need to copy it and then delete the file from the original directory.

➡ See also *directory; file; filename.*

copy protection: Refers to techniques used to prevent the unauthorized copying of software. The idea of copy-protected software was created by software manufacturers who wanted to prevent *software piracy*—users copying programs and giving them to friends and colleagues free of charge.

As enticing an idea as it may be, copy protection has not proved to be a viable strategy. For one, it is practically impossible to create software that cannot be copied by a knowledgeable programmer. Second, many consumers shy away from copy-protected software because backup copies are difficult to make. Thus, if their original copy of the software is damaged, the user must contact the manufacturer for a new copy. Finally, some copy-protection techniques can actually damage other software on the system. For these reasons, copy-protected software is becoming less common.

An alternative strategy for dealing with the problem of software piracy is *shareware,* where users are actually encouraged to copy and disseminate programs. Shareware publishers rely on people's honesty to pay for the products used.

➡ See also *backup; copy; shareware; software; software piracy.*

Courier font: A common monospaced (*fixed-pitch*) font. Most printers support the Courier font.

➡ See also *font; monospacing; fixed-pitch.*

CP/M: Abbreviation of *Control Program for Micro-processors.* Created by Digital Research Corporation, CP/M was one of the first operating systems for personal computers. However, Digital Research Corporation made a critical strategic error by not agreeing to produce an operating system for the first IBM PC. According to the folklore, the president of Digital Research was flying his airplane when IBM came to call. IBM marched out and never looked back.

Instead, IBM turned to Microsoft Corporation, which developed MS-DOS. By the mid 1980s, MS-DOS had become the standard operating system for IBM-compatible personal computers. Although still used on some old models, CP/M is practically obsolete.

➧ See also *DOS; operating system.*

cps: Abbreviation of *characters per second,* a unit of measure used to describe the speed of dot-matrix and daisy-wheel printers. The speed of laser and ink-jet printers is described in terms of pages per minute (ppm).

➧ See also *printer.*

CPU: Abbreviation of *central processing unit.* Pronounced *c-p-u,* the CPU is the brains of the computer. Sometimes referred to simply as the *processor* or *central processor,* the CPU is where most calculations take place. In terms of computing power, the CPU is the most important element of a computer system.

On large machines, CPUs require one or more printed circuit boards. On personal computers and small workstations, the CPU is housed in a single chip called a *microprocessor.*

Two typical components of a CPU are:

- the *arithmetic logic unit* (ALU), which performs arithmetic and logical operations
- the *control unit,* which extracts instructions from memory and decodes and executes them, calling on the ALU when necessary

In addition, main memory is sometimes considered part of the CPU.

➧ See also *chip; main memory; microprocessor; printed circuit board.*

CPU time: The amount of time the CPU is actually executing instructions. During the execution of most programs, the CPU sits idle much of the time while the computer fetches data from the keyboard or disk, or sends data to an output device. The CPU time of an executing program, therefore, is generally much less than the total execution time of the program. Multitasking operating systems take advantage of this by sharing the CPU among several programs.

CPU times are used for a variety of purposes: to compare the speed of two different processors, to gauge how CPU-intensive a program is, and to measure the amount of processing time being allocated to different programs in a multitasking environment.

➧ See also *CPU; multitasking.*

crash: (n) A serious computer failure. A computer crash means that the computer itself stops working or that a program aborts unexpectedly. A crash signifies either a hardware malfunction or a very serious software bug.

If your computer crashes, it is not your fault. If the program is good and your hardware is functioning properly, there is nothing you can do to make your system crash.

(v) To fail or break. Other terms for *crash* include *hang* and *bomb*.

➧ See also *bomb; bug; hang; head crash.*

CRC: Abbreviation of *cyclic redundancy check*, a common technique for detecting data transmission errors. A number of file transfer protocols, including Xmodem, use CRC in addition to *checksum*.

➡ See also *checksum; communications protocols; error detection; Xmodem.*

CRT: Abbreviation of *cathode-ray tube,* the technology used in most televisions and computer display screens. A CRT works by moving an electron beam back and forth across the back of the screen. Each time the beam makes a pass across the screen, it lights up phosphor dots on the inside of the glass tube, thereby illuminating the active portions of the screen (Figure 18). By drawing many such lines from the top to the bottom of the screen, it creates an entire screenful of images. A typical monitor redraws a screen 60 times per second.

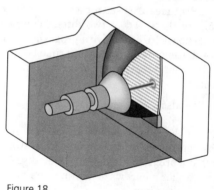

Figure 18
CRT

➡ See also *display screen; monitor.*

Ctrl: See under *Control key.*

cursor: (1) A special symbol, usually a solid rectangle or a blinking underline character, that signifies where the next character will be displayed on the screen. To type in different areas of the screen, you need to move the cursor. You can do this with the arrow keys, or with a mouse if your program supports it.

If you are running a graphics-based program, the cursor may appear as a small arrow, called a *pointer*. (The terms *cursor* and *pointer* are often used interchangeably.) In text processing, a cursor sometimes appears as an *I-beam pointer,* a special type of pointer that always appears between two characters. Note also that programs that support a mouse may use two cursors: a *text cursor*, which indicates where characters from the keyboard will be entered, and a *mouse cursor* for selecting items with the mouse.

➡ See also *arrow keys; display screen; graphics based; mouse; pixel; pointer.*

(2) A device, similar in appearance to a mouse, that is used to sketch lines on a digitizing tablet. Cursors for digitizers are sometimes called *pucks*.

➡ See also *digitizer; mouse.*

cursor control keys: Same as *arrow keys.*

cursor position: The position of the cursor on the display screen. While in text mode, a display screen is capable of displaying a certain number of lines and a certain number of characters on each line. The cursor position is represented by the line number and the character number and signifies where the next character will be displayed. For example, cursor position 1,1 always indicates the upper-leftmost corner position on the terminal. Cursor position 10,30 indicates the 30th character position on the 10th line.

➡ See also *cursor; display screen; text mode.*

customer support: Service that computer and software manufacturers, and third-party service companies, offer to customers. For personal computer products, the following are common customer support options:

mail-in service: The manufacturer will repair your equipment if you mail it in. Typical turn-around time is about four days. In some service plans, the manufacturer charges you for shipping expenses.

carry-in service: The manufacturer repairs your equipment, but you deliver it to a local service site. This is sometimes called *depot service*.

on-site contract: For a monthly or annual fee, a repair person comes to your site. (The fee is included in the purchase price of some machines.) Most on-site contracts guarantee that the service will be rendered within a fixed number of hours from when you report a problem.

hot lines: Many software manufacturers provide a phone number that you can call for advice and trouble-shooting. Often the number is toll-free. The quality of this type of support varies considerably from one company to another. Some hot lines are so good that they enable you to solve most problems yourself. Others are so bad that you are unable even to get through.

bulletin board system: Some companies maintain electronic bulletin boards staffed by service engineers. If you have a modem, you can report a problem to the bulletin board and a technician will respond. This can be convenient because bulletin boards are usually open 24 hours a day. Also, bulletin boards enable you to download software updates that correct known bugs.

➡ See also *bulletin board system; download.*

cut: In word processing, *cut* means to move a section of text from a document to a temporary buffer. This is one way to delete text. However, because the text is transferred to a buffer, it is not lost forever. You can copy the buffer somewhere else in the document or in another document, which is called *pasting*. To move a section of text from one place to another, therefore, you need to first cut it and then paste it.

Note that most word processors have only one buffer, sometimes called a *clipboard*. If you make two cuts in succession, the text from the original cut will be replaced by the text from the second cut.

Graphical user interfaces, such as MS-Windows and the Macintosh interface, allow you to cut and paste graphics as well as text.

➡ See also *buffer; clipboard; graphical user interface; paste; word processing.*

cut-sheet feeder: See under *sheet feeder.*

cyclic redundancy check: See *CRC.*

cylinder: A single track location on all the *platters* making up a hard disk. For example, if a hard disk has four platters, each with 600 tracks, then there will be 600 cylinders, and each cylinder will consist of 8 tracks (2 for each platter).

➡ See also *hard disk; platter; track.*

— D —

DA: Pronounced as separate letters, DA stands for *desk accessory.*

➡ See also *desk accessory.*

daisy-wheel printer: A type of printer that produces letter-quality type. A daisy-wheel printer works on the same principle as a ball-head typewriter. The daisy wheel is a disk made of plastic or metal on which characters stand out in relief along the outer edge. To print a character, the printer rotates the disk until the desired letter is facing the paper. Then a hammer strikes the disk, forcing the character to hit an ink ribbon, leaving an impression of the character on the paper. You can change the daisy wheel to print different fonts.

Daisy-wheel printers cannot print graphics, and in general they are noisy and slow, printing from 10 to about 75 characters per second. As the price of laser printers declines and the quality of dot-matrix printers improves, daisy-wheel printers are becoming obsolete.

➩ See also *font; letter quality; printer.*

DAT: Acronym for **d**igital **a**udio **t**ape, a relatively new type of storage medium that is increasingly being used for data storage. A DAT cartridge is slightly larger than a credit card and contains a magnetic tape that can hold from 700MB to 2.3G of data. It can support data transfer rates of about 10MB per minute. Like other types of tapes, DATs are *sequential-access* media.

The most common format for DAT cartridges is *DDS* (**d**igital **d**ata **s**torage).

➩ See also *gigabyte; mass storage; megabyte; sequential access; tape.*

data: (1) Information, usually formatted in a special way. All software is divided into two general categories: *data* and *programs.* Programs are collections of instructions for manipulating data.

Data can exist in a variety of forms—as numbers or text on pieces of paper, as bits and bytes stored in electronic memory, or as facts stored in a person's mind.

Strictly speaking, data is the plural of *datum,* a single piece of information. In practice, however, people use *data* as both the singular and plural form of the word.

➩ See also *program; software.*

(2) The term *data* is often used to distinguish binary machine-readable information from textual human-readable information. For example, some applications make a distinction between *data files* (files that contain binary data) and *text files* (files that contain ASCII data).

➠ See also *binary; ASCII.*

(3) In database management systems, data files are the files that store the database information, whereas other files, such as index files and data dictionaries, store administrative information.

➠ See also *database management system; data dictionary.*

database: (1) A collection of information organized in such a way that a computer program can quickly select desired pieces of data. You can think of a database as an electronic filing system.

Traditional databases are organized by *fields, records,* and *files.* A field is a single piece of information; a record is one complete set of fields; and a file is a collection of records. For example, a telephone book is analogous to a file. It contains a list of records, each of which consists of three fields: name, telephone number, and address (Figure 19).

An alternative concept in database design is known as *Hypertext.* In a Hypertext database, any object, whether it be a piece of text, a picture, or a film, can be linked to any other object. Hypertext databases are particularly useful for organizing large amounts of disparate information, but they are not designed for numerical analysis.

To access information from a database, you need a *database management system (DBMS).* This is a collection of programs that enables you to enter, organize, and select data in a database.

➠ See also *database management system; field; file; Hypertext; record.*

File

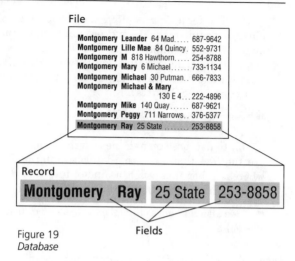

Figure 19
Database

(2) Increasingly, the term *database* is used as shorthand for *database management system*.

➠ See also *database management system*.

database management system (DBMS): A collection of programs that enables you to store, modify, and extract information from a database. There are many different types of DBMSs, ranging from small systems that run on personal computers to huge systems that run on mainframes. The following are examples of database applications:

- computerized library systems
- automated teller machines
- flight reservation systems
- computerized parts inventory systems

From a technical standpoint, DBMSs can differ widely. The terms *relational, network, flat, Hypertext,* and *hierarchical* all refer to the way a DBMS organizes information internally. The internal organization can affect how quickly and flexibly you can extract information.

Requests for information from a database are made in the form of a *query,* which is a stylized question. For example, the query

```
SELECT ALL WHERE NAME = "SMITH" AND
AGE > 35
```

requests all records in which the name field is SMITH and the age field is greater than 35. The set of rules for constructing queries is known as a *query language.* Different DBMSs support different query languages, although there is a semistandardized query language called SQL (structured query language). Sophisticated languages for managing database systems are called *fourth-generation languages,* or *4GLs* for short.

The information from a database can be presented in a variety of formats. Most DBMSs include a report writer program that enables you to output data in the form of a report. Many DBMSs also include a graphics component that enables you to output information in the form of graphs and charts.

➡ See also *database; flat-file database; fourth-generation language; Hypertext; query; relational database; report writer; SQL.*

data communications: See *communications.*

data compression: Storing data in a format that requires less space than usual. *Compressing* data is the same as *packing* data.

Data compression is particularly useful in communications because it enables devices to transmit the same amount of data in fewer bits. There are a variety of data compression techniques, but only a few have been standardized. The CCITT has defined a standard data compression technique for transmitting FAXes (Group 3 standard) and a compression standard for data communications through modems (CCITT V.42*bis*). In addition, there are software data compression formats, such as ARC and ZIP.

Data compression is also widely used in backup utilities, spreadsheet applications, and database management systems. Certain types of data, such as bit-mapped graphics, can be compressed to a small fraction of their normal size.

In recent years, *compression boards* have appeared in the marketplace. These are expansion boards that automatically compress data as it is written to a disk and then decompress the data when it is fetched. The data compression is invisible to the user but can effectively double or triple the capacity of a disk drive.

➡ See also *ARC; CCITT; communications; database management system; FAX machine; MNP; modem; pack; spreadsheet; standard; ZIP.*

data dictionary: In database management systems, a data dictionary is a file that defines the basic organization of a database. A data dictionary contains a list of all files in the database, the number of records in each file, and the names and types of each field. Most database management systems keep the data dictionary hidden from users to prevent them from accidentally destroying its contents.

Data dictionaries do not contain any actual data from the database, only bookkeeping information for managing it. Without a data dictionary, however, a database management system cannot access data from the database.

➡ See *database management system.*

data entry: The process of entering data into a computerized database or spreadsheet. Data entry can be performed by an individual typing at a keyboard or by a machine entering data electronically.

➡ See also *database; spreadsheet.*

data processing: A class of programs that organize and manipulate data, usually large amounts of numeric data. Accounting programs are the prototypical examples of data processing applications. In contrast, word processors, which manipulate text rather than numbers, are not usually referred to as data processing applications.

➡ See also *accounting software; application.*

data structure: In programming, the term *data structure* refers to a scheme for organizing related pieces of information. The basic types of data structures include:

- files
- lists
- arrays
- records
- trees
- tables

Each of these basic structures has many variations and allows different operations to be performed on the data.

➡ See also *array; file; record; tree structure.*

data type: In programming, classification of a particular type of information. It is easy for humans to distinguish between different types of data. We can usually tell at a glance whether a number is a percentage, a time, or an amount of money. We do this through special symbols—%, :, and $—that indicate the data's *type*. Similarly, a computer uses special symbols to keep track of the different types of data it processes.

Most programming languages require the programmer to *declare* the data type of every data object, and most database systems require the user to specify the type of each data field. The available data types vary from one programming language to another, and from one database application to another, but the following usually exist in one form or another:

integer: In more common parlance, *whole number*; a number that has no fractional part.

floating-point: A number with a decimal point. For example, 3 is an integer, but 3.5 is a floating-point number.

character (text): Readable text.

➡ See also *character; database; declare; field; floating-point number; integer; variable.*

dBASE: A popular database management system produced by Ashton Tate Corporation that runs on personal computers. The original version, called *Vulcan*, was created by Wayne Ratliff. In 1981, Ashton-Tate bought Vulcan and marketed it as dBASE II. Subsequent versions with additional features are known as dBASE III, dBASE III +, and dBASE IV.

All versions of dBASE run on IBM-compatible PCs and offer a relational database system with a fourth-generation language.

➡ See also *command driven; database management system; fourth-generation language; menu driven; query; query by example; relational database; user interface; windows.*

DBMS: See *database management system.*

debug: To find and remove errors (bugs) from a program or design.

➡ See also *bug.*

debugger: A special program used to find errors (bugs) in other programs. A debugger allows a programmer to stop a program at any point and examine and change the values of variables.

➡ See also *bug.*

decimal: Refers to numbers in base 10 (the numbers we use in everyday life). For example, the following are decimal numbers:

9

100345000

-256

Note that a decimal number is not necessarily a number with a decimal point in it. Numbers with decimal points (that is, numbers with a fractional part) are called *fixed-point* or *floating-point* numbers.

In addition to the decimal format, computer data is often represented in binary, octal, and hexadecimal formats.

➡ See also *binary; floating-point number; hexadecimal; integer; octal.*

declare: In programming, *to declare* is to define the name and data type of a variable or other programming construct. Many programming languages, including C and Pascal, require you to declare variables before using them.

➡ See also *data type; programming language; variable.*

decrement: To subtract. For example, if you count down consecutively from 10 to 0, you decrement by 1. If you count down by twos, you decrement by 2. The opposite of decrementing is *incrementing*.

➡ See also *increment.*

decryption: The process of decoding data that has been *encrypted* into a secret format. Decryption requires a secret *key* or *password*.

➡ See also *encryption; key; password; security.*

dedicated: Reserved for just one use. In communications, a *dedicated channel* is a line reserved exclusively for one type of communication. This is the same as a *leased line* or *private line*.

A *dedicated server* is a single computer in a network reserved for serving the needs of the network. For example, some networks require that one computer be set aside to manage communications between all the other computers. A dedicated server could also be a computer that manages printer resources. Note, however, that not all servers are dedicated. In some networks, it is possible for a computer to act as a server and perform other functions as well.

The opposite of dedicated is *general purpose*.

➡ See also *channel; expansion slot; network; server*.

de facto standard: A format, language, or protocol that has become a standard not because it has been approved by a standards organization but because it is widely used and recognized by the industry as being standard. For example, DOS is the de facto standard operating system for IBM-compatible PCs. Other de facto standards include:

- Hayes command set for controlling modems
- Kermit Communications Protocol
- Xmodem Communications Protocol
- Hewlett-Packard Printer Control Language (PCL) for laser printers.
- PostScript page description language for laser printers

➡ See also *Hayes compatibility; Kermit; PCL; PostScript; standard; Xmodem*.

default: A value or setting that a device or program automatically selects if you do not specify a substitute. For example, word processors have default margins and default page lengths that you can override or reset.

The *default disk drive* is the disk drive the computer accesses unless you specify a different disk drive. Likewise, the *default directory* is the directory the operating system searches unless you specify a different directory.

The default can also be an action that a device or program will take. For example, some word processors generate backup files *by default.*

delete: To remove or erase. For example, deleting a character means removing it from a file or erasing it from the display screen. Deleting a file means erasing it from a disk.

Delete key: Often abbreviated as *Del,* the Delete key is used to remove the character immediately under the cursor (or to the right of the insertion point). Note the difference between the Delete key, which deletes the character under the cursor, and the Backspace key, which deletes the character to the left of the cursor or insertion point.

➠ See also *backspace; insertion point; keyboard.*

delimiter: A punctuation character or group of characters that separates two names or two pieces of data, or marks the beginning or end of a programming construct. Delimiters are used in almost every computer application. For example, in specifying DOS pathnames, the backslash (\) is the delimiter that separates directories and filenames. Other common delimiters include the comma (,), semicolon (;), quotes ("), and braces ({}).

➠ See also *pathname.*

demand paging: In virtual memory systems, demand paging is a type of *swapping* in which pages of data are not copied from disk to RAM until they are needed. In contrast, some virtual memory systems use *anticipatory paging,* in which the operating system attempts to anticipate which data will be needed next and copies it to RAM before it is actually required.

➡ See also *paging; RAM; swap; virtual memory.*

density: How tightly information is packed together on a storage medium (tape or disk). A higher density means that data are closer together, so the medium can hold more information. Floppy disks can be *single-density, double-density, high-density,* or *extra-high-density.* To use a double-density, high-density, or extra-high-density disk, you must have a disk drive that supports the density level. *Density,* therefore, can refer both to the media and the device.

Table 9 shows the storage capacities of double- and high-density floppies on the IBM PC and the Apple Macintosh computer.

Table 9: Floppy Disk Densities

	5¼-INCHES		
	Single	Double	High
IBM	360K	720K	1.2MB
Mac	NA	NA	NA

	3½-INCHES		
	Single	Double	High
IBM	NA	720K	1.44MB
Mac	400K	800K	1.2MB

Note that the only difference between double-density and high-density disks is that the high-density disks were found to be higher quality during the testing process. High-quality disks are sold as high-density, and lower-quality disks are sold as double-density. It is often possible, therefore, to format a double-density disk as a high-density disk, but this practice is not encouraged.

➧ See also *disk; disk drive; double-density disk; FDHD; floppy disk; high-density disk.*

desk accessory (DA): On Apple Macintoshes, a desk accessory is a utility that is always available regardless of what application you are running. For example, Apple's Calculator is a desk accessory. Most desk accessories are utilities, which means that they are small, stand-alone programs designed to perform one small task.

On IBM PCs, desktop accessories are called *pop-up utilities* or *TSRs*.

➧ See also *memory resident; pop-up utility; TSR; utility.*

desktop: In graphical user interfaces, a *desktop* is the metaphor used to portray file systems. Such a desk-

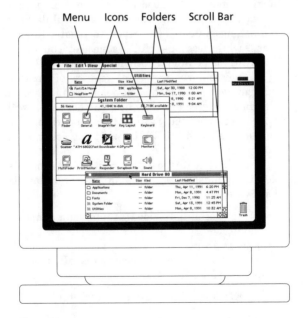

Figure 20
Macintosh Desktop

top consists of pictures, called *icons*, that show cabinets, files, folders, and various types of documents (that is, letters, reports, pictures). You can arrange the icons on the electronic desktop just as you can arrange real objects on a real desktop—moving them around, putting one on top of another, reshuffling them, and throwing them away (Figure 20).

➡ See also *graphical user interface; icon.*

desktop computer: Same as *personal computer.*

desktop publishing: Using a personal computer or workstation to produce high-quality printed documents. A desktop publishing system is a fancy and powerful word-processing system. It allows you to use different typefaces, specify various margins and justifications, and embed illustrations and graphs directly into the text. The most powerful desktop publishing systems enable you to create illustrations, while less powerful systems let you insert illustrations created by other programs.

A particularly important feature of desktop publishing systems is that they enable you to see on the display screen exactly how the document will appear when printed. Systems that support this feature are called *WYSIWYG*s (**w**hat **y**ou **s**ee **i**s **w**hat **y**ou **g**et).

In addition to the program itself, a complete desktop publishing system requires the following hardware:

- a high-resolution video adapter and graphics monitor
- a laser printer
- at least 1MB of main memory (usually more)
- a powerful CPU

The following devices are also useful:

- a mouse
- an optical scanner

Only the most powerful personal computers are capable of running desktop publishing software. To run the best desktop publishing systems, you need a workstation.

Until recently, the hardware costs made desktop publishing systems impractical for most uses. But as the prices of personal computers and workstations have fallen, desktop publishing systems have become increasingly popular for producing newsletters, brochures, and other documents that formerly required a typesetter.

➡ See also *CPU; justification; laser printer; main memory; monitor; mouse; optical scanner; page layout program; personal computer; typeface; word processing; workstation; WYSIWYG.*

DESQview: A popular program developed by Quarterdeck Office Systems that provides IBM PC users with a windowed, multitasking environment in which they can run other programs. DESQview is similar to Microsoft Windows, but is character based, whereas Windows is graphical.

➡ See also *character based; graphics based; Microsoft Windows; DOS; multitasking; window.*

destination: Many computer commands move data from one file to another or from one storage device to another. This is referred to as moving the data from the *source* to the *destination* (or *target*). The term is also used as an adjective, as in *destination file* or *destination device.*

device: Any machine or component that attaches to a computer. Examples of devices include disk drives, printers, mice, and modems. These particular devices fall into the category of *peripheral devices* because they are separate from the main computer. Display monitors and keyboards are also devices, but because they are integral parts of the computer, they are not considered peripheral.

Every device, whether peripheral or not, requires a program called a *device driver* that acts as a translator, converting general commands from an application into specific commands that the device understands.

➡ See also *computer; CONFIG.SYS; driver.*

device dependent: Like *machine-dependent, device-dependent* refers to programs that can run only on a certain type of hardware.

➡ See also *machine dependent.*

device driver: See *driver.*

dialog box: A box that appears on a display screen to present information or request input (Figure 21).

Dialog Box

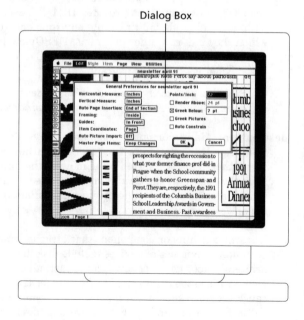

Figure 21
Dialog Box

Typically, dialog boxes are temporary—they disappear once you have entered the requested information.

In the Macintosh and Microsoft Windows interfaces, there is a convention that any menu option followed by ellipsis points (. . .) will, when selected, bring up a dialog box. Options without ellipsis points are executed directly.

➠ See also *box; graphical user interface; pop-up window; window.*

digital: Describes any system based on discontinuous data or events. Computers are digital machines because at their most basic level they can distinguish between just two values, 0 and 1, or off and on. There is no simple way to represent all the values in between, such as 0.25. All data that a computer processes must be encoded digitally, as a series of zeroes and ones.

The opposite of digital is *analog.* A typical analog device is a clock in which the hands move continuously around the face. Such a clock is capable of indicating every possible time of day. In contrast, a digital clock is capable of representing only a finite number of times (every tenth of a second, for example). (See Figure 3 at *analog.*)

In general, humans experience the world analogically. Vision, for example, is an analog experience because we perceive infinitely smooth gradations of shapes and colors. Most analog events, however, can be simulated digitally. Photographs in newspapers, for instance, consist of an array of dots that are either black or white. From afar, the viewer does not see the dots (the digital form), but only lines and shading, which appear to be continuous. Although digital representations are approximations of analog events, they are useful because they are relatively easy to store and manipulate electronically. The trick is in converting from analog to digital, and back again.

This is the principle behind compact discs (CDs). The music itself exists in an analog form, as waves in the air, but these sounds are then translated into a digital form that is encoded onto the disk. When you play a compact disc, the CD player reads the digital data, translates it back into its original analog form, and sends it to the amplifier and eventually the speakers.

Internally, computers are digital because they consist of discrete units called *bits* that are either on or off. But by combining many bits in complex ways, computers simulate analog events. In one sense, this is what computer science is all about.

➧ See also *analog; modem.*

digital audio tape: See *DAT.*

digital monitor: A monitor that accepts digital rather than analog signals. All monitors (except flat-panel displays) use CRT technology, which is essentially analog. The term *digital*, therefore, refers only to the type of input received from the video adapter. A digital monitor then translates the digital signals into analog signals that control the actual display.

In general, digital monitors support less resolution than analog monitors and are used only for low- and medium-quality graphics. The MDA, CGA, and EGA video standards, for example, specify digital signals. VGA and Super VGA, on the other hand, require an analog monitor. Some monitors are capable of accepting either analog or digital signals.

➧ See also *analog; analog monitor; digital; monitor; video adapter.*

Digital Video Interactive: See *DVI.*

digitize: To translate into a digital form. For example, optical scanners digitize images by translating them into bit maps. It is also possible to digitize sound, video, and any type of movement. In all these cases, digitization is performed by sampling at discrete intervals. To digitize sound, for example, a device measures pitch and volume many times per second. These numeric values can then be recorded digitally.

➡ See also *bit map; digital; optical scanner.*

digitizer: (1) An input device that enables you to enter drawings and sketches into a computer. A digitizer consists of an electronic tablet and a cursor or pen. A cursor (also called a *puck*) is similar to a mouse, except that it has a window with cross hairs for pinpoint placement, and it can have as many as 16 buttons. A pen (also called a *stylus*) looks like a simple ballpoint pen but uses an electronic head instead of ink. The tablet contains electronics that enable it to detect movement of the cursor or pen and translate the movements into digital signals that it sends to the computer.

For digitizers, each point on the tablet represents a point on the display screen in a fixed manner. This differs from mice, in which all movement is relative to the current cursor position. The static nature of digitizers makes them particularly effective for tracing drawings. Most modern digitizers also support a *mouse emulation mode,* in which the pen or cursor acts like a mouse.

Digitizers are also called *digitizing tablets, graphics tablets, touch tablets*, or simply *tablets*.

➡ See also *cursor; input device; mouse.*

(2) Any device, such as an optical scanner, that digitizes data.

➡ See also *digitize.*

digitizing tablet: See *digitizer.*

DIN connector: *DIN* stands for **Deutsche Industrinorm,** the standards-setting organization for

West Germany. A DIN connector is a connector that conforms to one of the many standards defined by DIN. DIN connectors are used widely in personal computers. For example, the keyboard connector for IBM PCs and compatibles is a DIN connector (see Figure 17 at *connector*).

➡ See also *connector; keyboard; standard.*

dingbat: A small picture, such as a star or a pointing finger, that can be inserted into a document (Figure 22). Many clip-art packages include a set of dingbats. One of the most popular sets, called Zapf dingbats, is represented as a PostScript font.

Figure 22
Dingbats

➡ See also *clip art; PostScript.*

DIP: Acronym for **d**ual **i**n-line **p**ackage, a type of *chip* housed in a rectangular casing with two rows of connecting pins on either side.

➡ See also *chip.*

DIP switch: A DIP (**d**ual **i**n-line **p**ackage) switch is a series of tiny switches built into circuit boards (Figure 23). The housing for the switches, which has the same shape as a chip, is the DIP.

DIP switches enable you to configure a circuit board for a particular type of computer or application. The installation instructions should tell you

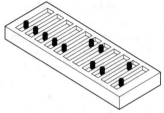

Figure 23
DIP Switches

how to set the switches. DIP switches are always toggle switches, which means they have two possible positions—on or off. (Instead of on and off, you may see the numbers 1 and 0.)

One of the advantages of OS/2 over DOS is that it allows you to configure circuit boards by entering software commands instead of setting DIP switches. This is also an advantage of EISA and MCA over the ISA bus.

➨ See also *chip; configuration; EISA; expansion board; ISA; MCA; OS/2; printed circuit board; toggle*.

direct access: Same as *random access*.

direct-connect modem: A modem that connects directly to a telephone line via modular connectors rather than requiring an acoustic coupler. Almost all modern modems are direct-connect.

➨ See also *acoustic coupler; modem*.

directive: Same as *command*.

direct memory access: See *DMA*.

directory: A special kind of file used to organize other files into a hierarchical structure. Directories contain bookkeeping information about files that are, figuratively speaking, beneath them. You can think

131

of a directory as a folder or cabinet that contains files and perhaps other folders. In fact, many graphical user interfaces, such as the Macintosh interface, use the term *folder* instead of *directory*.

Computer manuals often describe directories and file structures in terms of an *inverted tree,* as shown in Figure 24. The files and directories at any level are contained in the directory above them. To access a file, you may need to specify the names of all the directories above it. You do this by specifying a *path*.

The topmost directory in any file system is called the *root directory*. A directory that is below another directory is called a *subdirectory*.

To read information from, or write information into, a directory, you must use an operating system command. You cannot directly edit directory files. For example, the DIR command in DOS reads a directory file and displays its contents.

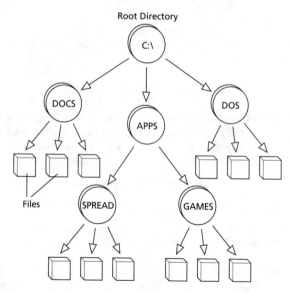

Figure 24
Directory Tree

➧ See also *file; file system; folder; hierarchical; path; root directory; tree structure.*

disk: A round plate on which data can be encoded. There are two basic types of disks: magnetic disks and optical disks.

A magnetic disk is like a phonograph record, except that the data is encoded as microscopic magnetized *needles* on the disk's surface rather than as grooves in the vinyl. Also, you can record and erase data on a magnetic disk any number of times, just as you can with a cassette tape. Magnetic disks come in a number of different forms:

floppy disk: A typical 5¼-inch floppy disk can hold 360K or 1.2MB. Microfloppies (3½-inch floppies) normally store 720K or 1.44MB of data. Bernoulli disks can hold 20MB or more.

hard disk: Hard disks can store anywhere from 5MB to more than 3GB. Hard disks are also from 2 to 20 times faster than floppy disks.

removable cartridge: Removable cartridges are hard disks encased in a metal or plastic cartridge, so you can remove them just like a floppy disk. Removable cartridges are very fast, often faster than fixed hard disks. A typical cartridge has a capacity of about 40MB.

Optical disks record data by burning microscopic holes in the surface of the disk with a laser. To read the disk, another laser beam shines on the disk and detects the holes by changes in the reflection pattern.

Optical disks have a much larger data capacity than magnetic disks, but they are somewhat slower and more expensive. Most optical disks are read-only.

Optical disks come in three forms:

CD-ROM: When you purchase CD-ROMs, they are already filled with data. You can read the data from a CD-ROM, but you cannot modify, delete, or write new data.

WORM: Stands for *write-once, read-many.* WORM disks can be written on once and then read any number of times; however, you need a special WORM disk drive to write data onto a WORM disk.

erasable optical (EO): EO disks (sometimes called *floptical disks*) can be read to, written to, and erased just like magnetic disks.

The machine that spins a disk is called a *disk drive.* Within each disk drive is one or more *heads* (often called *read/write heads*) that actually read and write data.

Accessing data from a disk is not as fast as doing so from main memory, but disks are cheaper and more stable. Unlike RAM, disks hold on to data even when the computer is turned off. Consequently, disks are the storage medium of choice for most types of data. Another storage medium is magnetic tape, but tapes are used less often than disks because they are *sequential-access* devices (to access data in the middle of a tape, the tape drive must pass through all the preceding data).

A new disk, called a *blank disk,* has no data on it. Before you can store data on a blank disk, you must *format* it. In DOS systems, disks are formatted with the FORMAT command. When you execute the FORMAT command, the operating system divides the disk into tracks and sectors and allocates space for directories and other bookkeeping information. Every operating system formats disks somewhat differently, so a disk formatted by one operating system usually cannot be read by another operating system.

➡ See also *CD-ROM; disk drive; erasable optical disk; floppy disk; format; hard disk; head; mass storage; optical disk; removable storage; sector; tape; track.*

disk cache: A disk cache is a portion of RAM used to speed up access to data on a disk. The RAM can be part of the disk drive itself (called a *hard disk cache*) or it can be general-purpose RAM in the computer that is reserved for use by the disk drive (called a *soft disk cache*). Hard disk caches are more effective, but they are also much more expensive (see Figure 10 at *cache*).

In both cases, a disk cache works by storing the most recently accessed data in the RAM cache. When a program needs to access new data, the operating system first checks to see if the data is in the cache before reading it from the disk. Because computers can access data from RAM much faster than from a disk, disk caching can significantly increase performance. Many cache systems also attempt to predict what data will be requested next so they can place that data in the cache ahead of time.

Although caching improves performance, there is some risk involved. If the computer crashes (due to a power failure, for example), the system may not have time to copy the cache back to the disk. In this case, whatever changes you made to the data will be lost. Usually, however, the cache system updates the disk frequently so that even if you lose some data, it will not be much. A special type of disk cache, called a *write-thru cache*, removes the risk of losing data because it only caches data for read operations; write operations are always sent directly to the disk.

➡ See also *buffer; cache; disk drive; RAM.*

disk crash: See under *head crash.*

disk drive: A machine that reads data from and writes data onto a disk. A disk drive resembles a stereo turntable in that it rotates the disk very fast. It has one or more heads that read and write data.

There are different types of disk drives for different types of disks. For example, a *hard disk drive* reads and writes hard disks, and a *floppy drive* accesses floppy disks. A magnetic disk drive reads magnetic disks, and an optical drive reads optical disks.

Disk drives can be either *internal* (housed within the computer) or *external* (housed in a separate box that connects to the computer).

The two most important features of disk drives are:

storage capacity: Floppy disk drives can support disks of anywhere from 200K (204,800 bytes) to 10MB (10,485,760 bytes). Hard disks start at about 5MB and go up to more than 3GB (about 3.1 billion bytes).

performance: The physical speed of a disk drive is expressed by how much time it takes to access a single piece of data—this is called the *access time*. Hard disk drives for personal computers have access times of from 12 to 80 milliseconds. Floppy disks are 2 to 20 times slower. In practical terms, however, a disk drive's performance has less to do with its access time than with other factors. Disk drives can improve their speed dramatically by caching data.

➡ See also *access time; cache; disk; interleaving; mass storage; optical disk.*

diskette: Same as *floppy disk.*

diskless workstation: A workstation or PC on a local-area network (LAN) that does not have its own disk. Instead, it stores files on a network file server. Diskless workstations can reduce the overall cost of a LAN because one large-capacity disk drive is usually less expensive than several low-capacity drives. In addition, diskless workstations can simplify backups and security because all files are in one place—on the file server. Also, accessing data from a large remote file server is often faster than accessing data from a small local storage device.

One disadvantage of diskless workstations, however, is that they are useless if the network fails.

When the workstation is a PC, it is often called a *diskless PC.*

➧ See also *disk drive; local-area network; server; workstation.*

disk operating system: See *DOS.*

disk optimizer: A program that makes a disk more efficient by *defragmenting* the disk. Fragmentation occurs naturally when a disk is used often.

➧ See also *fragmentation.*

disk pack: A stack of removable hard disks encased in a metal or plastic container.

➧ See also *hard disk; removable cartridge.*

display: (v) To make data or images appear on a monitor.

(n) Short for *display screen.*

display adapter: Same as *video adapter.*

display screen: The display part of a monitor. Most display screens work under the same principle as a television, using a cathode-ray tube (CRT). Consequently, the term *CRT* is often used in place of display screen.

➧ See also *CAD/CAM; desktop publishing; flat-panel display; graphics; laptop computer; monitor; resolution.*

distributed database: A database that consists of two or more data files located at different sites on a computer network. Because the database is distributed, different users can access it without interfering with one another. However, the DBMS must periodically check the scattered databases to make sure that they all have consistent data.

➡ See also *database; database management system; distributed processing; network.*

distributed processing: Refers to any of a variety of computer systems that use more than one computer, or processor, to run an application. This includes *parallel processing,* in which a single computer uses more than one CPU to execute programs. More often, however, distributed processing refers to local-area networks (LANs) designed so that a single program can run simultaneously at various sites. Most distributed processing systems contain sophisticated software that detects idle CPUs on the network and parcels out programs to utilize them.

Another form of distributed processing involves *distributed databases,* databases in which the data is stored across two or more computer systems. The database system keeps track of where the data is so that the distributed nature of the database is not apparent to users.

➡ See also *database management system; distributed database; local-area network; parallel processing.*

dithering: Creating new colors and shades by varying the pattern of dots. Newspaper photographs, for example, are dithered. If you look closely, you can see that different shades of gray are produced by varying the patterns of black and white dots (Figure 25). There are no gray dots at all. The more dither patterns that a device or program supports, the more shades of gray it can represent. In printing, dithering is usually called *halftoning,* and shades of gray are called *halftones.*

Note that *dithering* differs from *gray scaling.* In

gray scaling, each individual dot can have a different shade of gray.

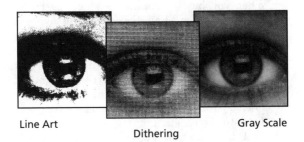

Line Art   Gray Scale

Dithering

Figure 25
Dithering

➠ See also *halftone; gray scaling; pixel.*

DMA: Abbreviation of **direct memory access**, a technique for transferring data from main memory to a device without passing it through the CPU. Computers that have DMA channels can transfer data to and from devices much more quickly than computers without a DMA channel can. This is useful for making quick backups and for *real-time* applications.

➠ See also *backup; channel; CPU; main memory; real time.*

document: (1) A text file, usually one produced by a word processor.

➠ See also *file; text; word processing.*

(2) On Apple Macintosh computers, *documents* are any data files associated with a particular application. For example, a document could be a text file, a graphics file, or a spreadsheet.

documentation: Instructions for using a computer device or program. Documentation can appear in a variety of forms, the most common being manuals. When you buy a computer product (hardware or software), it almost always comes with one or more manuals that describe how to install and operate the product. In addition, many software products include an on-line version of the documentation that you can display on your screen or print out on a printer. Another type of on-line documentation is a *help system,* which has the documentation embedded into the program.

Documentation is often divided into the following categories:

reference: Detailed descriptions of particular items presented in alphabetical order. Reference documentation is designed for people who are already somewhat familiar with the product but need reminders or very specific information about a particular topic.

installation: Describes how to install a program or device but not how to use it.

tutorial: Teaches a user how to use the product. Tutorials move at a slower pace than reference manuals and generally contain less detail.

Because the documentation often provides the only instruction you will ever receive, it is important that it be clear, complete, and accurate.

➡ See also *help; on-line.*

DOS: Acronym for *disk operating system.* The term *DOS* can refer to any operating system, but it is most often used as a shorthand for *MS-DOS* (*Microsoft disk operating system*) and *PC-DOS*. Developed by Microsoft for IBM, MS-DOS is the standard operating system for IBM-compatible personal computers. IBM sells almost the same operating system as PC-DOS. Both of these operating systems (Table 10) are known generically as *DOS systems*.

The initial versions of DOS were very simple and resembled another operating system called CP/M. Subsequent versions have become increasingly sophisticated as they have incorporated features of minicomputer operating systems. However, DOS still does not support multiple users or multitasking. In addition, DOS has a built-in limitation of 1MB of memory. To exceed this limit, you need a

Table 10: MS-DOS and PC-DOS Versions

There are nearly a dozen different versions of MS-DOS and PC-DOS. The following are the most important:

VERSION	DATE	NOTES
PC-DOS 2.0, 2.1, and 2.11	1983	Operating system for the PC/XT; supports hard disk drives
PC-DOS 3.0	1984	Operating system for the PC/AT; supports high-density floppy disk drives and *RAM disks*
MS-DOS 3.05	1984	Same as PC-DOS 3.0
PC-DOS 3.1	1985	Supports PC networks
PC-DOS 3.2	1985	Supports 3½-inch, 720K disk drives
MS-DOS 3.2	1986	Same as PC-DOS 3.2
PC-DOS 3.3	1987	Supports 3½-inch, 1.44MB disk drives, multiple hard disk partitions, improved hard disk backup, and the FASTOPEN command
PC-DOS 4.0	1988	Supports unlimited disk partition sizes, expanded memory, and a graphical shell
PC-DOS 4.1	1988	Corrects bugs in PC-DOS 4.0
MS-DOS 4.1	1988	Same as PC-DOS 4.1, but with additional bugs fixed
MS-DOS 5.0	1991	Adds utilities and accesses memory above 640K

special memory system called EMS (Expanded Memory Specification).

In 1988, Microsoft and IBM introduced a new operating system for IBM PCs and IBM-compatible personal computers called OS/2. Most programs written for DOS will also run under OS/2. OS/2 runs only on IBM PCs (or compatibles) with an Intel 80286 or later microprocessor.

Although DOS is the standard operating system for IBM-compatible personal computers, it is not the only operating system available. For example, Microsoft offers another operating system called Xenix that is very similar to UNIX.

➡ See also *DESQview; expanded memory; IBM PC; Intel microprocessors; Microsoft Windows; multitasking; operating system; OS/2; UNIX.*

dot-matrix printer: A type of printer that produces characters and illustrations by striking pins against an ink ribbon to print closely spaced dots in the appropriate shape. In general, dot-matrix printers are inexpensive and relatively fast. In addition, they are capable of printing graphics and usually support more than one font.

Dot-matrix printers vary in two important characteristics:

speed: Given in characters per second (cps), the speed can vary from about 50 to over 500 cps. Most dot-matrix printers offer different speeds depending on the quality of print desired.

print quality: Determined by the number of pins (the mechanisms that print the dots), it can vary from 9 to 24. The best dot-matrix printers (24 pins) can produce near letter-quality type, although you can still see a difference if you look closely.

In addition to these characteristics, you should also consider the noise factor. Compared to laser and ink-jet printers, dot-matrix printers are notorious for making a racket. Although the price of laser printers is dropping rapidly, dot-matrix printers are still much cheaper to operate. A page printed by a dot-matrix printer costs about a penny, whereas a laser-printed page costs two to three cents. In addition, most dot-matrix printers can print carbon copies, something laser printers cannot do.

➠ See also *pin; printer*.

dot pitch: A measurement that indicates the distance between each pixel on a display screen. Measured in millimeters, the dot pitch is one of the principal characteristics determining the quality of display monitors. The lower the number, the crisper the image. The dot pitch of color monitors for personal computers ranges from about 0.22 mm to 0.42 mm.

➠ See also *monitor; pixel*.

dots per inch: See *dpi*.

double click: Pressing and releasing a mouse button twice in rapid succession. Note that the second click must immediately follow the first, otherwise the program will interpret them as two separate clicks rather than one double click.

In Microsoft Windows and the Macintosh interface, you can use a double click to open files and applications. Both systems let you set the double click speed (the longest acceptable interval between each click).

➠ See also *click; Macintosh computer; Microsoft Windows; mouse*.

double-density disk: A floppy disk that has twice the storage capacity of a single-density floppy. Single-density disks are now practically obsolete. Double-density 5¼-inch disks for IBM PCs and compatibles can hold 360K of data. Double-density 3½-inch disks can hold 720K.

Although high-density disk drives can format

both high-density and double-density disks, double-density disks formatted by a high-density drive may not be readable by a double-density drive. Similarly, high-density drives may not be able to read disks that have been formatted by a double-density disk drive.

➥ See also *density; floppy disk.*

double precision: Refers to a type of floating-point number that has more precision (that is, more digits to the right of the decimal point) than a *single-precision* number. The term *double precision* is something of a misnomer because the precision is not really double. The word *double* derives from the fact that a double-precision number uses twice as many bits as a regular floating-point number. For example, if a single-precision number requires 32 bits, its double-precision counterpart will be 64 bits long.

The extra bits increase not only the precision but also the range of magnitudes that can be represented. The exact amount by which the precision and range of magnitudes are increased depends on what format the program is using to represent floating-point values. Most computers use a standard format known as the *IEEE floating-point format.*

➥ See also *floating-point number; IEEE.*

double-sided disk: A floppy disk with both sides prepared for recording data. You can store twice as much data on a double-sided disk, but you need to use a double-sided disk drive (most disk drives are double-sided).

➥ See also *disk drive; floppy disk.*

down: Not working. A computer system is said to be down when it is not available to users. This can occur because it is broken (that is, it has crashed), or because it has been made temporarily unavailable to users so that routine servicing can be performed.

➡ See also *crash*.

download: To copy data (usually an entire file) from a main source to a peripheral device. The term is often used to describe the process of loading a font into a laser printer. The font is first copied from a disk to the printer's local memory. A font that has been downloaded like this is called a *soft font* to distinguish it from the *hard* fonts that are permanently in the printer's memory.

The term *download* also describes the process of copying a file from a network file server to a computer on the network. In this case, the server is the main source of data, and the computers on the network are like peripheral devices. Downloading can also refer to copying a file from a *bulletin board service* to a personal computer.

➡ See also *bulletin board service; font; laser printer; main memory; network; peripheral device; server; soft font*.

downloadable font: Same as *soft font*.

downward compatible: Same as *backward compatible*.

DP: See *data processing*.

dpi: Abbreviation of *dots per inch*, which indicates the resolution of images. The more dots per inch, the higher the resolution. A common resolution for laser printers is 300 dots per inch. This means 300 dots across and 300 dots down, so there are 90,000 dots per square inch.

➡ See also *laser printer; resolution*.

draft mode: A printing mode in which the printer prints text as fast as possible without regard to the print quality. Most dot-matrix printers support two modes: draft mode and either *letter-quality* or *near letter-quality* mode.

➡ See also *dot-matrix printer; letter quality; mode; near letter quality; printer.*

draft quality: Describes print whose quality is less than near letter quality (see Figure 41 at *letter quality*). Most 9-pin dot-matrix printers produce draft-quality print.

➡ See also *dot-matrix printer; draft mode; letter quality; near letter quality; printer.*

drag: (1) In graphical user interfaces, *drag* refers to moving an icon or other image on a display screen. To drag an object across a display screen, you usually select the object with a mouse button and then move the mouse while keeping the mouse button pressed down.

(2) The term *drag* is also used more generally for any operation in which the mouse button is held down while the mouse is moved. For example, you would drag the mouse to select a block of text.

➡ See also *graphical user interface; icon; mouse; select.*

DRAM: Pronounced *dee-ram,* DRAM stands for *dynamic random access memory,* a type of memory used in most personal computers.

➡ See also *dynamic RAM.*

draw program: A graphics program that enables you to draw pictures on a display screen. You can then store the images in files, merge them into documents, and print them. Draw programs use *vector graphics,* which makes it easy to scale images to different sizes. This makes draw programs particularly effective for drafting and diagramming. In contrast, *paint programs* store images as *bit maps.*

→ See also *bit map; graphics; paint program; vector graphics*.

drive: Short for *disk drive*.

drive bay: An area of reserved space in a personal computer where hard or floppy disk drives (or tape drives) can be installed. The number of drive bays in a computer determines the total number of internal mass storage devices it can handle.

→ See also *disk drive; mass storage*.

driver: A program that controls a device. Every device, whether it be a printer, disk drive, or keyboard, must have a driver program. Many drivers, such as the keyboard driver, come with the operating system. For peripheral devices, you may need to load a new driver when you connect the device to your computer.

A driver acts like a translator between the device and programs that use the device. Each device has its own set of specialized commands that only its driver knows. In contrast, most programs access devices by using generic commands. The driver,

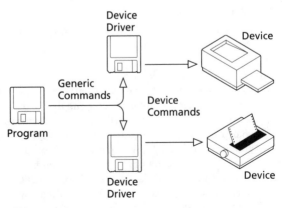

Figure 26
Device Driver

therefore, accepts generic commands from a program and then translates them into specialized commands for the device (Figure 26).

Most programs that allow you to print documents (such as word processors and database systems) come with drivers for the most popular printers. During the installation or *setup* session, you need to tell the program what type of printer you have so that it can install the correct driver.

➡ See also *CONFIG.SYS; device.*

drop-down menu: Same as *pull-down menu.*

DTP: See *desktop publishing.*

dual supertwist: See under *supertwist.*

dumb terminal: A display monitor that has no processing capabilities. A dumb terminal is simply an output device that accepts data from the CPU. In contrast, a *smart terminal* is a monitor that has its own processor for special features, such as bold and blinking characters. Dumb terminals are not as fast as smart terminals, and they do not support as many display features, but they are adequate for most applications.

➡ See also *display screen; intelligent terminal; smart terminal; terminal.*

dump: (n) The act of copying raw data from one place to another with little or no formatting for readability. Usually, *dump* refers to copying data from main memory to a display screen or a printer. Dumps are useful for diagnosing bugs. After a program fails, you can study the dump and analyze the contents of memory at the time of the failure. Dumps are usually output in a difficult-to-read form (that is, binary, octal, or hexadecimal), so a dump will not help you unless you know exactly what to look for.

(v) To output an image of computer memory.

duplex: Same as *full duplex*.

DVI: Abbreviation of *Digital Video Interactive*, a technology developed by RCA and now owned by Intel that enables a computer to store and display moving video images like those on television. The most difficult aspect of displaying TV-like images on a computer is overcoming the fact that each frame requires an immense amount of storage. A single frame can require up to 2MB of storage. Televisions display 30 frames per second, which can quickly exhaust a computer's mass storage resources. It is also difficult to transfer so much data to a display screen at a rate of 30 frames per second.

DVI overcomes these problems by using specialized processors to compress and decompress the data. Two competing video architectures are *CD-I* (Compact Disc-Interactive) and *JPEG* (Joint Photographic Experts Group).

➡ See also *CD-I; data compression; NTSC*.

Dvorak keyboard: A keyboard designed for speed typing. The Dvorak keyboard was designed in the 1930s by August Dvorak, a professor of education, and his brother-in-law, William Dealy. Unlike the traditional QWERTY keyboard, the Dvorak keyboard is designed so that most words fall in the middle row of keys. In addition, common letter combinations are positioned in such a way that they can be typed quickly (Figure 27).

The QWERTY keyboard, designed in the 1800s for mechanical typewriters, was actually intended to slow typists, in order to avoid jamming the keys. It has been estimated that in an average eight-hour day, a typist's hands travel 16 miles on a QWERTY keyboard, but only 1 mile on a Dvorak keyboard.

A number of computers, including the Apple IIc and IIGS, allow you to choose between the QWERTY and Dvorak keyboards. Also, you can

Figure 27
Dvorak Keyboard

often turn a QWERTY keyboard into a Dvorak keyboard by redefining the keys with macros.

In addition to the standard Dvorak keyboard, there are two additional Dvorak keyboards, a left-handed and right-handed keyboard. These keyboards are designed for people who have only one hand to type with.

➧ See also *keyboard; macro; QWERTY keyboard.*

DXF: Abbreviation of *Data Exchange File*, a two-dimensional graphics file format supported by virtually all PC-based CAD products. It was created by AutoDesk for the AutoCAD system.

➧ See also *CAD; graphics; graphics file formats.*

dynamic: Refers to actions that take place at the moment they are needed rather than in advance. For example, many programs perform *dynamic memory allocation,* which means that they do not reserve memory ahead of time, but seize sections of memory when needed. In general, such programs require less memory, although they may run a little more slowly.

The opposite of dynamic is *static*.

➧ See also *dynamic variable; static variable*.

dynamic RAM: A type of physical memory used in most personal computers. The term *dynamic* indicates that the memory must be constantly *refreshed* (reenergized) or it will lose its contents. RAM (random-access memory) is sometimes referred to as DRAM to distinguish it from *static RAM* (SRAM). Static RAM is faster and more stable than dynamic RAM, but it requires more power and is more expensive.

➧ See also *main memory; RAM; refresh; static RAM*.

dynamic resolution: A feature supported by some mice that causes the mouse resolution to depend on how fast the mouse is moved. When you move the mouse fast, the cursor moves proportionally further (the resolution is low). This is useful for jumping across the screen. Without this feature, you might need to sweep the mouse several times to move the cursor from one side of the display screen to the other. When you move the mouse slowly, the resolution increases to enable you to pinpoint specific pixels.

Dynamic resolution is also called *ballistic tracking, automatic acceleration, variable acceleration,* and *dynamic acceleration*.

➧ See also *mouse; resolution*.

dynamic variable: In programming, a dynamic variable is a variable whose address is determined when the program is run. In contrast, a *static* variable has memory reserved for it at compilation time.

➧ See also *static variable; variable*.

EBCDIC: Abbreviation of *Extended Binary-Coded Decimal Interchange Code.* Pronounced *eb-si-dik,* EBCDIC is an IBM code for representing characters as numbers (Table 11). Although it is widely used on large IBM computers, most other computers, including IBM PCs, use ASCII codes.

➧ See also *ASCII.*

edge connector: The part of a *printed circuit board* that plugs into a computer or device. The edge connector generally has a row of broad metallic tracks that provide the electrical connection (see Figure 56 at *printed circuit board*).

➧ See also *printed circuit board.*

editor: Sometimes called *text editor,* an editor is a program that enables you to create and edit text files. There are many different types of editors, but they all fall into two general categories:

line editors: A relatively primitive form of editor that requires you to specify a specific line of text before you can make changes to it.

screen-oriented editors: Also called *full-screen editors,* these editors enable you to modify any text that appears on the display screen by moving the cursor to the desired location.

The distinction between editors and word processors is not clear-cut, but in general, word processors provide more formatting features.

➧ See also *command driven; menu driven; word processing.*

Table 11. EBCDIC Codes

DECIMAL	HEXADECIMAL	CHARACTER
129	81	a
130	82	b
131	83	c
132	84	d
133	85	e
134	86	f
135	87	g
136	88	h
137	89	i
145	91	j
146	92	k
147	93	l
148	94	m
149	95	n
150	96	o
151	97	p
152	98	q
153	99	r
162	A2	s
163	A3	t
164	A4	u
165	A5	v
166	A6	w
167	A7	x
168	A8	y
169	A9	z
240	F0	0
241	F1	1
242	F2	2
243	F3	3
244	F4	4
245	F5	5
246	F6	6
247	F7	7
248	F8	8
249	F9	9
122	7A	:
123	7B	#
124	7C	@
125	7D	'
126	7E	=
127	7F	"
193	C1	A

Table 11. *(Continued)*

DECIMAL	HEXADECIMAL	CHARACTER
194	C2	B
195	C3	C
196	C4	D
197	C5	E
198	C6	F
199	C7	G
200	C8	H
201	C9	I
209	D1	J
210	D2	K
211	D3	L
212	D4	M
213	D5	N
214	D6	O
215	D7	P
216	D8	Q
217	D9	R
226	E2	S
227	E3	T
228	E4	U
229	E5	V
230	E6	W
231	E7	X
232	E8	Y
233	E9	Z
64	40	blank
76	4C	<
77	4D	(
78	4E	+
79	4F	|
80	50	&
90	5A	!
91	5B	$
92	5C	*
93	5D	)
94	5E	;
96	60	-
97	61	/
107	6B	,
108	6C	%
109	6D	_
110	6E	>
111	6F	?

EEMS: Abbreviation of *Enhanced Expanded Memory Specification*. EEMS is an enhanced version of the original EMS, which enables DOS applications to use more than 1MB of memory. EEMS was developed by AST, Quadram, and Ashton-Tate to improve the performance of the original version of EMS. Subsequently, Lotus, Intel, and Microsoft developed the LIM 4.0 version of EMS, which supports both the original EMS and EEMS.

➡ See also *expanded memory; LIM memory.*

EEPROM: Acronym for *electrically erasable programmable read-only memory*. An EEPROM is a special type of PROM that can be erased by exposing it to an electrical charge. Like other types of PROM, EEPROM retains its contents even when the power is turned off. Also like other types of ROM, EEPROM is not as fast as RAM.

A special type of EEPROM, referred to as *flash memory* or *flash EEPROM*, can be rewritten while it is in the computer rather than requiring a special device called a *PROM reader*.

➡ See also *EPROM; flash memory; memory; PROM; RAM; ROM.*

EGA: Abbreviation of *enhanced graphics adapter*, a graphics display system for IBM PCs and compatibles introduced by IBM in 1984. EGA supports 16 colors from a palette of 64 and provides a resolution of 640 by 350. This is better than CGA but not as good as VGA.

➡ See also *CGA; composite video; graphics; palette; resolution; RGB monitor; SVGA; VGA; video adapter; XGA.*

EIA (Electronics Industry Association) interface: Same as *RS-232C* interface.

8086: Short for the *Intel 8086 microprocessor*.

➔ See also *Intel microprocessors*.

8514/A: One of IBM's highest resolution video standards for PCs. It is designed to extend the capabilities of VGA. The 8514/A standard provides a resolution of 1,024 by 768 pixels and a palette of 262,000 colors, of which 256 can be displayed at one time. On monochrome displays, 8514/A provides 64 shades of gray.

True 8514/A systems rely on *interlacing*, a technique that makes it possible to provide resolution at low cost. Interlacing, however, carries a performance penalty, so some manufacturers produce *noninterlaced* 8514/A clones. 8514/A video adapters require an MCA (Micro Channel architecture) bus. Another video standard, SVGA, offers similar resolutions but works with ISA and EISA systems.

➔ See also *EISA; interlacing; ISA Micro Channel architecture; monochrome; palette; resolution; SVGA; video adapter; XGA*.

EISA: Acronym for *Extended Industry Standard Architecture*, a bus architecture designed for IBM PCs and compatibles using an Intel 80386 or 80486 microprocessor. EISA buses are 32 bits wide and support multiprocessing.

The EISA bus was designed by nine IBM competitors (sometimes called the *Gang of Nine*): AST Research, Compaq Computer, Epson, Hewlett-Packard, NEC Information Systems, Olivetti, Tandy, WYSE, and Zenith Data Systems. They designed the architecture to compete with IBM's own high-speed bus architecture called the *Micro Channel architecture (MCA)*.

The principal difference between EISA and MCA is that EISA is backward compatible with the ISA bus (also called the *AT bus*), while MCA is not. This means that computers with an EISA bus can use new EISA expansion cards as well as old AT expansion cards. Computers with an MCA bus can use only MCA expansion cards.

EISA and MCA are not compatible with each other. This means that the type of bus in your computer determines which expansion cards you can install.

➡ See also *backward compatible; bus; expansion board; Micro Channel architecture; multiprocessing*.

ELD: See *electroluminescent display*.

electrically erasable programmable read-only memory: See *EEPROM*.

electroluminescent display (ELD): A technology used to produce a very thin display screen, called a *flat-panel display*. ELDs are used in laptop and portable computers. An ELD works by sandwiching a thin film of phosphorescent substance between two plates. One plate is coated with vertical wires and the other with horizontal wires, forming a grid. When an electrical current is passed through a horizonal and vertical wire, the phosphorescent film at the intersection glows, creating a point of light, or *pixel*.

Other types of flat-panel displays include LCD displays and gas-plasma displays. Both are more common than ELDs. Gas plasma displays use almost the same technique as ELDs, but employ a gas instead of a phosphorescent film.

➡ See also *flat-panel display; gas-plasma display; laptop computer; LCD; pixel*.

electronic mail: Refers to computer applications that enable users to send messages to other users at different terminals. The messages can be notes entered from the keyboard or electronic files stored on disk. Most mainframes, minicomputers, and computer networks have an electronic-mail (E-mail) system. Some electronic-mail systems are confined to a single computer system or network, but others have gateways to other computer systems, enabling users to send electronic mail anywhere in the world. Companies that are fully computerized make extensive use of E-mail because it is fast, flexible, and reliable.

Most E-mail systems include a rudimentary text editor for composing messages, but many allow you to edit your messages using any editor you want. You then send the message to the recipient by specifying the recipient's username. You can also send the same message to several users at once. This is called *broadcasting*.

To see if you have any mail, you may have to check your electronic mailbox periodically, although most systems alert you when mail is received. After reading your mail, you can store it in a text file, forward it to other users, or delete it. Copies of memos can be printed out on a printer if you want a paper copy.

Most public carriers—AT&T, MCI, and Western Union, for example—offer electronic-mail services. For a small annual fee, you can set up a mailbox. You can then send mail to any other user who also has a mailbox on the same network. Usually, it takes only a few seconds or minutes for mail to arrive at its destination. This is a particularly effective way to communicate with a group because you can broadcast a message or document to everyone in the group at once.

In addition to public carriers, most bulletin board systems (BBSs), such as CompuServe, provide electronic-mail capabilities.

➡ See also *bulletin board system; CCITT; gateway; mailbox; network; public carrier; username; workgroup computing.*

elevator: Same as *scroll bar*.

E-mail: Short for *electronic mail*.

embedded command: In word processing, an embedded command is a sequence of special characters inserted into a document that affects the formatting of the document when it is printed. For example, when you change fonts in a word processor (by specifying bold type), the word processor inserts an embedded command that causes the printer to change fonts. Embedded commands can also control the display screen, causing it to display blinking characters or produce other special effects.

Embedded commands are usually invisible when you edit a file, but many word processors support a special mode that lets you see these commands.

➧ See also *command; font; word processing.*

EMS: Abbreviation of *Expanded Memory Specification.*

➧ See also *expanded memory.*

emulation: Refers to the ability of a program or device to imitate another program or device. Many printers, for example, are designed to emulate Epson printers because so much software is written for Epsons. By emulating an Epson printer, a printer can work with any software written for a real Epson. Emulation tricks the software into believing that a device is really some other device.

Communications software packages often include *terminal emulation drivers*. This enables your PC to emulate a particular type of terminal so that you can log on to a mainframe.

It is also possible for a computer to emulate another type of computer. For example, there are programs that enable an Apple Macintosh to emulate an IBM PC.

➧ See also *communications software; log on; mainframe; terminal.*

Encapsulated PostScript: See *EPS.*

encryption: The translation of data into a secret code. Encryption is the most effective way to achieve data security. To read an encrypted file, you must have access to a secret key or password that enables you to decrypt it.

➡ See also *password; security*.

End key: A special cursor control key on IBM PC keyboards. The End key has different meanings depending on which program is running. For example, it might move the cursor to the end of the line, the end of the page, or the end of the file.

➡ See also *keyboard*.

end of file: See *EOF*.

end of line: See *EOL*.

end user: The final or ultimate user of a computer system. The end user is the individual who uses the product after it has been fully developed and marketed. The term is useful because it distinguishes two classes of users, users who require a bug-free and finished product, and users who may use the same product for development purposes. The term *end user* usually implies an individual with a relatively low level of computer expertise. Unless you are a programmer or engineer, you are almost certainly an end user.

➡ See also *user*.

Enhanced Expanded Memory Specification: See *EEMS*.

enhanced graphics adapter: See *EGA*.

Enhanced Keyboard: A 101-key keyboard from IBM that supersedes the keyboard for the PC/AT computer. The most significant difference between the enhanced keyboard and previous models is that the enhanced keyboard has a row of 12 function keys at the top instead of 10 function keys grouped on the left side of the keyboard.

➡ See also *function keys; IBM PC; keyboard.*

Enhanced Small Device Interface: See *ESDI.*

Enter key: Same as *Return key.*

environment: (1) The state of a computer, usually determined by which programs are running and basic hardware and software characteristics. For example, when one speaks of running a program in a UNIX environment, it means running a program on a computer that has the UNIX operating system.

One ingredient of an environment, therefore, is the operating system. But operating systems include a number of different parameters. For example, many operating systems allow you to choose your command prompt or a default command path. All these parameters taken together constitute the environment.

➡ See also *operating system; parameter.*

(2) In DOS systems, the environment is an area in memory that the operating system and other programs use to store various types of miscellaneous information. For example, your word processor may use the environment area to store the location of backup files. You can view or modify the environment with the SET command.

➡ See also *DOS.*

EO: See *erasable optical disk.*

EOF mark: Short for *end-of-file mark*, a special character or sequence of characters that marks the end of a file. Operating systems need to keep track of where every file ends. There are two techniques for doing this: One is to put a special end-of-file mark at the end of each file. The other is to keep track of how many characters are in the file.

In many operating systems, including DOS and OS/2, the end-of-file mark is CTRL-Z. In UNIX, the end-of-file mark is CTRL-D.

EOL mark: Short for *end-of-line mark,* a special character or sequence of characters that marks the end of a line. For many programs, the EOL character is CTRL-M (carriage return) or CTRL-J (newline). End-of-line can also be abbreviated *EOLN.*

EPROM: Acronym for *erasable programmable read-only memory,* a special type of memory that retains its contents until it is exposed to ultraviolet light. The ultraviolet light clears its contents, making it possible to reprogram the memory. To write to and erase an EPROM, you need a special device called a *PROM programmer* or *PROM burner.*

An EPROM differs from a PROM in that a PROM can be written to only once and cannot be erased. EPROMs are used widely in personal computers.

➡ See also *memory; PROM.*

EPS: Abbreviation of *Encapsulated PostScript.* Pronounced as separate letters, EPS is the graphics file format used by the PostScript language.

EPS files can be either binary or ASCII. The term *EPS* usually implies that the file contains a representation of the graphics for display purposes. In contrast, *PostScript files* include only the Post-Script commands for printing the graphic.

➡ See also *ASCII; binary; graphics file formats; graphics; PostScript.*

erasable optical disk: A type of optical disk that can be erased and loaded with new data, just like magnetic disks. In contrast, most optical disks, called *CD-ROMs,* are read-only.

Although the technology is still young, erasable optical disks seem destined to become the future medium of choice. A single 5¼-inch optical disk can store as much as 1,000MB of data, about 800 times more than a typical floppy disk. The data access speed of optical disks varies considerably, from about 60 to 500 milliseconds. Though comparable to floppy disks, they are not yet as fast as magnetic hard disk drives.

Some erasable optical drives come with *autochangers*, which enable you to load more than one disk at a time. The autochanger automatically accesses the disk you need.

Erasable optical disks are often called *floptical disks*.

➤ See also *access time; CD-ROM; disk; floppy disk; mass storage; optical disk*.

erasable programmable read-only memory: See *EPROM*.

ergonomics: The science concerned with producing safe and comfortable machines for humans. For example, one branch of ergonomics deals with designing furniture that avoids causing backaches and muscle cramps. In the computer field, ergonomics plays an important role in the design of display terminals and keyboards.

Another term for ergonomics is *human engineering*.

error detection: In communications, *error detection* refers to a class of techniques for detecting garbled messages. Two of the simplest and most common techniques are called *checksum* and *CRC*. More sophisticated strategies include MNP and CCITT V.42.

➤ See also *CCITT; checksum; CRC; Kermit; MNP; Xmodem*.

ESC: Short for *Escape key*. For example, *ESC-Q* means *press the Escape key and then the Q key*.

➧ See also *escape character; Escape key*.

escape character: A special character that can have many different functions. It is often used to abort the current command and return to a previous place in the program. It is also used to send special instructions to printers and other devices. An escape character is generated with the *Escape key*, a special key that exists on most computer keyboards.

　　When the escape character is combined with other characters, it is called an *escape sequence*.

➧ See also *escape sequence; keyboard*.

Escape key: A key on computer keyboards that enables you to enter a nonprinting character called the *escape character*.

➧ See also *escape character; keyboard*.

escape sequence: A sequence of special characters that sends a command to a device or program. Typically, an escape sequence begins with an escape character, but this is not universally true.

➧ See also *escape character*.

ESDI: Abbreviation of *enhanced small device interface*, an interface standard developed by a consortium of the leading personal computer manufacturers for connecting disk drives to IBM PCs and compatibles. A descendant of the older ST-506 interface standard, ESDI supports relatively fast data rates (about 10–20 megabits per second) and large storage capacities (up to 1,000MB). ESDI is two to three times faster than the older *ST-506* standard.

　　Not all disk and tape drives support ESDI, but those that do are likely to be faster than those that do not. To use an ESDI drive, however, your computer must have an ESDI controller. A competing standard for high-speed disk drives is *SCSI*. For a lower-cost alternative to ESDI, see *IDE*.

➡ See also *controller; disk drive; IDE interface; mass storage; megabyte; SCSI; ST-506 interface; tape drive.*

Ethernet: A local-area network protocol developed by Xerox Corporation in cooperation with DEC and Intel. Today, however, Ethernet is the sole responsibility of DEC.

Ethernet uses a bus topology and supports data transfer rates of 10 megabits per second. Ethernet is supported by a wide variety of computers in addition to DEC machines and has been standardized in the IEEE 802.3 standard.

➡ See also *IEEE; local-area network; network; protocol; topology.*

even header: In word processing, a header that appears only on even-numbered pages.

➡ See also *header.*

even parity: Refers to the parity-checking mode in which each byte must have an even number of set bits.

➡ See also *parity checking.*

Excel: A powerful spreadsheet program from Microsoft Corporation that runs on Apple Macintosh computers and IBM PCs. Excel was the first spreadsheet program for Macintoshes and continues to dominate that market. For IBM PCs and compatibles, the leading spreadsheet program is Lotus 1-2-3.

➡ See also *Lotus 1-2-3; Macintosh computer; spreadsheet.*

exclusive OR: A Boolean operator that returns a value of TRUE only if both its operands have different values. Contrast with the *inclusive OR operator,* which returns a value of TRUE if *either* of its operands is TRUE.

➡ See also *Boolean operators*.

executable file: A file in a format that the computer can directly execute. Unlike source files, executable files cannot be read by humans. To transform a source file into an executable file, you need to pass it through a compiler or assembler.

In DOS systems, executable files have either a .COM or .EXE extension and are called *COM files* and *EXE files*, respectively.

➡ See also *assembler; COM file; compiler; EXE file; file; source code.*

execute: Same as *run*. *Execute* means to perform an action, as in executing a program or a command.

EXE file: In DOS systems, an EXE file is an executable file with an .EXE extension. Executable files are similar to COM files, but they have *relative* instead of *absolute addresses*. Consequently, they are usually somewhat larger and take a little longer to load. However, EXE files are not limited to 64K as COM files are, so most large programs are stored as EXE files.

➡ See also *absolute address; COM file; executable file; extension; file; filename; load; DOS; program; relative address.*

expanded memory: Expanded memory, known as EMS (**E**xpanded **M**emory **S**pecification), is a technique for utilizing more than 1MB of main memory in DOS-based computers. The limit of 1MB is built into the DOS operating system. The upper 384K is reserved for special purposes, leaving just 640K of *conventional memory* for programs.

One way to overcome this limit is to install an EMS system in your PC. EMS systems consist of two parts, the extra physical memory and the software to access the memory (known as an *EMS driver* or *expanded memory manager*). On PCs with an Intel 8088, 8086, or 80286 microprocessor, you can install EMS memory by inserting a special EMS memory board, such as Intel's Above Board. EMS memory boards come with the EMS driver, so it is not necessary to purchase any additional software. (Most memory boards can be configured as either extended or expanded memory.)

On 80386 machines, the microprocessor can automatically turn extended memory into expanded memory, so you do not need any special hardware (aside from the memory chips). You do need, however, an EMS driver. Versions 4.0 and later of DOS have a built-in EMS driver, and many PC compatibles come with the driver already installed. Otherwise, you can buy the driver separately.

You can also buy EMS programs that simulate EMS by using disk memory instead of RAM, but these systems are not as fast as real EMS systems.

There are several versions of EMS. The original versions, called *EMS 3.0* and *3.2,* enable programs to use an additional 8MB of memory, but for data only. An improved version developed by AST, Quadram and Ashton-Tate is known as *EEMS* (Extended **EMS**). EEMS enables programs to use extra memory for code as well as for data. The most recent version of EMS (created in 1987) is known as EMS 4.0 or *LIM 4.0,* LIM being the initials of the three companies that developed the specification: Lotus, Intel, and Microsoft. EMS 4.0 raises the available amount of memory to 32MB.

Until the release of Microsoft Windows 3.0 in 1990, expanded memory was the preferred way to add memory to a PC. The alternative method, called *extended memory*, was less flexible and could be used only by special programs such as RAM disks. Windows 3.0, however, contains an *extended memory manager* that enables programs to use extended memory without interfering with one another. In addition, Windows 3.0 can simulate expanded memory for those programs that need it. Increasingly, therefore, extended memory is becoming more popular than expanded memory.

➡ See also *conventional memory; DESQview; EEMS; expansion board; extended memory; IBM PC; Intel microprocessors; main memory; microprocessor; Microsoft Windows; DOS; RAM disk.*

expansion board: An electronic card that you can insert into a computer to give it added capabilities. Typically, expansion boards increase the amount of main memory or add graphics capabilities to a computer. A special kind of expansion board, called an *accelerator board,* makes a computer faster by adding a more powerful CPU.

Expansion boards for IBM PCs can be half-size, three-quarter-size, or full-size. Most IBM PCs and compatibles have slots for each type of board. A half-size board is sometimes called an *8-bit board* because it can transmit only 8 bits at a time. A full-size board is called a *16-bit* board.

Expansion boards are also called *expansion cards, add-ins,* and *add-ons.*

➡ See also *accelerator board; add-in; add-on; CPU; expansion slot; main memory; printed circuit board; video adapter.*

expansion bus: A collection of wires and protocols that allows the expansion of a computer by inserting printed circuit boards (*expansion boards*).

➡ See also *bus; expansion board; protocol.*

expansion slot: An opening in a computer where a circuit board can be inserted to add new capabilities to the computer. Many personal computers contain expansion slots for adding more memory, graphics capabilities, or support for special devices. The boards inserted into the expansion slots are called *expansion boards, expansion cards, add-ins,* and *add-ons.*

Expansion slots for IBM PCs and compatibles come in three sizes: *half-, three-quarter-,* and *full-size.*

➡ See also *expansion board; printed circuit board; slot.*

expert system: A computer application that performs a task that would otherwise be performed by a human expert. For example, there are expert systems that can diagnose human illnesses, make financial forecasts, and schedule routes for delivery vehicles. Some expert systems are designed to take the place of human experts, while others are designed to aid them.

Expert systems are part of a general category of computer applications known as *artificial intelligence.* To design an expert system, one needs a *knowledge engineer,* an individual who studies how human experts make decisions and translates the rules into terms that a computer can understand.

➡ See also *artificial intelligence.*

export: To format data in such a way that it can be used by another application. An application that can export data can send data directly to another application for processing, enabling the two programs to share the same data. One program, for example, could be a word processor, while the other could be a database management system.

The flip side of exporting is *importing.* Importing refers to the ability of an application to read and use data produced by a different application. Exporting implies that the sending application reformats the data for the receiving application, whereas importing implies that the receiving application does the reformatting.

➡ See also *import.*

expression: In programming, an expression is any legal combination of symbols that represents a value. Each programming language and application has its own rules for what is legal and illegal. For example, in the C language $x + 5$ is an expression, as is the character string *"MONKEYS."*

Every expression consists of at least one *operand* and can have one or more *operators*. Operands are values, whereas operators are symbols that represent particular actions. In the expression

$$x + 5$$

x and 5 are operands, and + is an operator.

Expressions are used in programming languages, database systems, and spreadsheet applications. For example, in database systems, you use expressions to specify which information you want to see. These types of expressions are called *queries*.

Expressions are often classified by the type of value that they represent. For example:

Boolean expressions: Evaluate to either TRUE or FALSE

integer expressions: Evaluate to whole numbers, like 3 or 100

floating-point expressions: Evaluate to real numbers, like 3.141 or -0.005

string expressions: Evaluate to character strings

➡ See also *Boolean expression; character string; data type; floating-point number; integer; operand; operator; query.*

extended ASCII: A set of codes that extends the basic ASCII set. The basic ASCII set uses 7 bits for each character, giving it a total of 128 unique symbols. The extended ASCII character set uses 8 bits, which gives it an additional 128 characters. The extra characters represent characters from foreign languages and special symbols for drawing pictures.

See *ASCII* for tables of ASCII and extended ASCII character codes.

➡ See also *ASCII*.

Extended Binary-Coded Decimal Interchange Code: See *EBCDIC*.

extended graphics array: See *XGA*.

Extended Industry Standard Architecture: See *EISA*.

extended memory: Memory above and beyond the standard 1MB of main memory that DOS supports. Extended memory is only available in PCs with an Intel 80286, 80386, or 80486 microprocessor.

Two types of memory can be added to a PC to increase memory beyond 1MB: *expanded memory* and *extended memory*. Expanded memory conforms to a published standard called *EMS* that enables DOS programs to take advantage of it. Extended memory, on the other hand, is not configured in any special manner and is therefore unavailable to most programs. It is most commonly used for RAM disks and print spoolers. In addition, some operating environments, such as OS/2, DESQview, and Microsoft Windows 3.0, are designed to run programs in *protected mode*, which enables them to use extended memory. Programs that use extended memory should conform to one of the standard schemes to avoid conflicts: Extended Memory Specification (XMS), DOS/Protected Mode Interface (DPMI), or Virtual Control Program Interface (VCPI).

Most memory expansion boards permit you to set switches to select whether the memory is to be installed as extended memory or expanded memory. Machines based on the Intel 80386 and 80486 microprocessors can convert extended memory into expanded memory.

➡ See also *DESQview; expanded memory; Intel microprocessors; main memory; memory; Microsoft Windows; DOS; OS/2; protected mode; RAM disk; spooling; XMS.*

Extended Memory Specification: See *XMS.*

extended VGA: See *Super VGA.*

extension: (1) An extra feature added to a standard programming language or system.

(2) One or several letters at the end of a filename. Filename extensions usually follow a period and indicate the type of information stored in the file (Table 12). In the filename *EDIT.COM*, for example, the extension is *COM*, which indicates that the file is a command file. (Depending on the operating system, the punctuation separating the extension from the rest of the filename may or may not be considered part of the extension itself.)

➡ See also *BAT file; COM file; EXE file; filename.*

Table 12: DOS Filename Extensions

The DOS operating system recognizes the following filename extensions:

.BAK	backup file
.BAT	batch file
.COM	command file
.EXE	executable file
.LIB	library file
.MAP	map file
.OBJ	object file

These extensions are reserved by the operating system and have special significance. You can invent your own extensions to keep track of different types of personal files.

external command: In DOS systems, an external command is any command that does not reside in the

COMMAND.COM file. This includes all other COM files, as well as EXE and BAT files. Commands in the COMMAND.COM file are called *internal commands*.

➡ See also *BAT file; COM file; command; EXE file; internal command; DOS.*

external modem: A modem that resides in a self-contained box outside the computer system. Contrast with an *internal modem*, which resides on a printed circuit board inserted into the computer (see Figure 47 at *modem*).

External modems tend to be slightly more expensive than internal modems. Many experts consider them superior because they contain lights that indicate how the modem is functioning. In addition, they can easily be moved from one computer to another.

➡ See also *modem; printed circuit board.*

facsimile machine: See *FAX machine.*

FAT: See *file allocation table.*

fatal error: An error that causes a program to abort. Normally, a fatal error returns you to the operating system. When a fatal error occurs, you may lose whatever data the program was currently processing. Although serious, fatal errors are less severe than crashes.

➡ See also *abort; crash.*

FAX: (v) To send a document via a FAX machine.

   (n) (1) A document that has been sent, or is about to be sent, via a FAX machine.

   (2) Short for **Facsimile machine.**

➡ See also *FAX machine.*

FAX board: See under *FAX modem.*

FAX machine: Abbreviation of *facsimile machine,* a FAX machine is a device that can send or receive pictures and text over a telephone line. FAX machines work by digitizing an image—dividing it into a grid of dots. Each dot is either on or off, depending on whether it is black or white. Electronically, each dot is represented by a bit that has a value of either 0 (off) or 1 (on). In this way, the FAX machine translates a picture into a series of zeros and ones (called a *bit map*) that can be transmitted like normal computer data. On the receiving side, a FAX machine reads the incoming data, translates the zeros and ones back into dots, and reprints the picture.

   The idea of FAX machines has been around since 1842, when Alexander Bain invented a machine capable of receiving signals from a telegraph wire and translating them into images on paper. In 1850, a London inventor named F. C. Blakewell received a patent for a similar machine, which he called a *copying telegraph.*

   But while the idea of FAX machines has existed since the 1800s, FAX machines did not become popular until the mid 1980s. The spark igniting the FAX revolution was the adoption in 1983 of a standard protocol for sending FAXes at rates of 9,600 bps. The standard was created by the CCITT standards organization and is known as the *Group 3* standard. Now, FAXes are commonplace in offices of all sizes. They provide an inexpensive, fast, and reliable method for transmitting correspondence, contracts, résumés, handwritten notes, and illustrations.

A FAX machine consists of an optical scanner for digitizing images on paper, a printer for printing incoming FAX messages, and a telephone for making the connection. The optical scanner generally does not offer the same quality of resolution as stand-alone scanners. Most printers on FAX machines are *thermal,* which means they require a special kind of paper.

All FAX machines conform to the CCITT Group 3 protocol. (There is a new protocol called Group 4, but it requires ISDN lines.) The Group 3 protocol supports two classes of resolution: 203 by 98 dpi and 203 by 196 dpi. The protocol also specifies a data compression technique and a maximum transmission speed of 9,600 bps.

Some of the features that differentiate one FAX machine from another include the following:

resolution: Group 3 FAX machines scan and print images at 203 by 98 dpi or 203 by 196 dpi.

speed: FAX machines transmit data at either 4,800 bps or 9,600 bps. A 9,600 bps FAX machine typically requires 10 to 20 seconds to transmit one page. A 4,800 bps machine takes twice as long.

printer type: Most FAX machines use a thermal printer that requires special paper that tends to turn yellow or brown after a period. More expensive FAX machines have printers that can print on regular bond paper.

paper size: The thermal paper used in most FAX machines comes in two basic sizes: 8.5-inches wide and 10.1-inches wide. Some machines accept only the narrow-sized paper.

paper cutter: Most FAX machines include a paper cutter because the thermal paper that most FAX machines use comes in rolls. The least expensive models and portable FAXes, however, may not include a paper cutter.

paper feeder: Some FAX machines have paper feeders so that you can send multiple-page docu-

ments without manually feeding each page into
the machine.

autodialing: FAX machines come with a variety
of dialing features. Some enable you to program
the FAX to send a document at a future time to
take advantage of the lowest telephone rates.

As an alternative to stand-alone FAX machines,
you can also put together a FAX system by purchasing separately a FAX modem and an optical scanner. You may not even need the optical scanner if
the documents you want to send are already in electronic form.

➡ See also *bit map; bps; CCITT; communications;
digitize; FAX modem; optical scanner; resolution; thermal printer.*

FAX modem: A device you can attach to a personal
computer that enables you to transmit electronic
documents as FAXes. A FAX modem is like a regular modem except that it is designed to transmit
documents to a FAX machine, or another FAX
modem, rather than to a computer. Some, but not
all, FAX modems do double duty as regular
modems. As with regular modems, FAX modems
can be either *internal* or *external.* Internal FAX
modems are often called *FAX boards.*

Documents sent through a FAX modem must
already be in an electronic form (that is, in a disk
file), and the documents you receive are likewise
stored in files on your disk. To create FAX documents from images on paper, you need an optical
scanner.

FAX modems come with communications software similar to communications software for regular modems. This software can give the FAX modem
many capabilities that are not available with stand-
alone FAX machines. For example, you can broadcast a FAX document to several sites at once. In
addition, FAX modems offer the following advantages over FAX machines:

price: FAX modems are less expensive. In addition, they require less maintenance because there are no moving parts. However, if you need to purchase an optical scanner in addition to the FAX modem, there is no price advantage.

convenience: FAX modems are more convenient if the documents you want to send are already in electronic form. With a FAX machine, you would first need to print the document. A FAX modem lets you send it directly.

speed: FAX modems can almost always transmit documents at the maximum speed of 9,600 bps, whereas not all FAX machines support such high data transmission rates.

image quality: The image quality of transmissions by FAX modems is usually superior because the documents remain in electronic form.

The principal disadvantage of FAX modems is that you cannot FAX paper documents unless you buy a separate optical scanner, which eliminates any cost advantages of FAX modems. Another problem with FAX modems is that each document you receive requires an enormous amount of disk storage (about 100K per page). Not only does this eat up disk storage, but it takes a long time to print such files.

➡ See also *broadcast; FAX machine; gray scaling; modem; optical scanner; polling.*

FCC: Abbreviation of *Federal Communications Commission.* Among other duties, the FCC is responsible for rating personal computers and other equipment as either Class A or Class B. The ratings indicate how much radiation a personal computer emits. Almost all personal computers satisfy Class A requirements, which means they are suitable for office use. Class B machines, which are suitable for use anywhere (including the home), must pass more stringent tests. Class B indicates that the machine's radio frequency (RF) emissions are so low that they do not interfere with other devices such as radios and TVs.

FDDI: Abbreviation of *Fiber-Optic **D**igital **D**evice **I**nterface*, a set of ANSI protocols for sending digital data over fiber optic cable. FDDI supports data rates of up to 100 mbps (megabits per second).

A proposed standard, called *FDDI-2*, supports the transmission of voice and video information as well as data.

➡ See also *fiber optics; network; protocol.*

FDHD: Short for *floppy **d**rive **h**igh **d**ensity,* FDHD refers to 3½-inch disk drives for Apple Macintosh computers that can accept double-density or high-density 3½-inch floppy disks. FDHDs can also read DOS-formatted floppy disks, which enables Macintosh computers and IBM PCs to share data. FDHD drives are often called *SuperDrives.*

➡ See also *density; floppy disk; Macintosh computer; DOS; SuperDrive disk drive.*

feathering: In desktop publishing, feathering is the process of adding space between all lines on a page or in a column to force vertical justification.

➡ See also *vertical justification.*

Federal Communications Commission: See *FCC.*

FF: See *form feed.*

Fiber-Optic Digital Device Interface: See *FDDI.*

fiber optics: A technology that uses glass (or plastic) threads (fibers) to transmit data. A fiber optic cable consists of a bundle of glass threads, each of which is capable of transmitting messages at close to the speed of light (Figure 28).

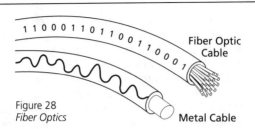

Figure 28
Fiber Optics

Fiber optics has several advantages over traditional metal communications lines:

- Fiber optic cables have a much greater bandwidth than metal cables. This means that they can carry more data.
- Fiber optic cables are less susceptible than metal cables to interference.
- Fiber optic cables are much thinner and lighter than metal wires.
- Data can be transmitted digitally (the natural form for computer data) rather than analogically.

The main disadvantage of fiber optics is that the cables are expensive to install. In addition, they are more fragile than wire and are difficult to split.

Fiber optics is a particularly popular technology for local-area networks. In addition, telephone companies are steadily replacing traditional telephone lines with fiber optic cables. In the future, almost all communications will employ fiber optics.

➡ See also *analog; bandwidth; communications; digital; FDDI; ISDN; local-area network.*

field: (1) A space allocated for a particular item of information. A tax form, for example, contains a number of fields: one for your name, one for your Social Security number, one for your income, and so on. In database systems, fields are the smallest units of information you can access (see Figure 19 at *database*).

Most fields have certain attributes associated with them. For example, some fields are numeric whereas others are textual, some are long while others are short. In addition, every field has a name, called the *field name*.

In database management systems, a field can be *required*, *optional*, or *calculated*. A *required field* is one in which you must enter data, while an *optional field* is one you can leave blank. A calculated field is one whose value is derived from some formula involving other fields. You do not enter data into a calculated field; the system automatically determines the correct value.

A collection of fields is called a *record*.

➡ See also *attribute; data type; database management system; record.*

(2) The phrase *in the field* refers to any geographical location other than the factory or office where a product was created. Similarly, a *field representative* is an employee who represents a company in distant locations.

file: A collection of data or information that has a name, called the *filename*. Almost all information stored in a computer must be in a file. There are many different types of files: data files, text files, program files, directory files, and so on. Different types of files store different types of information. For example, *program files* store programs, whereas *text files* store text.

Table 13 lists some common types of files.

➡ See also *binary format; command; compile; data; directory; executable file; library; map; object code; text.*

file allocation table (FAT): A table that the operating system uses to locate files on a disk. Due to fragmentation, a file may be divided into many sections that are scattered around the disk. The FAT keeps track of all these pieces.

Table 13: File Types

FILE TYPE	DESCRIPTION
Batch file	Same as *command file*–contains operating system commands
Binary file	Contains data or instructions in binary format
Command file	Contains operating system commands
Data file	Contains data
Directory file	Contains bookkeeping information about files that are *below* it
Executable file	Contains a program or commands in an executable format
Library file	Contains functions in object format
Map file	Contains a map of a program
Object file	Contains code that has been compiled
Text file	Contains textual data (that is, data that can be read by humans), including files you create with a text editor and any file in ASCII format.

In DOS systems, FATs are stored in *hidden files*, called *FAT files*.

⇨ See also *disk; file; fragmentation; operating system.*

file attribute: See under *attribute.*

file compression: See under *data compression* and *packed file.*

file defragmentation: See under *fragmentation.*

file fragmentation: See *fragmentation.*

file locking: See under *lock.*

file management: Refers to the system that an operating system or program uses to organize and keep track of files. For example, a *hierarchical file system* is one that uses directories to organize files into a tree structure (see Figure 24 at *directory*).

Although the operating system provides its own file management system, you can buy separate file management systems. These systems interact smoothly with the operating system but provide more features, such as improved backup procedures and stricter file protection.

➡ See also *directory; hierarchical.*

filename: The name of a file. All files have names. Different operating systems impose different restrictions on filenames. Most operating systems, for example, prohibit the use of certain characters in a filename and impose a limit on the length of a filename. In addition, many systems allow a filename extension that consists of one or more characters following the proper filename. The filename extension usually indicates what type of file it is.

Within a single directory, filenames must be unique. However, two files in different directories may have the same name. Some operating systems, such as UNIX, allow a file to have more than one name.

➡ See also *directory; extension; file.*

file server: See under *server.*

filter: (1) A program that accepts a certain type of data as input, transforms it in some manner, and then outputs the transformed data. For example, a program that sorts names is a filter because it accepts the names in unsorted order, sorts them, and then outputs the sorted names.

(2) A pattern through which data is passed. Only data that matches the pattern is allowed to pass through the filter.

Finder: The desktop management and file management system for Apple Macintosh computers. In addition to managing files and disks, the Finder is responsible for managing the Clipboard and Scrapbook and all desktop icons and windows.

Finder is a single-tasking program. The multitasking version of Finder is called MultiFinder.

➡ See also *clipboard; desktop; file management; icon; Multifinder; multitasking.*

firmware: Software (programs or data) that has been permanently written onto read-only memory. Firmware is a combination of software and hardware. ROMs and PROMs that have data or programs recorded on them are firmware.

➡ See also *hardware; PROM; ROM; software.*

fixed disk: Same as *hard disk.*

fixed-frequency monitor: A monitor that can only accept signals in one frequency range. In contrast, *multiscanning* monitors automatically adjust themselves to the frequency at which data is being sent.

➡ See also *monitor; multiscanning monitor.*

fixed length: Having a set length that never varies. In database systems, a field can have a *fixed* or a *variable* length. A variable-length field is one whose length can be different in each record, depending on what data is stored in the field.

The terms *fixed length* and *variable length* can also refer to the entire record. A fixed-length record is one in which every field has a fixed length. A variable-length record has at least one variable-length field.

➡ See also *database management system; field; record; variable length.*

fixed pitch: Refers to fonts in which every character has the same width. Most typewriters and inexpensive printers use fixed-pitch fonts. Newspapers, magazines, and books, however, usually use *proportional* fonts, in which different characters have different widths (see Figure 58 at *proportional pitch*).

The use of a fixed-pitch font is called *monospacing*.

➡ See also *font; monospacing; pitch; proportional pitch*.

fixed width: Same as *fixed pitch*.

➡ See also *fixed pitch; font*.

flag: (n) (1) A software or hardware mark that signals a particular condition or status. A flag is like a switch that can be either on or off. The flag is said to be *set* when it is turned on.

(2) A special mark indicating that a piece of data is unusual. For example, a record might contain an *error flag* to indicate that the record consists of unusual, probably incorrect, data.

(v) To mark an object to indicate that a particular event has occurred or that the object marked is unusual is some way.

flash memory: A special type of *EEPROM* that can be erased and reprogrammed inside a computer. Conventional EEPROMs require a special device called a *PROM reader*.

➡ See also *EEPROM*.

flatbed scanner: A type of *optical scanner* that consists of a flat surface on which you lay documents to be scanned. Flatbed scanners are particularly effective for bound documents.

➡ See also *optical scanner*.

flat-file database: A relatively simple database system in which each database is contained in a single file. In contrast, *relational* database systems can use multiple files to store a single database, and each file can have a different record format. Relational systems are more suitable for large applications, but flat databases are adequate for many small applications. Simple flat-file database systems that lack programming capabilities are called *file managers*.

➡ See also *database management system; file management; record; relational database.*

flat-panel display: A very thin display screen used in laptop computers. There are a variety of techniques for producing flat-panel displays:

liquid crystal display (LCD): Uses rod-shaped molecules that flow like liquid to direct light between two polarizing filters. This type of display usually produces bluish letters on top of a grayish-white background. Some color LCD displays are capable of displaying 16 or more colors.

gas plasma display: Uses an electric current to ionize gases, causing them to glow. This is similar to the technique used in neon signs. Gas-plasma displays usually produce orange images on top of a black background.

electroluminescent display (ELD): Similar to gas plasma but uses a layer of phosphor instead of gas. Electroluminescent displays are usually amber, although they can also be green.

thin film transistors (TFT): A special type of LCD screen, in which each pixel consists of three separate transistors, one each for red, green, and blue. The TFT technology provides the best resolution of the flat-panel techniques, but it is also the most expensive.

Most LCD screens are backlit to make them easier to read in bright environments. Gas-plasma and ELD displays are somewhat faster than LCD displays, but they require more power and are generally more expensive. All three techniques can produce low- to medium-quality displays.

➡ See also *backlighting; display screen; electroluminescent display; gas-plasma display; laptop computer; LCD; pixel; TFT.*

flat screen: Same as *flat-panel display.*

flat technology monitor: Often abbreviated as *FTM,* flat technology monitors are monitors that have a flat display screen to reduce glare. Conventional display screens are curved, which makes them more susceptible to reflections from external light sources.

Do not confuse flat technology monitors with *flat-screen displays.* Flat-screen displays are the display screens used in laptops and other portable computers.

➡ See also *CRT; flat-panel display; monitor.*

flicker: See *screen flicker.*

floating-point number: A real number (that is, a number that can contain a fractional part). The following are floating-point numbers:

$$3.0$$
$$-111.5$$
$$\frac{1}{2}$$
$$3E-5$$

The last example is a computer shorthand for scientific notation. It means $3*10^{-5}$ (or 10 to the negative 5th power multiplied by 3).

In essence, computers are integer machines and are capable of representing real numbers only by using complex codes. The most popular code for representing real numbers is called the *IEEE Floating-Point Standard.*

The term *floating point* is derived from the fact

that there is no fixed number of digits before and after the decimal point; that is, the decimal point can float. There are also representations in which the number of digits before and after the decimal point is set, called *fixed-point* representations. In general, floating-point representations are slower and less accurate than fixed-point representations, but they can handle a larger range of numbers.

Note that most floating-point numbers a computer can represent are just approximations. One of the challenges in programming with floating-point values is ensuring that the approximations lead to reasonable results. If the programmer is not careful, small discrepancies in the approximations can snowball to the point where the final results become meaningless.

➡ See also *FPU; IEEE; integer; precision; scientific notation.*

floating-point unit: See *FPU.*

floppy disk: A soft magnetic disk (Figure 29). It is called *floppy* because it flops if you wave it. Unlike most hard disks, floppy disks (often called *floppies*) are portable, because you can remove them from a disk drive. Disk drives for floppy disks are called *floppy drives.* Floppy disks are slower to access than hard disks and have less storage capacity, but they are much less expensive.

Floppies come in several sizes:

8-inch: The largest, and oldest, come in envelopes that are 8 square inches. These disks are now obsolete.

5¼-inch: The common size for personal computers made before 1987. This type of floppy is generally capable of storing between 100K and 1.2MB of data, although high-density disks for IBM PCs and compatibles can store up to 40MB. The most common sizes are 360K and 1.2MB.

3½-inch: Sometimes called a *microfloppy*, this type of disk is common in newer personal computers. *Floppy* is something of a misnomer for these disks, as they are encased in a rigid envelope. Despite their small size, microfloppies have a larger storage capacity than their cousins—from 400K to 43MB of data. The most common sizes for IBM PCs are 720K (double-density) and 1.44MB (high-density). Macintoshes support disks of 400K, 800K, and 1.2MB.

2-inch: This newest and smallest floppy is used in some laptop computers. Typically, it has a storage capacity of 720K.

Floppy disks can be single-sided or double-sided (data can be stored on both sides) and can be single-density, double-density, quad-density, high-density, or extra-high-density. The double-density disks are capable of storing twice as much data as the single-density disks, and the quad disks twice as much again. High-density disks have a capacity of up to 2MB. Extra-high-density disks can hold as much as 40MB of data.

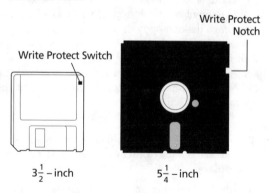

Write Protect Switch

Write Protect Notch

$3\frac{1}{2}$ – inch

$5\frac{1}{4}$ – inch

Figure 29
Floppy Disk

➧ See also *density; disk; FDHD; format; hard disk; mass storage; microfloppy disk; Super-Drive disk drive.*

floptical disk: Another name for *erasable optical disk.*

flush: (adj) Aligned along a margin. Text that is *flush left* is aligned along the left margin. *Flush-right* text is aligned along the right margin. For example:

This text is printed
flush left. It is aligned along
the left margin.

This text is printed
flush right. It is aligned along
the right margin.

The opposite of flush is *ragged*. The first example has a ragged right margin and the second has a ragged left margin. Text that is both flush left and flush right is said to be *justified*.

➠ See also *justify; margins; ragged.*

(v) To copy data from a temporary storage area such as RAM to a more permanent storage medium such as a disk.

folder: In the Macintosh environment, and for many programs that have graphical user interfaces, a folder is an object that can contain multiple documents. Folders are used to organize information. In the DOS and UNIX worlds, folders are called *directories*.

➠ See also *desktop; directory; file; graphical user interface; Macintosh computer.*

font: A design for a set of characters (Figure 30). A font is the combination of typeface and other qualities, such as size, pitch, and spacing. For example, Times Roman is a typeface that defines the shape of each character. Within Times Roman, however, there are many fonts to choose from—different sizes,

Helvetica

ABCDEFGHIJKLMNOPQRSTUVWXYZ
Fonts are designed for a set of characters. A font is the combination of

Courier

ABCDEFGHIJKLMNOPQRSTUVWXYZ
Fonts are designed for a set
of characters. A font is the

Times Roman

ABCDEFGHIJKLMNOPQRSTUVWXYZ
Fonts are designed for a set of characters. A
font is the combination of typeface and other

Optima

ABCDEFGHIJKLMNOPQRSTUVWXYZ
Fonts are designed for a set of characters.
A font is the combination of typeface and

Figure 30
Popular Fonts

italic, bold, and so on. (The term *font* is often used incorrectly as a synonym for *typeface*.)

The height of characters in a font is measured in *points*, each point being approximately 1/72 inch. For example, the text in this book is printed with 9-point type. The width is measured by *pitch*, which refers to how many characters can fit in an inch. Common pitch values are 10 and 12. A font is said to be *fixed pitch* if every character has the same width. If the widths vary depending on the shape of the character, it is called a *proportional font*.

Most word processors enable you to choose from among several supported fonts. Laser, ink-jet, and dot-matrix printers offer the widest selection of fonts. These printers support a certain set of built-in fonts, but you can expand this set by loading different fonts from software (*soft fonts*) or from font cartridges.

Computers and devices use two methods to represent fonts. *Bit-mapping* the fonts is the most common method. In a bit-mapped font, every character is represented by an arrangement of dots. To print a bit-mapped character, a printer simply locates the character's bit-mapped representation stored in memory and prints the corresponding dots. Each different font, even when the typeface is the same, requires a different set of bit maps.

The other method utilizes a *vector graphics system* to define fonts. In vector graphics systems, the shape or outline of each character of a font is defined geometrically. The typeface can be displayed in any size, so a single font description really represents innumerable fonts. For this reason, object-oriented fonts are called *scalable* fonts—they can be any size (scale). Other terms for object-oriented fonts are *outline fonts* and *vector fonts*. The most widely used scalable-font system is PostScript.

Aside from the scalability of vector fonts, their other main advantage over bit-mapped fonts is that they make the most of high-resolution devices. In the past, bit-mapped fonts looked the same whether printed on a 300-dpi printer or a 1,200-dpi printer. Now many laser printers support a *smoothing* feature that improves the appearance of bit-mapped fonts when printed at high resolutions. Vector fonts eliminate the problem altogether because the fonts are not designed for a particular resolution.

Despite the advantages of vector fonts, bit-mapped fonts are still widely used. One reason for this is that small vector fonts do not look very good on low-resolution devices, such as display monitors (which are low-resolution when compared with laser printers). Almost all computer systems, therefore, use bit-mapped fonts for screen displays. In addition, many professionals prefer to use bit-mapped fonts on high-resolution printers because characters can be individually tailored to the printing device.

An additional drawback of vector fonts is that every character must be generated as it is needed. This is a computation-intensive process that requires a powerful microprocessor to make it acceptably fast.

➧ See also *bit map; dpi; fixed pitch; font cartridge; page description language; pitch; point; PostScript; printer; proportional pitch; raster graphics; resolution; scalable font; soft font; typeface; vector graphics.*

font card: An *expansion board* that you insert into a printer so that it can print more fonts. Not all printers have a slot for a font card.

➧ See also *expansion board; font; printer; slot.*

font cartridge: A ROM cartridge that contains one or more fonts. By inserting the cartridge into a laser printer, you give the printer the ability to print different fonts. Another way to load fonts into a printer is to download them from the computer's storage device.

➧ See also *cartridge; download; font; laser printer; soft font.*

font family: A set of fonts all with the same typeface, but with different sizes and weights.

➧ See also *font; typeface.*

footer: In word processing, a footer is one or more lines of text that appear at the bottom of every page of a document. Once you specify what text should appear in the footer, the word processor automatically inserts it.

Most word processors allow you to use special symbols in the footer that represent changing values. For example, you can enter a symbol for the page number, and the word processor will replace the symbol with the correct number on each page. If you enter the date symbol, the word processor will insert the current date, which will change if necessary each time you print the document.

You can usually specify two different footers, one for odd-numbered pages (*odd footer*) and one for even-numbered pages (*even footer*).

➡ See also *header*.

footprint: The amount of floor or desk space required by a device. For example, a *small-footprint* computer is a computer whose dimensions (width and depth) are relatively small.

foreground: (1) In multiprocessing systems, the process that is currently accepting input from the keyboard or other input device is sometimes called the *foreground process*.

➡ See also *background; multiprocessing*.

(2) On display screens, the foreground consists of the characters and pictures that appear on the screen. The *background* is the uniform canvas behind the characters and pictures.

➡ See also *background*.

format: (v) (1) To prepare a storage medium, usually a disk, for reading and writing. When you format a disk, the operating system erases all bookkeeping information on the disk, tests the disk to make sure all sectors are reliable, marks bad sectors (that is, those that are scratched), and creates internal address tables that it later uses to locate information. You must format a disk before you can use it.

Note that reformatting a disk does not erase the data on the disk, only the address tables. Do not panic, therefore, if you accidentally reformat a disk that has useful data. A computer specialist should

193

be able to recover most, if not all, of the information on the disk. You can also buy programs that enable you to recover a disk yourself.

The previous discussion, however, applies only to *high-level* formats, the type of formats that most users execute. In addition, hard disks have a *low-level format*, which sets certain properties of the disk such as the interleave factor. The low-level format also determines what type of disk controller can access the disk (e.g., *RLL* or *MFM*).

Almost all hard disks that you purchase have already had a low-level format. It is not necessary, therefore, to perform a low-level format yourself unless you want to change the interleave factor or make the disk accessible by a different type of disk controller. Performing a low-level format erases all data on the disk.

➠ See also *controller; disk; hard disk; initialize; interleaving; low-level format; MFM; RLL; sector.*

(2) In the FORTRAN programming language, the FORMAT statement specifies how to print data.

(n) A particular arrangement. Almost everything associated with computers has a format.

form feed: A special character that causes the printer to advance one page length or to the top of the next page. In systems that use the ASCII character set, a form feed has a decimal value of 12. *Form feed* is sometimes abbreviated *FF*.

➠ See also *ASCII.*

forms software: A type of program that enables you to design and fill in forms on a computer. Most forms packages contain a number of sample forms that you can modify for your own purposes.

formula: (1) An equation or expression.

➡ See also *expression*.

(2) In spreadsheet applications, a formula is an expression that defines how one cell relates to other cells. For example, you might define cell C5 (column C, row 5) with the formula

$$+A4*D7$$

which means to multiply the value in cell A4 by the value in cell D7.

➡ See also *cell; expression; spreadsheet*.

FORTRAN: Acronym for *formula translator*, FORTRAN is the oldest high-level programming language. Designed by IBM in the late 1950s, it is still popular today, particularly for scientific applications that require extensive mathematical computations.

The two most common versions of FORTRAN are FORTRAN IV and FORTRAN 77. FORTRAN IV was approved as a USASI standard in 1966. FORTRAN 77 is a version of FORTRAN that was approved by ANSI in 1978 (they had expected to approve it in 1977, hence the name). FORTRAN 77 includes a number of features not available in older versions of FORTRAN. A new ANSI standard for FORTRAN is expected to be ratified in the near future.

➡ See also *ANSI; programming language*.

486: See under *Intel microprocessors*.

4GL: See *fourth-generation language*.

fourth-generation language: Often abbreviated *4GL*, fourth-generation languages are programming languages closer to human languages than typical high-level programming languages (see Figure 57 at *programming language*). Most 4GLs are used to access databases. For example, a typical 4GL command is

```
FIND ALL RECORDS WHERE NAME IS
"SMITH"
```

The other three generations of computer languages are:

first generation: machine language

second generation: assembly language

third generation: high-level programming languages

➡ See also *database management system; programming language; query; query language.*

FPU: Short for **f**loating-**p**oint **u**nit, a specially designed chip that performs *floating-point* calculations. Computers equipped with an FPU perform certain types of applications much faster than computers that lack one. In particular, graphics applications are faster with an FPU.

Some microprocessors, such as the Intel 80486, have a built-in FPU. With other microprocessors, you can usually add an FPU by inserting the FPU chip on the *motherboard*.

➡ See also *coprocessor; Intel microprocessors; floating-point number; motherboard.*

fragmentation: (1) Refers to the condition of a disk in which files are divided into pieces scattered around the disk. Fragmentation occurs naturally when you use a disk frequently, creating, deleting, and modifying files. It is undesirable because it slows down the speed at which data can be accessed.

In DOS systems, you can defragment a disk by copying all the files to a new disk with the COPY or XCOPY command. When you copy files using COPY or XCOPY, the operating system combines all the fragmented portions and creates a contiguous file. Do not use the DISKCOPY command, because it maintains the old file organization, including the fragmentation.

You can also buy software products, called *disk optimizers*, that defragment a disk in place, without copying files to a second medium.

➡ See also *copy; disk; disk optimizer; file; DOS.*

(2) Fragmentation can also refer to RAM that has small, unused holes scattered throughout it.

friction feed: A method of feeding paper through a dot-matrix or daisy-wheel printer. Friction-feed printers use plastic or rubber rollers to squeeze a sheet of paper and pull it through the printer.

The other principal form of feeding paper into a dot-matrix or daisy-wheel printer is through a *tractor feed,* in which sprocketed wheels on either side of the printer fit into holes in the paper. As the wheels revolve, the paper is pulled through the printer. Tractor-feed printers require special paper, whereas friction-feed printers can handle most types of cut-sheet paper, including envelopes. Many printers support both types of feeding mechanisms (see Figure 71 at *tractor feed*).

➡ See also *daisy-wheel printer; dot-matrix printer; sheet feeder; tractor feed.*

front end: (1) For software applications, *front end* is the same as *user interface*.

➡ See also *user interface.*

(2) In distributed processing applications, the machines that present an interface to users are often called *front ends*. The machines that actually perform calculations, database inquiries, and other processing functions are called *back ends*.

➡ See also *distributed processing.*

(3) Compilers, the programs that translate source code into object code, are often composed of two parts: a *front end* and a *back end*. The front end is responsible for checking syntax and detecting errors, whereas the back end performs the actual translation into object code.

➡ See also *compiler*.

FTM: See *flat technology monitor*.

full duplex: Refers to the transmission of data in two directions simultaneously. For example, a telephone is a full-duplex device because both parties can talk at once. In contrast, a walkie-talkie is a *half-duplex* device because only one party can transmit at a time.

Most modems have a switch that lets you choose between full-duplex and half-duplex modes. The choice depends on which communications program you are running.

In full-duplex mode, data you transmit does not appear on your screen until it has been received and sent back by the other party. This enables you to validate that the data has been accurately transmitted. If your display screen shows two of each character, it probably means that your modem is set to half-duplex mode when it should be in full-duplex mode.

➡ See also *communications; half duplex; modem*.

function: (1) In programming, the term *function* refers to a section of a program that performs a specific task. In this sense, a function is a type of procedure or routine. Some programming languages make a distinction between a *function*, which returns a value, and a *procedure*, which performs some operation but does not return a value.

Most programming languages come with a prewritten set of functions that are kept in a library.

You can also write your own functions to perform specialized tasks.

➡ See also *library; procedure; program; routine.*

(2) The term *function* is also used synonymously with *operation* and *command.* For example, you execute the *delete function* to erase a word.

➡ See also *command.*

function keys: Special keys on the keyboard that have different meanings depending on which program is running. Function keys are normally labeled F1 to F10 or F12. On older IBM PCs, for example, ten function keys are grouped on the left side of the keyboard; new PCs have the enhanced keyboard, with twelve function keys aligned along the top of the keyboard. In addition, some PCs have a special function key that you can use in association with any other key, plus an Alt (Alternate) key that behaves like a second function key.

➡ See also *Alt key; enhanced keyboard; keyboard.*

G

G: The symbol used for *giga* or *gigabyte.*

➡ See also *giga.*

gas-plasma display: A type of thin display screen called a *flat-panel display.* Gas-plasma displays are common in laptop and portable computers.

A gas-plasma display works by sandwiching neon gas between two plates. One plate is coated with vertical wires and the other with horizontal wires, forming a grid. When electric current is passed through a horizontal and vertical wire, the gas at the intersection glows, creating a point of light, or *pixel*. Images on gas-plasma displays generally appear as orange objects on top of a black background.

Other types of flat-panel displays include *LCD* displays and *electroluminescent displays* (ELDs).

➡ See also *electroluminescent display; flat-panel display; laptop computer; LCD; pixel.*

gateway: In networking, a gateway is a combination of hardware and software that links two different types of networks.

➡ See also *network.*

GB: See *gigabyte.*

GEM: A graphical user interface developed by Digital Research that is built into personal computers made by Atari, and is also used as an interface for some DOS programs. Like the Macintosh interface and Microsoft Windows, GEM provides a windowed environment for running programs.

GEM also refers to a special graphics file format used in GEM-based applications.

➡ See also *graphical user interface; Macintosh computer; Microsoft Windows.*

genlock: Short for *generator locking device,* a genlock is a device that enables a composite video machine, such as a TV, to simultaneously accept two signals. A genlock locks one set of signals while it processes the second set. This enables you to combine graphics from a computer with video signals from a second source such as a video camera.

➡ See also *composite video.*

GIF: A bit-mapped graphics file format used by CompuServe and many BBSs. GIF supports color and various resolutions. It also includes data compression, making it especially effective for scanned photos.

➡ See also *BBS; CompuServe; data compression; graphics formats; resolution.*

giga (G): (1) When decimal notation is used, giga stands for one billion. For example, a *gigavolt* is 1 billion volts.

(2) When applied to computers, which use the binary notation system, giga represents 2 to the 30th power, which is 1,073,741,824, a little more than 1 billion. A *gigabyte*, therefore, is about 1.073 billion bytes.

➡ See also *binary; mass storage; megabyte.*

gigabyte: 2 to the 30th power (1,073,741,824) bytes. One gigabyte is equal to 1,024MB. Gigabyte is often abbreviated as *G* or *GB*.

➡ See also *byte; giga; MB.*

gppm: Abbreviation for *graphics pages per minute*, the speed with which laser printers can print nontext pages. Typically, laser printers are rated in *pages per minute (ppm)*, but this refers only to the speed at which they print text pages. The gppm is always much less and may be the more important figure if you are using the printer to print documents that are graphics-intensive.

➡ See also *graphics; laser printer; ppm.*

graphical user interface: A program interface that takes advantage of the computer's graphics capabilities to make the program as easy as possible to use (Figure 31). Well-designed graphical user interfaces can free the user from learning complex command languages. On the other hand, many users find that they work more effectively with a

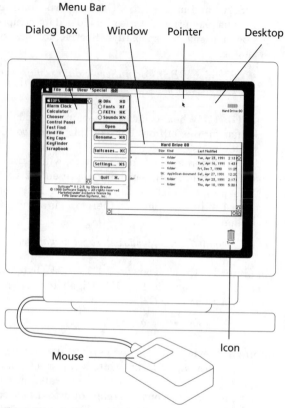

Menu Bar

Dialog Box   Window   Pointer   Desktop

Mouse

Icon

Figure 31
Graphical User Interface

command-driven interface, especially if they already know the command language.

Graphical user interfaces, such as the one used by the Apple Macintosh computer, feature the following basic components:

desktop: The area on the display screen where icons are grouped is often referred to as the desktop because the icons are intended to represent real objects on a real desktop.

windows: You can divide the screen into different areas. In each window, you can run a different program or display a different file. You can move windows around the display screen, and change their shape and size at will.

pointer: A symbol that appears on the display screen and that you move to select objects and commands. Usually, the pointer appears as a small angled arrow. Text-processing applications, however, use an *I-beam pointer* that is shaped like a capital *I*.

icons: Small pictures that represent commands, files, or windows. By moving the pointer to the icon and pressing a mouse button, you can execute a command or convert the icon into a window. You can also move the icons around the display screen as if they were real objects on your desk.

menus: Most graphical user interfaces let you execute commands by selecting a choice from a menu.

mouse: A small device that you move on a flat surface, such as your tabletop, to move the pointer. A mouse or other pointing device is an essential ingredient of graphical user interfaces.

The first graphical user interface was designed by Xerox Corporation's Palo Alto Research Center in the 1970s, but it was not until the 1980s and the emergence of the Apple Macintosh that graphical user interfaces became popular. One reason for their slow acceptance was that they require considerable CPU power and a high-quality monitor, which until recently were prohibitively expensive.

In addition to their visual components, graphical user interfaces also make it easier to move data from one application to another. A true graphical user interface, called a *GUI*, includes standard formats for representing text and graphics. Because the formats are well defined, different programs that run under a common GUI can share data. This makes it possible, for example, to copy a graph created by a spreadsheet program into a document created by a word processor.

Many DOS programs include some features of GUIs, such as menus, but are not *graphics based*. Such interfaces are sometimes called *graphical character-based user interfaces* to distinguish them from true GUIs.

A number of applications for IBM PCs and compatibles feature GUIs. Most of them are based either on Microsoft Windows (for DOS systems) or the Presentation Manager (for OS/2 systems). Both of these products provide programmers with tools to develop GUIs.

➨ See also *bit map; character based; desktop; GEM; graphics; I-beam pointer; icon; Macintosh computer; menu; Microsoft Windows; mouse; pointer; Presentation Manager; user interface; window.*

graphics: Pertains to any computer device or program that makes a computer capable of displaying and manipulating pictures. For example, laser printers and plotters are *graphics devices* because they permit the computer to output pictures. A *graphics monitor* is a display monitor that can display pictures. A *graphics board* (or *graphics card*) is a printed circuit board that, when installed in a computer, permits the computer to display pictures.

Many software applications include graphics components. Such programs are said to *support* graphics. For example, certain word processors support graphics because they let you draw or import pictures. All CAD/CAM systems support graphics. Some database management systems and spreadsheet programs support graphics because they let you display data in the form of graphs and charts. Such applications are often referred to as *business graphics*.

The following are also considered *graphics applications:*

paint programs: Allow you to create rough free-hand drawings. The images are stored as bit maps and can easily be edited.

illustration/design software: Supports more advanced features than paint programs, particularly for drawing curved lines. The images are usually stored in vector-based formats. Illustration/design programs are sometimes called *draw programs.*

presentation graphics software: Lets you create bar charts, pie charts, graphics, and other types of images for slide shows and reports. The charts can be based on data imported from spreadsheet applications.

animation software: Enables you to chain and sequence a series of images to simulate movement. Each image is like a frame in a movie.

CAD software: Enables architects and engineers to draft designs.

desktop publishing: Provides a full set of word-processing features as well as illustration features, so that you can create newsletters, advertisements, books, and other types of documents.

In general, applications that support graphics require a powerful CPU and a large amount of memory. Many graphics applications—for example, computer animation systems—require more computing power than is available on personal computers and will run only on powerful workstations or specially designed graphics computers. This is true of all three-dimensional computer graphics applications.

In addition to the CPU and memory, graphics software requires a graphics monitor and support for one of the many graphics standards. Some programs, for instance, require VGA graphics, which is one of IBM's advanced graphics systems for PCs. If your computer does not have built-in support for a specific graphics system, you can insert a video adapter card.

The quality of most graphics devices is determined by their *resolution*—how many points per square inch they can represent—and their color capabilities.

➡ See also *bit map; CAD; CAD/CAM; character based; clip art; CPU; database management system; desktop publishing; display screen; IBM PC; laser printer; main memory; monitor; Microsoft Windows; personal computer; plotter; presentation graphics; raster graphics; resolution; spreadsheet; vector graphics; video adapter; word processing; workstation.*

graphics based: Refers to software and hardware that treat objects on a display screen as bit maps or geometrical shapes rather than as characters. In contrast, *character-based* systems treat everything as ASCII or extended ASCII characters (see Figure 12 at *character-based*).

All graphics software, for example illustration programs and presentation software, is by definition graphics based. Systems that manipulate text can also be graphics based; for example, desktop publishing systems are essentially graphics-based word processors.

Traditionally, most DOS applications—word processors, spreadsheets, and database management systems—have been character based. This enables them to run on any IBM PC, even those with limited CPU, memory, and graphics capabilities. Increasingly, however, software manufacturers are spurning backward compatibility to create fully graphics-based applications.

Because the Macintosh is a graphical computer, all programs that run on a Macintosh computer are graphics based.

➤ See also *bit map; character based; desktop publishing; graphics; Macintosh computer; Microsoft Windows; Presentation Manager.*

graphics file formats: There are a number of different file formats for representing graphics images. The most common are:

BMP: The bit-mapped file format used by Microsoft Windows.

CGM (Computer Graphics Metafile): A format developed by several standards organizations, CGM is supported by many PC software products.

DXF (Data Exchange File): A format created by Autodesk. Almost all PC-based CAD systems support DFX.

EPS (Encapsulated PostScript): The file format for the PostScript language. EPS uses a combination of PostScript commands and TIFF or PICT formats.

GEM: The graphics file format used by GEM-based applications. GEM is a graphical user interface (GUI) developed by Digital Research.

GIF: The bit-mapped file format used by CompuServe and many other BBSs.

HPGL (Hewlett-Packard Graphics Language): One of the oldest file formats. Although it is not very sophisticated, it is supported by many PC-based graphics products.

IGES (Initial Graphics Exchange Specification): An ANSI standard for three-dimensional wire frame models. IGES is supported by most PC-based CAD systems.

PCX: Originally developed by ZSOFT for its PC Paintbrush program, PCX is a common graphics file format supported by many graphics programs, as well as most optical scanners and FAX modems.

PIC (Lotus Picture File): A relatively simple file format developed by Lotus for representing graphs generated by Lotus 1-2-3. PIC is supported by a wide variety of PC applications.

PICT: Developed by Apple Computer in 1984 as the standard format for storing and exchanging graphics files. PICT is an object-oriented graphics file format used by the Apple MacDraw program. It is supported by almost all graphics programs that run on a Macintosh.

TIFF (Tagged Image File Format): The standard file format for storing images as bit maps.

WMF (Windows Metafile Format): A file format for exchanging graphics between Microsoft Windows applications.

➡ See also *CGM; DXF; EPS; GEM; graphics; HPGL; IGES; PCX; PIC; PICT; TIFF; WMF.*

graphics mode: Many video adapters support several different modes of resolution, all of which are divided into two general categories: *character mode* and *graphics mode.* In character mode, the display screen is treated as an array of blocks, each of which can hold one ASCII character. In graphics mode, the display screen is treated as an array of pixels. Characters and other shapes are formed by turning on combinations of pixels.

Of the two modes, graphics mode is the more sophisticated. Programs that run in graphics mode can display an unlimited variety of shapes and fonts, whereas programs running in character mode are severely limited. Programs that run entirely in graphics mode are called *graphics-based* programs.

➡ See also *character based; graphics based; pixel; video adapter.*

graphics pages per minute: See *gppm.*

graphics tablet: Same as *digitizer.*

gray scaling: The use of many shades of gray to represent an image. *Continuous-tone* images, such as black-and-white photographs, use an almost unlimited number of shades of gray. Conventional computer hardware and software, however, can only represent a few shades of gray (typically 16 to 256). Gray scaling is the process of converting a continuous-tone image to an image that a computer can manipulate.

While gray scaling is an improvement over monochrome, it requires large amounts of memory because each dot is represented by from 4 to 8 bits. At a resolution of 300 dpi, you would need about 6MB to represent a single 8½-by-11-inch page using 256 shades of gray. This can be reduced somewhat through data compression techniques, but gray scaling still requires a great deal of memory.

Many optical scanners are capable of gray scaling, using from 16 to 256 different shades of gray. However, gray scaling is only useful if you have an output device—monitor or printer—that is capable of displaying all the shades. Most color monitors are capable of gray scaling, but the images are generally not as good as on dedicated gray-scaling monitors.

Note that gray scaling is different from *dithering*. Dithering simulates shades of gray by altering the density and pattern of black and white dots. In gray scaling, each individual dot can have a different shade of gray (see Figure 25 at *dithering*).

➡ See also *continuous tone; data compression; dithering; monitor; optical scanner; resolution.*

greeking: In desktop publishing systems, *greeking* refers to the approximation of text characters on a screen display (Figure 32). Greeking is often used by word processors that support a *preview* function. In preview mode, the word processor attempts to show what a document will look like when printed. Frequently, however, the graphics display capabili-

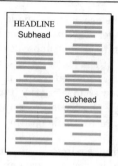

Figure 32
Greeking

ties of the monitor are not sufficient to show all fonts. To give a general idea of what the text will look like and how page layout will appear, the word processor uses graphics symbols to approximate the text. These symbols suggest greek letters, hence the term *greeking*.

➧ See also *desktop publishing; font; graphics; layout; preview; word processing.*

Group 3 protocol: The universal protocol defined by the CCITT for sending FAXes.

➧ See also *CCITT; FAX machine.*

Group 4 protocol: A protocol defined by CCITT for sending FAXes over ISDN networks.

➧ See also *CCITT; FAX machine; ISDN.*

groupware: A class of software that helps groups of colleagues (*workgroups*) attached to a local-area network organize their activities. Typically, groupware supports the following operations:

- scheduling meetings and allocating resources
- electronic mail
- password protection for documents

- telephone utilities
- electronic newsletters

Groupware is sometimes called *workgroup productivity software.*

➡ See also *electronic mail; local-area network; scheduler; workgroup computing.*

GUI: Acronym for *graphical user interface.* Pronounced *goo-ee*, a GUI is a user interface that utilizes the graphics capabilities of a computer to make programs as easy as possible to use.

➡ See also *graphical user interface.*

gutter: In desktop publishing, the space between columns in a multiple-column document.

➡ See also *desktop publishing.*

GW-BASIC: A dialect of the BASIC programming language that comes with many versions of the DOS operating system.

➡ See also *BASIC.*

— H —

hacker: A slang term for a computer enthusiast. Among professional programmers, the term *hacker* implies an amateur or a programmer who lacks formal training. Depending on how it is used, the term can be either complimentary or derogatory, although it is developing an increasingly derogatory connotation. The pejorative sense of *hacker* is becoming more prominent largely because the popular press has coopted the term to refer to individuals who gain unauthorized access to computer systems for the purpose of stealing and corrupting data.

➡ See also *programmer*.

half duplex: Refers to the transmission of data in just one direction at a time. For example, a walkie-talkie is a half-duplex device because only one party can talk at a time. In contrast, a telephone is a *full-duplex* device because both parties can talk simultaneously.

Most modems contain a switch that lets you select between half-duplex and full-duplex modes. The correct choice depends on which program you are using to transmit data through the modem.

In half-duplex mode, each character transmitted is immediately displayed on your screen. (For this reason, it is sometimes called *local echo*—characters are echoed by the local device.) In full-duplex mode, transmitted data is not displayed on your monitor until it has been received and returned (remotely echoed) by the other device. If you are running a communications program and every character appears twice, it probably means that your modem is in half-duplex mode when it should be in full-duplex mode, and every character is being both locally and remotely echoed.

➡ See also *communications; full duplex; modem*.

half height: IBM PCs and compatibles support both full-height and half-height disk drives. The half-height models take up less space but usually have less storage capacity.

➡ See also *bay; disk drive*.

halftone: In printing, a halftone is a shade of gray. Halftones are created through a process called *dithering*, in which the density and pattern of black and white dots are varied to simulate different shades of gray. If you look closely at a newspaper, you can see that the photographs are printed using halftones.

➧ See also *dithering*.

handle: In graphics programs, a handle is an outline of a graphical object, often with small black squares. To select an object, you move the pointer to one of the handles and click a mouse button (see Figure 8 at *Bézier curves*).

➧ See also *graphics; pointer*.

handshaking: The process by which two devices initiate communications. Handshaking begins when one device sends a message to another device indicating that it wants to establish a communications channel. The two devices then send several messages back and forth that enable them to agree on a communications protocol.

➧ See also *communications; protocol*.

hang: To crash in such a way that the computer does not respond to input from the keyboard or mouse. If your computer is hung, you usually need to reboot it, although sometimes hitting the correct sequence of control characters will free it up.

➧ See also *bomb; crash*.

hanging indent: Same as *hanging paragraph*.

hanging paragraph: In word processing, a hanging paragraph is a paragraph that has all lines but the first indented. For example:

```
This is an example of a hanging
  paragraph. The entries in this
  book are set as hanging para-
  graphs. A hanging paragraph is
  also known as a hanging indent.
```

With many word processors, you can create hanging paragraphs by specifying a negative indentation for the first line of each paragraph.

➧ See also *word processing*.

hard: The term *hard* is used to describe anything that physically exists. In contrast, the term *soft* refers to concepts and symbols.

➧ See also *hardware; software*.

hard card: A hard disk drive on an expansion card. Unlike most disk drives that are either external to the computer or fit in one of the disk drive bays, a hard card slips into an expansion slot. Hard cards are generally faster than conventional disk drives, and they are easier to install. Their storage capacities, however, are more limited.

➧ See also *bay; expansion board; expansion slot; hard disk*.

hard coded: Unchangeable. Hard-coded features are built into the hardware or software in such a way that they cannot be modified.

hardcopy: A printout of data stored in a computer. It is considered *hard* because it exists physically on paper, whereas a *soft* copy exists only electronically.

➧ See also *hard; soft*.

hard disk: A magnetic disk on which you can store computer data. The term *hard* is used to distinguish it from a soft, or *floppy,* disk. Hard disks hold more data and are faster than floppy disks. A hard disk, for example, can store anywhere from 10MB to 3,000MB, whereas floppies have a storage capacity of from 100K to 20MB.

The disk drives for hard disks are called *hard disk drives* or *Winchester drives,* Winchester being the name of the first popular hard disk drive technology developed by IBM in 1973.

Hard disk drives for PCs generally have access times of 30 milliseconds or less. Changing the *interleave factor,* however, can have an effect on access times. In addition, many disk drives improve their performance through a technique called *caching.*

A single hard disk usually consists of several *platters.* Each platter requires two read/write heads, one for each side. All the read/write heads are attached to a single access arm so that they cannot move independently. Each platter has the same number of *tracks,* and a track location that cuts across all platters is called a *cylinder.* For example, a typical 20MB hard disk for an IBM PC has two platters (four sides) and 615 cylinders.

There are several interface standards for passing data between a hard disk and a computer. The most common are:

ST-506: The standard interface on all PC/XT and PC/AT computers. The ST-506 standard supports both MFM and RLL encoding formats.

SCSI (Small Computer System Interface): The standard interface for Apple Macintoshes, SCSI is also popular on UNIX systems and is available on many PC compatibles.

ESDI (Enhanced Small Device Interface): A high-speed interface for IBM's newest generation of computers. ESDI is about twice as fast as ST-506.

IDE (Integrated Drive Interface): Not as fast as ESDI, but faster than ST-506.

Note that SCSI and ESDI disk drives will not run on a PC/XT or PC/AT computer unless you add a special disk controller.

In general, hard disks are less portable than floppies, although it is now possible to buy removable hard disks. There are two types of removable hard disks: *disk packs* and *removable cartridges.*

➡ See also *access time; cache; controller; cylinder; disk; disk drive; disk pack; ESDI; floppy disk; IDE interface; interleaving; mass storage; MFM; platter; removable cartridge; RLL; SCSI; ST-506 interface; track; Winchester disk drive.*

hard disk drive: The mechanism that reads and writes data on a hard disk.

➡ See also *disk drive; hard disk.*

hard hyphen: See under *hyphenation.*

hard return: A *return* is the process of jumping from the end of one line of text to the beginning of the next line. Word processors utilize two types of returns: *hard returns* and *soft returns.*

A hard return is an actual symbol inserted into the text. Usually, it consists of two characters—the ASCII characters for carriage return and line feed. The hard-return characters are usually invisible, but most word processors support a mode that lets you see them. Whenever you press the Return or Enter key while editing a document, the word processor inserts a hard return.

Hard returns cause the word processor to start a new line regardless of how margins are set. Therefore, if a document contains hard returns, the lines will end at the same place even if you change the margins. In contrast, soft returns depend on how the margins are set.

➡ See also *carriage return; Enter key; line feed; return; soft return.*

hardware: Refers to objects that you can actually touch, like disks, disk drives, display screens, keyboards, printers, boards, and chips. In contrast, software is untouchable. Software exists as ideas, concepts, and symbols, but it has no substance.

Books provide a useful analogy for describing the difference between software and hardware. The pages and the ink are the hardware, while the words, sentences, paragraphs, and the overall meaning are the software. A computer without software is like a book full of blank pages—you need software to make the computer useful just as you need words to make a book meaningful.

➡ See also *software*.

Hayes compatibility: Hayes Microcomputer Products is one of the leading manufacturers of modems and has developed a language for controlling modems that has become the de facto standard. Any modem that recognizes Hayes modem commands is said to be *Hayes-compatible*. This is very useful because many communications programs use Hayes modem commands.

➡ See also *communications; de facto standard; modem*.

head: The mechanism that reads data from or writes data to a magnetic disk or tape. If the head becomes dirty, it will not work properly. This is one of the first things to check if your disk drive or tape drive begins to malfunction.

The head is sometimes called a *read/write head*. Double-sided floppy disk drives have two heads, one for each side of the disk. Hard disk drives have many heads, two for each *platter*.

➡ See also *disk drive; head crash; platter*.

head crash: A serious disk drive malfunction. A head crash usually means that the head has scratched or burned the disk. In a hard disk drive, the head normally hovers a few microinches from the disk. If the head becomes misaligned or if dust particles come between it and the disk, it can touch the disk. When this happens, you usually lose much of the data on the hard disk and will need to replace both the head and the disk. For this reason, it is important to operate disk drives, particularly hard disk drives, in as clean an environment as possible. Even smoke particles can cause a head crash.

Head crashes are less common for floppy disks, as the head touches the disk anyway under normal operation.

Another term for *head crash* is *disk crash*.

➡ See also *crash; disk; disk drive; head.*

header: (1) In word processing, a line of text that appears at the top of each page of a document. Once you specify the text that should appear in the header, the word processor automatically inserts it.

Most word processors allow you to use special symbols in the header that represent changing values. For example, you can enter a symbol for the page number, and the word processor will automatically replace the symbol with the correct number on each page. If you enter the date symbol, the word processor will insert the current date, which will change if necessary each time you print the document.

Most word processors allow you to specify two different headers, one for odd-numbered pages (*odd headers*) and one for even-numbered pages (*even headers*).

➡ See also *footer; word processing.*

(2) In file management, a header is a region at the beginning of each file where bookkeeping information is kept. For example, the header may contain the date the file was created, the date it was last updated, and the file's size. The header can be accessed only by the operating system or by specialized programs. When you edit a file, for example, you will not see the header.

➡ See also *file management.*

helical-scan cartridge: A type of magnetic tape that uses the same technology as VCR tapes. The term *helical scan* usually refers to 8 mm tapes, although 4 mm tapes (called *DAT tapes*) use the same technology. The 8 mm helical-scan tapes have data capacities from 2.5GB to 5GB.

➡ See also *DAT; mass storage; tape.*

Help: On-line documentation. Many programs come with the instruction manual, or a portion of the manual, integrated into the program. If you encounter a problem or forget a command while running the program, you can summon the documentation by pressing a designated *Help key* or entering a *HELP command.* On IBM PCs and compatibles, the Help key is often the function key labeled *F1.*

Once you summon the Help system, the program often displays a menu of Help topics. You can choose the appropriate topic for whatever problem you are currently encountering. The program will then display a *Help screen* that contains the desired documentation.

Some programs are more sophisticated, displaying different Help messages depending on where you are in the program. Such systems are said to be *context sensitive.*

➡ See also *context sensitive; documentation; function keys; on-line.*

Hercules graphics: A graphics display system for IBM PCs and compatibles developed by Van Suwannukul, founder of Hercules Computer Technology. Suwannukul developed the system so that he could produce his doctoral thesis on IBM PC equipment using his native Thai alphabet.

First offered in 1982, the original Hercules system filled a void left by IBM's MDA (**m**onochrome **d**isplay **a**dapter) system. MDA produces high-resolution monochrome text but cannot generate graphics. Hercules systems generate both high-resolution text and graphics for monochrome monitors. The resolution is 720 by 348.

Although originally a monochrome system, Hercules now offers color graphics video adapters as well. You can install a Hercules system into a PC by plugging in a Hercules expansion board.

➡ See also *CGA; graphics; MDA; monochrome; pixel; resolution; video adapter.*

heterogeneous network: A network that includes computers and other devices from different manufacturers. For example, local-area networks (LANs) that connect IBM PCs with Apple Macintosh computers are heterogeneous.

➡ See also *local-area network; network.*

Hewlett-Packard Graphics Language: See *HPGL.*

hex: Short for *hexadecimal.*

hexadecimal: Refers to the base-16 number system, which consists of 16 unique symbols: the numbers 0

Table 14: Table of Hexadecimal Values

DECIMAL	HEXADECIMAL	BINARY
0	0	0000
1	1	0001
2	2	0010
3	3	0011
4	4	0100
5	5	0101
6	6	0110
7	7	0111
8	8	1000
9	9	1001
10	A	1010
11	B	1011
12	C	1100
13	D	1101
14	E	1110
15	F	1111

to 9 and the letters A to F (Table 14). For example, the decimal number 15 is represented as F in the hexadecimal numbering system. The hexadecimal system is useful because it can represent every byte (8 bits) as two consecutive hexadecimal digits. It is easier for humans to read hexadecimal numbers than binary numbers.

To convert a value from hexadecimal to binary, you merely translate each hexadecimal digit into its 4-bit binary equivalent. For example, the hexadecimal number

3F8A

translates to the following binary number:

0011 1111 1000 1010

➡ See also *binary; decimal; octal.*

hidden file: In DOS systems, a hidden file is a file with a special *hidden attribute* turned on, so that the file is not normally visible to users. For example, hidden files are not listed when you execute the DOS DIR command. However, most file management utilities allow you to view hidden files.

DOS hides some files, such as MSDOS.SYS and IO.SYS, so that you will not accidentally corrupt them. You can also turn on the hidden attribute for any normal file, thereby making it invisible to casual snoopers.

➡ See also *attribute; file allocation table; file management.*

hierarchical: Refers to systems that are organized in the shape of a pyramid, with each row of objects linked to objects directly beneath it. Hierarchical systems pervade everyday life (Figure 33). The army, for example, which has generals at the top of the pyramid and privates at the bottom, is a hierarchical system. Similarly, the system for classifying plants and animals according to species, family, genus, and so on, is also hierarchical.

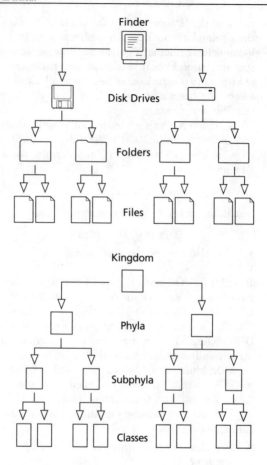

Figure 33
Hierarchical Systems

Hierarchical systems are as popular in computer systems as they are in other walks of life. The most obvious example of a hierarchical system in computers is a file system, in which directories have files and subdirectories beneath them. Such a file organization is, in fact, called a *hierarchical file system*.

In addition to file systems, many data structures for storing information are hierarchical in form. Menu-driven programs are also hierarchical, because they contain a *root menu* at the top of the pyramid and *submenus* below it.

➡ See also *directory; file management; menu driven; tree structure.*

high-density disk: A high-quality floppy disk capable of holding more data than a *double-density* disk. High-density 5¼-inch disks for IBM PCs and compatibles can hold 1.2MB of data. High-density 3½-inch disks can store 1.44MB.

Although high-density disk drives can format both high-density and double-density disks, double-density disks formatted by a high-density drive may not be readable by a double-density drive. Similarly, high-density drives may not be able to read disks that have been formatted by a double-density disk drive.

➡ See also *density; floppy disk.*

high-level language: A programming language such as FORTRAN, COBOL, or Pascal that enables a programmer to write programs that are more or less independent of a particular type of computer. Such languages are considered high-level because they are closer to human languages and further from machine languages. In contrast, assembly languages are considered low-level because they are very close to machine languages (see Figure 57 at *programming language*).

The main advantage of high-level languages over low-level languages is that they are easier to read, write, and maintain. Ultimately, programs written in a high-level language must be translated into machine language by a compiler or interpreter. Such programs are generally larger and slower than programs written directly in a low-level language.

The first high-level programming languages were designed in the 1950s. Now there are dozens of different languages, including the following:

- Ada
- ALGOL
- BASIC
- COBOL
- C
- FORTRAN
- LISP
- Pascal
- PROLOG

➡ See also *Ada; assembly language; BASIC; C; COBOL; compile; FORTRAN; LISP; low-level language; machine language; Pascal; programming language.*

high memory: In DOS-based systems, high memory refers to the first 64K above 1MB.

➡ See also *conventional memory; DOS; expanded memory; extended memory; TSR.*

high resolution: See under *resolution.*

Home key: A key on IBM PC keyboards that controls cursor movement. Usually, the Home key moves the cursor to the top left corner of the screen or to the beginning of the file, but it can have other meanings depending on which program is running.

➡ See also *keyboard.*

host: A computer system that is accessed by a user working at a remote location. Typically, the term is used when there are two computer systems connected by modems and telephone lines. The system that contains the data is called the host, while the computer at which the user sits is called the remote.

➡ See also *remote control.*

hot key: A user-defined key sequence that executes a memory-resident program. DOS systems allow you to keep a certain number of programs in main memory at all times. Such programs are called *TSRs* (**t**erminate and **s**tay **r**esident). Because they are always in main memory, you can execute TSRs from within other applications. This is particularly useful for programs such as calendars and calculators that you use frequently.

When you install a TSR program, you define a special key (usually a function key or control character) that invokes the TSR whenever it is pressed. This is called a *hot key*. When choosing which keys will be hot keys, be careful to choose those that do not have different meanings in the applications you use.

➧ See also *control character; function keys; memory resident; TSR*.

hot link: (n) A link between two applications such that changes in one affect the other. For example, some desktop publishing systems let you establish hot links between documents and databases or spreadsheets. When data in the spreadsheet changes, the corresponding charts and graphs in the document change accordingly.

(v) To establish a link between two applications.

➧ See also *database; link; spreadsheet*.

HP-compatible printer: Hewlett-Packard was one of the first companies to produce a laser printer for IBM PCs, and most software products include drivers for HP printers. The drivers control the printers through a language called *PCL (**p**rinter **c**ontrol language)*. Other manufacturers of laser printers design their printers so that they, too, understand PCL, making them able to emulate HP printers. In this way, their printers are HP-compatible and are thus automatically supported by many software products.

No non-HP printer, however, is 100 percent HP-compatible. Manufacturers claim HP compatibility even if their printers only recognize a subset of PCL commands. Note also that there are different versions of PCL. A printer may be able to emulate an HP LaserJet Plus but not a LaserJet II. Finally, HP laser printers support font cartridges, and not all HP-compatible printers can accept the same cartridges.

While HP's PCL is the de facto standard for laser printers that connect to IBM PCs, the de facto printer control language for Apple Macintosh computers is Adobe PostScript.

➡ See also *compatibility; driver; emulation; font cartridge; laser printer; PCL; PostScript.*

HPGL: Abbreviation of *Hewlett-Packard Graphics Language*, a two-dimensional graphics file format supported by a wide variety of PC products.

➡ See also *graphics; graphics file formats.*

human engineering: Same as *ergonomics.*

HyperCard software: A programming environment for the Macintosh introduced by Apple in 1987. The HyperCard model consists of *cards,* and collections of cards, called *stacks.* You can connect the cards in various ways, and leaf through them the way you would with a set of Rolodex cards. In addition to data, each card can contain graphics and *buttons* (which perform various database operations).

Each object in a HyperCard system—stack, card, text field, button, or background—can have a *script* associated with it. A script is a set of instructions that specify what actions should take place when a user selects an object with the mouse or when some other event occurs.

HyperCard offers a consistent and simple interface, making it ideal for certain types of databases and utilities. It is often used to customize the desktop or control peripheral devices. Writing Hyper-Card applications is known as *authoring*.

➡ See also *authoring tool; button; database management system; Hypertext; script*.

Hypertext: A special type of database system, invented by Ted Nelson in the 1960s, in which objects (text, pictures, music, programs, and so on) can be creatively linked to each other. When you select an object, you can see all the other objects that are linked to it. You can move from one object to another even though they might have very different forms. For example, while reading a document about Mozart, you might click on the phrase *Violin Concerto in A Major,* which could display the written score or perhaps even invoke a recording of the concerto. Clicking on the name *Mozart* might cause various illustrations of Mozart to appear on the screen. The icons that you select to view associated objects are called *Hypertext links* or *buttons*.

Hypertext systems are particularly useful for organizing and browsing through large databases that consist of disparate types of information. There are several Hypertext systems available for Apple Macintosh computers and IBM PCs that enable you to develop your own databases. Such systems are often called *authoring systems*. HyperCard software from Apple Computer is the most famous.

➡ See also *authoring tool; button; click; database management system; HyperCard software; icon; link; Macintosh computer; multimedia*.

hyphenation: In word processing, hyphenation refers to splitting a word that would otherwise extend beyond the right margin. Not all word processors support hyphenation, and of those that do support it, not all perform it correctly.

Word processors use two basic techniques to perform hyphenation. The first employs an internal dictionary of words that indicates where hyphens may be inserted. The second uses a set of logical formulas to make hyphenation decisions. The dictionary method is more accurate but is usually slower. The most sophisticated programs use a combination of both methods.

Most word processors allow you to override their own hyphenation rules and define yourself where a word should be divided.

Hyphens inserted automatically by a hyphenation utility are called *discretionary* or *soft hyphens*. Hyphens that you add explicitly by entering the dash character are called *hard hyphens*.

➧ See also *word processing; word wrap*.

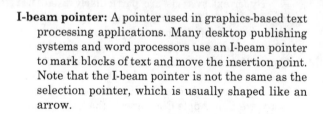

I-beam pointer: A pointer used in graphics-based text processing applications. Many desktop publishing systems and word processors use an I-beam pointer to mark blocks of text and move the insertion point. Note that the I-beam pointer is not the same as the selection pointer, which is usually shaped like an arrow.

➧ See also *graphics based; insertion point; Macintosh computer; pointer*.

IBM PC: Refers to a family of personal computers produced by IBM. In this book, and in most other computer literature, the term *IBM PC* also refers to all computers that are compatible with IBM PCs. These are also called *IBM clones, IBM compatibles,* or simply *compatibles*. The term *PC* is also frequently used to cover all IBM PCs and compatibles. This is a bit confusing because *PC* is the model name of the first IBM PC, introduced in 1981. But now most people use the term *PC* to refer to any IBM PC or to any personal computer.

All IBM PCs are based on Intel microprocessors, starting with the 8088 and increasing in power up to the Intel 80486. The first two models, the PC and PC/XT, both use an 8088 chip. The only difference is that the XT includes a hard disk drive and more expansion slots.

In 1984, IBM introduced the PC/AT, which was the first IBM PC to use the more powerful Intel 80286 microprocessor. The PC, PC/XT, and PC/AT are all considered *first-generation* PCs. In 1987, IBM began its second generation of PCs, the PS/2 line. The PS/2 generation of PCs offers three main improvements over first-generation PCs:

- 3½ inch microfloppies—on all PS/2 models
- VGA graphics—on all PS/2 models after the Model 30
- MCA (Micro Channel architecture)—on all PS/2 models after the Model 30

The first two features can easily be added to first-generation machines, and many PC compatibles already include them. The third feature refers to a new bus architecture. The MCA bus is not compatible with the older AT bus, so it requires a new set of add-on boards.

All IBM PCs are software-compatible to a large degree. This means that they can run the same programs without modification and share data files. This compatibility exists largely because most software producers create software that will run on an 8088 microprocessor, and the 8088 is upward compatible with all other Intel microprocessors. Increasingly, however, software companies are beginning to write programs specifically for the 80286 or 80386 processor. These programs will not run on less powerful microprocessors.

IBM supports two operating systems for its PCs, both originally produced by Microsoft Corporation. The first, DOS, runs on all IBM PCs. (IBM sells DOS by the name *PC-DOS.*) The second operating system, OS/2, runs only on models with an Intel 80286 or 80386 microprocessor and at least 2MB of memory. Microsoft continues to be responsible for DOS development, but as of 1990, IBM itself is doing the bulk of OS/2 development.

Table 15 lists IBM PCs in order of speed and power. Note that two machines that have the same CPU may run at different clock speeds, making one faster than the other.

➨ See also *CGA; clock speed; compatibility; DOS; expanded memory; extended memory; Intel microprocessors; MCGA; Micro Channel architecture; microfloppy; microprocessor; OS/2; personal computer; VGA; XGA.*

icon: On a display screen, a small picture that represents an object or program. Icons are very useful in applications that use windows, because with the click of a mouse button you can shrink an entire window into a small icon. (This is sometimes called *minimizing.*) To redisplay the window, you merely move the pointer to the icon and click (or *double click*) a mouse button. (This is sometimes called *restoring* or *maximizing*).

Icons are a principal feature of graphical user interfaces (see Figure 20 at *desktop*).

➨ See also *click; double click; graphical user interface; graphics; Macintosh computer; mouse; pointer; Presentation Manager; window.*

IDE interface: Abbreviation of either *Intelligent Drive Electronics* or *Integrated Drive Electronics*, depending on whom you ask. It is a low-cost alternative to SCSI and ESDI interfaces. An IDE is a hard disk drive interface for IBM PCs and compatibles, in which the controller is integrated into the disk

Table 15: IBM PC Models

MODEL	CPU	BUS	GRAPHICS	NOTES
PC	8088	PC	CGA	Discontinued
PC/XT	8088	XT	EGA	Discontinued
XT/286	80286	XT	EGA	Discontinued
PC/AT	80286	AT	VGA	Discontinued
PS/2 Model 25	8086 8MHz	AT	MCGA	
PS/2 Model 25-286	80286 10MHz	AT	VGA	
PS/2 Model 30-286	80286 10MHz	AT	VGA	
PS/2 Model 50Z	80286 10MHz	MCA	VGA	
PS/2 Model 55SX	80386SX 16MHz	MCA	VGA	Configured as a diskless workstation for LANs
PS/2 Model 55LS	80386SX 16MHz	MCA	VGA	Tower configuration version of the 55SX
PS/2 Model 65SX	80386SX 16MHz	MCA	VGA	
PS/2 Model P70-386	80386 16-20MHz	MCA	VGA	Portable version of the PS/2 Model 70
PS/2 Model 70-386	80386 16-25MHz	MCA	VGA	
PS/2 Model 70-486	80486 25MHz	MCA	VGA	
PS/2 Model 80-386	80386 20-25MHz	MCA	VGA	
PS/2 Model 90XP	80486 25-33MHz	MCA	XGA	
PS/2 Model 95XP	80486 25-33MHz	MCA	XGA	Tower configuration version of the Model 90XP

drive. IDE interfaces support data transfer rates of about 7.5 megabits per second.

➧ See also *ESDI; hard disk drive; interface; SCSI; ST-506 interface.*

identifier: Same as *name*. The term *identifier* is usually used for variable names.

➧ See also *name; variable.*

IEEE: Abbreviation of *Institute of Electrical and Electronics Engineers*, pronounced *I-triple-E*. Founded in 1963, the IEEE is an organization composed of engineers, scientists, and students. The IEEE is best known for developing standards for the computer and electronics industry. In particular, the IEEE standards for computer networks and floating-point representations are widely followed.

➧ See also *Ethernet; floating-point number; network; token-ring network.*

IGES: Acronym for *Initial Graphics Exchange Specification*, an ANSI graphics file format for three-dimensional wire-frame models.

➧ See also *ANSI; graphics; graphics file formats.*

ImageWriter: Refers to any in a family of dot-matrix printers that Apple offers for the Macintosh computer. There are several versions, including the ImageWriter I, ImageWriter II, and the ImageWriter LQ. The last is a 24-pin letter-quality printer. In addition to these Apple printers, many printer manufacturers make Macintosh-compatible printers that you can use in place of an ImageWriter.

Laser printers for the Macintosh are called *LaserWriters*.

➧ See also *dot-matrix printer; LaserWriter; letter quality; Macintosh computer; printer.*

impact printer: Refers to a class of printers that work by banging a head or needle against an ink ribbon to make a mark on the paper. This includes dot-matrix printers, daisy-wheel printers, and line printers. In contrast, laser and ink-jet printers are *nonimpact printers*. The distinction is important because impact printers tend to be considerably noisier than nonimpact printers but are useful for multipart forms such as invoices.

➡ See also *daisy-wheel printer; dot-matrix printer; ink-jet printer; laser printer; line printer; printer.*

import: To use data from another application. The ability to import data is very important in software applications because it means that one application can complement another. Many programs, for example, are designed to be able to import data from dBASE databases. This allows you to store your data using dBASE but to manipulate it with some other program.

The opposite of importing is *exporting*, which refers to the ability to send data from one application to another. Exporting implies that the sending application reformats the data for the receiving application, whereas importing implies that the receiving application does the reformatting.

➡ See also *export.*

inclusive OR operator: A Boolean operator that returns a value of TRUE if *either* of its operands is TRUE. Contrast with the *exclusive OR operator,* which returns a value of TRUE only if both operands have different values.

➡ See also *Boolean operators.*

increment: (v) To add a fixed amount. For example, if you count consecutively from 1 to 10, you increment by one. If you count by twos, you increment by two.

A large proportion of computer software consists of loops of instructions in which one or more values are incremented each time the loop is executed.

➡ See also *decrement; loop.*

(n) An amount that is added. For example, if you count by threes, the increment is three.

incremental backup: A backup procedure that backs up only those files that have been modified since the previous backup. Contrast with a full backup, in which all files are backed up regardless of whether they have been modified since the last backup. Incremental backups are also called *archival backups.*

➡ See also *archival backup; backup.*

Industry Standard Architecture (ISA) bus: The bus architecture used in the IBM PC/XT and PC/AT. The AT version of the bus is called the *AT bus* and has become a de facto industry standard. Two successors to the ISA bus are IBM's Micro Channel architecture (MCA) and the Extended ISA (EISA).

➡ See also *AT bus; bus; EISA; Micro Channel architecture; standard.*

init: A type of program for Macintoshes. Inits are usually small utilities that are executed each time you start up (or restart) a Macintosh. Like *cdevs*, they must be placed in the system folder to function properly.

➡ See also *cdev; system folder; utility.*

Initial Graphics Exchange Specification: See *IGES.*

initialize: (1) On Apple Macintosh computers, *initializing* a disk means *formatting* it.

➡ See also *format.*

(2) In programming, *initialize* means to assign a starting value to a variable.

➮ See also *assign; variable.*

(3) *Initialize* can refer to the process of starting up a program or system.

ink-jet printer: A type of printer that works by spraying ionized ink at a sheet of paper. Magnetized plates in the ink's path direct the ink onto the paper in the desired shapes. Ink-jet printers are capable of producing very high quality print (letter quality), approaching that produced by laser printers. A typical ink-jet printer provides a resolution of 300 dpi and supports about a dozen built-in fonts. You can often add additional fonts with font cartridges or by downloading fonts from a disk.

In general, the price of ink-jet printers is lower than that of laser printers. However, they are also considerably slower, printing between one and two pages per minute. Another drawback of ink-jet printers is that they require a special type of ink that tends to smudge.

➮ See also *dots per inch; download; font; font cartridge; laser printer; printer.*

input: (n) Whatever goes into the computer. Input can take a variety of forms, from commands you enter from the keyboard to data from another computer or device. A device that feeds data into a computer, such as a keyboard or mouse, is called an *input device.*

(v) The act of entering data into a computer.

➮ See also *I/O; output.*

input device: Any machine that feeds data into a computer. For example, a keyboard is an input device, whereas a display monitor is an output device.

Input devices other than the keyboard are sometimes called *alternate input devices*. Mice, trackballs, and light pens are all alternate input devices.

➡ See also *device; I/O; light pen; mouse; output;
trackball.*

input/output: See *I/O.*

insert: To place an object between two other objects.
Inserting characters, words, paragraphs, and documents is common in word processing. Note that *insert* differs from *append*, which means to add at the
end.

Most computer keyboards have an *Insert key*,
which turns *insert mode* on and off.

➡ See also *append; insert mode; Ins key.*

insertion point: In graphics-based programs, the insertion point is the point where the next characters
typed from the keyboard will appear on the display
screen. The insertion point is usually represented
by a blinking vertical line. You can reposition the
insertion point by pressing arrow keys or by moving
the I-beam pointer.

➡ See also *arrow keys; graphics based; I-beam
pointer; insert mode; pointer; word processing.*

insert mode: Most text editors and word processors
have two text entry modes from which you can
choose. In *insert mode,* the editor inserts all characters you type at the cursor position (or to the right
of the insertion point). With each new insertion, the
editor pushes over characters to the right of the
cursor or pointer to make room for the new character.

If insert mode is turned off, the editor over-
writes existing characters instead of inserting the
new ones before the old ones. This is often called
overstrike (or *overwrite*) *mode*. Most PC keyboards

have an *Ins key* that lets you switch back and forth between insert and overwrite modes.

For most programs, the default text entry mode is insert mode.

➡ See also *Ins key; insertion point; overstrike; word processing*.

Ins key: *Ins* stands for ***insert***. The Ins key on a computer keyboard turns the insert mode on and off. The Ins key does not work for all programs, but most word processors and text editors support it.

➡ See also *insert mode*.

Institute of Electrical and Electronics Engineers: See *IEEE*.

instruction: A basic command. The term *instruction* is often used to describe the most rudimentary programming commands. For example, a computer's *instruction set* is the list of all the basic commands in the computer's machine language.

➡ See also *CISC; command; machine language; RISC*.

integer: A whole number. The following are integers:

> 0
> 1
> -125
> 144457

In contrast, the following are *not* integers:

> .5
> -1.0
> 1.3E4
> "string"

The first three are *floating-point* numbers; the last is a *character string*.

Integers, floating-point numbers, and character strings constitute the basic data types that most computers support. There are often different sizes of integers available; for example, IBM PCs support short integers, which are 2 bytes, and long integers, which are 4 bytes.

➡ See also *character string; data type; floating-point number.*

integrated: (1) A popular computer buzzword that refers to two or more components merged together into a single system. For example, any software product that performs more than one task can be described as *integrated.*

(2) Increasingly, the term *integrated software* is reserved for applications that combine word processing, database management, spreadsheet functions, and communications into a single package.

integrated circuit (IC): Another name for a chip, an IC is a small electronic device made out of a semiconductor material. The first integrated circuit was developed in the 1950s by Jack Kilby of Texas Instruments and Robert Noyce of Fairchild Semiconductor.

Integrated circuits are used for a variety of devices, including microprocessors, audio and video equipment, and automobiles. Integrated circuits are often classified by the number of transistors and other electronic components they contain:

SSI (small-scale integration): Up to 100 electronic components per chip

MSI (medium-scale integration): From 100 to 3,000 electronic components per chip

LSI (large-scale integration): From 3,000 to 100,000 electronic components per chip

VLSI (very large-scale integration): From 100,-000 to 1,000,000 electronic components per chip

ULSI (ultra large-scale integration): More than 1 million electronic components per chip

➡ See also *chip; semiconductor.*

Integrated Drive Electronics: See *IDE.*

integrated services digital network: See *ISDN.*

Intellifont: A *scalable font* technology that is part of Hewlett-Packard's *PCL 5* page description language.

➡ See also *page description language; PCL; scalable font.*

intelligent terminal: A terminal (monitor and keyboard) that contains processing power. Intelligent terminals include memory and a processor to perform special display operations. In contrast, a *dumb terminal* has no processing capabilities; it must rely entirely on the central computer. A *smart terminal* has some processing capabilities, but not as much as an intelligent terminal.

➡ See also *display screen; dumb terminal; monitor; smart terminal; terminal.*

Intel microprocessors: Microprocessors made by Intel Corporation form the foundation of all IBM PCs and compatibles. See Table 16 for a partial list of Intel microprocessors.

Models after the 8086 are often referred to by the last three digits (for example, the *286* or *386*). All the microprocessors can run at various clock rates. The 80286, for example, supports clock rates of from 6 to 20 MHz.

All Intel microprocessors (except the 80860) are backward compatible, which means that they can run programs written for a less powerful processor. The 80286, for example, can run programs written

Table 16: Intel Microprocessors

MICROPROCESSOR	REGISTER WIDTH (BITS)	BUS WIDTH (BITS)	NOTES
8088	16	8	Used in the original IBM PC and PC/XT.
8086	16	16	
80286	16	16	Supports virtual memory and an address space of 16MB; is 5 to 20 times faster than the 8088
80386SX	32	16	Compatible with both the 80286 and the 80386
80386	32	32	Built-in multitasking and virtual memory, has an address space of 4GB; is 2 to 4 times faster than the 80286
80486	32	32	Similar to the 386 but much faster; uses a built-in *memory cache* to avoid *wait states*; includes a floating-point coprocessor
80860	64	64	RISC architecture; supports clock speeds up to 50MHz; pipeline architecture enables it to execute three instructions simultaneously

for the 8086 and 8088. Until the 80386, most software developers took advantage of this fact by writing software that would run on the 8088, and hence all other microprocessors. The 80386, however, offers special programming features not available on previous models. Software written specifically for the 80386, therefore, may not run on older microprocessors.

The 80386 microprocessor is a full 32-bit chip (32-bit data registers and 32-bit buses). It can support up to four gigabytes of main memory. In addition, the 386 supports as much as 16 terabytes of virtual memory.

➧ See also *bus; clock rate; downward compatible; IBM PC; main memory; memory cache; microprocessor; multitasking; register; RISC; virtual memory; wait state.*

Intelligent Drive Electronics: See *IDE.*

interactive: Accepting input from a human. Interactive computer systems are programs that allow users to enter data or commands. Most popular programs, for example, word processors and spreadsheet applications, are interactive.

A noninteractive program is one that, when started, continues without requiring human contact. A compiler is a noninteractive program, as are all *batch-processing* applications.

➧ See also *batch processing; compiler.*

interface: (n) Something that connects two separate entities. For example, a *user interface* is the part of a program that connects the computer with a human operator (user).

There are also interfaces to connect programs, to connect devices, and to connect programs to devices. An interface can be a program or a device, such as an electrical connector.

➧ See also *user interface.*

(v) To communicate. For example, two devices that can transmit data between each other are said to *interface with each other*. This use of the term is scorned by language purists because *interface* has historically been used as a noun.

interlacing: A display technique that enables a monitor to provide more resolution. With interlacing monitors, the electron guns draw only half the horizontal lines with each pass (for example, all odd lines on one pass and all even lines on the next pass). Because an interlacing monitor refreshes only half the lines at one time, it can display more lines, giving it greater resolution. Another way of looking at it is that interlacing provides the same resolution as noninterlacing, but less expensively.

A shortcoming of interlacing is that the reaction time is slower, so programs that depend on quick refresh rates (e.g., animation), may experience flickering or streaking. Given two monitors that offer the same resolution, the noninterlacing one will generally be better.

➡ See also *CRT; monitor; refresh; resolution.*

interleaving: (1) Refers to the way *sectors* on a disk are organized. In one-to-one interleaving, the sectors are placed sequentially around each track. In two-to-one interleaving, sectors are staggered so that consecutively numbered sectors separated by an intervening sector (Figure 34).

The purpose of interleaving is to make the disk drive more efficient. The disk drive can access only one sector at a time, and the disk is constantly spinning beneath the read/write head. This means that by the time the drive is ready to access the next sector, the disk may have already spun beyond it. If a data file spans more than one sector and if the sectors are arranged sequentially, the drive will need to wait a full rotation to access the next chunk of the file. If instead the sectors are staggered, the

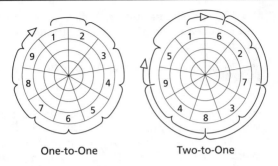

One-to-One Two-to-One

Figure 34
Interleaving

disk will be perfectly positioned to access sequential sectors.

The optimum interleaving factor depends on the speed of the disk drive, the operating system, and the application. On DOS systems, most disk drives work best with a one-to-one interleave factor. (However, your disk controller must be able to support one-to-one interleaving.) For OS/2, two-to-one interleaving is often better. The only way to find the best interleaving factor is to experiment with various factors and various applications.

In DOS, you can change the interleave factor through the DEBUG program. However, this requires that you perform a low-level format, which destroys all data on the disk. To change the interleave factor without destroying the data, you need a special disk utility program.

➧ See also *controller; disk; disk drive; sector; track.*

(2) *Interleaving* can also refer to main memory. In this case, the main memory is divided into two or more sections, and the CPU accesses each section alternately. This is effective because the CPU is often much faster than memory. Rather than waiting for memory to catch up (through wait states),

the CPU can operate at its maximum speed, accessing first one section of main memory and then the other.

➡ See also *access time; clock speed; CPU; memory; wait state.*

internal command: In DOS systems, internal commands are any that reside in the COMMAND.COM file. This includes the most common DOS commands, such as COPY and DIR. Commands that reside in other COM files, or in EXE or BAT files, are called *external commands.*

➡ See also *command; external command; DOS.*

internal font: Same as *resident font.*

internal modem: A modem that resides on an expansion board that plugs into a computer. In contrast, an *external modem* is a stand-alone box that attaches to a computer via cables (see Figure 47 at *modem*).

➡ See also *expansion board; external modem; modem.*

International Standards Organization: See *ISO.*

interpreter: A program that executes instructions written in a high-level language. There are two ways to run programs written in a high-level language. The most common is to *compile* the program; the other method is to pass the program through an interpreter.

An interpreter translates high-level instructions into an intermediate form, which it then executes. In contrast, a compiler translates high-level instructions directly into machine language. Compiled programs generally run much faster than interpreted programs. The advantage of an interpreter, however, is that it does not need to go through the compilation stage during which machine instructions are generated. This process can be time-consuming if the program is long. The interpreter, on the other hand, can immediately execute high-level programs. For this reason, interpreters are sometimes used during the development of a program, when a programmer wants to add small sections at a time and test them quickly. In addition, interpreters are often used in education because they allow students to program interactively.

Both interpreters and compilers are available for most high-level languages. However, BASIC and LISP are especially designed to be executed by an interpreter. In addition, page description languages, such as PostScript, use an interpreter. Every PostScript printer, for example, has a built-in interpreter that executes PostScript instructions.

➡ See also *BASIC; compile; LISP; page description language; PostScript; programming language.*

interprocess communication (IPC): A capability supported by some operating systems that allows one *process* to communicate with another process. The processes can be running on the same computer or on different computers connected through a network.

IPC enables one application to control another application and for several applications to share the same data without interfering with one another. IPC is required in all multiprocessing systems, but is not generally supported by single-process operating systems such as DOS. OS/2 and UNIX support IPC.

➡ See also *multiprocessing; network; operating system; process.*

interrupt: (n) A signal informing a program that an event has occurred. When a program receives an interrupt signal, it takes a specified action (which can be to ignore the signal). Interrupt signals can cause a program to suspend itself temporarily in order to service the interrupt.

Interrupt signals can come from a variety of sources. For example, every keystroke generates an interrupt signal. Interrupts can also be generated by other devices, such as a printer, to indicate that some event has occurred. These are called *hardware interrupts*. Interrupt signals initiated by programs are called *software interrupts*.

(v) To send an interrupt signal.

inverse video: Same as *reverse video*.

inverted tree: See under *tree structure*.

invocation: The execution of a program or function.

➧ See also *invoke*.

invoke: To activate. One usually speaks of *invoking* a function or routine in a program. In this sense, the term *invoke* is synonymous with *call*.

➧ See also *call; function; routine*.

I/O: Short for *input/output*. I/O refers to any operation, program, or device whose purpose is to enter data into a computer or to extract data from a computer.

One usually uses the term *I/O* to distinguish noncomputational parts of a program from other parts that are strictly computational, or to distinguish certain devices from other devices. For example, a printer is an I/O device, whereas a CPU is a computational device.

All computer applications contain both I/O and computational parts. A word-processing system, for instance, contains various I/O components (for entering, displaying, and printing text) as well as non-I/O components (for checking spelling, searching for words, and so on).

➧   See also *input; output.*

IPC: See *interprocess communication.*

IRMA board: A popular expansion board for IBM PCs
and Macintoshes that enables these personal computers to emulate IBM 3278 and 3279 mainframe
terminals. In other words, personal computers with
IRMA boards can function as both stand-alone computers and as terminals connected to a mainframe
computer. IRMA boards are made by a company
called DCA.

➧   See also *emulation; expansion board; mainframe; stand-alone; terminal.*

ISA: See *Industry Standard Architecture.*

ISA bus: ISA stands for *Industry Standard Architecture.* The ISA bus is the bus used on IBM PC/XTs
and IBM PC/ATs. The version of the bus used on
ATs is called the *AT bus.*

➧   See also *AT bus; bus; IBM PC.*

ISDN: Abbreviation of *integrated services digital network*, an international communications standard
for sending voice, video, and data over telephone
lines. ISDN requires special metal wires and supports data transfer rates of 64,000 bps.

   The original version of ISDN employs baseband
transmission. A proposed version, called *B-ISDN*,
uses broadband transmission and will be able to
support transmission rates of 1,500,000 bps. B-ISDN
requires fiber optic cables.

➧   See also *broadband ISDN; FDDI; fiber optics;
standard.*

ISO: Acronym for *International Standards Organization.* Founded in 1946, ISO is an international organization composed of national standards bodies

from over 75 countries. For example, ANSI (American National Standards Institute) is a member of ISO. ISO has defined a number of important computer standards, the most significant of which is perhaps OSI (Open Systems Interconnection), a standardized architecture for designing networks.

➡ See also *ANSI; network; standard.*

italic: In typography, *italic* refers to fonts with characters slanted to the right. An italic font often includes one or more character shapes, such as the *a* and the *f*, that differ from those in the roman font of the same family.

iteration: A single pass through a group of instructions. Most programs contain loops of instructions that are executed over and over again. The computer *iterates* through the loop, which means that it repeatedly executes the loop.

➡ See also *loop.*

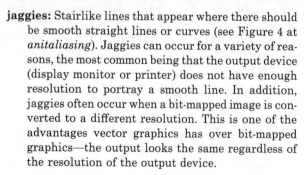

jaggies: Stairlike lines that appear where there should be smooth straight lines or curves (see Figure 4 at *anitaliasing*). Jaggies can occur for a variety of reasons, the most common being that the output device (display monitor or printer) does not have enough resolution to portray a smooth line. In addition, jaggies often occur when a bit-mapped image is converted to a different resolution. This is one of the advantages vector graphics has over bit-mapped graphics—the output looks the same regardless of the resolution of the output device.

The effect of jaggies can be reduced somewhat by a graphics technique known as *antialiasing*. Antialiasing smooths out jagged lines by surrounding the jaggies with shaded pixels. In addition, some printers can reduce jaggies with a technique known as *smoothing*.

➧ See also *antialiasing; bit map; pixel; resolution; smoothing; vector graphics.*

job: A task performed by a computer system. For example, printing a file is a job. Jobs can be performed by a single program or by a collection of programs.

➧ See also *program; task.*

join: In relational databases, a *join operation* is a query that retrieves data from two separate databases. The two databases must be *joined* by at least one common field. That is, the *join field* is a member of both databases.

➧ See also *database; field; query; relational database.*

joystick: A lever that moves in all directions and controls the movement of a pointer or some other display symbol (Figure 35). A joystick is similar to a mouse, except that with a mouse the cursor stops

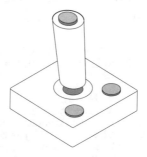

Figure 35
Joystick

moving as soon as you stop moving the mouse. With a joystick, the pointer continues moving in the direction the joystick is pointing. To stop the pointer, you must return the joystick to its upright position. Most joysticks include two buttons called *triggers*.

Joysticks are used mostly for computer games, but they are also used occasionally for CAD/CAM systems and other applications.

➡ See also *mouse; pointer*.

jumper: A metal bridge that closes an electrical circuit (Figure 36). Typically, a jumper consists of a plastic plug that fits over a pair of protruding pins. Jump-

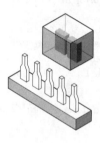

Figure 36
Jumper

ers are sometimes used to configure expansion boards. By placing a jumper plug over a different set of pins, you can change a board's parameters.

➡ See also *configure; expansion board*.

justification: Alignment of text along a margin. For example, the following is both left- and right-justified:

```
This text is  left- and right-justi-
fied because the left and right
margins are  aligned.   Note,  how-
ever,  that  t h e justification
does not look  very  good because
the  text  is  printed  with a
fixed-pitch font.
```

The text above looks a bit funny because there are wide gaps between some letters but not between others. To produce good-looking justification, the word processor and printer must be capable of microspacing; that is, they must be able to separate letters by less than a full space. In addition, justified text always looks better when a *proportional font* is used. For example:

> This text is left- and right-justified, and microspacing is in effect. The text is printed with a proportional font. Compare this to the previous example, which did not use microspacing.

Vertical justification refers to adjusting the vertical space between lines so that columns and pages have an even bottom margin. One vertical justification technique, called *feathering*, inserts an even amount of space between each line so that the page or column has a specified vertical length.

➡ See also *feathering; microspacing; pitch; proportional pitch; vertical justification; word processing*.

justify: In word processing, to align text along the left and right margins.

➡ See also *justification*.

K: (1) Short for *kilo* or *kilobyte*. In decimal systems, *kilo* stands for 1,000, but in *binary* systems, a *kilo* is 1,024 (2 to the 10th power). Technically, therefore, a kilobyte is 1,024 bytes, but it is often used loosely as a synonym for 1,000 bytes. For example, a computer that has 256K main memory can store approximately 256,000 bytes (or characters) in memory at one time.

A *megabyte* is 2 to the 20th (approximately 1 million) and a *gigabyte* is 2 to the 30th (approximately 1 billion).

To distinguish between a decimal K (1,000) and a binary K (1,024), the IEEE has suggested following the convention of using a small *k* for a decimal kilo and a capital *K* for a binary kilo, but this convention is by no means strictly followed.

➡ See also *binary; byte; giga; IEEE; megabyte; memory.*

(2) When used to describe memory chips, *K* stands for *kilobit* (1,024 bits). This is equivalent to 128 bytes. Most memory chips come in sizes of either 256 kilobits (64K bytes) or 1 *megabit* (256K bytes).

➡ See also *chip.*

KB: Short for *kilobyte* (1,024 bytes).

➡ See also *K.*

Kermit: A file-transfer *protocol* developed at Columbia University. Kermit can be used by modems and communications software to send files over telephone lines. Although it is a relatively slow protocol, Kermit is noted for its transmission accuracy. Kermit is not in the public domain, but since Columbia University allows people to use the protocol without payment, almost all communications products support it.

There are actually two versions of Kermit, the original version and a later version called *Super Kermit.* Unlike standard Kermit, Super Kermit supports *full-duplex* transmission, which makes it much faster.

Other file-transfer protocols used by slow- to medium-speed modems include Xmodem and Ymodem.

➡ See also *CCITT; communications; full duplex; MNP; modem; protocol; Xmodem; Ymodem.*

kerning: In typography, *kerning* refers to adjusting the space between characters, especially by placing two characters closer together than normal (Figure 37). Kerning, which is used with proportional fonts, makes certain combinations of letters, such as WA, MW, TA, and VA, look better.

Only the most sophisticated word processors and desktop publishing systems perform kerning. Normally, you can activate or deactivate kerning for particular fonts.

OCTAVE
Before

OCTAVE
After

Figure 37
Kerning

➡ See also *desktop publishing; font; word processing.*

key: (1) A button on a keyboard.

(2) In database management systems, a key is a field that you use to sort data. It can also be called a *key field*, *sort key*, or *key word*. For example, if you sort records by age, then the age field is a key. Most database management systems allow you to have more than one key so that you can sort records in different ways.

➡ See also *database management system; field.*

(3) A password or table needed to decipher encoded data.

➡ See also *encryption; password.*

keyboard: The set of typewriterlike keys that enables you to enter data into a computer. Computer keyboards are similar to electric-typewriter keyboards but contain additional keys. The keys on computer keyboards are often classified as follows:

alphanumeric keys—letters and numbers

punctuation keys—comma, period, semicolon, and so on.

special keys—function keys, control keys, arrow keys, Caps Lock key, and so on.

The standard layout of letters, numbers, and punctuation is known as a *QWERTY keyboard* because the first five keys on the top row of letters spell *QWERTY*. The QWERTY keyboard was designed in the 1800s for mechanical typewriters and was actually designed to slow typists down in order to avoid jamming the keys. Another keyboard design, which has letters positioned for speed typing, is the *Dvorak keyboard.*

There is no standard computer keyboard, although many manufacturers imitate the keyboards of IBM PCs. There are actually three different IBM PC keyboards: the original PC keyboard, with 84 keys; the AT keyboard, also with 84 keys; and the *enhanced keyboard*, with 101 keys. They are shown in Figure 38. The three differ somewhat in the placement of function keys, the Control key, the Return key, and the Shift keys. Despite the placement differences, almost all computer keyboards contain the special-purpose keys shown in Table 17.

In addition to these keys, IBM keyboards contain the following keys: PgUp, PgDn, Home, End, Ins, Pause, Num Lock, Scroll Lock, Break, Caps Lock, Prt Sc.

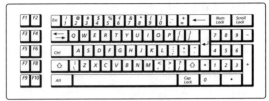

XT Keyboard

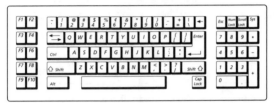

AT (Standard)

AT (Enhanced)

Figure 38
Keyboards

Table 17: Special Keys on IBM PC Keyboards

Alt key	Short for *Alternate,* this key is like a second Control key.
Arrow keys	Most keyboards have four arrow keys that enable you to move the cursor (or insertion point) up, down, right, or left. Used in conjunction with the Shift, Fn, or Alt keys, the arrow keys can move the cursor more than one position at a time, but this depends on which program is running.

255

Table 17: *(continued)*

Backspace key	Deletes the character just to the left of the cursor (or insertion point) and moves the cursor to that position.
Caps Lock key	A toggle key that, when activated, causes all alphabetic characters to be uppercase.
Ctrl key	Short for *Control*, this key is used in conjunction with other keys to produce *control characters*. The meaning of each control character depends on which program is running.
Delete key	Sometimes labeled *Del*, deletes the character at the current cursor position but does not move the cursor. For graphics-based applications, the Delete key deletes the character to the right of the *insertion point*.
Enter key	Used to enter commands or to move the cursor to the beginning of the next line. Sometimes labeled *Return* instead of *Enter*.
Esc key	Short for *Escape*, this key is used to send special codes to devices and to exit (or *escape*) from programs.
Fn key	Short for *Function*, this key is used in conjunction with other keys to produce special actions that vary depending on which program is running.
Function keys	Special keys labeled F1 to Fx, x being the number of function keys on the keyboard. These keys have different meanings depending on which program is running.
Return key	Another name for the Enter key.

There are several different types of keyboards for the Apple Macintosh. All of them are called *ADB keyboards* because they connect to the Apple Desktop bus (ADB). The two main varieties of Macintosh keyboards are the *standard* keyboard and the *extended* keyboard, which has 15 additional special-function keys.

➡ See also *ADB; alphanumeric; Alt key; arrow keys; Backspace key; Break key; Caps Lock key; Control key; cursor; Delete key; Dvorak keyboard; End key; enhanced keyboard; Enter key; Escape key; function keys; Home key; Ins key; insertion point; Macintosh computer; Num Lock key; Pause key; PgDn key; PgUp key; Print Screen key; QWERTY keyboard.*

keyboard buffer: See under *buffer*.

keyboard template: See under *template*.

keypad: See under *numeric keypad*.

keystroke: The pressing of a key. The efficiency of a software program is sometimes measured by the number of keystrokes it requires to perform a specific function. The fewer the keystrokes, claim some software producers, the faster and more efficient the program. The number of keystrokes, however, is generally less important than other characteristics of the software.

keyword: (1) In text editing and database management systems, a *keyword* is an index entry that identifies a specific record or document.

(2) In programming, a keyword is a word that is reserved by a program because the word has a special meaning. Keywords can be commands or parameters. Every programming language has a set of keywords that cannot be used as variable names. Keywords are sometimes called *reserved names*.

➡ See also *command; parameter; variable.*

kilobyte: 2 to the 10th (1,024) bytes.

➡ See also *K.*

kludge: A derogatory term that refers to a poor design. Like *hacks*, kludges use nonstandard techniques. But whereas a hack connotes a clever solution to a problem, a kludge implies that the solution is inelegant.

➡ See also *hack.*

label: (1) A name.

➡ See also *name.*

(2) For mass storage devices, a label is the name of a storage volume. It is sometimes referred to as a *volume label.* Each operating system has its own set of rules for labeling volumes. The label provides a mnemonic name that indicates what type of information is stored on the *media.*

➡ See also *disk; mass storage; volume.*

(3) In spreadsheet programs, a label is any descriptive text placed in a cell.

➡ See also *cell; spreadsheet.*

(4) In programming languages, a label refers to a particular location in a program, usually a particular line of source code.

(5) The term *label* is also commonly used to mean a small, sticky piece of paper that you can place on an object to identify it. For example, you can paste labels on floppy disks to indicate what data is stored on them.

LAN: See *local-area network.*

landscape: In word processing and desktop publishing, the terms *portrait* and *landscape* refer to whether the document is oriented vertically or horizontally (Figure 39). A page with landscape orientation, typical for spreadsheets, is wider than it is tall.

Not all printers are capable of generating text in landscape mode. Of those that are, some require special landscape versions of their fonts; others can rotate the standard portrait fonts 90 degrees.

Orientation is also a characteristic of monitors.

Landscape   Portrait

Figure 39
Landscape vs. Portrait

➡ See also *monitor; portrait; printer; word processing.*

language: A system for communicating. Written languages use symbols (that is, characters) to build words. The entire set of words is the language's *vocabulary*. The ways in which the words can be meaningfully combined are defined by the language's *syntax* and *grammar*. The actual meaning of words and combinations of words is defined by the language's *semantics*.

In computer science, human languages are known as *natural languages*. Unfortunately, computers are not sophisticated enough to understand natural languages. As a result, we must communicate with computers using special computer languages. There are many different classes of computer languages, including *machine languages, programming languages,* and *fourth-generation languages*.

➧ See also *artificial intelligence; fourth-generation language; machine language; natural language; programming language; syntax.*

laptop computer: A small, portable computer—small enough that it can sit on your lap. The principal difference between a laptop computer and a personal computer is the display screen. Laptop computers use a variety of techniques, known as *flat-panel technologies,* to produce a lightweight and nonbulky display screen. As a result, when folded up, laptop computers are the size of a small briefcase (Figure 40). Laptops are often divided into two types—*clamshells* and *lunchboxes*—based on their shape and the way they fold up.

The weight of laptop computers varies from a low of a few pounds to a high of about 20 pounds. The smallest laptop computers (those that weigh under 6 pounds) are often called *notebook computers*.

The quality of laptop display screens varies considerably. In general, laptop display screens display fewer lines than normal display screens and are difficult to read in bright environments. In addition, most do not support high-quality graphics or multiple colors.

Figure 40
Laptop Computer

In terms of computing power, modern laptop computers are nearly equivalent to personal computers. They have the same CPUs, memory capacity, and disk drives. However, all this power in a small package is expensive. Laptop computers cost about twice as much as equivalent regular-sized computers.

Most laptop computers come with battery packs that enable you to run them without plugging them in. However, the batteries need to be recharged every few hours.

➡ See also *display screen; flat-panel display; notebook computer; personal computer.*

large-scale integration: Refers to the placement of thousands of electronic components on a single integrated circuit. The term is often abbreviated *LSI*.

➡ See also *chip; integrated circuit.*

laser printer: A type of printer that utilizes a laser beam to produce an image on a drum. The light of the laser alters the electrical charge on the drum wherever it hits. The drum is then rolled through a reservoir of toner, which is picked up by the charged portions of the drum. The toner is then transferred to the paper through a combination of heat and pressure. This is also the way copy machines work.

Because an entire page is transmitted to a drum before the toner is applied, laser printers are sometimes called *page printers*. There are two other types of page printers that fall under the category of *laser printers* even though they do not use lasers at all. One uses an array of *LEDs* to expose the drum, and the other uses *LCDs*. Once the drum is charged, however, they both operate like a real laser printer.

Laser printers produce very high-quality print and are capable of printing an almost unlimited variety of fonts. Most laser printers come with a basic set of fonts, called *internal* or *resident* fonts, but you can add additional fonts in one of two ways:

font cartridges: Laser printers have slots in which you can insert font cartridges, ROM boards on which fonts have been recorded. The advantage of font cartridges is that they use none of the printer's memory.

soft fonts: All laser printers come with a certain amount of RAM memory, which you can usually increase by adding memory boards in the printer's expansion slots. You can then copy fonts from a disk to the printer's RAM. This is called *downloading* fonts. A font that has been downloaded is often referred to as a *soft font*, to distinguish it from the *hard fonts* available on font cartridges. The more RAM a printer has, the more fonts that can be downloaded at one time.

Some word processors support the commands necessary to download fonts. If your word processor does not support downloading, you can purchase special downloading programs.

In addition to text, laser printers are very adept at printing graphics. However, most printers require at least 1MB of RAM to produce high-quality graphics.

Because laser printers are *nonimpact* printers,

they are much quieter than dot-matrix or daisy-wheel printers. They are also relatively fast, although not as fast as some dot-matrix printers. The speed of laser printers ranges from about 4 to 20 pages of text per minute (ppm). A rate of 6 ppm is equivalent to about 40 characters per second (cps).

Laser printers are controlled through *page description languages (PDLs)*. There are two de facto standards for PDLs:

HP: Hewlett-Packard (HP) was one of the pioneers of laser printers and has developed a Printer Control Language (PCL) to control output. Almost all software products for IBM PCs and compatibles include an HP driver so that they can print documents on an HP-compatible printer. Many laser printers claim to be HP-compatible, but the compatibility is never 100 percent. There are several versions of PCL, so a printer may be compatible with one but not another. In addition, many printers that claim compatiblity cannot accept HP font cartridges.

PostScript: The de facto standard for Apple Macintosh printers. It is also possible to connect a PostScript printer to an IBM PC, but some IBM software is designed exclusively for HP printers and does not support PostScript printers.

➡ See also *download; driver; expansion slot; font; font cartridge; graphics; HP-compatible printer; LCD; LED; liquid crystal shutter printer; non-impact printer; object-oriented; page description language; PCL; PostScript; printer; RAM; resident font; scalable font; smoothing; soft font; toner.*

LaserWriter: Any printer in a family of Apple laser printers designed to run off a Macintosh computer. There are many models of the LaserWriter, including the ones shown in Table 18.

In addition to these Apple printers, many laser printers available from other manufacturers are compatible with Macintosh computers. In general, they fall into two categories: PostScript printers and QuickDraw printers. PostScript printers support more fonts, but they are also more expensive.

Table 18: LaserWriter Models

LaserWriter	The original LaserWriter. Although adequate for most applications, it has trouble producing solid black areas. It comes with only 1.5MB of RAM, which limits the number of fonts you can use.
LaserWriter Plus	A faster version of the original LaserWriter.
LaserWriter II SC	A second-generation LaserWriter that can produce darker and more solid blacks than previous versions. It is not a PostScript printer, however, and comes with only 1MB of RAM.
LaserWriter II NT	The *NT* stands for *new technology*. This is a PostScript printer built around a Motorola 68020 microprocessor, which makes it considerably faster than earlier models.
LaserWriter II NTX	An expandable version of the *NT* that lets you insert up to 12MB of RAM.
Personal LaserWriter	A slower and less expensive version of the LaserWriter II NTX.

➥ See also *font; laser printer; Macintosh computer; Motorola microprocessors; PostScript; printer; QuickDraw; RAM.*

launch: In the Macintosh world, launch means to load and run a program.

➡ See also *load*.

LAWN: See *local-area wireless network*.

layout: (1) In word processing and desktop publishing, layout refers to the arrangement of text and graphics. The layout of a document can determine which points are emphasized, and whether the document is aesthetically pleasing.

While no computer program can substitute for a professional layout artist, a powerful desktop publishing system can make it easier to lay out professional-looking documents. A WYSIWYG aids layout considerably because it allows you to lay out a document on the display screen and see what it will look like when printed.

➡ See also *desktop publishing; word processing; WYSIWYG*.

(2) In database management systems, *layout* refers to the way information is displayed. You can change the layout by selecting different fields.

➡ See also *database management system; field; report writer*.

LCD: Abbreviation of *liquid crystal display*, a type of display used in digital watches and many laptop computers. LCD displays utilize two sheets of polarizing material with a liquid crystal solution between them. An electric current passed through the liquid causes the crystals to align so that light cannot pass through them. Each crystal, therefore, is like a shutter, either allowing light to pass through or blocking the light.

Monochrome LCD images usually appear as blue or dark gray images on top of a grayish-white background. There are also color LCD displays, which use two basic techniques for producing color: **Double supertwisted nematic** (DSTN) display is the less expensive of the two technologies, but its colors are not particularly sharp and it has slow reaction times. The other technology, called *thin film transistor* (TFT) or *active-matrix*, produces color images that are even sharper than traditional CRT displays, but the technology is very expensive.

Most LCD screens used in laptop computers are monochrome and are backlit to make them easier to read in bright environments. An especially clear type of backlit LCD display is known as a *supertwist display*.

Other types of display screens used in laptop computers include *gas-plasma displays* and *electroluminescent displays*.

➠ See also *backlighting; electroluminescent display; flat-panel display; gas-plasma display; liquid crystal shutter printer; page-white display; supertwist*.

leading: In typography, *leading* refers to the vertical space between lines of text. The word derives from the fact that typographers once used thin strips of lead to separate lines. Now, the leading value also includes the size of the font. For example, 10-point text with 2 points of spacing between lines would mean a leading of 12 points.

Many word processors and all desktop publishing systems allow you to specify the leading. In addition, some systems automatically adjust leading so that columns and pages have even bottom margins. This feature is called *vertical justification*.

➠ See also *font; justification; point; vertical justification*.

leaf: Items at the very bottom of a hierarchical tree structure. In hierarchical file systems, files are leaves because they can have nothing below them. Directories, on the other hand, are *nodes*.

➡ See also *hierarchical; node; tree structure.*

learn mode: A mode in which a program learns. The term is usually used to describe a process of defining *macros*. Once you switch the program into learn mode, it will record all subsequent keystrokes you make. You can then assign these keystrokes to a function key to create a macro.

➡ See also *macro.*

LED: Abbreviation of *light-emitting diode*, an electronic device that lights up when electricity is passed through it. LEDs are usually red. They are good for displaying images because they can be relatively small, and they do not burn out. LEDs are also used in some laserlike printers.

➡ See also *LCD; printer.*

left justify: To align text along the left margin. *Left-justified* text is the same as *flush-left* text.

➡ See also *flush; justify.*

letter quality (LQ): Refers to print that has the same quality as that produced by a typewriter. Computer printers are divided into two classes: those that produce letter-quality type, such as laser, ink-jet, and daisy-wheel printers; and those that do not, including most dot-matrix printers (Figure 41).

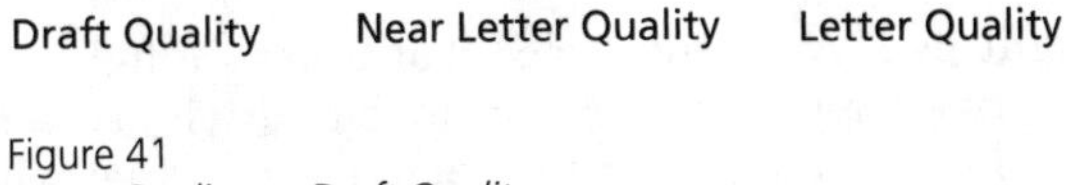

Draft Quality   Near Letter Quality   Letter Quality

Figure 41
Letter Quality vs. Draft Quality

The term *letter quality* is really something of a misnomer now, because laser printers produce print that is considerably better than that produced by a typewriter.

Many dot-matrix printers produce a high-quality print known as *near letter quality*. You have to look closely to see that the print is not really letter quality. A lower classification of print quality is called *draft quality*.

➡ See also *daisy-wheel printer; dot-matrix printer; draft quality; ink-jet printer; laser printer; near letter quality; printer.*

LF key: See *line feed.*

library: (1) A collection of files.

(2) In programming, a library is a collection of precompiled routines that a program can use. The routines, sometimes called *modules*, are stored in object format. Libraries are particularly useful for storing frequently used routines because you do not need to explicitly link them to every program that uses them. The linker automatically looks in libraries for routines that it does not find elsewhere.

➡ See also *linker; module; object code; routine.*

light bar: On a display screen, a highlighted region that indicates a selected component in a menu. The light bar can be produced by using a different color or by reversing the image so that black-on-white text becomes white-on-black.

➡ See also *menu; reverse video.*

light-emitting diode: See *LED.*

light pen: An input device that utilizes a light-sensitive detector to select objects on a display screen. A light pen is similar to a mouse, except that with a light pen you can move the pointer and select objects on the display screen by directly pointing to the objects with the pen (Figure 42).

Light pens are more precise than mice because the light-sensitive detector can recognize individual pixels. For this reason, light pens are used in applications that require extreme precision, such as CAD/CAM applications.

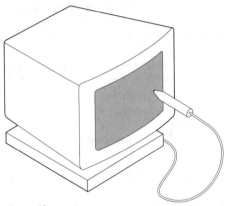

Figure 42
Light Pen

➠ See also *CAD/CAM; display screen; input device; mouse; pixel; pointer.*

LIM memory: A technique for adding memory to DOS systems. LIM memory lets you exceed the 1MB memory limit imposed by DOS. The name derives from the initials of the three companies that designed the technique—Lotus, Intel, and Microsoft—and is sometimes referred to as *LIM 4.0,* which is its official name.

➠ See also *expanded memory.*

line editor: A primitive type of editor that allows you to edit only one line of a file at a time. EDLIN is a line editor that comes with the DOS operating system.

➡ See also *editor; word processor.*

line feed: Often abbreviated *LF,* a line feed is a code that moves the cursor on a display screen down one line. Most computers use a combination of a line feed and a carriage return character to move the cursor to the beginning of the next line, the line feed moving the cursor down one line and the carriage return moving it to the beginning of the line. When you press the Return or Enter key while editing a file, the word processor inserts a line feed and carriage return.

On printers, a line feed advances the paper one line. Many printers have a button labeled *LF* that executes a line feed when pressed. (Note, however, that the printer must be in off-line mode to execute a line feed.)

In the ASCII character set, a line feed has a decimal value of 10.

➡ See also *ASCII; carriage return; off-line.*

line printer: A high-speed printer capable of printing an entire line at one time. A fast line printer can print as many as 3,000 lines per minute. The main disadvantages of line printers are that they can print only one font, they cannot print graphics, the print quality is low, and they are very noisy.

➡ See also *printer.*

link: (v) (1) To bind together.

(2) In programming, the term *link* refers to execution of a *linker.*

➡ See also *linker.*

(3) In spreadsheet programs, *linking* refers to the ability of a worksheet to take its data for particular cells from another worksheet. Two or more files are thus *linked* by common cells.

➡ See also *cell; spreadsheet.*

(n) (1) In communications, a link is a line or channel over which data is transmitted.

➡ See also *channel; communications.*

(2) In data management systems, a link is a pointer to another record. You can connect one or more records by inserting links into them.

➡ See also *database management system; record.*

(3) In many operating systems (UNIX, for example), a link is a pointer to a file. Links make it possible to reference a file by several different names and to access a file without specifying a full *path.*

➡ See also *filename; path; UNIX.*

link edit: To run a linker.

➡ See also *linker.*

linker: Also called *link editor* and *binder,* a linker is a program that combines object modules to form an executable program (see Figure 15 at *compile*). Many programming languages allow you to write different pieces of code, called *modules,* separately. This simplifies the programming task because you can break a large program into small, more manageable pieces. Eventually, though, you need to put all the modules together. This is the job of the linker.

In addition to combining modules, a linker also replaces symbolic addresses with real addresses. Therefore, you may need to link a program even if it contains only one module.

Most operating systems supply a linker. In DOS and OS/2, you execute the linker with the LINK command. In UNIX, the equivalent command is *ld.*

➡ See also *address; compile; executable file; module; object code.*

liquid crystal display: See *LCD.*

liquid crystal shutter printer: A type of printer similar to a laser printer. Instead of using a laser to create an image on the drum, however, it shines a light through a liquid crystal panel. Individual pixels in the panel either let the light pass or block the light, thereby creating an image composed of dots on the drum.

Liquid crystal shutter printers produce print quality equivalent to that of laser printers.

➡ See also *laser printer; LCD; pixel.*

LISP: Acronym for *list processor*, a high-level programming language especially popular for artificial intelligence applications. LISP was developed in the early 1960s by John McCarthy at MIT.

➡ See also *artificial intelligence; programming language.*

list: (v) To display data in an ordered format. For example, the LIST command in BASIC displays lines of a program.

(n) Any ordered set of data.

listing: A printout of text, usually a source program.

➡ See also *printout; source code.*

load: (1) To install. For example, to load a disk means to mount it in a disk drive.

(2) To copy a program from a storage device into memory. Every program must be loaded into memory before it can be executed. Usually the loading process is performed invisibly by a part of the operating system called the *loader.* You simply enter the name of the program you want to run, and the operating system loads it and executes it for you.

➡ See also *loader; main memory; operating system; program.*

(3) In programming, *load* means to copy data from main memory into a data register.

➡ See also *main memory; register*.

loader: An operating system utility that copies programs from a storage device to main memory, where they can be executed. In addition to copying a program into main memory, the loader can also replace virtual addresses with physical addresses.

Most loaders are invisible: that is, you cannot directly execute them, but the operating system uses them when necessary.

➡ See also *load; main memory; program; utility; virtual memory*.

local: In networks, *local* refers to files, devices, and other resources at your workstation. Resources located at other *nodes* on the networks are *remote*.

➡ See also *local-area network; network; node; remote; workstation*.

local-area network (LAN): A computer network that spans a relatively small area. Most LANs are confined to a single building or group of buildings. However, one LAN can be connected to other LANs over any distance via telephone lines and radio waves.

Most LANs connect workstations and personal computers. Each *node* (individual computer) in a LAN has its own CPU with which it executes programs, but it is also able to access data from anywhere in the LAN. LANs are also used to combine CPUs so that multiple CPUs scattered across a network can execute a single program. This is known as *distributed processing*. LANs also make it possible to send electronic mail among users. The principal benefit derived from LANs, therefore, is the ability to share data between many machines and users.

Many experts believe that LANs will eventually replace minicomputers. The advantage of LANs is that they are more flexible: It is relatively easy to add new devices and computers to the system, and most LANs support devices from different vendors. It is possible, for example, to mix IBM PCs and Apple Macintosh computers on the same LAN.

One disadvantage of LANs is that they are more difficult to manage because there are so many different software and hardware locations. On a minicomputer, all the software (and most of the hardware) is centralized.

There are many different types of LANs, *token-ring networks, Ethernets,* and *ARCnets* being the most common for IBM PCs. Most Apple Macintosh networks are based on Apple's *AppleTalk* network system, which is built into Macintosh computers.

The following characteristics differentiate one LAN from another:

topology: The geometric arrangement of devices on the network. For example, devices can be arranged in a ring or in a straight line.

protocols: The rules and encoding specifications for sending data. The protocols also determine whether the network uses a peer-to-peer or client/server architecture.

media: Devices can be connected by twisted-pair wire, coaxial cables, or fiber optic cables. Some networks do without connecting media altogether, communicating instead via radio waves.

LANs are capable of transmitting data at very fast rates, much faster than data can be transmitted over a telephone line; but the distances are limited, and there is also a limit on the number of computers that can be attached to a single LAN (between 15 and 500 computers per LAN).

➡ See also *AppleTalk; ARCnet; client/server architecture; CPU; distributed processing; electronic mail; Ethernet; NetWare; network; node; peer-to-peer architecture; personal computer; protocol; token-ring network; topology; TOPS; workstation.*

local-area wireless network (LAWN): A type of local-area network that uses high-frequency radio waves rather than wires to communicate between nodes.

➡ See also *local-area network.*

local echo: Same as *half duplex.*

LocalTalk: The cabling scheme supported by the *AppleTalk* network protocol for Macintosh computers. Most local-area networks that use AppleTalk, such as *TOPS,* also conform to the LocalTalk cable system. Such networks are sometimes called *LocalTalk networks.*

Although LocalTalk networks are relatively slow, they are popular because they are easy and inexpensive to install and maintain.

➡ See also *AppleTalk; local area network; Macintosh computer; TOPS.*

lock: To make a file or other piece of data inaccessible. *File locking* is a critical component of all multi-user computer systems, including local-area networks. When multiple users share files, the operating system must ensure that two or more users do not attempt to modify the same file simultaneously. It does this by *locking* the file as soon as the first user opens it. All subsequent users may read the file, but they cannot write to it until the first user is finished.

In addition to file locking, many database management systems support *record locking,* in which a single record, rather than an entire file, is locked. This enables different users to access different records within the same file without interfering with one another.

➠ See also *database management system; file; local-area network; multi-user; operating system; record.*

logical: Refers to a user's view of the way data or systems are organized. The opposite of logical is *physical*, which refers to the real organization of a system. For example, a logical description of a file is that it is a collection of data stored together. This is the way files appear to users. Physically, however, a single file can be divided into many pieces scattered across a disk.

➠ See also *fragmentation; physical.*

logical operator: Same as *Boolean operator.*

log in: Same as *log on.*

log off: Same as *log out.*

log on: To make a computer system recognize you so that you can begin a computer session. Most personal computers have no log-on procedure—you just turn the machine on and begin working. For larger systems, however, you usually need to enter a *username* and *password* before the computer system will allow you to execute programs. This is also true of most networks.

➠ See also *password; username.*

log out: To end a session at the computer. For personal computers, you can log out simply by turning the machine off. On larger computers, where you share computer resources with other users, there is generally an operating system command that lets you log off.

look-and-feel: Refers to the general appearance and operation of a user interface. This is a hot legal issue because many software companies are claiming that competitors who copy the look-and-feel of their products are infringing on their copyright protection. To date, the courts have not ruled definitively on this matter.

➨ See also *user interface*.

loop: In programming, a loop is a series of instructions that is repeated over and over again. Each pass through the loop is called an *iteration*. Loops constitute one of the most basic and powerful programming concepts.

➨ See also *iteration*.

Lotus 1-2-3: A spreadsheet program designed for IBM-compatible personal computers by Lotus Corporation in 1982. Lotus 1-2-3 was the first publicly available program to combine graphics, spreadsheet functions, and data management (three functions, hence the name). Its relative ease of use and flexibility made it an enormous success and contributed to the acceptance of personal computers in business.

➨ See also *spreadsheet*.

low-level format: Hard disks must be formatted twice before they can be used. The first format, called a *low-level* format, sets the interleave factor and prepares the disk for a particular type of disk controller. This is generally performed at the factory.

➨ See also *controller; format; interleaving*.

low-level language: A machine language or an assembly language. Low-level languages are closer to the hardware than are high-level programming languages, which are closer to human languages.

➡ See also *assembly language; high-level language; language; machine language; programming language.*

lowercase: Small letters, as opposed to capital letters. The word *yes*, for example, is in lowercase, while the word *YES* is in uppercase. For many programs, this distinction is very important. Programs that distinguish between lowercase and uppercase are said to be *case sensitive.*

➡ See also *case sensitivity; uppercase.*

low resolution: See under *resolution.*

LPT: A name frequently used by operating systems to identify a printer. Although LPT stands for *line printer terminal,* it is used more generally to identify any type of printer.

➡ See also *printer.*

LQ: See *letter quality.*

LSI: See *large-scale integration.*

luggable: Same as *transportable.*

lunchbox: See under *laptop computer.*

—— M ——

M: Abbreviation for *mega.*

Mac: Short for *Macintosh computer.*

machine address: Same as *absolute address.*

machine code: See under *machine language*.

machine dependent: Refers to a software application that runs only on a particular model of computer. Programs that run on a variety of computers are called *machine independent*.

Almost all programs have some machine dependencies (that is, they run somewhat differently on different computers), but the degree of independence can vary widely. Machine-independent programs give you more flexibility: if you buy a new computer, you can continue using the same software package instead of learning a new one. On the other hand, machine-dependent programs often take advantage of special hardware features of a particular computer, making the programs faster.

Another term for *machine dependent* is *device dependent*, but whereas *machine dependent* usually refers to the computer, *device dependent* can refer to a dependency on any device, like a printer.

➠ See also *application*.

machine independent: Able to run on a variety of computers.

➠ See also *machine dependent*.

machine language: The lowest-level programming language. Machine languages are the only languages understood by computers. While easily understood by computers, machine languages are almost impossible for humans to use because they consist entirely of numbers. Programmers, therefore, use either a high-level programming language or an assembly language. An assembly language contains the same instructions as a machine language, but the instructions and variables have names instead of being just numbers (see Figure 57 at *programming language*).

Programs written in high-level languages are translated into assembly language or machine language by a *compiler*. Assembly language programs are translated into machine language by a program called an *assembler*.

Every CPU has its own unique machine language. Programs must be rewritten or recompiled, therefore, to run on different types of computers.

➭ See also *assembler; assembly language; compiler; CPU; high-level language; low-level language; programming language*.

machine readable: In a form that a computer can accept. Machine-readable data includes files stored on disk or tape, or data that comes from a device connected to a computer. Even typewritten pages can be considered machine-readable if you have an **o**ptical **c**haracter **r**ecognition (OCR) system. A handwritten letter, on the other hand, is not machine-readable because there is no way to directly feed the letter into a computer.

➭ See also *optical character recognition*.

Macintosh computer: A popular model of computer made by Apple Computer (Figure 43). Introduced in 1984, the Macintosh features a graphical user interface (GUI) that utilizes windows, icons, and a mouse to make it relatively easy for novices to use the computer productively. Rather than learning a complex set of commands, you need only point to a selection on a menu and click a mouse button.

Moreover, the GUI is embedded into the operating system. This means that all applications that run on a Macintosh computer have a similar user interface. Once a user has become familiar with one application, he or she can learn new applications relatively easily.

The Macintosh family of computers is not compatible with the IBM family of personal computers. They have different microprocessors and different file formats. This makes it difficult (though not im-

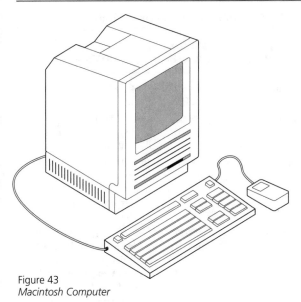

Figure 43
Macintosh Computer

possible) to share data between the two types of computers.

Since the Macintosh interface's arrival on the marketplace and its enthusiastic acceptance by customers, numerous software producers have produced similar interfaces. For example, the OS/2 operating system for IBM personal computers includes a graphical user interface (*Presentation Manager*) similar in many respects to the Macintosh interface, and Microsoft offers a Mac-like GUI for DOS-based systems called *Windows*.

There are a number of different Macintosh models, with varying degrees of speed and power, as shown in Table 19. All models are available in many different configurations—different monitors, disk drives, and memory. All Macintosh computers use a microprocessor from the Motorola 68000 family, so that programs written for one Macintosh computer

Table 19: Macintosh Computer Models

MODEL	MICRO-PROCESSOR	COMMENTS
Macintosh	68000 8-MHz	1984; 128K RAM; 400K floppy drive; discontinued
Mac Plus	68000 8-MHz	1986; 1MB RAM; 800K floppy drive; SCSI interface; discontinued
Macintosh SE	68000 8-Mhz	1987; 1–8MB RAM; 800K floppy drive; optional built-in 20MB hard drive; one expansion slot; discontinued
Macintosh II	68020 16-MHz	1987; 1–8MB RAM; 800K floppy drive; built-in 40MB hard drive; color graphics option; 6 expansion slots; discontinued
Macintosh IIx	68030 16-MHz	1988; 1–8 MB RAM; 1.4-MB SuperDrive; 80MB hard drive; NuBus; discontinued
Macintosh SE/30	68030 16-MHz	1989; 1–8MB RAM; 1.4MB SuperDrive; 80MB hard drive; NuBus; supports color and gray scales
Macintosh IIcx	68030 16-MHz	1989; 1–8MB RAM; 1.4MB SuperDrive; 40MB hard drive; smaller version of IIx; discontinued
Mac Portable	68000 16-MHz	1989; Portable version of the Mac; 1MB RAM; 1.4MB SuperDrive; 40MB hard drive; weighs about 16 pounds
Macintosh IIci	68030 25-MHz	1989; 1–8MB RAM; 1.4MB SuperDrive; 40MB hard drive
Macintosh IIfx	68030 40-MHz	1990; 4–16MB RAM; 1.4MB SuperDrive; 80MB hard drive

Table 19: *(continued)*

MODEL	MICRO-PROCESSOR	COMMENTS
Classic	68000 8-MHz	1990; Apple's entry-level Mac; 1–4MB RAM; 1.4MB SuperDrive
Mac LC	68020 16-MHz	1990; LC stands for "Low-Cost Color"; 2–8MB RAM; 1.4MB SuperDrive; 40MB hard drive; 12-inch RGB Display
Mac IIsi	68030 20-MHz	1990; replacement for the IIcx; 2–16MB RAM; 1.4MB SuperDrive; 40MB hard drive

will run on any other Macintosh computer (with a few exceptions).

➡ See also *application; graphical user interface; IBM PC; microprocessor; Motorola microprocessors; mouse; NuBus; OS/2; Presentation Manager; SCSI; SuperDrive; user interface; Microsoft Windows.*

macro: (1) A symbol, name, or key that represents a list of commands, actions, or keystrokes. Many programs allow you to create macros so that you can enter a single character or word to perform a whole series of actions. Suppose, for example, that you are editing a file and want to indent every third line five spaces. If your word processor supports macros, you can create one that consists of the following keystrokes:

Move Cursor to Beginning of Line

Move Cursor Down 1 Line

Move Cursor Down 1 Line

Move Cursor Down 1 Line

Insert 5 Spaces

Now you can enter the name of the macro, and the word processor will perform all these commands at once.

You can also use macros to enter words or phrases that you use frequently. For example, you could define a macro to contain all the keystrokes necessary to begin a letter—your name, address, and the date. Then, whenever you write a letter, you just press the macro key to include the letter header.

In a way, macros are like simple programs or batch files. Some applications support sophisticated macros that even allow you to use variables and flow control structures such as loops.

➠ See also *batch file; command; loop; program.*

(2) In dBASE programs, a macro is a variable that points to another variable where the data is actually stored. In most other applications, this would be called a *link*.

➠ See also *dBASE; link.*

magnetic disk: See under *disk*.

magnetic tape: See under *tape*.

mail: See *electronic mail*.

mailbox: An area in memory or on a storage device where electronic mail is placed. In electronic mail systems, each user has a private mailbox. When the user receives electronic mail, the mail system automatically puts it in the mailbox.

The mail system allows you to scan mail that is

in your mailbox, copy it to a file, delete it, print it, or forward it to another user. If you want to save mail, it is a good idea to copy it to a file, because files tend to be more stable than mailboxes.

➡ See also *electronic mail*.

mail merge: A feature supported by many word processors that enables you to generate form letters. To use a mail-merge system, you first store a set of information, like a list of names and addresses, in one file. In another file, you write a letter, substituting special symbols in place of names and addresses (or whatever other information will come from the first file). For example, you might write:

```
Dear NAME:
Our records show that your address
is:
   STREET
   CITY, STATE ZIP
   If this is incorrect, . . .
```

When you execute the merge command, the word processor automatically generates letters by replacing symbols (NAME, STREET, CITY, STATE, and ZIP) in the second file with the appropriate data from the first file (see Figure 45 at *merge*).

The power and flexibility of mail-merge systems varies considerably from one word processor to another. Some word processors support a full set of logical operators that enable you to specify certain conditions under which information should be merged. Also, some merge systems allow you to merge data from several files at once.

➡ See also *Boolean operator; merge; word processing*.

main memory: Refers to physical memory that is internal to the computer. The word *main* is used to distinguish it from external mass storage devices such as disk drives. Another term for main memory is *RAM*.

The computer can manipulate only data that is in main memory. Therefore, every program you execute and every file you access must be copied from a storage device into main memory. The amount of main memory on a computer is crucial because it determines how many programs can be executed at one time and how much data can be readily available to a program.

Because computers often have too little main memory to hold all the data they need, computer engineers invented a technique called *swapping,* in which portions of data are copied into main memory as they are needed. Swapping occurs when there is no room in memory for needed data. When one portion of data is copied into memory, an equal-sized portion is copied (swapped) out to make room. Another technique, called *virtual memory*, enables a computer to access larger amounts of data than main memory can hold at one time, but it is a relatively slow process. Therefore, the more memory a computer has and the more it can avoid swapping, the faster it will be able to execute large programs.

Now, most IBM PCs and compatibles come with a minimum of 640K main memory. This is adequate for some applications, but you may need more memory to run sophisticated applications, particularly those that include graphics. You can usually increase the amount of memory by inserting extra memory in the form of chips or memory expansion boards.

Note, however, that DOS has a built-in limit of 1MB (of which only 640K is normally available to programs). To use more than 1MB, you can employ a special system called *EMS* (Expanded Memory Specification) that overcomes the limitations imposed by DOS. Also, some programs such as Microsoft Windows 3.0 are able to use *extended memory*.

Main memory is distinct from *user memory*. User memory is the memory actually available to run programs. This is less than the amount of main memory because most systems reserve a portion of main memory for the operating system. A PC with 1MB main memory, for example, typically reserves 384K for system use, leaving 640K for user programs. On IBM PCs, the user memory is called *conventional memory*.

➡ See also *chip; conventional memory; expanded memory; expansion board; extended memory; K; loader; megabyte; memory; RAM; swapping; user memory; virtual memory.*

mainframe: A very large and expensive computer capable of supporting hundreds of users simultaneously. In the hierarchy that starts with a simple microprocessor (in watches, for example) at the bottom and moves to supercomputers at the top, mainframes are just below supercomputers. In some ways, mainframes are more powerful than supercomputers because they support more simultaneous programs. But supercomputers can execute a single program faster than a mainframe. The distinction between small mainframes and minicomputers is vague, depending really on how the manufacturer wants to market its machines.

Unisys and IBM are the largest manufacturers of mainframes.

➡ See also *computer; microprocessor; minicomputer; supercomputer.*

map: (n) A file showing the structure of a program after it has been compiled. The *map file* lists every variable in the program along with its memory address. This information is useful for debugging purposes. Normally a compiler will not produce a map file unless you explicitly ask for it by specifying the appropriate compiler option.

➡ See also *compile; debug; option.*

(v) (1) To make logical connections between two entities. Because programs cannot translate directly from human concepts to computer numbers, they translate incrementally through a series of layers. Each layer contains the same amount of information as the layer above but in a form somewhat closer to the form that the computer understands. This activity of translating from one layer to another is called *mapping*.

The term *map* is often used to describe programming languages. For example, C is an efficient programming language because it *maps well* onto the machine language. What this means is that it is relatively easy to translate from the C language to machine languages.

➡ See also *programming language*.

(2) To copy a set of objects from one place to another while preserving the objects' organization. For example, when loaded, programs on a disk are mapped into memory. Graphics images in memory are mapped onto a display screen.

➡ See also *load*.

map file: See under *map*.

margins: In word processing, the strips of white space around the edge of the paper. All text falls between the margins. Most word processors allow you to specify the widths of margins. The wider the margins, the narrower the page.

If your word processor performs *word wrap,* it will automatically adjust the length of the lines when you change the widths of the margins.

➡ See also *word processing; word wrap*.

mass storage: Refers to various techniques and devices for storing large amounts of data. The earliest storage devices were punched paper cards, which were used as early as 1804 to control silk-weaving looms. Modern mass storage devices include all types of disk drives and tape drives. Mass storage is distinct from *memory,* which refers to temporary storage areas within the computer. Unlike memory, mass storage devices retain data even when the computer is turned off.

The main types of mass storage are:

floppy disks: Relatively slow and have a small capacity, but they are portable, inexpensive, and reliable.

hard disks: Faster and have more capacity than floppy disks, but they are also more expensive. Some hard disk systems are portable (*removable cartridges*), but most are not.

optical disks: Unlike floppy and hard disks, which use electromagnetism to encode data, optical disk systems use a laser to read and write data. Optical disks have the largest storage capacity of the mass storage devices, but they are not as fast as hard disks. Also, they are relatively expensive, and most optical disks are read-only.

tapes: Relatively inexpensive and can have very large storage capacities, but they do not permit random access of data.

Mass storage is measured in *kilobytes* (1,024 bytes), *megabytes* (1,024 kilobytes), and *gigabytes* (1,024 megabytes).

➡ See also *disk; floppy disk; gigabyte; hard disk; K; main memory; megabyte; memory; optical disk; random access; tape.*

math coprocessor: See under *coprocessor.*

mathematical expression: Any expression that represents a numeric value.

➡ See also *expression.*

matrix: A two-dimensional array; that is, an array of rows and columns.

➡ See also *array*.

maximize: In graphical user interfaces, maximizing refers to enlarging a window to its maximum size.

➡ See also *graphical user interface; window; zoom*.

MB: (1) Short for *megabyte* (1,084,576 bytes). A hard disk that has 20MB of storage should be capable of storing nearly 21 million characters. Manufacturers of mass storage devices sometimes play fast and loose with the term *megabyte,* however, using it to mean just one million bytes.

(2) When used to describe memory chips, *MB* stands for *megabit* rather than *megabyte*. A megabit is 1,048,576 bits or 128K (one eighth of a megabyte).

➡ See also *chip; K*.

Mbyte: Short for *megabyte*.

MCA: See *Micro Channel architecture*.

MCGA: Abbreviation of *multicolor/graphics array* (or *memory controller gate array*), the graphics system built into IBM PS/2 Models 25 and 30. It provides graphics capabilities equal to or greater than MDA and CGA, but it is not as powerful as EGA or VGA. Like VGA, MCGA uses analog signals.

➡ See also *CGA; EGA; graphics; IBM PC; MDA; monitor; VGA; video standards*.

MDA: Abbreviation of *monochrome display adapter*, a monochrome video standard for IBM PCs and compatibles. MDA supports high-resolution monochrome text but does not support graphics or colors. The resolution for text is 720 by 350 pixels.

➡ See also *graphics; Hercules graphics; monitor;*

monochrome; pixel; resolution; VGA; video standards.

mean time between failures: See *MTBF*.

media: (1) Objects on which data can be stored. These include hard disks, floppy disks, and tapes.

➡ See also *disk; mass storage*.

(2) In computer networks, *media* refers to the cables linking workstations together. There are many different types of transmission media, the most popular being twisted-pair wire (normal electrical wire), coaxial cable (the type of cable used for cable television), and fiber optic cable (cables made out of glass).

➡ See also *fiber optics; local-area network; network*.

meg (MB): Short for *megabyte*. See under *MB*.

mega: In decimal systems, the prefix *mega* means one million, but in binary systems, *mega* stands for 2 to the 20th power, or 1,084,576. One megabyte, therefore, is 1,084,576 bytes (this is equivalent to 1,024K).

➡ See also *giga; K; megabyte*.

megabyte (MB): 1,084,576 bytes.

➡ See also *MB*.

megaflop: See *MFLOP*.

megahertz: See *MHz*.

memory: Internal storage areas in the computer. The term *memory* identifies data storage that comes in the form of chips, and the word *storage* is used for memory that exists on tapes or disks. Moreover, the term *memory* is usually used as a shorthand for *physical memory,* which refers to the actual chips capable of holding data. Some computers also use virtual memory, which expands physical memory onto a hard disk.

Every computer comes with a certain amount of physical memory, usually referred to as *main memory* or *RAM.* You can think of main memory as an array of boxes, each of which can hold a single byte of information. A computer that has 640K bytes of memory, therefore, can hold 640K bytes (about 650,-000 characters) of information.

There are several different types of memory:

RAM (random-access memory): The same as main memory. When used by itself, the term *RAM* refers to *read and write* memory; that is, you can both write data into RAM and read data from RAM. This is in contrast to ROM, which permits you only to read data. Most RAM is *volatile,* which means that it requires a steady flow of electricity to maintain its contents. When the power is turned off, whatever data was in RAM is lost.

ROM (read-only memory): Computers almost always contain some read-only memory that holds instructions for starting up the computer. Unlike RAM, ROM cannot be written to.

PROM (programmable read-only memory): A PROM is a memory chip on which you can store a program. But once the PROM has been used, you cannot wipe it clean and use it to store something else. Like ROMs, PROMs are nonvolatile.

EPROM (erasable programmable read-only memory): An EPROM is a special type of PROM that can be erased by exposing it to ultraviolet light.

EEPROM (electrically erasable programmable read-only memory): An EEPROM is a special type of PROM that can be erased by exposing it to an electrical charge.

➡ See also *chip; EEPROM; EPROM; K; main memory; mass storage; PROM; RAM; ROM; virtual memory; VRAM.*

memory cache: See under *cache.*

memory controller gate array: See *MCGA.*

memory dump: See under *dump.*

memory effect: The property of nickel-cadmium (NiCad) batteries that causes them to lose their capacity for full recharging if they are recharged before they are fully drained. The term derives from the fact that the battery appears to have a *memory* for the amount of charging it can sustain. If it is recharged when it is already full, it will sustain only a small charge the next time as well, even if it is fully drained.

➡ See also *NiCad battery.*

memory resident: Permanently in memory. Normally, a computer does not have enough memory to hold all the programs you use. When you want to run a program, therefore, the operating system is obliged to free some memory by copying data or programs from main memory to a disk. This process is known as *swapping.*

Certain programs, however, can be marked as being *memory resident,* which means that the operating system is not permitted to swap them out to a storage device; they will always remain in memory.

The programs and data used most frequently are the ones that should be memory resident. This includes central portions of the operating system and special programs, such as calendars and calculators, that you want to be able to access immediately.

Another term for *memory resident* is *RAM resident.* In DOS systems, memory-resident programs are called *pop-up utilities* or *TSRs* (terminate and stay resident). On Apple Macintosh computers, memory-resident programs are called *desk accessories (DAs)*.

➧ See also *desk accessory; memory; operating system; swap; TSR.*

menu: A list of commands or options from which you can choose (Figure 44). Most applications now have a menu-driven component. You can choose an item from the menu by specifying the item's code (a number or letter) or by simply pointing to the item with a mouse and clicking one of the mouse buttons.

The antithesis of a menu-driven program is a *command-driven* system, in which you must explicitly enter the command you want rather than choose from a list of possible commands. Menu-driven systems are simpler and easier to learn but

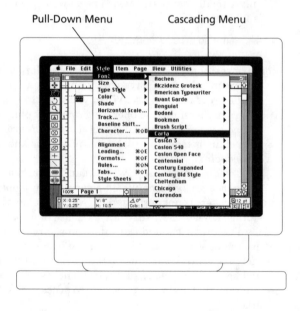

Figure 44
Menus

are generally not as flexible as command-driven systems, which lend themselves more naturally to interaction with programs.

There are several different types of menus:

pop-up menu: A menu that appears temporarily when you click the mouse button on a selection. Once you make a selection from a pop-up menu, the menu usually disappears.

cascading menu: A submenu that opens when you select a choice from another menu.

pull-down menu: A special type of pop-up menu that appears directly beneath the command you selected.

moving-bar menu: A menu in which options are highlighted by a bar that you can move from one item to another. Most menus are moving-bar menus.

menu bar: A menu arranged horizontally. Each menu option is generally associated with another pull-down menu that appears when you make a selection.

tear-off menu: A pop-up menu that you can move around the screen like a window. Pop-up menus are usually attached to the menu selection that caused them to pop up.

➡ See also *command; command driven; graphical user interface; user interface.*

menu bar: A horizontal menu that appears on top of a window. Usually, each option in a menu bar is associated with a pull-down menu.

➡ See also *menu; window.*

menu driven: Refers to programs whose user interface employs menus. The antithesis of a menu-driven program is a *command-driven* program.

➡ See also *command driven; menu; user interface.*

merge: (1) To combine two files in such a way that the resulting file has the same organization as the two individual files. For example, if two files contain a list of names in alphabetical order, merging the two files results in one large file with all the names still in alphabetical order.

Note that *merge* is different from *append*. Append means to combine two files by adding one of them to the end of the other.

(2) In word processing, *mail merge* refers to generating form letters by combining one file containing a list of names, addresses, and other information with a second file containing the text of the letter (Figure 45).

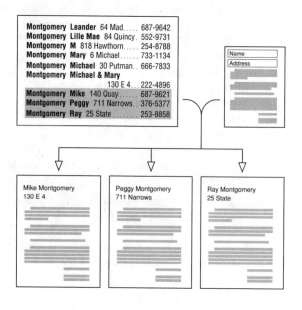

Figure 45
Mail Merge

➽ See also *mail merge*.

message box: Same as *alert box.*

MFLOP: Short for *mega floating-point operations per second,* MFLOPs are a common measure of the speed of computers used to perform *floating-point* calculations. Another common measure of computer speed and power is *MIPS* (**m**illion **i**nstructions **pe**r **s**econd), which indicates integer performance.

➡ See also *floating-point number; MIPS.*

MFM: Abbreviation of *modified frequency modulation,* an encoding scheme used by many PC disk drives. A competing scheme, known as RLL (run length limited), produces faster data access speeds and can increase a disk's storage capacity by up to 50 percent.

Technically, any disk drive can use MFM or RLL. The one it uses depends on the disk controller.

MFM is sometimes referred to as *ST-506,* which is the interface used for MFM disk drives.

➡ See also *controller; disk drive; RLL; ST-506 interface.*

MFP: See *multifunction peripheral.*

MHz: The abbreviation for *megahertz.* One MHz represents one million cycles per second. The speed of microprocessors, called the *clock speed,* is measured in megahertz. For example, a microprocessor that runs at 25MHz executes 25 million cycles per second. Each computer instruction requires a fixed number of cycles, so the clock speed determines how many instructions per second the microprocessor can execute. To a large degree, this controls how powerful the microprocessor is. The other chief factor in determining a microprocessor's power is its data width (that is, how many bits it can manipulate at one time).

➡ See also *clock speed; microprocessor.*

micro: (1) Short for *microprocessor*.

(2) Short for *personal computer*.

(3) A prefix meaning *one millionth*. For example, a *microsecond* is one millionth of a second.

(4) Something very small. For example, a *microfloppy* is a small floppy disk.

➤ See also *microfloppy disk*.

Micro Channel architecture (MCA): A bus architecture for high-end IBM PS/2 computers and future IBM personal computers. It is called a *bus architecture* because it defines how peripheral devices and internal components communicate across the computer's expansion bus. MCA was introduced by IBM in 1987.

MCA was designed to take the place of the older AT bus, the architecture used on IBM PC/ATs and compatibles. Unlike the AT bus, MCA is a multiprocessing bus (it can support more than one CPU) and allows for wider bandwidths and faster clock speeds. The original version of MCA runs at 10MHz and the second version at nearly twice that speed (the AT bus runs at 8MHz); the MCA bus has a 32-bit data path (the AT bus data path is 16 bits wide). In addition, MCA enables users to configure boards entirely in software, without needing to physically set switches.

IBM is pushing for MCA to replace the AT bus as the new standard for personal computer bus architectures. However, MCA has been received by manufacturers and consumers with considerable reluctance. Because the MCA bus is incompatible with the AT bus, manufacturers of add-on boards must design completely new boards rather than simply modify their old boards.

As an alternative to MCA, a number of hardware and software companies have joined together to produce a different bus architecture called EISA (Extended Industry Standard Architecture). EISA is similar to MCA but is backward compatible with the AT bus. This means that EISA uses the same connectors as the AT bus, so old-style AT boards can fit in EISA computers.

➡ See also *add-on; architecture; AT bus; bandwidth; bus; clock speed; EISA; multiprocessing; switch.*

microcomputer: Same as *personal computer*.

Microcom Networking Protocol: See *MNP*.

microfloppy disk: A small floppy disk (see Figure 29 at *floppy disk*). Microfloppy disks come enclosed in hard, 3½ square-inch casings. Although smaller than older-style floppies, microfloppies have greater storage capacity.

IBM PCs and compatibles support two types of microfloppies:

- **double-density** microfloppies hold 720K.
- **high-density** microfloppies can store 1.44MB.

➡ See also *density; disk; floppy disk.*

microjustification: Refers to the use of microspacing to justify text.

➡ See also *microspacing.*

microprocessor: A silicon chip that contains a CPU. In the world of personal computers, the terms *microprocessor* and *CPU* are used interchangeably. At the heart of all personal computers and most workstations sits a microprocessor. Microprocessors also control the logic of almost all digital devices, from clock radios to fuel-injection systems for automobiles.

The leading manufacturers of microprocessors for personal computers are Intel and Motorola (Table 20). IBM personal computers are based on microprocessors made by Intel, whereas the Apple Macintosh computers (as well as many UNIX workstations) use Motorola microprocessors.

Two basic characteristics differentiate microprocessors:

bandwidth: The number of bits processed in a single instruction.

clock speed: Given in megahertz, the clock speed determines how many instructions per second the processor can execute.

In both cases, the higher the value, the more powerful the CPU. For example, a 32-bit microprocessor that runs at 25MHz is more powerful than a 16-bit microprocessor that runs at 8MHz.

Table 20: Popular Microprocessors

The following list shows some popular microprocessors in approximate order of speed and power

MICRO-PROCESSOR	REGISTER WIDTH	BUS WIDTH	CLOCK SPEED (MHZ)
Intel 8080	8	8	2
Zilog Z80	8	8	2
MOS Technology 6502	8	8	1
Intel 8088	16	8	5, 8
Intel 8086	16	16	5, 8, 10
Intel 80286	16	16	8, 10, 12.5
Harris 80C286	16	16	12.5, 25
Motorola 68000	32	16	8
Motorola 68010	32	16	16 to 25
Intel 80386SX	32	16	16, 20, 25
Motorola 68020	32	32	16, 25
Intel 80386	32	32	16, 20, 25, 33
Motorola 68030	32	32	16, 25, 33, 40
Intel 80486	32	32	25, 33, 40, 50
Intel 80860	64	64	50

In addition to bandwidth and clock speed, microprocessors are classified as being either RISC (reduced instruction set computer) or CISC (complex instruction set computer).

➧ See also *bandwidth; chip; CISC; clock speed; CPU; Intel microprocessors; Motorola microprocessors; register; RISC.*

Microsoft Excel: See *Excel.*

Microsoft Windows: A software product developed by Microsoft Corporation that provides developers with tools to build graphics-based applications (Figure 46). MS-Windows is often called an *operating environment* because it changes the way DOS and DOS applications appear to users. In addition to providing a graphical user interface for DOS, MS-Windows also provides a consistent set of tools and file formats so that all programs using MS-Windows can interact smoothly.

Figure 46
MS-Windows Desktop

Unlike other operating environments, such as DESQview, MS-Windows requires that programs be written specifically for it. Programs that have not been developed especially for MS-Windows cannot take advantage of most MS-Windows features. While this limits the influence of MS-Windows, it also enforces consistency—because all programs that use MS-Windows use the same tools, they share a common look and feel. This is one of the reasons the Macintosh computer has been so successful. Moreover, all Windows-designed programs use the same file formats so that graphics can easily be copied from one application to another.

Version 3.0 of Windows, released in 1990, uses protected mode for 286- and 386-based computers. This enables it to make full use of extended memory (it can also simulate expanded memory for those programs that need it). In addition, Windows 3.0 supports virtual memory.

➡ See also *DESQview; DOS; expanded memory; extended memory; graphical user interface; graphics; IBM PC; icon; Intel microprocessors; multitasking; OS/2; Presentation Manager; protected mode; user interface; virtual memory; window.*

microspacing: The insertion of variable-sized spaces between letters in order to justify text. For example, the following justified text uses microspacing:

> This text is right- and left-justified and is microspaced. Compare with the following example, which is not microspaced.

Without microspacing, the text would look like the following:

```
This  text  is  right-  and  left-
j u s t i f i e d   a n d   i s   n o t
microspaced. Compare with the
previous  example,  which  is  mi-
crospaced.
```

Some word processors are capable of microspacing. To print microspaced text, however, you need a high-quality printer. Most daisy-wheel printers and inexpensive dot-matrix printers are not capable of microspacing (see Figure 58 at *proportional pitch*).

➡ See also *justification; printer.*

MIDI: Acronym for *musical instrument digital interface*, a standard adopted by the electronic music industry in 1983 for representing sounds in a form that computers can use. At minimum, a MIDI representation of a sound includes values for the note's pitch, length, and volume. It can also include additional characteristics, such as instrument type and vibrato.

The MIDI standard is supported by most synthesizers, so sounds created on one synthesizer can be played and manipulated on another synthesizer. Computers that have a MIDI interface can record sounds created by a synthesizer and then manipulate the data to produce new sounds. For example, you can change the key of a composition with a single keystroke.

A number of software programs are available for composing and editing music that conform to the MIDI standard. They offer a variety of functions: for instance, when you play a tune on a keyboard connected to a computer, a music program can translate what you play into a written score.

The most popular personal computers for MIDI processing are the Apple Macintosh, Atari ST, and the Commodore Amiga. The latter two come with a built-in MIDI port. You can buy add-on MIDI interfaces for the Macintosh computer and IBM PC.

➡ See also *Amiga; IBM PC; interface; Macintosh computer; port; standard.*

mini: Short for *minicomputer.*

minicomputer: A midsized computer. In size and

power, minicomputers lie between *workstations* and *mainframes*. In the past decade, the distinction between large minicomputers and small mainframes has blurred, however, as has the distinction between small minicomputers and workstations. But in general, a minicomputer is a multiprocessing system capable of supporting from 10 to about 200 users simultaneously.

The most popular model of minicomputer is the VAX made by Digital Equipment Corporation. Other large manufacturers of minicomputers include IBM, Data General, and Prime Computer.

➡ See also *computer; mainframe; multiprocessing; workstation.*

minifloppy: A 5¼-inch floppy disk.

➡ See also *floppy disk.*

minimize: In graphical user interfaces, to convert a window into an icon.

➡ See also *graphical user interface; icon; window.*

MIPS: Acronym for *million instructions per second.* A common measure of a computer's speed and power, MIPS measures roughly the number of machine instructions that a computer can execute in one second. However, different instructions require more or less time than others, and there is no standard method for measuring MIPS. In addition, MIPS refers only to the CPU speed, whereas real applications are generally limited by other factors, such as I/O speed. A machine with a high MIPS rating, therefore, might not run a particular application any faster than a machine with a low MIPS rating.

Despite these problems, the MIPS rating can give you a general idea of a computer's speed. The IBM PC/XT computer, for example, is rated at ¼ MIPS, and the PC/AT runs at a little over 1 MIPS. Powerful workstations have ratings of over 20 MIPS.

➦ See also *CPU; MFLOPS*.

MIS: Short for *management information system*. MIS refers to a class of software that provides managers with tools for organizing and evaluating their department. Typically, MIS systems are written in COBOL and run on mainframes or minicomputers.

➦ See also *COBOL; mainframe; minicomputer; software*.

MNP: Abbreviation of *Microcom Networking Protocol*, a communications protocol developed by Microcom, Inc., that is used by many high-speed modems. MNP supports several different classes of communication, each higher class providing additional features. Modems can support one or more classes. Class 4 automatically varies the transmission speed based on the quality of the line. Class 5 provides data compression. Class 6 attempts to detect the highest transmission speed of the modem at the other end of the connect and transmit at that speed.

The most common levels of MNP support are Class 4 and Class 5, frequently called *MNP-4* and *MNP-5*. Using the data compression techniques provided by MNP-5, computers can achieve throughputs of over 48,000 bps using 2,400 bps modems.

Because MNP is built into the modem hardware, it affects all data transmission. In contrast, software protocols, such as *Xmodem, Ymodem, Zmodem*, and *Kermit*, affect only file transfer operations.

➦ See also *communications protocol; data compression; Kermit; modem; Xmodem; Ymodem; Zmodem*.

mode: The state or setting of a program or device. For example, when a word processor is in *insert mode*, characters that you type are inserted at the cursor position. In *overstrike mode*, characters typed replace existing characters.

The term *mode* implies a choice—that you can change the setting and put the system in a different mode.

➡ See also *insert mode; overstrike.*

modem: Acronym for **mo**dulator-**dem**odulator. A modem is a device that enables a computer to transmit data over telephone lines (Figure 47). Computer information is stored digitally, whereas information transmitted over telephone lines is transmitted in the form of analog waves. A modem converts between these two forms. (Note that fiber optic telephone lines send data digitally, so they do not require modems.)

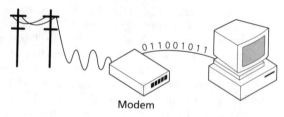

Figure 47
Modem

Fortunately, there is one standard interface for connecting external modems to computers called *RS-232.* Consequently, any external modem can be attached to any computer that has an RS-232 port, which almost all personal computers have. There are also modems that come as an expansion board that you can insert into a vacant expansion slot. These are sometimes called *onboard* or *internal* modems and are more machine specific.

While the modem interfaces are standardized, a number of different protocols for formatting data to be transmitted over telephone lines exist. Some, like CCITT V.22 and V.32, are official standards, while others have been developed by private companies. Most modems have built-in support for the more common protocols—at slow data transmission speeds at least, most modems can communicate with each other. At high transmission speeds, however, the protocols are less standardized.

Aside from the transmission protocols that they support, the following characteristics distinguish one modem from another:

baud rate and bps: How fast the modem can transmit and receive data. At slow rates, modems are measured in terms of baud rates. The slowest rate is 300 baud (about 25 cps). At higher speeds, modems are measured in terms of bps. The fastest modems run at 9,600 bps, although they can achieve even higher data transfer rates by compressing the data. The most common rate is 1,200 bps (about 120 cps). At this rate, it takes about 15 seconds to fill a screen with data. Obviously, the faster the transmission rate, the faster you can send and receive data. Note, however, that you cannot receive data any faster than it is being sent. If the device sending data to your computer is sending it at 300 baud, you must receive it at 300 baud. It does not always pay, therefore, to have a very fast modem. In addition, some telephone lines are unable to transmit data reliably at very high rates.

voice/data: Many modems support a switch to change between voice and data modes. In data mode, the modem acts like a regular modem. In voice mode, the modem acts like a regular telephone. Modems that support a voice/data switch have a built-in loudspeaker and microphone for voice communication.

auto-answer: An auto-answer modem enables your computer to receive calls in your absence. This is only necessary if you offer some type of computer service that people can call in to use.

data compression: Some modems perform data compression, which enables them to send data at faster rates. However, the modem at the receiving end must be able to decompress the data using the same compression technique.

error detection: There are a variety of error-detection techniques designed to ensure that data is transmitted accurately. The most universal is *parity checking*. More sophisticated techniques, such as *Xmodem, Kermit,* and *MNP,* are also available.

To get the most out of a modem, you should have a *communications software package,* a program that simplifies the task of transferring data.

➡ See also *analog; baud rate; bps; broadband ISDN; CCITT; communications; communications protocol; communications software; data compression; digital; fiber optics; full duplex; half duplex; Hayes compatibility; Kermit; MNP; parity checking; port; protocol; RS-232; Xmodem.*

modified frequency modulation: See *MFM.*

modular architecture: Refers to the design of any system composed of separate components that can be connected together. The beauty of modular architectures is that you can replace or add any one component (module) without affecting the rest of the system. The opposite of a modular architecture is an *integrated* architecture, in which no clear divisions exist between components.

The term *modular* can apply to both hardware and software. *Modular software design,* for example, refers to a design strategy in which a system is composed of relatively small and autonomous routines that fit together.

➡ See also *architecture; integrated; module.*

Modula-2: A programming language designed by Niklaus Wirth, the author of Pascal. Wirth created Modula-2 in the late 1970s to answer many of the criticisms leveled at Pascal, which he had created ten years earlier. In particular, Modula-2 addresses Pascal's lack of support for separate compilation of modules and multitasking. Although Modula-2 found support in academia, it is not often used for applications.

➡ See also *compile; multitasking; Pascal; programming language.*

module: (1) In software, a module is a part of a program. Programs are composed of one or more independently developed modules that are not combined until the program is linked. A single module can contain one or several routines.

➡ See also *link; program; routine.*

(2) In hardware, a module is a self-contained component.

➡ See also *modular architecture.*

monitor: (1) Another term for *display screen.* The term *monitor,* however, usually refers to the entire box, whereas *display screen* can mean just the screen. In addition, the term *monitor* often implies graphics capabilities.

There are many ways to classify monitors. The most basic is in terms of color capabilities, which separates monitors into three classes:

monochrome: Monochrome monitors actually display two colors, one for the background and one for the foreground. The colors can be black and white, green and black, or amber and black.

gray-scale: A gray-scale monitor is a special type of monochrome monitor capable of displaying different shades of gray.

color: Color monitors can display from 16 to over 1 million different colors. They are sometimes called *RGB* monitors because they accept three separate signals—red, green, and blue.

Color and gray-scaling monitors are often classified by the number of bits they use to represent each pixel. For example, an 8-bit monitor represents each pixel with 8 bits. The more bits per pixel, the more colors and shades of gray the monitor can display.

After this classification, the most important aspect of a monitor is its screen size. Like televisions, screen sizes are measured in diagonal inches, the distance from one corner to the opposite corner diagonally. A typical size for *VGA* monitors is 14 inches. Monitors that are 16 or more inches diagonally are often called *full-page* monitors. In addition to their size, monitors can be either *portrait* (height greater than width) or *landscape* (width greater than height). Larger landscape monitors can display two full pages, side by side.

The resolution of a monitor indicates how densely packed the pixels are. In general, the more pixels (often expressed in dots per inch), the sharper the image.

Another common way of classifying monitors is in terms of the type of signal they accept: *analog* or *digital*. Digital monitors are often called *TTL monitors*. The type of monitor you need depends on what graphics video adapter you are using. MDA, CGA, and EGA require a digital monitor, but VGA, super VGA, 8514/A, and other high-resolution color standards require analog monitors. Some monitors are capable of accepting either type of signal.

Most monitors are *fixed frequency*, which means that they accept input at only one frequency. Another type of monitor, called a *multiscanning monitor,* automatically adjusts to the frequency of the signals being sent to it. This means that it can accept input from different types of video adapters. Like fixed-frequency monitors, multiscanning monitors accept TTL, analog, or both types of input.

Other factors that determine a monitor's quality include the following:

bandwidth: The range of signal frequencies the monitor can handle. This determines how much data it can process.

refresh rate: How many times per second the screen is refreshed (redrawn).

interlaced or noninterlaced: Interlacing is a technique that enables a monitor to have more resolution, but it reduces the monitor's reaction speed.

dot pitch: The amount of space between each pixel. The smaller the dot pitch, the sharper the image.

convergence: The clarity and sharpness of each pixel.

➭ See also *analog monitor; bandwidth; CGA; convergence; digital monitor; display screen; dot pitch; dots per inch; EGA; fixed-frequency monitor; graphics; gray scaling; interlacing; MDA; monochrome; multiscanning monitor; pixel; refresh; resolution; RGB monitor; super VGA; TTL monitor; VGA; video adapter.*

(2) A program that *observes* a computer. For example, some monitor programs report how often another program accesses a disk drive or how much CPU time it uses.

monochrome: One color. Monitors can be either monochrome or color. Monochrome monitors actually use two colors, one for the display image (the foreground) and one for the background.

Monochrome monitors generally produce a sharper image than color monitors, but color monitors are useful for certain types of graphics programs. Note, however, that almost all software is designed to run on both monochrome and color monitors, so choosing between a color or monochrome monitor does not limit your software choices, even though some applications look better on a color monitor.

A special type of monochrome display is a *gray-scaling* monitor, which is capable of displaying from 16 to 256 different shades of gray.

➡ See also *background; foreground; graphics; gray scaling; monitor.*

monochrome display adapter: See *MDA.*

monospacing: Refers to fonts in which each character has the same width. The opposite of monospacing is *proportional spacing,* in which different characters have different widths. For example, in a proportionally spaced font, the letter *o* would be wider than the letter *i.* Proportionally spaced fonts look more professional, but monospaced fonts are often superior for tabular data because the uniform width of each character makes alignment of columns easier.

Most printed matter, including this book, uses proportional spacing. Display screens, however, usually display text with a monospaced font (unless you are using a WYSIWYG).

➡ See also *font; proportional spacing; WYSIWYG.*

motherboard: The main circuit board of a microcomputer. The motherboard contains the connectors for attaching additional boards. Typically, the motherboard contains the CPU, memory, serial and parallel ports, and all the controllers required to control standard peripheral devices, such as the display screen, keyboard, and disk drive. Other circuit boards are called *add-ons* or *expansion boards* if they attach to the expansion bus, or *daughterboards* if they attach directly to an expansion board.

Because the motherboard contains the CPU, all other chips attached to the motherboard can access the CPU directly without going through the bus. For this reason, it is a good idea to fill up the motherboard completely before adding expansion boards. For example, to add memory to your system, you may be able to insert chips directly onto the motherboard instead of purchasing a separate memory board.

IBM refers to motherboards on PCs as *system boards*. (For the PS/2 line of computers, IBM calls the motherboards *planar boards*.) On most IBM PCs and compatibles, it is possible to replace the motherboard to upgrade to a faster microprocessor. Replacing the motherboard is somewhat more difficult and more expensive than adding an accelerator board, but it has two advantages:

The motherboard contains the bus, ROM, and main memory. Replacing it, therefore, improves performance of all of these components in addition to adding a faster CPU. Also, by replacing everything at once, you can avoid potential compatibility problems.

Replacing the motherboard avoids using up one of the expansion slots.

➡ See also *add-on; bus; chip; controller; CPU; expansion board; microprocessor; port; printed circuit board.*

Motorola microprocessors: Motorola Corporation is one of the leading manufacturers of microprocessors. Motorola microprocessors are used in all Apple Macintosh computers and in most workstations, including workstations made by NEXT and Hewlett-Packard.

➡ See also *microprocessor.*

mouse: A device that controls the movement of the cursor or pointer on a display screen. A mouse is a small object you can roll along a hard, flat surface (Figure 48). Its name is derived from its shape, which looks a bit like a mouse, and the fact that it is connected to the computer by a wire that one can imagine to be the mouse's tail. As you move the mouse, the pointer on the display screen moves in

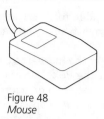

Figure 48
Mouse

the same direction. Mice contain at least one button and sometimes as many as three, which have different functions depending on what program is running.

Invented by Douglas Engelbart of Stanford Research Center in 1963, and pioneered by Xerox in the 1970s, the mouse is one of the great breakthroughs in computer ergonomics because it frees the user to a large extent from using the keyboard. In particular, the mouse is important for menu-driven applications because you can simply point to your command choice and click a mouse button. Such applications are often called *point-and-click* programs. The mouse is also useful for graphics programs that allow you to draw pictures by using the mouse like a pen, pencil, or paintbrush.

There are three types of mice:

mechanical: Has a rubber or metal ball on its underside that can roll in all directions. Sensors within the mouse detect the direction and move the screen pointer accordingly.

optical: Uses a laser to detect the mouse's movement. You must roll the mouse along a special mat with a grid so that the optical mechanism has a frame of reference. Optical mice respond more quickly and precisely than mechanical mice, but they are also more expensive.

optomechanical: Uses a combination of the mechanical and optical technologies. Unlike optical mice, however, optomechanical mice do not require gridded mats.

The resolution of a mouse determines how sensitive it is to movement. The resolution is measured by the number of points (or pixels) that can be detected with each inch of mouse movement. The resolution is usually stated in terms of dots per inch (dpi), counts per inch (cpi), or points per inch (ppi). A 300 dpi mouse, for example, can detect 300 distinct points each time you move it one inch. A high resolution means that you can pinpoint pixels on the display screen more easily. But it also means that you must move the mouse farther to move the cursor. Many mice let you select from several resolutions.

In addition, some mice support a feature called *dynamic resolution,* which means that the resolution depends on how fast you move the mouse. When you move the mouse fast, the cursor moves proportionally farther. This is useful for jumping across the screen. Without this feature, you might need to sweep the mouse across the table or mat several times to move the cursor from one side of the display screen to the other. Dynamic resolution is also called *ballistic tracking*, *automatic acceleration*, *variable acceleration*, and *dynamic acceleration.*

Mice connect to IBM PCs in one of two ways. *Serial mice* connect directly to an RS-232C serial port. This is the simplest type of connection. *Bus mice* connect to the *bus* through an interface card. This is somewhat more complicated because you need to configure and install an *expansion board.* The choice between these two connections depends on whether you have a free serial port. If you do, it is usually simpler to connect a serial mouse.

Mice connect to Macintosh computers through the ADB (Apple Desktop bus) port. IBM PS/2s also have a special port for attaching a mouse.

➡ See also *ADB; bus; cursor; ergonomics; expansion board; graphical user interface; menu driven; pointer; serial port; trackball.*

mousepad: A pad you can place on a desktop or other surface and over which you can move a mouse. Mousepads provide more traction than smooth surfaces such as glass and wood, so they make it easier to move a mouse accurately.

For mechanical mice, mousepads are optional. Optical mice, however, require special mousepads on which a grid has been drawn.

➡ See also *mouse*.

mouse pointer: See under *pointer*.

moving-bar menu: A common type of menu in which options are selected by moving a highlighted bar over them. You can move the bar with a mouse or with arrow keys, or sometimes with the Tab key.

➡ See also *menu*.

MS-DOS: See under *DOS*.

MS-Windows: See *Microsoft Windows*.

MTBF: Short for *mean time between failures*. MTBF ratings are measured in hours and indicate the sturdiness of hard disk drives and printers.

Typical disk drives for personal computers have MTBF ratings of about 40,000 hours. This means that at least half of the disk drives with such a rating will fail once in the first 40,000 hours of operation. Most working conditions are not ideal, so MTBF ratings can be considered as only approximate guidelines for judging the hardiness of disk drives. The fact that MTBF ratings exist at all, however, underscores the fact that every disk drive will eventually fail if run long enough.

➡ See also *disk drive*.

multicolor/graphics array: See *MCGA*.

MultiFinder: The multitasking version of *Finder* for Apple Macintosh computers. This is the part of the operating system responsible for managing the desktop—locating documents and folders and handling the Clipboard and Scrapbook.

➡ See also *clipboard; desktop; Finder; Macintosh computer; multitasking; operating system.*

multifrequency monitor: A type of video monitor capable of accepting signals at more than one frequency range. This enables the monitor to support several different video standards. Typically, multifrequency monitors for IBM PCs and compatibles support MDA, Hercules, CGA, VGA, and sometimes super VGA.

Multifrequency monitors differ somewhat from *multiscanning* monitors. Multiscanning monitors can support video signals at any frequency level within its range, whereas multifrequency monitors support only a select number of frequency levels. However, because almost all video signals conform to one of a handful of video standards, the greater potential of multiscanning monitors is generally not utilized.

➡ See also *monitor; multiscanning monitor; video adapter.*

multifunction peripheral (MFP): A device that combines the functions of a number of I/O devices that are normally separate. A typical MFP supports photocopying, laser printing, and FAXes. Some MFPs also support a voice/FAX/data phone-line switcher.

➡ See also *FAX machine; I/O device; laser printer.*

multimedia: Refers to computer applications that combine audio and video components with computer functions. For example, multimedia training systems for truck drivers consist of a large display screen and sound system that simulate driving conditions. The system is attached to a computer that analyzes the driver's movements and responds accordingly. In addition, computerized animation is considered a multimedia application.

Multimedia applications have not had a large impact on the business and home markets due to the prohibitively high cost of computational power and mass storage required. However, the emergence of the *optical disk* technology may significantly boost multimedia applications. Some experts believe that multimedia systems will create a computing revolution in the 1990s.

➡ See also *authoring tool; optical disk.*

multiprocessing: (1) Refers to a computer system's ability to support more than one process (program) at the same time. Multiprocessing operating systems enable several programs to run concurrently. UNIX is one of the most widely used multiprocessing systems, but there are many others, including OS/2 for high-end IBM PCs. Multiprocessing systems are much more complicated than single-process systems because the operating system must allocate resources to competing processes in a reasonable manner.

➡ See also *multitasking; OS/2; process; UNIX.*

(2) Refers to the utilization of multiple CPUs in a single computer system. This is also called *parallel processing.*

➡ See also *CPU; distributed processing; parallel processing.*

multiscanning monitor: A type of monitor that automatically adjusts to the signal frequency of the video display board to which it is connected. Consequently, multiscanning monitors can display images based on almost any graphics display system, including MDA, Hercules, EGA, VGA, and SVGA.

In contrast, fixed-frequency monitors respond to only one, or a few, frequencies, so they can connect to a limited number of video display boards. However, fixed-frequency monitors are less expensive than multiscanning monitors and usually produce sharper images.

Multiscanning monitors are sometimes called *multisync*, *multifrequency*, and *variable-frequency* monitors. Increasingly, however, the term *multifrequency monitor* is reserved for monitors that support a fixed number of video frequencies. In contrast, multiscanning monitors scan the incoming signals and set themselves to whatever frequency range they are receiving. In practice, there is little difference between the two types of monitors because most video signals conform to one of a handful of video standards.

➡ See also *analog monitor; digital monitor; EGA; fixed-frequency monitor; Hercules graphics; MDA; monitor; SVGA; VGA; video adapter; video standards.*

multisync monitor: Same as *multiscanning* or *multifrequency monitor.*

multitasking: The ability to execute more than one *task* at the same time, a task being a program. The terms *multitasking* and *multiprocessing* are often used interchangeably, although multiprocessing sometimes implies that more than one CPU is involved.

In multitasking, only one CPU is involved, but it switches from one program to another so quickly that it gives the appearance of executing all of the programs at the same time.

There are two basic types of multitasking: *preemptive* and *cooperative*. In preemptive multitasking, the operating system parcels out CPU *time slices* to each program. In cooperative multitasking, each program can control the CPU for as long as it needs it. If a program is not using the CPU, however, it can allow another program to use it temporarily. OS/2 and UNIX use preemptive multitasking, whereas MultiFinder (for Macintosh computers) uses cooperative multitasking.

➧ See also *MultiFinder; multiprocessing; operating system; OS/2; UNIX.*

multi-user: Refers to computer systems that support two or more simultaneous users. All mainframes and minicomputers are multi-user systems, but most personal computers and workstations are not. Another term for *multi-user* is *time sharing.*

➧ See also *mainframe; minicomputer.*

musical instrument digital interface: See *MIDI.*

N

name: A sequence of one or more characters that uniquely identifies a file, variable, account, or other entity. Computer systems impose various rules about naming objects. For example, there is often a limit to the number of characters you can use, and not all characters are allowed.

Names are sometimes called *identifiers.*

➧ See also *extension; filename; variable.*

nanosecond: A billionth of a second. Many computer operations, such as the speed of memory chips, are measured in nanoseconds. *Nanosecond* is often abbreviated as *ns.*

➩   See also *access time.*

National Television Standards Committee: See
NTSC.

natural language: A human language. For example,
English, French, and Chinese are natural languages. Computer languages, such as FORTRAN
and C, are not.

Probably the single most challenging problem
in computer science is to develop computers that
can understand natural languages. So far the complete solution to this problem has proved elusive,
although a great deal of progress has been made.
Fourth-generation languages are the programming
languages closest to natural languages.

➩   See also *fourth-generation language; language.*

near letter quality: A quality of print that is not quite
letter quality, but is better than draft quality (see
Figure 41 at *letter quality*). Many dot-matrix printers produce near letter quality print.

Near letter quality is often abbreviated *NLQ.*

➩   See also *dot-matrix printer; draft quality; letter
quality; printer.*

NetBIOS: An IBM program that augments the DOS
BIOS by adding special functions for local-area networks (LANs). Almost all LANs for IBM PCs are
based on the NetBIOS. Some LAN manufacturers
have even extended it, adding additional network
capabilities.

➩   See also *BIOS; local-area network.*

NetWare: A popular local-area network (LAN) operating system developed by Novell Corporation. Net-
Ware is a software product that runs on a variety of
different types of LANs, from Ethernets to IBM
token-ring networks. It provides users and pro-

grammers with a consistent interface that is independent of the actual hardware used to transmit messages.

➠ See also *Ethernet; local-area network; operating system; token ring network.*

network: A group of two or more computer systems linked together. There are many types of computer networks, including:

local-area networks (LANs): The computers are geographically close together (that is, in the same building).

wide-area networks (WANs): The computers are farther apart and are connected by telephone lines or radio waves.

ISDNs: The computers are connected by special telephone lines that permit the transmission of voice, video, and data at the same time.

In additon to these types, the following characteristics are also used to categorized different types of networks:

topology: The geometric arrangement of a computer system. Common topologies include a bus, star, and ring (see Figure 68 at *topology*).

protocol: The protocol defines a common set of rules and signals that computers on the network use to communicate. One of the most popular protocols for LANs is called *Ethernet.* Another popular LAN protocol for IBM PCs is the *IBM token-ring network.*

architecture: Networks can be broadly classified as using either a *peer-to-peer* or *client/server* architecture.

Computers on a network are sometimes called *nodes.* Computers and devices that allocate resources for a network are called *servers.*

➡ See also *architecture; Ethernet; FDDI; ISDN; local-area network; node; protocol; server; token-ring network; topology; wide-area network.*

network interface card (NIC): A *printed circuit board* you insert into a computer so the computer can be connected to a network. Most NICs are designed for a particular type of network, protocol, and media, although some can serve multiple networks.

➡ See also *local-area network; media; network; printed circuit board; protocol.*

neural network: A type of computing that attempts to imitate the way a human brain works. Rather than using a digital model, in which all computations manipulate zeros and ones, a neural network works by creating connections between *processing elements*, the computer equivalent of neurons. The organization and weights of the connections determine the output. Neural networks are particularly effective for predicting events when the networks have a large database of prior examples to draw on. Strictly speaking, a neural network implies a nondigital computer, but neural networks can be simulated on digital computers. The field of neural networks was pioneered by Bernard Widrow of Stanford University in the 1950s. To date, there are very few commercial applications of neural networks, but the approach is beginning to prove useful in certain areas, such as voice recognition and weather prediction.

➡ See also *artificial intelligence; digital; voice recognition.*

newline: Same as *line feed.*

NIC: See *network interface card.*

NiCad battery pack: NiCad stands for *nickel-cadmium*, the materials used in the battery packs for many laptop computers. NiCad batteries can provide considerable power, but they need to be recharged every three or four hours. Full recharging can take as much as twelve hours, although newer batteries can be recharged in just a few hours.

NiCad batteries have several interesting properties, the most important of which is that they work best after they have been fully drained and then recharged. If they are only partially drained and then recharged, they lose their capacity to be fully charged. This is called *the memory effect*.

Even with full drainage (called *deep discharging*), all batteries have a limit to the number of times they can be recharged. The maximum for most NiCad batteries is one thousand recharges.

➡ See also *laptop computer*.

NLQ: Stands for *near letter quality*.

node: (1) In networks, a node is a processing location in the network. A node can be a computer or some other device, such as a printer.

➡ See also *network*.

(2) In tree structures, a node is a point where two or more lines meet.

➡ See also *tree structure*.

noise: In communications, *noise* is interference that destroys the integrity of signals on a line. Noise can come from a variety of sources, including radio waves, nearby electrical wires, lightning, and bad connections. One of the major advantages of fiber optic cables over metal cables is that they are much less susceptible to noise.

➡ See also *communications; fiber optics*.

nonimpact printer: A type of printer that does not operate by striking a head against a ribbon. Examples of nonimpact printers include laser printers and ink-jet printers. The term *nonimpact* is important primarily in that it distinguishes quiet printers from noisy (impact) printers.

➦ See also *impact printer; ink-jet printer; laser printer; printer.*

noninterlaced: Refers to monitors and video standards that do not use interlacing techniques to improve resolution. Although interlacing increases resolution, it increases screen flicker and reduces reaction time.

➦ See also *screen flicker; interlacing; monitor.*

nonvolatile memory: Types of memory that retain their contents when power is turned off. ROM is nonvolatile, whereas RAM is *volatile.*

➦ See also *memory; RAM; ROM.*

NOR operator: A Boolean operator that returns a value of TRUE only if both operands are FALSE.

➦ See also *Boolean operators.*

notebook computer: An extremely lightweight personal computer. Notebook computers typically weigh less than 6 pounds and are small enough to fit easily in a briefcase. In contrast, laptop computers can weigh as much as 20 pounds and usually require their own carrying case.

A special type of notebook computer, sometimes called a *slate PC*, uses an electronic pen rather than a keyboard for entering input.

➦ See also *laptop computer; slate PC.*

NOT operator: A Boolean operator that returns TRUE if its operand is FALSE, and FALSE if its operand is TRUE.

➦ See also *Boolean operators.*

ns: Short for *nanosecond*.

NSFnet: A wide-area network developed under the auspices of the National Science Foundation (NSF). NSFnet is replacing ARPANET as the main government network linking universities and research facilities.

➡ See also *ARPANET; network; wide-area network.*

NTSC: Abbreviation of *National Television Standards Committee*. The NTSC is responsible for setting television and video standards in the United States (in Europe and the rest of the world, the dominant television standards are PAL and SEACAM). The NTSC standard for television defines a *composite video* signal with a refresh rate of 60 half-frames (interlaced) per second. Each frame can contain 16 million different colors.

The NTSC standard is incompatible with most computer video standards, which generally use *RGB* video signals. However, you can insert special video adapters into your computer that convert NTSC signals into computer video signals and vice versa.

➡ See also *composite video; interlacing; RGB monitor; standard; video adapter.*

NuBus: The expansion bus for all versions of Macintosh computers starting with the Macintosh II.

➡ See also *expansion bus; Macintosh computer.*

null character: A character that has all its bits set to 0. A null character, therefore, has a numeric value of 0, but it has a special meaning when interpreted as text. In some programming languages, notably C, a null character is used to mark the end of a character string. In database and spreadsheet applications, null characters are often used as padding and are displayed as spaces.

➡ See also *character string; padding.*

null-modem cable: A specially designed cable that allows you to connect two computers directly to each other via their communications ports (RS-232 ports). Null modems are particularly useful with portable computers because they enable the portable computer to exchange data with a larger system.

➡ See also *modem; port; RS-232C.*

number cruncher: (1) A computer whose dominant characteristic is its ability to perform large amounts of numerical computations quickly. Supercomputers, for example, are sometimes called number crunchers. In addition, the term *number cruncher* is often applied to powerful workstations.

➡ See also *supercomputer; workstation.*

(2) The term *number cruncher* is sometimes applied to programs. For example, statistical programs are number crunchers because their main task is to perform mathematical calculations.

(3) Less frequently, the term *number cruncher* refers to individuals who use a computer primarily for analyzing numbers.

numeric coprocessor: See under *coprocessor.*

numeric keypad: A separate set of keys on some keyboards that contain the numbers 0 through 9 and a decimal point arranged as on an adding machine (Figure 49). Numeric keypads make it easier to enter large amounts of numeric data.

Frequently, the keys on the numeric keyboard also serve as cursor control keys. Their meanings, therefore, depend on what mode the numeric keypad is in. In *numeric mode,* they represent numbers; in *cursor control mode,* they are like arrow keys. Keyboards that support these dual functions contain an additional key that enables you to switch modes. The name of this key varies—on many keyboards it is labeled *Num Lock.*

Figure 49
Numeric Keypad

➠ See also *arrow keys; keyboard; mode; Num Lock key.*

Num Lock key: A key that switches the numeric keypad from numeric mode to cursor control mode, and vice versa. In numeric mode, the keys represent numbers even when they are combined with the Shift key, Function key, or Control key. Otherwise, these combinations may have different meanings.

The Num Lock key is a toggle key, meaning that it changes the current mode. If the numeric keypad is already locked in numeric mode, pressing the Num Lock key releases it.

➠ See also *numeric keypad; toggle.*

— O —

OA: See *office automation.*

object code: The code produced by a *compiler* (see Figure 15 at *compiler*). Programmers write programs in a form called *source code*. The source code consists of instructions in a particular language, like C or FORTRAN. Computers, however, can only execute instructions written in a low-level language called *machine language*.

To get from source code to machine language, the programs must be transformed by a compiler. The compiler produces an intermediary form called object code. Object code is often the same as or similar to a computer's machine language. The final step in producing an executable program is to transform the object code into machine language, if it is not already in this form. This can be done by a number of different types of programs, called *assemblers, binders, linkers,* and *loaders.*

➡ See also *assembler; assembly language; code; compile; link; load; machine language.*

object oriented: (1) In programming, *object oriented* refers to a type of programming in which programmers define not only the data type of a data structure, but also the types of operations (functions) that can be applied to the data structure. In this way, the data structure becomes an *object* that includes both data and functions. In addition, programmers can create relationships between one object and another. For example, objects can *inherit* characteristics from other objects.

One of the principal advantages of object-oriented programming techniques over conventional

programming techniques is that they enable programmers to create modules that do not need to be
changed when a new type of object is added. A programmer can simply create a new object that inher-
its many of its features from existing objects. This
makes object-oriented programs easier to modify.

To perform object-oriented programming, one
needs an object-oriented programming language.
C++ and Smalltalk are two of the more popular
languages, and there are also object-oriented versions of Pascal.

Object-oriented programming is often referred
to by its initials, *OOP*.

➡ See also *data structure; function; module; programming language.*

(2) In graphics, the term *object oriented* refers to
a particular way of representing graphical objects,
such as lines, arcs, circles, and rectangles. Instead
of representing a graphical image as a bit map, an
object-oriented system represents each object with
a mathematical description. This enables the system to manipulate objects more freely. In an object-
oriented system, for example, you can overlap
objects but still access them individually, which is
impossible in a bit-mapped system. Also, object-oriented images profit from high-quality output devices. The higher the resolution of a monitor or
printer, the sharper an object-oriented image will
look. In contrast, bit-mapped images always appear
the same regardless of a device's resolution.

One of the most widely used formats for object-
oriented graphics is PostScript. PostScript is a page
description language (PDL) that makes it possible
to describe objects and manipulate them in various
ways. For example, you can make objects smaller or
larger, turn them at various angles, and change
their shading and color. A font described in Post-
Script, therefore, can easily be transformed into an-

other font by changing its size or boldness. Object-oriented fonts are called *outline fonts, scalable fonts,* or *vector fonts.*

Object-oriented graphics is also called *vector graphics*, whereas bit-mapped graphics is sometimes called *raster graphics.*

➡ See also *bit map; font; graphics; graphics file formats; page description language; PostScript; raster graphics; scalable font; vector graphics.*

OCR: See *optical character recognition.*

octal: Refers to the base-8 number system, which uses just eight unique symbols (0, 1, 2, 3, 4, 5, 6, and 7). Programs often display data in octal format because it is relatively easy for humans to read and can easily be translated into binary format, which is the most important format for computers (Table 21). By contrast, decimal format is the easiest for-

Table 21: Octal and Binary Equivalents

In octal format, each digit represents three binary digits, as shown:

OCTAL	BINARY
0	000
1	001
2	010
3	011
4	100
5	101
6	110
7	111

With this table it is easy to translate between octal and binary. For example, the octal number 3456 is 011 100 101 110 in binary.

mat for humans to read because it is the one we use in everyday life, but translating between decimal and binary formats is relatively difficult.

➧ See also *binary; decimal; hexadecimal.*

odd header: In word processing, an odd header is a header that appears only on odd-numbered pages.

➧ See also *header.*

odd parity: The mode of parity checking in which each byte contains an odd number of set bits.

➧ See also *parity checking.*

OEM: Stands for *original equipment manufacturer,* which is a misleading term for a company that has a special relationship with computer producers. OEMs buy computers in bulk and customize them for a particular application. They then sell the customized computer under their own name. The term is really a misnomer because OEMs are not the *original* manufacturers—they are the customizers.

Another term for OEM is *VAR (value-added reseller).*

office automation: Refers to computer systems that serve a variety of office operations, such as word processing, accounting, and electronic mail. Office automation almost always implies a network of computers with a variety of available programs.

➧ See also *electronic mail; network; word processing.*

off-line: Not connected. For example, all printers have a switch that allows you to turn them off-line. While the printer is off-line, you can perform certain commands like advancing the paper *(form feed),* but you cannot print documents sent from the computer. The opposite of off-line is *on-line.*

➡ See also *form feed; on-line.*

offset: (1) Refers to a value added to a base address to produce a second address. For example, if B represents address 100, then the expression

$$B+5$$

would signify the address 105. The 5 in the expression is the offset.

Specifying addresses using an offset is called *relative addressing* because the resulting address is relative to some other point. Another word for *offset* is *displacement.*

➡ See also *address; base address; relative address.*

(2) In desktop publishing, the offset is the amount of space along the edge of the paper. Its purpose is to allow room for the binding. The offset is sometimes called the *gutter.*

➡ See also *desktop publishing; gutter.*

(3) In printing, *offset printing* refers to a technique whereby ink is transferred to paper by a rubber roller. Most print shops use offset printing to produce large volumes of high-quality documents.

on-board: Literally, on a circuit board. *On-board memory,* for example, refers to memory chips on the motherboard. *On-board modems* are modems that are on expansion boards.

➡ See also *expansion board; motherboard; on-board modem; printed circuit board.*

on-board modem: Another term for an *internal* modem; that is, a modem that comes as an expansion board you can insert into a computer.

➡ See also *modem.*

1-2-3: See *Lotus 1-2-3*.

on-line: (1) Turned on and connected. For example, printers are on-line when they are ready to receive data from the computer. You can also turn a printer *off-line*. While the printer is off-line, you can perform certain tasks, such as advancing the paper, but you cannot send data to it. Most printers have an on-line button you can press to turn the machine on- or off-line.

➠ See also *off-line; printer*.

(2) Refers to a feature that can be used without exiting an application. For example, an *on-line Help System* is a Help System that you can access while running the program. In this usage, the term *on-line* is a bit redundant because almost all Help Systems are on-line.

➠ See also *help*.

on-line service: A database service you can log onto through a modem. There are thousands of on-line services covering a wide variety of specialized fields. Some of the better-known services include:

BRS: A general-purpose database service that boasts the world's largest medical database.

CompuServe: A large general-purpose service that has gateways to many other services.

Dialog: The largest public database service.

LEXIS: The leading legal database service.

NEXIS: The world's most extensive database for publications.

➠ See also *bulletin board system; database; modem*.

OOP: Stands for *object-oriented programming*.

➠ See also *object oriented*.

OOPL: Stands for *object-oriented programming language*.

➡ See also *object oriented*.

open: (1) To prepare a file for reading, writing, or execution. Whenever you access a file (that is, you edit a text file or run a program file), the operating system opens the file. Opening a file can be simple or complex depending on the operating system. For example, in a multiprocessing operating system, in which different users can share the same resources, the operating system must decide whether the file can be accessed simultaneously by more than one user, and if so, it must ensure that different users do not try to modify the file's contents at the same time.

After you have finished with a file, the operating system closes it. If you have modified the file, it replaces the old version with the new. It then makes the file available to other programs and users.

If you exit a program abnormally (for example, you turn off the power in the middle of an editing session), the operating system will have no opportunity to close files that are open. You may then receive an error message the next time you try to access these files; the operating system will report that the files are already open. To solve this problem, you will need to explicitly close the files. The procedure for doing this depends on the operating system.

➡ See also *close; file; operating system*.

(2) In graphical user interfaces, *open* means to expand an icon into a window.

➡ See also *graphical user interface; icon; window*.

open architecture: An architecture whose specifications are public. This includes officially approved standards as well as privately designed architectures whose specifications are made public by the designers. The opposite of *open* is *proprietary*.

The great advantage of open architectures is that anyone can design add-on products for it. By making an architecture public, however, a manufacturer allows others to duplicate its product. The IBM PC, for example, is based on open architectures, and has spawned an entire industry of IBM clones.

➡ See also *add-on; architecture; clone; proprietary; standard.*

operand: In all computer languages, expressions consist of two types of components: *operands* and *operators*. Operands are the objects that are manipulated and operators are the symbols that represent specific actions. For example, in the expression

$$5 + x$$

x and 5 are operands and $+$ is an operator. All expressions have at least one operand.

➡ See also *expression; operator.*

operating environment: The environment in which users run programs. For example, the DOS environment consists of all the DOS commands available to users. The Macintosh environment, on the other hand, is a graphical user interface that uses icons and menus instead of commands.

A number of software products provide an alternative operating environment for DOS. The two most popular are DESQview and Microsoft Windows, both of which enable you to divide your display screen into several windows and run a different application in each one. In addition, they perform functions normally associated with operating systems, such as memory management and multitasking.

There is a thin line between operating environments and shells. Historically, shells are the interfaces to operating systems. They do not actually add any new capabilities; they simply provide a better user interface. So-called intelligent shells, however, actually extend an operating system's capabilities, so there is little difference between intelligent shells and operating environments.

Operating environments are sometimes called *control programs*.

➡ See also *DESQview; environment; graphical user interface; Microsoft Windows; operating system; shell.*

operating system: The most important program that runs on a computer. Every general-purpose computer must have an operating system to run other programs. Operating systems perform basic tasks, such as recognizing input from the keyboard, sending output to the display screen, keeping track of files and directories on the disk, and controlling peripheral devices such as disk drives and printers (Figure 50). Table 22 describes several operating systems.

For large systems, the operating system has even greater responsibilities and powers. It is like a traffic cop—it makes sure that different programs and users running at the same time do not interfere with each other. The operating system is also responsible for *security*, ensuring that unauthorized users do not access the system.

Operating systems can be classified as follows:

multi-user: Allows two or more users to run programs at the same time. Some operating systems permit hundreds or even thousands of concurrent users.

multiprocessing: Allows a single user to run two or more programs at the same time. Each program being executed is called a *process*. Most multiprocessing systems support more than one user.

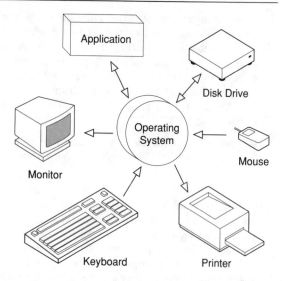

Figure 50
Operating System

multitasking: Allows a single process to run
more than one task. In common parlance, the
terms *multitasking* and *multiprocessing* are
often used interchangeably even though they
have slightly different technical meanings.

real-time: Responds to input instantly. General-
purpose operating systems, such as DOS and
UNIX, are not real time.

Operating systems provide a software platform
on top of which other programs, called *application
programs,* can run. The application programs must
be written to run on top of a particular operating
system. Your choice of operating system, therefore,
determines to a great extent the applications you
can run. For IBM-compatible personal computers,
the most popular operating systems are DOS and
OS/2, but others are available, such as Xenix.

As a user, you normally interact with the operating system through a set of commands. For exam-

Table 22: Operating Systems

There are many different operating systems. Listed here are some popular systems and a description of their salient characteristics. Consult the entry for each particular operating system for more information.

CP/M	One of the first operating systems for small computers. CP/M was initially used on a wide variety of personal computers, but it was eventually overshadowed by DOS.
MS-DOS	Runs on all IBM-compatible personal computers. MS-DOS is a single-user, single-tasking operating system. IBM sells practically the same operating system but calls it *PC-DOS*.
OS/2	The successor to DOS. OS/2 is a relatively powerful operating system that runs only on top-of-the-line IBM-compatible personal computers (that is, computers with an Intel 80286 or later microprocessor). OS/2 is generally compatible with MS-DOS but contains many additional features; for example, it is multitasking and supports virtual memory.
UNIX	Runs on a wide variety of personal computers and workstations. UNIX has become the de facto standard for workstations. It is a powerful multi-user, multiprocessing operating system. UNIX is the operating system of choice for many software development projects because it is flexible and runs on a wide array of computers.
Xenix	A version of UNIX that runs on IBM PCs and compatibles.

ple, the DOS operating system contains commands such as COPY and RENAME for copying files and changing the names of files, respectively. The commands are accepted and executed by a part of the operating system called the *command processor* or *command line interpreter*.

➤ See also *command processor; CP/M; DOS; file
management; multiprocessing; multitasking;
multi-user; OS/2; real time; UNIX; Xenix.*

operator: (1) A symbol that represents a specific action. For example, a plus sign (+) is an operator
that represents addition. The basic mathematic operators are

Operator	Action
+	addition
−	subtraction
*	multiplication
/	division

In addition to these operators, many programs
and programming languages recognize other operators that allow you to manipulate numbers and text
in more sophisticated ways. For example, *Boolean
operators* enable you to test the truth or falsity of
conditions, and *relational operators* let you compare
one value to another.

➤ See also *Boolean operator; expression; operand;
relational operator.*

(2) A computer operator is an individual who is
responsible for mounting tapes and disks, making
backups, and generally ensuring that a computer
runs properly.

optical character recognition: Often abbreviated
OCR, optical character recognition refers to the
branch of computer science that involves reading
text from paper and translating the images into a
form that the computer can manipulate (for example, into ASCII codes). An OCR system enables you
to take a book or a magazine article and feed it
directly into an electronic computer file.

All OCR systems include an optical scanner for
reading text, and sophisticated software for analyzing images. Most OCR systems use a combination of

hardware (specialized circuit boards) and software to recognize characters, although some inexpensive systems do it entirely through software. Advanced OCR systems can read text in a large variety of fonts, but they still have difficulty with handwritten text.

The potential of OCR systems is enormous because they enable users to harness the power of computers to access printed documents. OCR is already being used widely in the legal profession, where searches that once required hours or days can be accomplished in a few seconds.

➡ See also *ASCII; font; optical scanner; printed circuit board.*

optical disk: A storage medium from which data is read and to which it is written by lasers. Optical disks can store much more data—up to 1,000MB—than magnetic media, such as floppies and hard disks. There are three types of optical disks:

CD-ROM: Like audio CDs, CD-ROMs come with data already encoded onto them. The data is permanent and can be read any number of times, but CD-ROMs cannot be modified.

WORM: Stands for *write-once, read-many*. With a WORM disk drive, you can write data onto a WORM disk, but only once. After that, the disk behaves just like a CD-ROM.

erasable: This technology is still young, but some manufacturers are now producing optical disks that can be erased and loaded with new data, just like magnetic disks. These are often referred to as *EO* (**e**rasable **o**ptical) disks or *floptical disks*.

These three technologies are not compatible with one another; each requires a different type of disk drive and disk. Even within one category, there are many competing formats, although CD-ROMs are relatively standardized.

Although optical disks have huge storage capacities, they are not as fast as magnetic disks. In addition, the optical disk technology is not yet mature. There is no standard format for optical disks, and the lifetime of data stored on them is unknown. Finally, the optical disk technology is still expensive. For these reasons, optical disks are not used widely, although they are becoming a popular medium for long-term backup.

➡ See also *CD-ROM; disk; erasable optical disk; mass storage; ROM; WORM.*

optical fiber: See under *fiber optics.*

optical mouse: See under *mouse.*

optical scanner: A device that can read text or illustrations printed on paper and translate the information into a form the computer can use. A scanner works by *digitizing* an image—dividing it into a grid of boxes and representing each box with either a zero or a one, depending on whether the box is filled in. (For color and gray scaling, the same principle applies, but each box is then represented by several bits.) The resulting matrix of bits, called a *bit map,* can then be stored in a file, displayed on a screen, and manipulated by programs (Figure 51).

Optical scanners do not distinguish text from illustrations; they represent all images as bit maps. Therefore, you cannot directly edit text that has been scanned. To edit text read by an optical scanner, you need an *optical character recognition (OCR)* system to translate the image into ASCII characters.

Scanners differ from one another in the following respects:

resolution: The denser the bit map, the higher the resolution. Typically, scanners support resolutions of from 75 to 300 dpi, 300 dpi being the same resolution used by most laser printers.

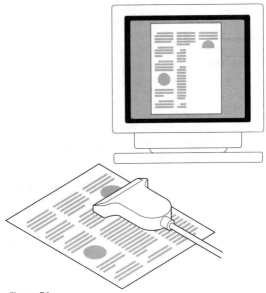

Figure 51
Optical Scanner

size and shape: Some scanners are small hand-held devices that you move across the paper. These hand-held scanners are often called *half-page* scanners because they can only scan 2 to 5 inches at a time. Hand-held scanners are adequate for small pictures and photos, but they are difficult to use if you need to scan an entire page of text or graphics.

Larger scanners include machines into which you can feed sheets of paper. These are called *sheet-fed* scanners. Sheet-fed scanners are excellent for loose sheets of paper, but they are unable to handle bound documents.

A second type of large scanner, called a *flatbed scanner,* is like a photocopy machine. It consists of a board on which you lay books, magazines, and other documents that you want to scan.

Overhead scanners (also called *copyboard* scanners) look somewhat like overhead projectors. You place documents faceup on a scanning bed, and a small overhead tower moves across the page.

gray scaling: Some scanners are capable of representing various shades of gray. This is particularly useful for scanning photographs and illustrations, or anything that is in color. The number of shades of gray that the scanner can represent varies anywhere from 16 to 256.

color: Some scanners are capable of producing color images, but they are considerably more expensive than monochrome or gray-scaling scanners.

➠ See also *ASCII; bit map; FAX machine; font; gray scaling; optical character recognition; resolution.*

option: (1) In command-driven interfaces, an option is an addition to a command that changes or refines the command in a specified manner. As the term implies, options are just that—they are not required.

In the DOS operating system, options are preceded by a slash (/). Other operating systems and applications have different rules for specifying options.

Another word for option is *switch.*

➠ See also *command; command driven.*

(2) In graphical user interfaces, an option is a choice in a *dialog box.*

➠ See also *graphical user interface; dialog box.*

Option key: A key on Macintosh keyboards that you use in concert with other keys to generate special characters and commands. On IBM PCs and compatibles, the corresponding key is called an *Alt key.*

➠ See also *Alt key; keyboard; Macintosh computer.*

original equipment manufacturer: See *OEM*.

OR operator: A Boolean operator that returns a value
of TRUE if either of its operands is TRUE. This is
called an *inclusive OR operator*. There is also an
exclusive OR operator (often abbreviated *XOR*) that
returns a value of TRUE only if both operands have
different values.

➡ See also *Boolean operator*.

orphan: In word processing, an orphan is the first line
of a paragraph that appears as the last line of a
page. Orphans are considered bad form in page layout, so many word processors allow you to avoid
them.

   A *widow* is the opposite of an orphan. It is the
last line of a paragraph that appears as the first line
of a page. As with orphans, you can direct most
word processors to avoid widows.

➡ See also *widow; word processing*.

OS/2: An operating system developed by Microsoft Corporation and IBM that runs on certain models of
IBM-compatible personal computers. OS/2 was designed to take the place of DOS for IBM's most
powerful personal computers and runs only on computers that have an Intel 80286 or later microprocessor and at least 2MB of memory.

   Version 1.0 of OS/2 has a command interface
almost identical to the DOS interface. The later
versions include a Presentation Manager that provides a graphical user interface similar to Microsoft Windows.

   Aside from the Presentation Manager, the big-
gest difference between DOS and OS/2 is that OS/2
is a *multitasking* operating system. This means that
it is capable of running several programs at the
same time. Both DOS and OS/2 are single-user operating systems.

   OS/2 supports up to 16MB of memory, whereas

the limit for DOS is 1MB (although you can exceed the DOS limit with *expanded* or *extended memory*). Another important feature of OS/2 is that it supports interprocess communication, the ability to send data and messages from one process to another.

OS/2 is backward compatible with DOS, which means that it can run all DOS programs. However, programs written specifically to run under OS/2 will not run under DOS.

Many of the features offered by OS/2 (such as the graphical user interface, multitasking, and more main memory) can be added to DOS systems through programs such as *Microsoft Windows* and *DESQview*. For this reason—combined with the expense of purchasing a machine that has enough CPU power and memory to run OS/2—the new operating system has not caught on in the marketplace as quickly as many expected.

➨ See also *backward compatible; DESQview; DOS; expanded memory; graphical user interface; IBM PC; IBM-compatible; main memory; Microsoft Windows; multitasking; operating system; Presentation Manager.*

outline font: A *scalable font* in which the outlines of each character are geometrically defined. The most popular language for defining outline fonts is *PostScript.*

An outline font is *scalable* because, given a geometrical description of a typeface, a printer or other display device can generate the characters at any size (scale). Aside from offering innumerable sizes of each font, outline fonts have the added advantage that they make the most of an output device's resolution. The more resolution a printer or monitor has, the better an outline font will look. The only disadvantage of outline fonts is that they require expensive hardware (or slow software) to produce the output.

➧ See also *bit map; font; PostScript; resolution; scalable font; typeface; vector graphics.*

output: (n) Anything that comes out of a computer. Output can be meaningful information or gibberish, and it can appear in a variety of forms—as binary numbers, as characters, as pictures. Output devices include display screens, lights, loudspeakers, and printers.

(v) To give out. For example, display screens output images, printers output print, and loudspeakers output sounds.

➧ See also *I/O.*

output device: Any machine capable of representing information from a computer. This includes display screens, printers, plotters, and synthesizers.

➧ See also *device; output.*

overflow error: An error that occurs when the computer attempts to handle a number that is too large for it. Every computer has a well-defined range of values that it can represent. If during execution of a program it arrives at a number outside this range, it will experience an overflow error. Overflow errors are sometimes referred to as *overflow conditions.*

overlaid windows: Windows arranged so that they overlap each other. Overlaid windows resemble a stack of pieces of paper lying on top of one another; only the topmost window is displayed in full. You can move a window to the top or bottom of the stack by clicking one of the mouse buttons. This is known as *popping* or *pushing,* respectively.

Overlaid windows are also called *cascading* windows. Windows that do not overlap are called *tiled windows.* See Figure 52 for a comparison of both types of windows.

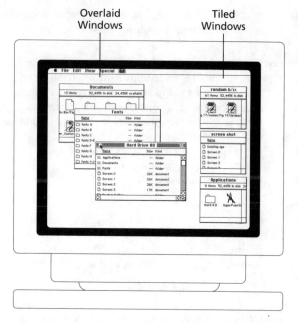

Figure 52
Overlaid Windows vs. Tiled Windows

➡ See also *pop; push; tiled windows; window.*

overstrike: To type over an existing character. Most
word processors and text editors allow you to
choose between two modes: *overstrike* and *insert.* In
overstrike mode, every character you type is displayed at the cursor position. If a character is already at that position, it is replaced. In insert mode,
each character you type is inserted at the cursor
position. This means that existing characters are
moved over to make room for the new character,
but they are not replaced.

Overstrike mode is also called *overwrite mode*

➡ See also *insert mode.*

overwrite mode: See under *overstrike.*

pack: To compress data.

➡ See also *data compression; packed file.*

packed file: A file in a compressed format. Many operating systems and applications contain commands that enable you to pack a file so that it takes up less memory. For example, suppose you have a text file containing ten consecutive space characters. Normally, this would require ten bytes of storage. However, a program that packs files would replace the space characters by a special *space-series* character followed by the number of spaces being replaced. In this case, the ten spaces would require only two bytes. This is just one packing technique—there are many others. One disadvantage of packed files, however, is that they can be read only by the program that packed them because they contain special codes.

Some modems automatically pack data before transmitting it across communications lines. This can produce faster communication because fewer bytes need to be sent. However, the modem on the receiving side must be capable of *unpacking* the data.

Packing is often referred to as *data compression,* particularly when it involves data communications.

➡ See also *data compression; modem.*

pad character: A character used to fill empty space. Many applications have fields that must be a particular length. For example, in a database application, you may have a field that is ten characters in length. If you use only four of the allotted characters, the program itself must fill in the remaining six characters with pad characters.

Some applications allow you to choose the character to be used as padding.

➡ See also *database; field; null character.*

padding: Filling in unused space.

➡ See also *pad character.*

page: (n) (1) A fixed amount of data.

(2) In word processing, a page is a page of text. Most text-processing applications recognize a hierarchy of components, starting with a *character* at the lowest level, followed by a *word,* a *line,* a *paragraph,* and a *page.* Applications permit certain operations for each type of component; for example, you can delete a character, a word, a line, and sometimes an entire page. For pages, you can also specify formatting characteristics (for example, whether the page should be right-justified or not). You can also usually specify the page length.

(3) In virtual memory systems, a page is a fixed number of bytes recognized by the operating system (usually 512 or 1,024).

➡ See also *main memory; paging; segment; swap; virtual memory.*

(v) (1) To display one page (or screenful) of a document at a time. To contrast, see *scroll.*

(2) To copy a page of data from main memory to a mass storage device, or vice versa. Paging is one form of swapping.

➡ See also *paging; swap; virtual memory.*

page break: The end of a page of text. In word-processing systems, you can enter special codes, called *hard* page breaks, that cause the printer to advance to the next page. Without hard page breaks, the word processor automatically begins a new page after a page has been filled (this depends on the number of lines per page). In this case, the page break is called a *soft* page break.

➡ See also *hard; soft; word processing.*

page description language: Often abbreviated *PDL,* a page description language is a language for describing the layout and contents of a printed page. The best-known PDLs are Adobe PostScript and Hewlett-Packard PCL (Printer Control Language), both of which are used to control laser printers.

PostScript is *object oriented,* meaning that it describes a page in terms of geometrical objects such as lines, arcs, and circles.

This object-oriented approach differs markedly from the *bit-map* approach used by the original versions of PCL (those up to PCL 5, released in 1990), in which each character or object is described as a grid of *on* or *off* dots.

➡ See also *bit map; font; laser printer; object oriented; PCL; PostScript; scalable font; typeface.*

Page Down key: Often abbreviated *PgDn,* the Page Down key is supported on many keyboards. Its meaning differs from one program to another, but it usually moves the cursor down a set number of lines.

page eject: Same as *form feed.*

page fault: See under *paging.*

page layout program: A program that enables you to format pages of text and graphics. Page layout tools support a variety of fonts and special graphics functions for manipulating pictures. Some word-processing systems support their own page layout functions, but page layout programs designed specifically for this purpose are also available. They generally lack sophisticated editing capabilities, however.

➡ See also *desktop publishing; font.*

page-mode memory: A special type of RAM divided into discrete sections, called *pages.* Within any page of memory, the CPU can access memory quickly without resorting to wait states. Typically, a page is 2K bytes.

➡ See also *CPU; memory; RAM; wait state.*

page preview: See *preview.*

Page Up key: Often abbreviated *PgUp,* the Page Up key is supported on many keyboards. Its meaning differs from one program to another, but it usually moves the cursor up a set number of lines.

page-white display: A special type of LCD display screen that uses supertwist technology to produce a high contrast between the foreground and background.

➡ See also *flat-panel display; LCD; supertwist.*

pagination: (1) Refers to numbering pages in a document.

(2) Refers to dividing a document into pages. Most word processors automatically paginate documents based on a page size that you specify. Some word processors enable you to avoid widows and orphans during pagination.

➡ See also *orphan; widow; word processing.*

paging: A technique used by virtual memory operating systems to help ensure that the data you need is available as quickly as possible. The operating system copies a certain number of pages from your storage device to main memory. When a program needs a page that is not in main memory, the operating system copies the required page into memory and copies another page back to the disk. One says that the operating system *pages* the data. Each time a page is needed that is not currently in memory, a *page fault* occurs.

This type of virtual memory is called *paged virtual memory*. Another form of virtual memory is *segmented virtual memory* (see Figure 74 at *virtual memory*).

➡ See also *main memory; operating system; page; segment; swap; virtual memory.*

paint program: A graphics program that enables you to draw pictures on the display screen. The pictures are stored as bit maps (raster graphics). In contrast, *draw programs* use vector graphics (object-oriented images), which scale better.

Most paint programs provide the *tools* listed in Table 23 in the form of icons. By selecting an icon, you can perform functions associated with the tool.

In addition to these tools, paint programs also provide easy ways to draw common shapes such as straight lines, rectangles, circles, and ovals.

Table 23: Paint Tools

TOOL	FUNCTION
Brush	For freehand painting using the currently selected pattern and color. Most paint programs provide differently shaped brushes for different styles of painting.
Eraser	For erasing selected areas of the display screen.
Lasso	For selecting parts of an illustration.
Pencil	For drawing freehand lines.
Scissors	For cutting a section of a painting.
Spray Paint	For spray painting in the current pattern and color.

➡ See also *bit map; draw program; graphics; object-oriented; raster graphics; scale; vector graphics.*

palette: (1) In computer graphics, a palette is the complete set of available colors. Most graphics systems let you use only a fraction of the colors available from the palette at one time. For example, EGA systems allow you to use 16 colors from a palette of 64. On monochrome systems, the term *palette* is sometimes used to refer to the available fill patterns.

➡ See also *EGA; graphics; video adapter.*

(2) In paint and illustration programs, a palette is a collection of symbols that represent drawing tools. For example, a simple palette might contain a paintbrush, a pencil, and an eraser.

➡ See also *draw program; graphics; paint program.*

palmtop: A small computer that literally fits in your palm. Compared to full-size computers, palmtops are severely limited, but they are extremely practical for certain functions such as phone books and calendars.

➡ See also *portable.*

paper feed: The device or the method that moves paper through a printer. For example, a *tractor-feed* mechanism is one that pulls the paper with a rotating wheel whose nubs catch in holes on either side of the paper.

➡ See also *printer.*

paper-white display: A high-quality monochrome monitor that displays characters in black against a white background. Paper-white displays are often easier to look at than black, amber, or green displays, especially for flat-panel displays for laptop computers. Paper-white displays for laptop computers are sometimes called *page-white displays*.

➡ See also *display screen; flat-panel display; monitor; page-white display*.

parallel: Refers to processes that occur simultaneously. Printers and other devices are said to be either *parallel* or *serial*. *Parallel* means the device is capable of receiving more than one bit at a time (that is, it receives several bits *in parallel*). Most modern printers support a parallel interface.

➡ See also *parallel port; port; printer; serial*.

parallel interface: A channel capable of transferring more than one bit simultaneously. Almost all personal computers come with at least one parallel interface that is reserved for connecting a printer. The other type of interface is a *serial interface*.

➡ See also *channel; parallel; parallel port; serial port*.

parallel port: A parallel interface for connecting an external device such as a printer. Most personal computers have both a parallel port and a serial port. On IBM PCs and compatibles, the parallel port uses a 25-pin connector (type DB-25) and is used almost exclusively to connect printers. It is often called a *Centronics interface* after the company that designed the original standard for parallel communication between a computer and printer. (The modern parallel interface is based on a design by Epson.)

The serial port is for connecting other devices, such as modems and mice, although you can also use it to connect certain types of printers.

➡ See also *Centronics parallel interface; parallel; port; serial port*.

parallel processing: The simultaneous use of more than one CPU to execute a program. Ideally, parallel processing makes a program run faster because there are more engines (CPUs) running it. In practice, it is often difficult to divide a program in such a way that separate CPUs can execute different portions without interfering with each other.

Most computers have just one CPU, but some models have several. There are even computers with thousands of CPUs. With single-CPU computers, it is possible to perform parallel processing by connecting the computers in a network. However, this type of parallel processing requires very sophisticated software called *distributed processing* software.

Note that parallel processing differs from multitasking, in which a single CPU executes several programs at once.

➡ See also *CPU; distributed processing; multitasking.*

parameter: (1) Characteristic. For example, *specifying parameters* means defining the characteristics of something. In general, parameters are used to customize a program. For example, file names, page lengths, and font specifications could all be considered parameters.

(2) In programming, the term *parameter* is synonymous with *argument*, a value that is passed to a routine.

➡ See also *argument; routine.*

parameter RAM (PRAM): On Macintosh computers, parameter RAM is a small portion of RAM used to store information about the way the system is configured. For example, parameter RAM holds the date and time, desktop pattern, mouse settings, volume settings, and other control data set with the Control Panel. Parameter RAM is powered by a battery, so it does not lose its contents when the power is turned off.

➡ See also *configure; Control Panel; Macintosh computer; memory; RAM.*

parent directory: Refers to the directory above another directory. Every directory, except the *root directory*, lies beneath another directory. The higher directory is called the *parent directory*, and the lower directory is called a *subdirectory*. In DOS and UNIX systems, the parent directory is identified by two dots (. .).

➡ See also *directory; root directory.*

parity: The quality of being either odd or even. The fact that all numbers have a parity (they are either odd or even) is commonly used in data communications to ensure the validity of data. This is called *parity checking*.

➡ See also *parity checking.*

parity bit: See under *parity checking.*

parity checking: In communications, parity checking refers to the use of *parity bits* to check that data has been transmitted accurately. The parity bit is added to every seven bits that are transmitted. The parity bit for each byte (seven data bits plus a parity bit) is set so that all bytes have either an odd number or an even number of set bits.

Assume, for example, that two devices are communicating with even parity (the most common form of parity checking). As the transmitting device sends data, it counts the number of set bits in each group of seven bits. If the number of set bits is even, it sets the parity bit to 0; if the number of set bits is odd, it sets the parity bit to 1. In this way, every byte has an even number of set bits. On the receiving side, the device checks each byte to make sure that it has an even number of set bits. If it finds an odd number of set bits, the receiver knows there was an error during transmission.

The sender and receiver must both agree to use parity checking and to agree on whether parity is to be odd or even. If the two sides are not configured with the same *parity sense*, communication will be impossible.

Parity checking is the most basic form of error detection in communications. Although it detects many errors, it is not foolproof, because it cannot detect situations in which two or four consecutive bits are changed due to electrical noise. There are many other more sophisticated protocols for ensuring transmission accuracy, such as MNP and CCITT V.42.

Parity checking is used not only in communications but also to test memory storage devices. IBM personal computers, for example, perform a parity check on memory every time you boot the machine.

➡ See also *CCITT; communications; communications protocol; MNP; modem.*

park: To lock the *read/write head* of a hard disk drive in a safe position so that the disk will not be damaged while moving the drive. Parking the disk is particularly important for portable and laptop computers, which are moved frequently. The disk will automatically *unpark* itself once you turn the power on.

Many disk drives support *automatic head parking,* in which the drive automatically parks the head whenever the power is turned off.

➡ See also *disk drive; head; head crash.*

partition: (v) To divide memory or mass storage into isolated sections. In DOS systems, you can partition a disk, and each partition will behave like a separate disk drive. This is particularly useful for disk drives larger than 32MB because this is the disk size limit imposed by versions of DOS through Version 3.3. By partitioning a large disk, you can utilize the entire disk for DOS applications. (Some disk drives come with drivers that support partitions larger than 32MB, even for old versions of DOS.)

Partitioning is also useful if you run more than one operating system. For example, you might reserve one partition for DOS and another for OS/2.

On Apple Macintosh computers, there are two types of partitioning: *hard* and *soft*. Hard partitioning is the same as DOS partitioning—the disk is physically divided into different sections. Soft partitioning, on the other hand, does not physically affect the disk at all, but it fools the Finder into believing that the disk is partitioned. The advantage of this is that you can partition the disk without affecting the data on it. With hard partitioning, it is usually necessary to reformat the entire disk.

➤ See also *disk drive; DOS; driver; Finder; hard; mass storage; soft; Xenix.*

(n) A section of main memory or mass storage that has been reserved for a particular application.

Pascal: A high-level programming language developed by Niklaus Wirth in the late 1960s. The language is named after Blaise Pascal, a seventeenth-century French mathematician who constructed one of the first mechanical adding machines.

Pascal is best known for its affinity to structured programming techniques. The nature of the language forces programmers to design programs methodically and carefully. For this reason, it is a popular teaching language.

Despite its success in academia, Pascal has had only modest success in the business world. Part of the resistance to Pascal by professional programmers stems from its inflexibility and lack of tools for developing large applications. For these reasons, many programmers prefer the C language.

To address some of these criticisms, Wirth designed a new language called Modula-2. Modula-2 is similar to Pascal in many respects, but it contains additional features.

➡ See also *C; Modula-2; programming language.*

password: A secret series of characters that enables a user to access a file, computer, or program. On multi-user systems, each user must enter his or her password before the computer will respond to commands. The password helps ensure that unauthorized users do not access the computer. In addition, data files and programs may require a password.

Ideally, the password should be something that nobody could guess. In practice, most people choose a password that is easy to remember, such as their name or their initials. This is one reason it is relatively easy to break into most computer systems.

➡ See also *log on; security.*

paste: To copy a section of text from a buffer (or clipboard) to a file. In word processing, blocks of text are moved from one place to another by cutting and pasting. When you cut a block of text, the word processor removes the block from your file and places it in a temporary holding area (a buffer). You can then paste the material in the buffer somewhere else.

➡ See also *buffer; clipboard; cut; word processing.*

path: (1) In DOS systems, a path is a list of directories where the operating system looks for executable files if it is unable to find the file in the working directory (Figure 53). You can specify the list of directories with the PATH command.

➡ See also *DOS; executable file; working directory.*

(2) Another name for *pathname*.

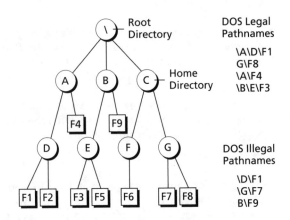

Figure 53
DOS Paths

➨ See also *pathname*.

pathname: A sequence of symbols and names that identifies a file. Every file has a name, called a *filename,* so the simplest type of pathname is just a filename. If you specify a filename as the pathname, the operating system looks for that file in your current working directory. However, if the file resides in a different directory, you must tell the operating system how to find that directory. You do this by specifying a path that the operating system must follow.

The pathname always starts from your working directory or from the root directory. Each operating system has its own rules for specifying paths. In DOS systems, for example, the root directory is named \, and each subdirectory is separated by an additional backslash. In UNIX, the root directory is named /, and each subdirectory is followed by a slash.

➭ See also *directory; filename; root directory; working directory.*

Pause key: A key that you can use to temporarily halt the display of data. Generally, you use the Pause key to freeze data that is being scrolled across the display screen. To continue scrolling, you can press any key.

On DOS and OS/2 systems, an alternative to using the Pause key is to use the MORE command, which displays one screenful of data at a time.

➭ See also *scroll; toggle.*

PC: (1) Short for *personal computer* or *IBM PC*. Some Macintosh aficionados object to classifying Macintosh computers as PCs, preferring to reserve the term for IBM PCs and compatibles. Nevertheless, the term is often used to refer to all personal computers, including Macintoshes, Amigas, and a host of others.

➭ See also *IBM PC; Macintosh computer; personal computer.*

(2) *PC* can stand for *printed circuit*, so a *PC board* is a printed circuit board.

➭ See also *printed circuit board.*

PCB: Short for *printed circuit board.*

PC-DOS: The name IBM uses to market the MS-DOS operating system developed by Microsoft, Inc.

➭ See also *DOS*

PC FAX: Same as *FAX modem.*

PCL: Abbreviation of *Printer Control Language*, the *page description language* used by the HP LaserJet and compatible printers. Unlike the PostScript PDL, most versions of PCL use *raster graphics* rather than *vector graphics*. Starting with PCL 5, however, HP supports a *scalable font* technology called *Intellifont*.

➧ See also *HP-compatible printer; Intellifont; laser printer; page description language; Post-Script; raster graphics; scalable font; vector graphics.*

PCX: Originally developed by ZSOFT for its PC Paintbrush program, PCX is a graphics file format for graphics programs running on IBM PCs and compatibles. It is used by most optical scanners, FAX programs, and desktop publishing systems. Another common format is *TIFF*.

➧ See also *desktop publishing; FAX machine; graphics file formats; graphics; optical scanner; TIFF.*

PDL: See *page description language.*

peer-to-peer architecture: A type of network in which each workstation has equivalent capabilities and responsibilities. This differs from *client/server architectures*, in which some workstations are dedicated to serving the others. Peer-to-peer networks are generally simpler and less expensive, but they usually do not offer the same performance under heavy loads. One of the most popular peer-to-peer networks for personal computers is TOPS.

➧ See also *client/server architecture; local-area network; TOPS; workstation.*

pel: Short for *pixel.*

peripheral: Short for *peripheral device.*

peripheral device: Any external device attached to a computer. Examples of peripherals include printers, disk drives, display monitors, keyboards, and mice.

➡ See also *device*.

personal computer: A small, relatively inexpensive
computer designed for an individual user. In price,
personal computers range anywhere from about
$100 to over $10,000. All are based on the microprocessor technology that enables manufacturers
to put an entire CPU on one chip. Businesses use
personal computers for word processing, accounting, desktop publishing, and for running spreadsheet and database management applications. At
home, the most popular use for personal computers
is for playing games.

Personal computers first appeared in the late
1970s. One of the first and most popular personal
computers was the Apple II, introduced in 1977 by
Apple Computer.

During the late 1970s and early 1980s, new models and competing operating systems seemed to appear daily. Then, in 1981, IBM entered the fray with
its first personal computer, known as the *IBM PC*.
The IBM PC quickly became the personal computer
of choice, and most other personal computer manufacturers fell by the wayside. One of the few companies to survive IBM's onslaught was Apple
Computer, which remains a major player in the personal computer marketplace.

Other companies adjusted to IBM's dominance
by building IBM clones, computers that were internally almost the same as the IBM PC, but that cost
less. Because IBM clones use the same microprocessors as IBM PCs, they are capable of running the
same software.

The principal characteristics of personal computers are that they are single-user systems and are
based on microprocessors. At the high end, however, the distinction between personal computers
and workstations has faded. High-end models of the
Apple Macintosh computer and the IBM PC offer
the same computing power and graphics capability

as low-end workstations by Sun, Hewlett-Packard, and DEC.

➡ See also *Amiga; clone; CPU; IBM PC; Macintosh computer; microprocessor; workstation.*

personal information manager: See *PIM.*

PgDn key: See *Page Down key.*

PgUp key: See *Page Up key.*

Phoenix BIOS: Phoenix Corporation is the largest producer of BIOS chips for IBM PC clones. Phoenix BIOSes have a reputation for exactly duplicating BIOSes produced by IBM.

➡ See also *BIOS; clone.*

physical: Refers to anything pertaining to hardware. The opposite of physical is *logical* or *virtual,* which describe software objects. For example, *physical memory* refers to the actual RAM chips installed in a computer. *Virtual memory,* on the other hand, is an imaginary storage area used by programs.

A *physical data structure* refers to the actual organization of data on a storage device. The *logical data structure* refers to how the information appears to a program or user. For example, a data file is a collection of information stored together. This is its logical structure. Physically, however, a file could be stored on a disk in several scattered pieces.

➡ See also *fragmentation; hardware; logical; software; virtual memory.*

PIC: Short for *Lotus **Pic**ture File,* the graphics file format used to represent graphics generated by Lotus 1-2-3.

➡ See also *graphics; graphics file formats; Lotus 1-2-3.*

pica: In typesetting, a pica is a unit of measurement equal to approximately 1/6 of an inch, or exactly 12 points.

➡ See also *point*.

PICT file format: An object-oriented graphics file format developed by Apple Computer in 1984. PICT uses QuickDraw and is supported by almost all graphics programs that run on Macintosh computers. In addition to QuickDraw representations, PICT files can also store bit maps.

The original PICT format supports 8 colors. A new version of PICT, called PICT2, supports at least 256 colors.

➡ See also *graphics; graphics file formats; Macintosh computer; object oriented; QuickDraw.*

PIM: Acronym for *personal information manager*, a type of software application designed to help users organize random bits of information. Although the category is fuzzy, most PIMs enable you to enter various kinds of textual notes—reminders, lists, dates—and to link these bits of information together in useful ways. Many PIMs also include calendar, scheduling, and calculator programs. One of the best-known PIMs for IBM PCs is called *Side-Kick.*

➡ See also *application; calculator; calendar; scheduler.*

pin: (1) In dot-matrix printers, pins are the devices that press on the ink ribbon to make dots on the paper. Printers are classified by how many pins they have on the printer head. The more pins a printer has, the higher quality type it is capable of producing. Dot-matrix printers can have anywhere from 9 to 24 pins. A 24-pin printer can produce letter-quality print.

➧ See also *dot-matrix printer; letter quality; near letter quality; printer.*

(2) A male lead on a connector.

➧ See also *connector.*

(3) Silicon chips have an array of thin metal feet (pins) on their undersides that enables them to be attached to a circuit board. The pins are very delicate and easily bent. If they are damaged, the chip will not sit correctly and will malfunction.

➧ See also *chip.*

pin feed: Same as *tractor feed.*

pipe: A temporary software connection between two programs or commands. Normally, the operating system accepts input from the keyboard and sends output to the display screen. Sometimes, however, it is useful to use the output from one command as the input for a second command, without passing the data through the keyboard or display screen. Pipes were invented for these situations (Figure 54).

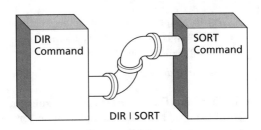

Figure 54
Pipes

One of the best examples of pipe usage is linking the command that lists files in a directory to a command that sorts data. By piping the two commands together, you can display the files in sorted order. In UNIX and DOS, the pipe symbol is a vertical bar (|). The DOS command to list files in alphabetical order, therefore, would be:

```
DIR | SORT
```

➧ See also *input; output.*

piracy: See *software piracy.*

pitch: (1) In word processing, *pitch* refers to the number of characters printed per inch. Pitch is one characteristic of a font. Common pitch values are 10 and 12.

In *fixed-pitch* fonts, every character has the same width. In *proportional-pitch* fonts, different characters have different widths, depending on their size. For example, the letter *d* would be wider than the letter *i*. Proportional-pitch fonts are also called *proportionally spaced* fonts, or simply *proportional fonts*. For proportional fonts, the pitch value is an average.

➧ See also *font; proportional pitch.*

(2) In graphics, *dot pitch* refers to the spacing between pixels on a monitor. The smaller the dot pitch, the sharper the image.

➧ See also *dot pitch; monitor.*

pixel: Short for *Picture Element,* a pixel is a single point in a graphic image. Graphics monitors display pictures by dividing the display screen into millions of pixels, arranged in rows and columns. The pixels are so close together that they appear connected.

The number of bits used to represent each pixel determines how many colors or shades of gray can be displayed. For example, an 8-bit color monitor uses 8 bits for each pixel, making it possible to display 256 different colors or shades of gray.

On color monitors, each pixel is actually composed of three dots—a red, a blue, and a green one. Ideally, the three dots should all converge at the same point, but all monitors have some convergence error that can make color pixels appear fuzzy.

The quality of a display monitor largely depends on its resolution, how many pixels per inch it has. The denser the pixels, the better the image will look. High-resolution monitors utilize over a million pixels.

➡ See also *convergence; graphics; gray scaling; monitor; resolution.*

planar board: IBM refers to the motherboards for its PS/2 computers as *planar boards* to distinguish them from the motherboards for its earlier PCs, which it calls *system boards*. The PS/2 planar boards contain all the functions of the PS/2 system boards and add video circuitry, input and output ports, and floppy disk circuitry.

➡ See also *IBM PC; motherboard; port.*

plasma display: A type of flat-panel display that works by sandwiching an ionized gas between two wired panels. In one panel the wires are placed in vertical rows, and in the other they are placed in horizontal rows. Together, the two panels form a grid. An individual point (pixel) can then be charged by passing a current through the appropriate x-coordinate and y-coordinate wires. When the gas is charged, it glows a bright orange.

➡ See also *flat-panel display; pixel.*

platform: The underlying hardware or software for a system. For example, the platform might be an IBM-compatible PC with an Intel 80386 processor, running DOS Version 4.1. The platform could also be UNIX machines on an Ethernet network.

The platform defines a standard around which a system can be developed. Once the platform has been defined, software developers can produce appropriate software and managers can purchase appropriate hardware and applications.

platter: A round magnetic plate that constitutes part of a hard disk. Hard disks typically contain two, four, or eight platters. Each platter requires two read/write heads, one for each side.

➧ See also *hard disk*.

plot: To produce an image by drawing lines. You can program a computer to plot images on a display screen or on paper.

➧ See also *plotter*.

plotter: A device that draws pictures on paper based on commands from a computer (Figure 55). Plotters differ from printers in that they draw lines using a pen. As a result, they can produce continuous lines, whereas printers can only simulate lines by printing a closely spaced series of dots. Multicolor plotters use different-colored pens to draw different colors.

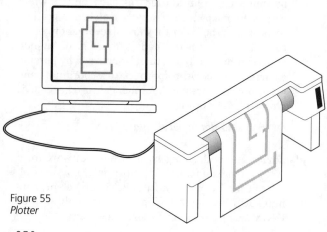

Figure 55
Plotter

In general, plotters are considerably more expensive than printers. They are used in engineering applications where precision is mandatory.

➥ See also *printer*.

plug: A connector used to link together devices.

➥ See also *connector*.

plug compatible: Refers to a device's ability to connect to other devices made by a different manufacturer without any alterations. For example, many companies sell plug-compatible expansion boards for IBM PCs. These are circuit boards that you can insert without modification into an IBM PC to give the computer added capabilities.

➥ See also *compatible; expansion board*.

point: (v) To move the pointer on a display screen in order to select an item. Graphical user interfaces, such as the Macintosh interface, are often called *point-and-click* interfaces because a user typically points to an object on the screen and then clicks a button on the mouse.

➥ See also *graphical user interface; mouse; pointer*.

(n) In typography, a point is about 1/72 of an inch and is used to measure the height of characters. (Technically, a point is .0138 inches, a little less than 1/72 of an inch.) This paragraph, for example, is printed in 9-point type.

The height of the characters is one characteristic of fonts. Some fonts are referred to as *fixed-point fonts* because their representation allows for only one size. In contrast, a *scalable font* is one that is represented in such a way that the size can easily be changed.

➥ See also *font; scalable font*.

pointer: (1) In graphical user interfaces such as the Macintosh and MS-Windows interfaces, a pointer is a small arrow or other symbol on the display screen that moves as you move the mouse. You can select commands and options by positioning the tip of the arrow over the desired choice and clicking a mouse button.

Many text-processing programs use an *I-beam pointer*.

Pointers are often referred to as *mouse pointers*.

➡ See also *graphical user interface; I-beam pointer*.

(2) In programming, a pointer is a special type of variable that holds a memory address (that is, it *points* to a memory location).

➡ See also *address; variable*.

pointing device: A device with which you can control the movement of the pointer to select items on a display screen. Examples of pointing devices include mice, trackballs, joysticks, and light pens.

➡ See also *input device; joystick; light pen; mouse; pointer; trackball*.

polling: Making continuous requests for data from another device. For example, modems that support polling can call another system and request data.

➡ See also *modem*.

pop: Given a stack of items, *popping* one of the items means to pull it off the stack. Although originally coined to describe manipulation of data stacks, the term is often used in connection with display windows. When two or more windows overlap, you can pop one of them so that it is the topmost window.

The opposite of pop is *push*, which means to move an object onto a stack.

➡ See also *pop-up window; push; stack; window*.

pop-up utility: A program installed to be *memory resi-dent* so that you can always execute it by pressing a special key, called a *hot key.* When you press the hot key, the pop-up utility appears, regardless of which application you are currently running. When you exit the pop-up utility, the system returns you to your previous program.

In DOS systems, pop-up utilities are also called *TSRs.* On Macintosh computers, pop-up utilities are known as *desk accessories.*

➡ See also *desk accessory; hot key; memory resi-dent; TSR.*

pop-up window: A window that suddenly appears (pops up) when you select an option with a mouse or press a special function key. Usually, the pop-up window contains a menu of commands and stays on the screen only until you select one of the com-mands. It then disappears.

A special kind of pop-up window is a *pull-down menu,* which appears just below the item you se-lected, as if you had pulled it down.

➡ See also *graphical user interface; pull-down menu; window.*

port: (n) An interface on a computer to which you can connect a peripheral device such as a printer. Per-sonal computers have various types of ports. Inter-nally, there are several ports for connecting disk drives, display screens, and keyboards. Externally, personal computers have ports for connecting modems, printers, mice, and other peripheral de-vices.

Ports can be *serial, parallel,* or *SCSI,* and they can be different sizes (that is, they can have a dif-ferent number and arrangement of pinholes). Al-most all personal computers come with a serial RS-232C port or RS-422 port for connecting a modem or mouse and a parallel port for connecting a printer. On IBM PCs and compatibles, the parallel port is a Centronics interface that uses a 25-pin connector. SCSI (**S**mall **C**omputer **S**ystem Interface) ports support higher transmission speeds than conventional ports and enable you to attach up to seven devices to the same port. All Apple Macintosh computers since the Macintosh Plus have a SCSI port.

➡ See also *Centronics parallel interface; communications; interface; modem; mouse; parallel; parallel port; peripheral device; RS-232C; SCSI; serial; serial port.*

(v) To move a program from one type of computer to another. To port an application, you need to rewrite sections that are machine dependent, and then recompile the program on the new computer. Programs that can be ported easily are said to be *portable.*

➡ See also *compile; machine dependent; portable.*

portable: (1) When used to describe hardware, *portable* means small and lightweight. For example, a portable computer is a computer small enough to carry.

➡ See also *laptop computer; notebook computer; transportable.*

(2) When used to describe software, *portable* means that the software has the ability to run on a variety of computers. *Portable* and *machine independent* mean the same thing—that the software does not depend on a particular type of hardware.

➡ See also *machine independent.*

portrait: In word processing and desktop publishing, the terms *portrait* and *landscape* refer to different orientations of the paper—vertical and horizontal (see Figure 39 at *landscape*). A page with portrait orientation, typical for letters, memos, and other text documents, is taller than it is wide.

Not all printers are capable of generating text in landscape mode.

Orientation is also a characteristic of monitors.

➧ See also *landscape; monitor; printer; word processing*.

PostScript: A **p**age **d**escription **l**anguage (PDL) developed by Adobe Systems. PostScript is primarily a language for printing documents on laser printers, but it can be adapted to produce images on other types of devices.

PostScript is an *object-oriented language*, meaning that it treats images, including fonts, as collections of geometrical objects rather than as bit maps. PostScript fonts are called *outline fonts* because the outline of each character is defined. They are also called *scalable fonts* because their size can be changed with PostScript commands. Given a single typeface definition, a PostScript printer can thus produce a multitude of fonts. In contrast, many printers represent fonts with bit maps. To print a bit-mapped typeface with different sizes, these printers require a complete set of bit maps for each size.

The principal advantage of object-oriented (*vector*) graphics over bit-mapped graphics—aside from scalable fonts—is that object-oriented images take advantage of high-resolution output devices whereas bit-mapped images do not. A PostScript drawing looks much better when printed on a 600 dpi printer than on a 300 dpi printer. A bit-mapped image looks the same on both printers. Another advantage of object-oriented graphics is that the images generally require less memory than bit-mapped images.

PostScript has become one of two de facto standards for laser printers. The other is Hewlett-Packard's **P**rinter **C**ontrol **L**anguage (PCL). Older versions of PCL use bit maps to represent fonts, but starting with version 5, PCL supports a scalable font technology called *Intellifont*.

PostScript is dominant in the Macintosh world, while PCL dominates the IBM PC and compatible market. Nevertheless, most software products (word processors, spreadsheet applications, and database management systems) are capable of generating output for either type of printer.

Every PostScript printer contains a built-in interpreter that executes PostScript instructions. If your laser printer does not come with PostScript support, you may be able to purchase a cartridge that contains PostScript.

➡ See also *bit map; de facto standard; EPS; font; font cartridge; graphics; HP-compatible printer; Intellifont; interpreter; laser printer; Laser-Writer; object oriented; outline font; page description language; PCL; printer; QuickDraw; resolution; scalable font; soft font; typeface; vector graphics.*

power down: To turn a machine off.

power supply: The component that supplies power to a computer. Most personal computers can be plugged into standard electrical outlets. The power supply then pulls the required amount of electricity and converts the AC current to DC current. It also regulates the voltage to eliminate spikes and surges common in most electrical systems. Not all power supplies, however, do an adequate voltage-regulation job, so a computer is always susceptible to large voltage fluctuations.

Power supplies are rated in terms of the number of watts they generate. The more powerful the computer, the more watts it needs. The power supplies for IBM PC/XT computers, for example, supply about 130 watts of power, whereas the power supplies for PC/AT computers provide 200 watts. If you upgrade to a faster CPU or add too many expansion boards, you may need to add a stronger power supply as well.

➡ See also *UPS*.

power up: To turn a machine on.

power user: A sophisticated user of personal computers. A power user is typically someone who has considerable experience with computers and utilizes
the most advanced features of applications.

➡ See also *user*.

ppm: Stands for *pages per minute* and is used to measure the speed of certain types of printers, particularly laser printers. An average speed for laser
printers printing text is 8 ppm.

   Note that the ppm advertised for printers applies only to text. Complex graphics can slow a
printer down considerably. Increasingly, the abbreviation *gppm* is being used for graphics pages
per minute.

➡ See also *laser printer; printer*.

PRAM: See *parameter RAM*.

precision: When used to describe floating-point numbers, *precision* refers to the number of bits used to
hold the fractional part. The more precision a system uses, the more exactly it can represent fractional quantities.

   Floating-point numbers are often classified as
single precision or *double precision*. A double-precision number uses twice as many bits as a single-
precision value, so it can represent fractional
quantities much more exactly.

➡ See also *double precision; floating-point number*.

presentation graphics: A type of business software
that enables users to create highly stylized images
for slide shows and reports. The software includes

functions for creating various types of charts and graphs and for inserting text in a variety of fonts. Most systems enable you to import data from a spreadsheet application to create the charts and graphs.

Presentation graphics is often called *business graphics*.

➧ See also *graphics; spreadsheet.*

Presentation Manager: A windowing program developed by Microsoft Corporation to run under the OS/2 operating system. Presentation Manager is similar to MS-Windows, the windowing product that Microsoft designed for the DOS operating system.

Presentation Manager gives users a graphical user interface similar to the interface on Apple Macintosh computers.

➧ See also *DOS; graphical user interface; OS/2; Microsoft Windows.*

preview: In word processing, *previewing* refers to formatting a document for the printer, but then displaying it on the display screen instead of printing it (see Figure 32 at *greeking*). Previewing allows you to see exactly how the document will appear when printed. If you have a WYSIWYG, previewing is unnecessary because the display screen always resembles the printed version. For word processors that are not WYSIWYGs, however, previewing is the next-best thing. If your word processor does not support previewing, you may be able to buy a separate program that allows you to preview documents.

➧ See also *greeking; thumbnail; word processing; WYSIWYG.*

primary storage: A somewhat dated term for *main memory*. Mass storage devices, such as disk drives and tapes, are sometimes called *secondary storage*.

➠ See also *main memory; mass storage.*

printed circuit board: A thin, rectangular plate on which chips and other electronic components are placed (Figure 56). Computers consist of one or more boards, often called *cards* or *adapters*. Circuit boards fall into the following categories:

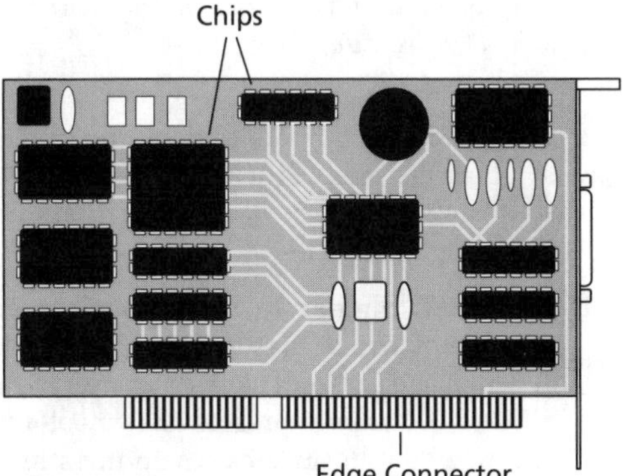

Figure 56
Printed Circuit Board

motherboard: The principal board that has connectors for attaching devices to the bus. Typically, the motherboard contains the CPU, memory, and basic controllers for the system. On IBM PCs, the motherboard is often called the *system board*. IBM calls the motherboards for PS/2 computers *planar boards*.

expansion board: Any board that plugs into one of the computer's expansion slots. Expansion boards include controller boards, LAN cards, and video adapters.

daughterboard: Any board that attaches directly to an expansion board.

controller board: A board that contains a controller for a peripheral device. When you attach new devices, such as a disk drive or graphics monitor, to a computer, you often need to add a controller board.

LAN card: A board that enables a PC to be connected to a local area network (LAN).

video adapter: A board that contains a controller for a graphics monitor.

➡ See also *controller; expansion board; expansion slot; local-area network; motherboard; planar board; video adapter.*

printer: A device that prints text or illustrations on paper. There are many different types of printers. In terms of the technology utilized, printers fall into the following categories:

daisy-wheel: Similar to a ball-head typewriter, this type of printer has a plastic or metal wheel on which the shape of each character stands out in relief. A hammer presses the wheel against a ribbon, which in turn makes an ink stain in the shape of the character on the paper. Daisy-wheel printers produce letter-quality print but cannot print graphics.

dot-matrix: Creates characters by striking pins against an ink ribbon. Each pin makes a dot, and combinations of dots form characters and illustrations.

ink-jet: Sprays ink at a sheet of paper. Ink-jet printers produce high-quality text and graphics.

laser: Uses the same technology as copy machines. Laser printers produce very high-quality text and graphics.

liquid crystal shutter: Similar to a laser printer, but uses liquid crystals rather than a laser to produce an image on the drum.

line printer: Contains a chain of characters or pins that print an entire line at one time. Line printers are very fast, but produce low-quality print.

thermal printer: An inexpensive printer that works by pushing heated pins against heat-sensitive paper. Thermal printers are widely used in calculators and FAX machines.

Printers are also classified by the following characteristics:

quality of type: The output produced by printers is said to be either *letter quality* (as good as a typewriter), *near letter quality,* or *draft quality.* Only daisy-wheel, ink-jet, and laser printers produce letter-quality type. Some dot-matrix printers claim letter-quality print, but if you look closely, you can see the difference.

speed: Measured in characters per second (cps) or pages per minute (ppm), the speed of printers varies widely. Daisy-wheel printers tend to be the slowest, printing about 30 cps. Line printers are fastest (up to 3,000 lines per minute). Dot-matrix printers can print up to 500 cps, and laser printers range from about 4 to 20 text pages per minute.

impact or nonimpact: Impact printers include all printers that work by striking an ink ribbon. Daisy-wheel, dot-matrix, and line printers are impact printers. Nonimpact printers include laser printers and ink-jet printers. The important difference between impact and nonimpact printers is that impact printers are much noisier.

graphics: Some printers (daisy-wheel and line printers) can print only text. Other printers can print both text and graphics.

fonts: Some printers, notably dot-matrix printers, are limited to one or a few fonts. In contrast, laser and ink-jet printers are capable of printing an almost unlimited variety of fonts. Daisy-wheel printers can also print different fonts, but you need to change the daisy wheel, making it difficult to mix fonts in the same document.

381

➠ See also *daisy-wheel printer; dot-matrix printer; draft quality; font; graphics; impact printer; ink-jet printer; laser printer; letter quality; line printer; liquid crystal shutter printer; near letter quality; nonimpact printer; thermal printer.*

printout: A printed version of text or data. Another term for printout is *hardcopy.*

Print Screen key: Often abbreviated *Prt Sc,* the Print Screen key is a useful key supported on many IBM PCs and compatibles. Pressing the Print Screen key causes the computer to send whatever images and text are currently on the display screen to the printer. This is particularly useful for obtaining hardcopies of data that result from DOS commands. For example, the DIR command lists files in a directory. To get a hardcopy of this list, you merely press the Print Screen key.

Note that the Print Screen key is only guaranteed to work with DOS commands. It may be turned off in applications.

➠ See also *hardcopy.*

print server: See under *server.*

print spooling: See under *spooling.*

procedure: (1) Same as *routine, subroutine,* and *function.* A procedure is a section of a program that performs a specific task.

➠ See also *routine.*

(2) An ordered set of tasks for performing some action.

process: (n) An operating system concept that refers to the combination of a program being executed and bookkeeping information used by the operating system. Whenever you execute a program, the operating system creates a new process for it. The process is like an envelope for the program: it identifies the program with a *process number* and attaches other bookkeeping information to it.

Some operating systems, such as UNIX, are capable of running many processes at the same time and are called *multiprocessing* operating systems.

In most operating systems, there is a one-to-one relationship between the process and the program, but some operating systems allow a single process to run more than one program at a time. Such systems are called *multitasking* operating systems.

➧ See also *multiprocessing; multitasking; operating system; program.*

(v) To perform some useful operations on data.

processor: Short for microprocessor or CPU.

➧ See also *CPU; microprocessor.*

program: (n) An organized list of instructions that, when executed, causes the computer to behave in a predetermined manner. Without programs, computers are useless.

A program is like a recipe. It contains a list of ingredients (called *variables*) and a list of directions (called *statements*) that tell the computer what to do with the variables. The variables can represent numeric data, text, or graphical images.

There are many programming languages—C, Pascal, BASIC, FORTRAN, COBOL, and LISP are just a few. These are all *high-level* languages. One can also write programs in *low-level* languages called *assembly languages*, although this is more difficult. Low-level languages are closer to the language used by a computer, while high-level languages are closer to human languages.

Eventually, every program must be translated into a *machine language* that the computer can understand. This translation is performed by *compilers, interpreters,* and *assemblers.*

When you buy software, you normally buy an executable version of a program. This means that the program is already in machine language—it has already been compiled and assembled and is ready to execute.

➧ See also *assembler; assembly language; compiler; executable file; hardware; high-level language; instruction; interpreter; language; low-level language; machine language; programming language; software; statement; variable.*

(v) To write programs.

programmable read-only memory: See *PROM.*

programmer: An individual who writes programs.

➧ See also *program.*

programming language: A vocabulary and set of grammatical rules for instructing a computer to perform specific tasks. The term *programming language* usually refers to *high-level* languages, such as BASIC, C, COBOL, FORTRAN, and Pascal. Each language has a unique set of keywords (words that it understands) and a special syntax for organizing program instructions.

High-level programming languages, while simple compared to human languages, are more complex than the languages the computer actually understands, called *machine languages.* Each different type of CPU has its own unique machine language.

Lying between machine languages and high-level languages are languages called *assembly languages* (Figure 57). Assembly languages are similar to machine languages, but they are much easier to program in because they allow a programmer to

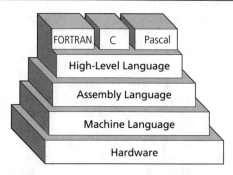

Figure 57
Hierarchy of Programming Languages

substitute names for numbers. Machine languages consist of numbers only.

Lying above high-level languages are languages called *fourth-generation languages* (usually abbreviated *4GL*). 4GLs are far removed from machine languages and represent the class of computer languages closest to human languages.

Regardless of what language you use, eventually you need to convert your program into machine language so that the computer can understand it. There are two ways to do this:

- *compile* the program
- *interpret* the program

See *compile* and *interpreter* for more information about these two methods.

The question of which language is best is one that consumes a lot of time and energy among computer professionals. Every language has its strengths and weaknesses. For example, FORTRAN is a particularly good language for processing numerical data, but it does not lend itself very well to organizing large programs. Pascal is very good for writing well-structured and readable programs, but it is not as flexible as the C programming language.

The choice of which language to use depends on the type of computer the program is to run on, what sort of program it is, and the expertise of the programmer.

➡ See also *assembly language; compiler; fourth-generation language; high-level language; interpreter; language; machine language; object oriented; syntax.*

PROM: Acronym for *programmable read-only memory*. A PROM is a memory chip on which data can be written only once. Once a program has been written onto a PROM, it remains there forever. Unlike main memory, PROMs retain their contents when the computer is turned off.

The difference between a PROM and a ROM (read-only memory) is that a PROM is manufactured as blank memory, whereas a ROM is programmed during the manufacturing process. To write data onto a PROM chip, you need a special device called a *PROM programmer* or *PROM burner*. The process of programming a PROM is sometimes called *burning* the PROM.

An *EPROM* (erasable programmable read-only memory) is a special type of PROM that can be erased by exposing it to ultraviolet light. Once it is erased, it can be reprogrammed.

➡ See also *EPROM; main memory; memory; ROM.*

prompt: A symbol on a display screen indicating that the computer is waiting for input. The symbol used depends on the program that is running. It can be a greater-than sign (>), a colon (:), a backslash (\), or a number of other symbols. Some operating systems allow you to define your own prompt, so you could define it to be, for example, *Good Morning:*.

Once the computer has displayed a prompt, it waits for you to enter some information. Generally, it will wait forever, but some programs have built-in time-outs that cause the program to continue execution after it has waited a specified amount of time.

➧ See also *time-out*.

proportional font: A font in which different characters have different *pitches* (widths). Proportional fonts are also called *proportional-pitch fonts*. The opposite of a proportional font is a *fixed-pitch* font.

➧ See also *font, pitch, proportional pitch*.

proportional pitch: The pitch of a font is determined by how the width of each character is handled. A proportional-pitch font is one in which different characters have different widths; the letter *i*, for example, would be narrower than the letter *q* and the letter *m* wider. This book uses a proportional-pitch font.

The opposite of proportional pitch is *fixed pitch*. In a fixed-pitch font, each character has the same width. Nongraphics display screens display text in a fixed-pitch font. (See Figure 58 for an example of both types of fonts.) Almost all printers, with the

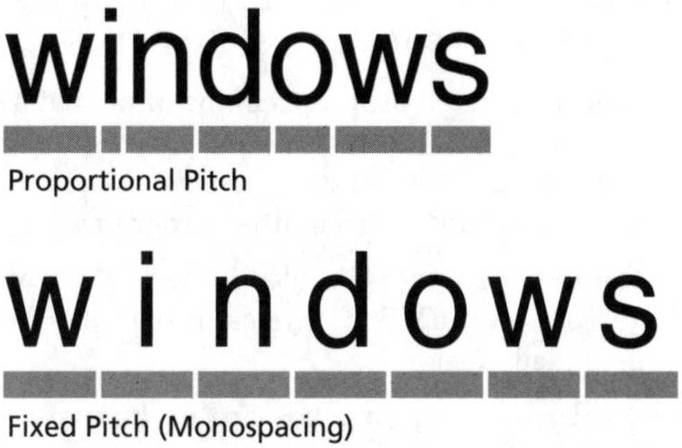

windows

Proportional Pitch

w i n d o w s

Fixed Pitch (Monospacing)

Figure 58
*Proportional-pitch Fonts vs.
Fixed-pitch Fonts*

387

exception of line printers, are able to print with either proportional-pitch or fixed-pitch fonts.

The use of a proportional-pitch font is called *proportional spacing*.

➧ See also *fixed pitch; font; pitch.*

proportional spacing: See under *proportional pitch.*

proprietary: Privately owned and controlled. In the computer industry, *proprietary* is the opposite of *open.* A proprietary design or technique is one that is owned by a company. It also implies that the company has not divulged specifications that would allow other companies to duplicate the product.

Increasingly, proprietary architectures are seen as a disadvantage. Consumers prefer open and standardized architectures, which allow them to mix and match products from different manufacturers.

➧ See also *architecture; open architecture; standard.*

protected mode: A type of memory utilization available on Intel 80286, 80386, and 80486 microprocessors. In protected mode, these processors provide the following features:

protection: Each program can be allocated a certain section of memory. Other programs cannot use this memory, so each program is protected from interference from other programs.

extended memory: Enables a single program to access up to 16MB of physical memory (15MB of extended memory).

virtual memory: Expands the *address space* to over 1GB.

multitasking: Enables the microprocessor to switch from one program to another so the computer can execute several programs at once.

Unfortunately, the DOS operating system is not designed to take advantage of these features. To run programs in protected mode, you need a more sophisticated operating system, such as OS/2 or UNIX, or a DOS operating environment such as Microsoft Windows.

➨ See also *DOS; expanded memory; extended memory; Intel microprocessors; main memory; Microsoft Windows; multitasking; OS/2; UNIX; virtual memory.*

protocol: An agreed-upon format for transmitting data between two devices. The protocol determines the following:

- the type of error checking to be used
- how the sending device will indicate that it has finished sending a message
- how the receiving device will indicate that it has received a message

There are a variety of standard protocols from which programmers can choose. Each has particular advantages and disadvantages; for example, some are simpler than others, some are more reliable, and some are faster.

From a user's point of view, the only interesting aspect about protocols is that your computer or device must support the right ones if you want to communicate with other computers. The protocol can be implemented either in hardware or in software.

➨ See also *communications; communications protocol; modem.*

Prt Sc key: See *Print Screen key.*

PS/2 computer: *PS/2* stands for Personal System/2, IBM's second generation of personal computers. There are many PS/2 models, with model numbers ranging from 25 to 95 (Table 24). One of the chief

Table 24: IBM PS/2 Models

MODEL	PROCESSOR	GRAPHICS	BUS
25	8086	MCGA	AT
30-286	80286	VGA	AT
50Z	80286	VGA	MCA
55SX	80386SX	VGA	MCA
65SX	80386SX	VGA	MCA
70-386	80386	VGA	MCA
70-486	80486	VGA	MCA
80	80386	VGA	MCA
90	80486	XGA	MCA
95	80486	XGA	MCA

differences between the PS/2 computers and the first-generation machines (PC, XT, and AT) is that most of the PS/2 models come with built-in VGA graphics. However, you can add VGA to first-generation machines by inserting an add-on board.

➡ See also *AT bus; IBM PC; Intel microprocessors; Micro Channel architecture; microprocessor; VGA; video adapter.*

public carrier: A government-regulated organization that provides telecommunication services to the public. This includes AT&T, MCI, and Western Union. Most public carriers provide *electronic-mail* services that enable you to send messages and documents over a telephone line to other computer users.

➡ See also *electronic mail.*

public-domain software: Refers to any program that is not copyrighted. Public-domain software is free and can be used without restrictions. The term *public-domain software* is often used incorrectly to include *shareware*, inexpensive software that is nevertheless copyrighted.

➡ See also *shareware*.

pull-down menu: A menu of commands or options that appears when you select an item with a mouse. The item you select is generally at the top of the display screen, and the menu appears just below it, as if you had pulled it down. Typically, the menu lasts only as long as you keep the mouse button pressed.

➡ See also *command; menu; option; pop-up window*.

punctuation: Like punctuation in human languages, punctuation in programming languages serves to separate words and phrases. But unlike human punctuation, which is often optional, computer punctuation is strictly required.

push: In programming, *push* means to place a data item onto a stack. The opposite of push is *pop,* which means to remove an object from a stack.

➡ See also *pop; stack*.

QBE: See *query by example*.

QIC: The abbreviation for *quarter-inch cartridge.* QIC tapes are among the most popular tapes used for backing up personal computers. There are many different types of QIC tapes, as shown in Table 25. They are divided into two general classes: full-size and minicartridge. The full-size cartridges are often referred to as *DC 6000* cartridges, and minicartridges are called *DC 2000* cartridges.

Table 25: QIC Standards

QIC TYPE	CAPACITY	CARTRIDGE SIZE
QIC-24	60MB	Full
QIC-40	40MB	Mini
QIC-80	80MB 120MB	Mini
QIC-100	20MB 40MB	Mini
QIC-120	125MB	Full
QIC-128	86MB 128MB	Mini
QIC-150	150MB 250MB	Full
QIC-380	380MB	Mini
QIC-525	320MB 525MB	Full
QIC-1000	1.01GB	Full
QIC-1350	1.35GB	Full
QIC-2000	2GB	Mini

The QIC-40 and QIC-80 standards are sometimes referred to as *floppy tape* standards because they are designed to use a personal computer's existing floppy disk drive controller instead of requiring a customized controller.

The various QIC standards are controlled by a consortium of manufacturers called Quarter-Inch Cartridge Drive Standards, Inc. The term *QIC*, therefore, is used to refer both to the type of tape and to the standards-producing organization.

➡ See also *mass storage; tape.*

quarter-inch cartridge: See *QIC.*

query: (n) A request for information from a database. There are three general methods for posing queries:

choosing parameters from a menu: In this method, the database system presents a list of parameters from which you can choose. This is perhaps the easiest way to pose a query because the menus guide you, but it is also the least flexible.

query by example (QBE): In this method, the system presents a blank record and lets you specify the fields and values that define the query.

query language: Many database systems require you to make requests for information in the form of a stylized query that must be written in a special *query language*. This is the most complex method because it forces you to learn a specialized language, but it is also the most powerful.

➧ See also *database management system; field; menu; query language; query by example; record.*

(v) To make a request for information from a database.

query by example: In database management systems, *query by example* (QBE) refers to a method of forming queries in which the database program displays a blank record with a space for each field. You can then enter conditions for each field that you want to be included in the query. For example, if you wanted to find all records where the AGE field is greater than 65, you would enter *65* in the AGE field blank.

QBE systems are considered easier to learn than formal query languages.

➧ See also *database management system; field; query language; query; record.*

query language: A specialized language for requesting information from a database. For example, the query

> SELECT ALL WHERE age > 30 AND name =
> "Smith"

requests all records in which the name-field is
"Smith" and the AGE field has a value greater than
30. The de facto standard for query languages is
SQL, although few database systems for personal
computers support a full-scale SQL. PC database
systems that do support SQL are often able to translate the query given in their own language into an
SQL query. This enables them to communicate with
other types of databases.

➡ See also *database management system; query;
SQL*.

queue: (v) To line up. In computer science, *queuing*
refers to lining up jobs for a computer or device. For
example, if you want to print a number of documents, the operating system (or a special print
spooler) queues the documents by placing them in a
special area called a *buffer* or *queue*. The printer
then pulls the documents off the queue one at a
time. Another term for this is *print spooling*.

The order in which a system executes jobs on a
queue depends on the priority system being used.
Most commonly, jobs are executed in the same
order that they were placed on the queue, but in
some schemes certain jobs are given higher priority.

➡ See also *buffer; job; operating system; spooling*.

(n) (1) A group of jobs waiting to be executed.
(2) In programming, a queue is a data structure
in which elements are removed in the same order
they were entered. This is often referred to as FIFO
(first in, first out). In contrast, a *stack* is a data
structure in which elements are removed in the reverse order from which they were entered. This is
referred to as LIFO (last in, first out).

➥ See also *data structure; stack.*

QuickDraw: The underlying graphics display system for Apple Macintosh computers. The QuickDraw system enables programs to create and manipulate graphical objects. Because all Macintosh programs use QuickDraw, they all share a common look.

There are several versions of QuickDraw that offer different color capabilities. The different versions are often distinguished by the number of bits they use to represent each pixel. For example, 32-bit QuickDraw uses 32 bits for each pixel.

QuickDraw is currently used primarily for displaying images on monitors, but some printers use it as well. In general, QuickDraw printers do not offer as many fonts as PostScript printers, but Apple has announced plans to enhance QuickDraw by adding scalable fonts.

➥ See also *graphics; Macintosh computer; pixel; PostScript; scalable font.*

QWERTY keyboard: Refers to the arrangement of keys on a standard English computer keyboard or typewriter. The name derives from the first six characters on the top alphabetic line of the keyboard.

The arrangement of characters on a QWERTY keyboard was designed over one hundred years ago to prevent jamming on mechanical typewriters by separating commonly used letter combinations. The arrangement does not lend itself, therefore, to fast typing.

With the emergence of ball-head electric typewriters and computer keyboards, on which jamming is not an issue, new keyboards designed for speed typing have been invented. The best-known is called a *Dvorak keyboard.* Despite their more rational designs, these new keyboards have not received wide acceptance.

➥ See also *Dvorak keyboard; keyboard.*

radio buttons: In graphical user interfaces, radio buttons are groups of buttons, of which only one can be on at a time. When you select one button, all the others are automatically deselected.

➡ See also *button; graphical user interface; select.*

ragged: In text processing, *ragged* means not aligned along a margin. The opposite of ragged is *flush* or *justified*. For example, the following text has a ragged right margin:

```
This  text  is  printed  with  a
ragged  right  margin.  Each  line
ends   at   a   different   spot.
```

Most word processors allow you to choose between ragged and justified margins. In general, ragged margins look more like print produced by a typewriter, while justified margins look more like print produced by a typesetter (for example, most books, magazines, and newspapers use justified margins). However, justified text looks good only if your word processor and printer are capable of printing proportionally spaced text.

➡ See also *flush; font; justify; proportional pitch.*

RAM: Acronym for *random access memory*, a type of computer memory that can be accessed randomly; that is, any byte of memory can be accessed without touching the preceding bytes. RAM is the most common type of memory found in computers and other devices, such as printers.

There are two basic types of RAM:

- *dynamic RAM*
- *static RAM*

The two types differ in the technology they use to hold data, dynamic RAM being the more common type. Dynamic RAM needs to be refreshed thousands of times per second. Static RAM needs to be refreshed less often, which makes it faster; but it is also more expensive than dynamic RAM. Both types of RAM are *volatile,* meaning that they lose their contents when the power is turned off.

In common usage, the term *RAM* is synonymous with *main memory*, the memory available to programs. For example, a computer with 640K RAM has approximately 640,000 bytes of memory that programs can use. In contrast, *ROM* (read-only memory) refers to special memory used to store programs that boot the computer and perform diagnostics. Most personal computers have a small amount of ROM (a few K bytes). In fact, both types of memory (ROM and RAM) allow random access. To be precise, therefore, RAM should be referred to as *read-write RAM* and *read-only RAM*.

➡ See also *boot; K; main memory; memory; ROM; static memory; VRAM.*

RAM cache: (1) Same as *cache memory.*

➡ See also *cache.*

(2) On Apple Macintosh computers, the term *RAM cache* refers to a *disk cache.*

➡ See also *disk cache.*

RAM disk: Refers to RAM that has been configured to simulate a disk drive. You can access files on a RAM disk as you would access files on a real disk. RAM disks, however, are approximately a thousand times faster than hard disk drives. They are particularly useful, therefore, for applications that require frequent disk accesses.

Because they are made of normal RAM, RAM disks lose their contents once the computer is turned off. To use a RAM disk, therefore, you need to copy files from a real hard disk at the beginning of the session and then copy the files back to the hard disk before you turn the computer off. Note that if there is a power failure, you will lose whatever data is on the RAM disk. (Some RAM disks come with a battery backup to make them more stable.)

The DOS operating system enables you to convert extended memory into a RAM disk with the VDISK command. VDISK stands for *virtual disk*, another name for RAM disks.

➡ See also *disk; extended memory; RAM.*

RAM resident: Same as *memory resident.*

random access: Refers to the ability to access data at random. The opposite of *random access* is *sequential access.* To go from point A to point Z in a sequential-access system, you must pass through all intervening points. In a random-access system, you can jump directly to point Z (Figure 59).

The terms *random access* and *sequential access* are often used to describe data files. A random-ac

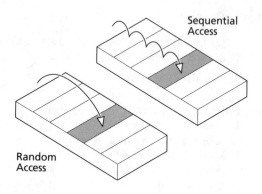

Figure 59
Random Access vs. Sequential Access

cess data file enables you to read or write information anywhere in the file. In a sequential-access file, you can only read and write information sequentially, starting from the beginning of the file.

Both types of files have advantages and disadvantages. If you are always accessing information in the same order, a sequential-access file is faster. If you tend to access information randomly, random access is better.

Random access is sometimes called *direct access*.

➡ See also *access; sequential access.*

random-access memory: See *RAM.*

range: In spreadsheet applications, a range is one or more contiguous cells. For example, a range could be an entire row or column, or multiple rows or columns. The only restrictions on ranges is that all the cells of the range must be contiguous and the entire range must be rectangular in shape; that is, you cannot have a range consisting of three cells in one column and four cells in the next.

Once you have defined a range, you can perform functions on it. This is a powerful feature because it allows you to manipulate a set of cells with one expression.

➡ See also *cell; expression; function; spreadsheet.*

raster graphics: Refers to hardware and software that represent graphics images as bit maps (see Figure 9 at *bit map*). The other method for representing images is known as *vector graphics.*

➡ See also *bit map; graphics; vector graphics.*

RDBMS: Short for *relational database management system.*

➡ See also *database management system; relational database.*

read: (v) To copy data from a storage medium, such as a disk, to main memory, where it can be utilized by a program.

(n) The act of reading. For example, *a fast disk drive performs 100 reads per second.*

readme file: A small text file that comes with many software packages and contains information not included in the official documentation. Typically, readme files describe how to install the software and print the documentation, and they often contain a list of known bugs. If you see a readme file, you should read it. It may save you a lot of headaches.

read-only memory: See *ROM*.

read/write head: See *head*.

real address: Same as *absolute address*.

real mode: An execution mode supported by the Intel 80286, 80386, and 80486 processors. In real mode, these processors imitate the Intel 8088 and 8086 microprocessors, although they run much faster. The other mode available on the 80286, 80386, and 80486 is called *protected mode*. In protected mode, programs can access extended memory and virtual memory. Protected mode also supports multitasking. The 80386 and 80486 microprocessors support a third mode called *virtual 8086 mode*. In virtual mode, these microprocessors can run several real-mode programs at once.

The DOS operating system was not designed to take advantage of protected mode, so it always executes programs in real mode. OS/2 and Microsoft Windows 3.0, however, can run in either real mode or protected mode. Only machines equipped with an 80386 or 80486 microprocessor can run two programs at once in different modes.

➡ See also *DOS; extended memory; Intel micro-processors; Microsoft Windows; multitasking; OS/2; protected mode; virtual memory.*

real time: Occurring immediately. The term is used to describe a number of different computer features. For example, real-time operating systems are systems that respond to input immediately. They are used for such tasks as navigation, in which the computer must react to a steady flow of new information without interruption. Most general-purpose operating systems are not real-time because they can take a few seconds, or even minutes, to react.

Real time can also refer to events simulated by a computer at the same speed that they would occur in real life. In graphics animation, for example, a real-time program would display objects moving across the screen at the same speed that they would actually move.

➡ See also *operating system.*

real-time clock: A clock that keeps track of the time even when the computer is turned off. Real-time clocks run on a special battery that is not connected to the normal power supply. In contrast, clocks that are not real-time do not function when the computer is off.

Do not confuse a computer's real-time clock with its CPU clock. The CPU clock regulates the execution of instructions.

➡ See *clock speed, CPU.*

reboot: To restart a computer.

➡ See also *boot.*

recalculate: In spreadsheet programs, *recalculation* refers to computing the values of cells in a spreadsheet. Recalculation is necessary whenever you change a formula or enter new data into one or more cells. Depending on the size and complexity of your spreadsheet, recalculation can be a time-consuming process. One criterion for evaluating spreadsheet programs, therefore, is how fast they recalculate.

To make recalculation faster, many spreadsheet programs support *minimal recalculation* (also called *optimal recalculation*), in which the program calculates only the values of cells that will change. In addition, some spreadsheets support *background recalculation*, which allows you to perform other operations while a recalculation is in progress.

➥ See also *background; cell; formula; spreadsheet.*

record: (1) In database management systems, a complete set of information. Records are composed of *fields,* each of which contains one item of information. A set of records constitutes a *file.* For example, a personnel file might contain records that have three fields: a name field, an address field, and a phone-number field (see Figure 19 at *database*).

➥ See also *database management system; field; file.*

(2) Some programming languages allow you to define a special data structure called a record. Generally, a record is a combination of other data objects. For example, a record might contain three integers, a floating-point number, and a character string.

➥ See also *data structure; data type.*

record locking: See under *lock.*

red-green-blue monitor: See *RGB monitor.*

redirection: In operating system shells, *redirection* refers to directing input and output to files and devices other than the default I/O devices. By default, input generally comes from the keyboard or mouse, and output goes to the display monitor. With a redirection operator, you can override these defaults so that a command or program takes input from some other device and sends output to a different device.

In DOS and UNIX systems, the redirection operators are < for input and > for output. For example, the DOS command

```
sort < c:\list > c:\sorted
```

takes input from a file called *list*, sorts it, and sends output to a file called *sorted*.

➡ See also *default; device; DOS; file; I/O; operating system; operator; shell; UNIX.*

redlining: In word processing, *redlining* refers to marking text that has been edited. Typically, redlining is used when two or more people are producing a document; each individual can *redline* the text he or she has added or edited. The redlined text will then appear in a special color (or as bold) so that others can see the changes that have been made.

Many word processors offer an automatic redlining feature, enabling the word processor to compare two documents and redline the differences. This allows you to edit a document and then add the redlining marks when you are finished.

➡ See also *word processing.*

reduced instruction set computer: See *RISC.*

refresh: To recharge a device with power or information. For example, *dynamic RAM* needs to be refreshed thousands of times per second or it will lose the data stored in it.

Similarly, display monitors must be refreshed many times per second. The refresh rate for a monitor is measured in hertz (Hz) and is also called the *vertical frequency.* The old standard for monitor refresh rates was 60Hz, but a new standard developed by VESA sets the refresh rate at 72Hz for VGA and Super VGA.

➡ See also *dynamic RAM; interlacing; monitor; SVGA; VESA; VGA; XGA.*

register: A storage area within the CPU. All data must be represented in a register before it can be processed. For example, if two numbers are to be multiplied, both numbers must be in registers, and the result is also placed in a register. (The register can contain the address of a memory location where data is stored rather than the actual data itself.)

The number of registers that a CPU has and the size of each (number of bits) help determine the power and speed of a CPU. For example, a 32-bit CPU is one in which each register is 32 bits wide. Therefore, each CPU instruction can manipulate 32 bits of data.

Usually, the movement of data in and out of registers is completely transparent to users, and even to programmers. Only assembly language programs can manipulate registers. In high-level languages, the compiler is responsible for translating high-level operations into low-level operations that access registers.

➡ See also *compiler; CPU; microprocessor.*

relational database: A type of database that stores data in the form of a table. Relational databases are powerful because they require few assumptions about how data is related or how it will be extracted from the database. As a result, the same database can be viewed in many different ways.

Another feature of relational systems is that a single database can be spread across several files. This differs from *flat-file databases,* in which each database is self-contained in a single file. Relational databases are more suitable for large applications.

Almost all full-scale database systems for personal computers use a relational database. Small database systems, however, use other designs that provide less flexibility in posing queries.

➡ See also *database management system; flat-file database; query.*

relational expression: See under *relational operator.*

relational operator: An operator that compares two values. Table 26 lists the most common relational operators.

Table 26: Relational Operators

SYMBOL	MNEMONIC	MEANING
=	EQ	Equal to
< > (or !=)	NE	Not equal to
>	GT	Greater than
> =	GE	Greater than or equal to
<	LT	Less than
< =	LE	Less than or equal to

For example, the expression

$$x < 5$$

means *x is less than 5.* This expression will have a value of TRUE if the variable x is less than 5; otherwise the value of the expression will be FALSE.

Relational operators are sometimes called *comparison operators.* Expressions that contain relational operators are called *relational expressions.*

➡ See also *Boolean logic; expression; operator.*

relative address: An address specified by indicating its distance from another address, called the *base address.* For example, a relative address might be $B + 15$, B being the base address and 15 the distance (called the *offset*).

There are two types of addressing: *relative addressing* and *absolute addressing*. In absolute addressing, you specify the actual address (called the *absolute address*) of a memory location (see Figure 1 at *address*).

Relative and absolute addressing are used in a variety of circumstances. In programming, you can use either mode to identify locations in main memory or on mass storage devices. In spreadsheet applications, you can use either mode to designate a particular *cell*.

➡ See also *absolute address; address; base address; cell; memory; offset.*

remote: In networks, *remote* refers to files, devices, and other resources that are not connected directly to your workstation. Resources at your workstation are considered local.

➡ See also *local-area network; local; network; workstation.*

remote control: Refers to a program's ability to access a computer system from a remote location. Remote-control programs for PCs enable you to access data stored on your home system even when you are traveling.

➡ See also *host; local; remote.*

removable cartridge: A type of disk drive system in which hard disks are enclosed in plastic or metal cartridges so that they can be removed like floppy disks. Removable cartridges combine the best aspects of hard and floppy disks. They are as fast as hard disks—often faster—and have the portability of floppy disks. The storage capacity of a typical removable cartridge can range from 20MB to 150MB, much more than the capacity of floppy disks.

A mass storage system similar to removable cartridges is *removable hard disks*. The only difference is that the mechanisms for spinning the disk are enclosed in the cartridge. The principal advantage of removable hard disks over removable cartridges is that removable hard disks are somewhat faster.

➡ See also *cartridge; disk; hard disk; mass storage*.

removable hard disk: See under *removable cartridge*.

report generator: Same as *report writer*.

report writer: A program, usually part of a database management system, that extracts information from one or more files and presents the information in a specified format. Most report writers allow you to select records that meet certain conditions and to display selected fields in rows and columns. You can also format data into pie charts, bar charts, and other diagrams. Once you have created a format for a report, you can save the format specifications in a file and continue reusing it for new data.

The report writer is one of the most important components of a database management system because it determines how much flexibility you have in outputting data.

➡ See also *database management system; field; record*.

reserved word: A special word reserved by a programming language or by a program. You are not allowed to use reserved words as variable names. For example, in BASIC and COBOL, the word *IF* is reserved because it has a special meaning.

Reserved words are sometimes called *keywords*.

➡ See also *keyword; variable*.

reset button: A button or switch on many computers that allows you to reset the computer without turning the power off, then on again. When you press the reset button, the computer will enter its start-up procedure as if you had turned the power off and then on again. Generally, you would use the reset button only when a program error has caused your computer to *hang*.

Note that on IBM PCs and compatibles, pressing the reset button is somewhat different from performing a warm reboot by pressing the Ctrl-Alt-Del reboot keys. When you perform a warm reboot, the system does not repeat the initial start-up stages during which memory is checked.

➡ See also *boot; hang; reboot.*

resident: (1) See *memory resident.*
(2) See *resident font.*

resident font: Also called an *internal font* or *built-in font,* a resident font is a font built into the hardware of a printer. All dot-matrix and laser printers come with one or more resident fonts. You can add additional fonts by inserting font cartridges or downloading soft fonts.

➡ See also *download; font; font cartridge; printer; soft font.*

resize: See under *size.*

resolution: Refers to the sharpness and clarity of an image. The term is most often used to describe monitors and printers. In the case of dot-matrix and laser printers, the resolution indicates the number of dots per inch. For example, a 300 dpi printer is one that is capable of printing 300 distinct dots in a line 1 inch long. This means it can print 90,000 dots per square inch.

For graphics monitors, the resolution signifies the number of dots (pixels) on the entire screen. For example, a 640-by-480 pixel screen is capable of displaying 640 distinct dots on each of 480 lines, or about 3 million pixels.

Printers and monitors are often classified as *high resolution,* *medium resolution,* or *low resolution* (Figure 60). The actual resolution ranges for each of these grades is constantly shifting as the technology improves.

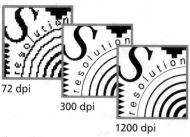

Figure 60
Resolution

➡ See also *dots per inch; monitor; pixel; printer; video adapter.*

restore: In graphical user interfaces, to *restore* means to return a window to its original size.

➡ See also *graphical user interface; size; window; zoom.*

return: A *return* is a special code that causes a word processor or other application to advance to the beginning of the next line. A *soft return* is a return that the application inserts automatically when you reach the end of a line. A *hard return* is a return that you explicitly enter by pressing the Return or Enter key.

➡ See also *hard return; Return key; soft return.*

Return key: Almost all computer keyboards have a key marked *Return* or *Enter;* the two names are synonymous. The Return key moves the cursor (or insertion point) to the beginning of the next line. But more important, it returns control to whatever program is currently running. After a program requests information from you (by displaying a prompt), it will usually not respond to your input until you have pressed the Return key. This allows you to correct typing mistakes or to reconsider your entry before it is too late. In many applications, pressing the Return key moves the cursor to the next field.

In word-processing programs, pressing the Return key inserts a hard return into a document.

In technical documentation, the Return key is often signified by a ⏎.

➡ See also *cursor; hard return; insertion point; keyboard; prompt.*

reverse video: A display method that causes a portion of the display to appear like a negative of the regular display. If the display screen normally displays light images against a dark background, putting it in *reverse video mode* will cause it to display dark images against a light background.

Many programs use reverse video to highlight items, such as selected menu lines. Also, some systems allow you to change the mode for all displays, so you can choose the display that is most comfortable for you. Some people prefer dark images on a light background, while others prefer light images on a dark background.

➡ See also *background; display screen; foreground.*

RGB monitor: Stands for *red, green, blue.* An RGB monitor is one that requires separate signals for each of the three colors. This differs from color televisions, for example, which use composite video signals, in which all the colors are mixed together.

In general, RGB monitors produce sharper images than composite monitors.

An RGB monitor consists of a vacuum tube with three electron guns—one each for red, green, and blue—at one end and the screen at the other end. The three electron guns fire electrons at the screen, which contains a phosphorous coating. When the phosphors are excited by the electron beams, they glow, creating a display.

Older RGB monitors have a refresh rate of 60Hz (they refresh the display 60 times per second). New monitors have a refresh rate of 72Hz, which reduces flickering. RGB monitors can accept either *analog* or *digital* input.

➧ See also *composite video; monitor.*

right justify: See under *justify.*

ring network: See *token-ring network.*

RISC: Acronym for *reduced instruction set computer*, a type of computer that utilizes an architecture in which the CPU recognizes a relatively limited number of instructions. Until the mid-1980s, the tendency among computer manufacturers was to build increasingly complex CPUs that had ever-larger sets of instructions. At that time, however, a number of computer manufacturers decided to reverse this trend by building CPUs capable of executing only a very limited set of instructions. The advantage of reduced instruction set computers is that they can execute their instructions very fast because the instructions are so simple. The disadvantage is that RISC computers sometimes require two or more instructions to perform an operation that can be performed by a single instruction on a more conventional computer. Since the emergence of RISC computers, conventional computers have been referred to as *CISCs (complex instruction set computers).*

There is still considerable controversy among experts about the ultimate value of RISC architectures. Its proponents argue that RISC machines are both cheaper and faster, and are therefore the machines of the future. Skeptics note that by making the hardware simpler, RISC architectures put a greater burden on the software. They argue that this is not worth the trouble because conventional microprocessors are becoming increasingly fast and cheap anyway.

To some extent, the argument is becoming moot because CISC and RISC implementations are becoming more and more alike. Today's RISC chips support as many instructions as yesterday's CISC chips.

➡ See also *CPU; instruction; microprocessor; workstation.*

RLL: Abbreviation of *run length limited*, an encoding scheme used to store data on some IBM PC hard disks. Although RLL produces fast data access times and increases a disk's storage capacity, it is not as prevalent as another encoding scheme called *MFM (modified frequency modulation)*.

Technically, any disk drive can use either encoding method. The one used depends on the disk controller.

➡ See also *controller; disk drive; MFM.*

robotics: The field of computer science concerned with creating robots, devices that can move and react to sensory input. Robotics is one branch of *artificial intelligence*.

Robots are now widely used in factories to perform high-precision jobs such as welding and riveting. They are also used in special situations that would be dangerous for humans—for example, in cleaning toxic wastes or defusing bombs.

Although great advances have been made in the field of robotics during last decade, robots are still not very useful in everyday life, as they are too clumsy to perform ordinary household chores.

➡ See also *artificial intelligence*.

ROM: Acronym for *read-only memory*, computer memory on which data has been prerecorded. Once data has been written onto a ROM chip, it cannot be removed and can only be read.

Unlike main memory (RAM), ROM retains its contents even when the computer is turned off. ROM is referred to as being *nonvolatile*, whereas RAM is *volatile*.

Most personal computers contain a small amount of ROM that stores critical programs such as the program that boots the computer. In addition, ROMs are used extensively in calculators and peripheral devices such as laser printers, whose fonts are often stored in ROMs.

A variation of a ROM is a *PROM (programmable read-only memory)*. Unlike ROMs, you can buy blank PROMs and write data onto them yourself, assuming that you have a special device called a *PROM programmer*.

➡ See *boot, memory, PROM, RAM*.

roman: In typography, *roman* refers to fonts with characters that are straight up and down rather than slanted. A font designed with characters slanted to the right is *italic*.

➡ See also *font; italic*.

ROM-BIOS: See *BIOS*.

root directory: The top directory in a file system (see Figure 24 at *directory*). The root directory is provided by the operating system and has a special name; for example, in DOS systems the root directory is called \. The root directory is sometimes referred to simply as the *root*.

➶ See also *directory; file management.*

routine: A section of a program that performs a particular task. Programs consist of *modules,* each of which contains one or more routines. The term *routine* is synonymous with *procedure, function,* and *subroutine.*

➶ See also *module; program.*

RS-232C: A standard interface approved by the Electronics Industry Association (EIA) for connecting serial devices (see Figure 17 at *connector*). Almost all modems conform to the RS-232C standard and most personal computers have an RS-232C *port* for connecting a modem or other device. In addition to modems, many display screens, mice, and serial printers are designed to connect to an RS-232C *port.*

The RS-232C standard supports two types of connectors—a 25-pin D-type connector (DB-25) and a 9-pin D-type connector (DB-9). The type of serial communications used by PCs requires only 9 pins so either type of connector will work equally well.

Although RS-232C is still the most common standard for serial communication, the EIA has recently defined successors to RS-232C called *RS-422* and *RS-423.* The new standards are backward compatible so that RS-232 devices can connect to an RS-422 port.

In 1987, the EIA upgraded and changed the name of RS-232C. The new name is EIA-232D, but the standard is generally still referred to by its old name.

➶ See also *serial; backward compatible; communications; connector; interface; modem; port; protocol; RS-422 and 423; serial; standard.*

RS-422 and 423: Standard interfaces approved by the Electronics Industry Association (EIA) for connecting serial devices. The RS-422 and RS-423 standards are designed to replace the older RS-232C standard because they support higher data rates and greater immunity to electrical interference. All Apple Macintosh computers contain an RS-422 port that can also be used for RS-232C communication.

➡ See also *communications; connector; interface; modem; port; protocol; RS-232C; standard.*

rule: (1) In word processing, a rule is a straight line that separates columns of text or illustrations.

(2) In expert systems, a rule is a conditional statement that tells the system how to react to a particular situation.

➡ See also *expert system.*

ruler: In word processing, a ruler is a line running across the display screen (Figure 61). It measures

Ruler

Figure 61
Ruler

the page layout in points, picas, or inches. It is sometimes called the *ruler line* and is particularly useful for setting margins and tabs. Sophisticated desktop publishing systems and page layout programs sometimes support *movable rulers* that you can move around the display screen to measure particular items of text or graphics.

➡ See also *desktop publishing; margins; page layout program; pica; point; word processing.*

run: To execute a program.

run length limited: See *RLL.*

runtime error: An error that occurs during the execution of a program. In contrast, *compile-time* errors occur while a program is being compiled. Runtime errors indicate bugs in the program or problems that the designers had anticipated but could do nothing about. For example, running out of memory will often cause a runtime error.

Note that runtime errors differ from bombs or crashes in that you can often recover gracefully from a runtime error.

➡ See also *bug; compiler; crash; bomb.*

runtime version: A version of a program that has been bundled in with another application. For example, many Microsoft Windows–based applications come with a runtime version of Windows. This is not the full-featured version of Windows that you would buy as a separate product, but rather an abbreviated version that contains enough features to let you run the application. If you have the full version of Windows, or of some other program, you do not need the runtime version.

➡ See also *application; Microsoft Windows; program.*

sans serif: Refers to a category of typefaces that do not use *serifs,* small lines at the ends of characters. Popular sans serif fonts include Helvetica, Avant Garde, and Geneva. Serif fonts include Times Roman, Courier, New Century Schoolbook, and Palatino (see Figure 73 at *typeface*).

➡ See also *font.*

save: In word processing, *save* means to copy a file from a temporary area to a more permanent storage medium. When you edit a file on a computer, the word processor copies the entire file, or portions of the file, into an area of main memory called a *buffer.* Any changes you make to the file are made to the copy in the buffer, not to the real file on the disk. The buffer is temporary—as soon as you exit the program or turn off the computer, the buffer disappears. To record your modifications to the file on the disk, you must save the file. When you do this, the word processor copies the contents of the buffer back to the file on the disk, replacing the previous version of the file.

Because computers can break down at any moment, it is a good idea to save your files periodically. Otherwise, you will lose all the work you have accomplished during an editing session. Many word processors automatically save files at regular intervals, which can be specified by the user, for example, every half hour. These intermediate saves are sometimes called *snapshots.*

The same principles of saving files with a word processor apply to other applications, such as database management and spreadsheet applications.

➡ See also *buffer; file; word processor.*

scalable font: A font represented in an object-oriented graphics language such as PostScript. Such fonts are called *scalable* because the representation of the font defines the shape of each character (the typeface) but not the size. Given a typeface definition, a scalable-font system can produce characters at any size (or *scale*).

Aside from offering innumerable sizes of each font, scalable fonts have the added advantage in that they make the most of an output device's resolution. The more resolution a printer or monitor has, the better a scalable font will look. A major disadvantage of scalable fonts is that they take longer to print because the printer must convert the geometrical definition of each character into a bit map that it can print.

Scalable fonts are often called *outline fonts* because the most common method of representing scalable fonts is to define the outline of each character. Scalable fonts are also called *object-oriented fonts* or *vector fonts*.

➡ See also *font; object oriented; outline font; PostScript; typeface; vector graphics.*

scale: To change the size of an object while maintaining its shape. Most graphics software, particularly vector-based packages, allow you to scale objects freely.

Another word for *scale* is *resize*.

➡ See also *graphics; scalable font; vector graphics.*

scanner: See *optical scanner.*

scheduler: (1) A software product designed to help a group of colleagues schedule meetings and other appointments. The scheduler program allows members of a group to view each others' calendars so that they can choose a convenient time. Once a time has been selected, the scheduler can automatically send out reminders through electronic mail and can even reserve resources such as conference rooms and overhead projectors.

Most schedulers come as part of an electronic mail system.

➧ See also *electronic mail*.

(2) In operating systems, a scheduler is a program that coordinates the use of shared resources, such as a printer.

➧ See also *operating system*.

scientific notation: A format for representing real (floating-point) numbers. Instead of writing the full number, scientific notation represents values as a number between 1 and 10 multiplied by 10 to some power. In the notation, the 10 is replaced by an uppercase or lowercase *E*. Table 27 shows some examples.

Table 27: Scientific Notation

NUMBER IN NORMAL NOTATION	IN SCIENTIFIC NOTATION
34,567.0	3.4567E4
0.0004	4.0E-4
1,000,000,000.0	1.0E9
-37.456	-3.7456E2
-0.00349	-3.49E-3

Scientific notation is much simpler for very large and very small numbers, such as the second and third example. Most programming languages, and many numeric applications, allow you to enter and display numbers using scientific notation.

➧ See also *floating-point number*.

screen: See *display screen*.

screen capture: Refers to the act of copying what is currently displayed on a screen to a file or printer. If the system is in graphics mode, the screen capture will result in a graphics file containing a bit map of the image. If the system is in text mode, the screen capture will normally load a file with ASCII codes.

➯ See also *ASCII; bit map; graphics mode; screen dump; text mode.*

screen dump: Refers to the act of copying what is currently on a display screen to a printer. IBM PCs and compatible computers have a key on the keyboard labeled *Prt Sc,* which stands for *Print Screen.* Not all applications, however, support this key.

➯ See also *dump; keyboard; screen capture.*

screen flicker: The phenomenon whereby a display screen appears to flicker. Screen flicker results from a variety of factors, the most important of which is the monitor's *refresh rate,* the speed with which the screen is redrawn. If the refresh rate is too slow, the screen will appear to glimmer. Another factor that affects screen flicker is the persistence of the screen phosphors. Low-persistence phosphors fade more quickly than high-persistence monitors, making screen flicker more likely. Screen flicker can also be affected by lighting. Finally, screen flicker is a subjective perception that affects people differently. Some people perceive screen flicker where others do not.

➯ See also *interlacing; monitor; refresh.*

screen saver: A small program that helps prevent *ghosting,* the permanent etching of a pattern on a display screen. Ghosting can occur if the same pattern is displayed on a display screen for a long period of time and occurs more often with monochrome monitors than with color monitors.

Screen savers come in two varieties: *screen*

blankers and *screen animators*. Screen blankers work by blacking out the screen or at least dimming it. Screen animators display a constantly shifting pattern of animated objects so that there is no time for any one pattern to burn itself into the screen.

Both types of screen saver can be activated manually by a command or automatically when the program determines that the same image has been on the screen for a specified duration. Most portable computers come with a built-in screen dimmer, although the purpose of this utility is more to conserve energy than to save the screen.

➡ See also *display screen; monitor.*

script: Another term for *macro* or *batch file,* a script is a list of commands that can be executed without user interaction. A *script language* is a simple programming language with which you can write scripts.

Apple Computer uses the term *script* to refer to programs written in its HyperCard language.

➡ See also *batch file; HyperCard software; macro.*

scroll: To view consecutive lines of data on the display screen. The term *scroll* means that once the screen is full, each new line appears at the edge of the screen and all other lines move over one position. For example, when you scroll down, each new line appears at the bottom of the screen and all the other lines move up one row, so that the top line disappears.

The term *vertical scrolling* refers to the ability to scroll up or down. *Horizontal scrolling* means that the image moves sideways.

The display should move smoothly, as if it were a piece of paper being moved up, down, or sideways. In practice, however, scrolling is not always so smooth.

The scrolling method of viewing documents does not recognize page boundaries. One advantage to scrolling, therefore, is that you can look at the end of one page and the beginning of the next page at the same time.

Another method of viewing data is called *paging*, whereby an entire page is displayed at once. Each subsequent page replaces the previous page on the screen.

➠ See also *page*.

scroll bar: A bar that appears on the side of a window to indicate which part of a list or document is currently in the window's frame. The scroll bar makes it easy to tell at a glance whether you are at the beginning, middle, or end of a file.

Typically, a scroll bar has arrows at either side, a gray or colored area in the middle, and an indicator box that moves from one side to the other to reflect your position in the document. By pointing at the gray area and clicking the mouse button, you can jump to the corresponding point in the list or document. For example, if you click on the top portion of the gray area, the top portion of the list appears in the window; if you click on the middle of the gray area, you move to the middle of the list. By clicking on the arrows, you can move forward or backward one page frame. You can also drag the indicator box to any point in the scroll bar to scroll more quickly.

Many windowing systems support both horizontal and vertical scroll bars, as shown in Figure 62.

➠ See also *click; drag; graphical user interface; window.*

SCSI: Abbreviation of *small computer systems interface*. Pronounced *scuzzy*, SCSI is a parallel interface standard used by Apple Macintosh computers, some IBM PC compatibles, and many UNIX systems for attaching peripheral devices to computers. All Apple Macintosh computers starting with the Macintosh Plus come with a SCSI port for attach-

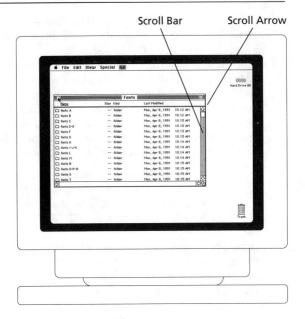

Figure 62
Scroll Bar

ing devices such as disk drives and printers. SCSI interfaces provide for faster data transmission rates (up to 32 megabits per second) than standard serial and parallel ports. In addition, you can attach up to seven devices to a single SCSI port, so that SCSI is really an I/O bus rather than simply an interface.

Although SCSI is an ANSI standard, there are many variations of it, so two SCSI interfaces may be incompatible. For example, SCSI supports several types of connectors.

Older IBM PCs and compatibles adhere to different interface standards—*ST-506*, *IDE*, and *ESDI* for tape drives, and *Centronics* for printers. You can, however, attach SCSI devices to an IBM PC or compatible by inserting a SCSI board in one of the expansion slots. Most high-end new PCs come with

SCSI built in. Note, however, that the lack of a single SCSI standard means that some devices may not work with some SCSI boards.

A new standard, called *SCSI-2*, provides a wider data bus (16 or 32 bits) than the original SCSI specification (8 bits). It is designed for use with the new bus architectures such as *MCA* and *EISA*, and seems destined to become that standard I/O bus for personal computers and workstations. SCSI-2 can support data rates as fast as 40MB per second.

➡ See also *ANSI; Macintosh computer; bus; Centronics parallel interface; connector; EISA; ESDI; expansion slot; IDE interface; interface; MCA; peripheral device; port; ST-506 interface.*

search and replace: A feature supported by most word processors that lets you replace a character string (a series of characters) with another string wherever the first string appears in the document. Most word processors have two search and replace modes. In the first mode, the word processor automatically makes all the replacements in the file. In the second mode, the word processor requires you to approve each replacement. This is safer because you may not want to make the change everywhere.

➡ See also *character string; word processing.*

secondary storage: Same as *mass storage.*

sector: The smallest unit that can be accessed on a disk. When you format a disk, the operating system divides it into tracks and sectors (Figure 63). The tracks are concentric circles around the disk and the sectors are segments within each circle. For example, a formatted disk might have 40 tracks, with each track divided into 10 sectors. The operating system and disk drive keep tabs on where information is stored on the disk by noting its track and sector number (see Figure 34 at *interleaving*).

Generally, every track has the same number of

Sector   Track   Zoned-bit Recording

Figure 63
Disk Sectors

sectors, but some high-capacity hard disk drives use a technique called *zoned-bit recording* in which tracks on the outside of the disk contain more sectors than those on the inside.

A sector that cannot be used due to a physical flaw on the disk is called a *bad sector*.

➠ See also *bad sector; disk; format; track.*

security: Refers to techniques for ensuring that data stored in a computer cannot be read or compromised. Most security measures involve data encryption and passwords. Data encryption is the translation of data into a form that is unintelligible without a deciphering mechanism. A password is a secret word or phrase that gives a user access to a particular program or system.

➠ See also *encryption; password.*

seek time: Refers to the time a program or device takes to locate a particular piece of data. For disk drives, the terms *seek time* and *access time* are often used interchangeably.

➠ See also *access time; disk drive.*

segment: In virtual memory systems, a segment is a variable-sized portion of data that is swapped in

425

and out of main memory. Contrast with *page,* which is a fixed-sized portion of data.

➡ See also *main memory; page; swap; virtual memory.*

select: In graphical user interfaces, you usually need to select an object—an icon, file, folder, and so on— before you can do anything with it. To select an object, you move the pointer to the object and click a mouse button.

➡ See also *click; graphical user interface; icon; pointer.*

semantics: In linguistics, semantics is the study of meanings. In computer science, the term is frequently used to differentiate the meaning of an instruction from its format. The format, which covers the spelling of language components and the rules controlling how components are combined, is called the language's *syntax.* For example, if you misspell a command, it is a syntax error. If, on the other hand, you enter a legal command that does not make any sense in the current context, it is a semantic error.

➡ See also *programming language, syntax.*

semiconductor: A material that is neither a good conductor of electricity (like copper) nor a good insulator (like rubber). The most common semiconductor material is silicon. Computer chips, both for CPU and memory, are composed of semiconductor materials.

Semiconductors make it possible to miniaturize electronic components. Not only does miniaturization mean that the components take up less space, it also means that they are faster and require less energy.

➡ See also *chip.*

sequential access: Refers to reading or writing data records in sequential order; that is, one record after the other. To read record 10, for example, you would first need to read records 1 through 9. This differs from *random access,* in which you can read and write records in any order (see Figure 59 at *random access*).

Some programming languages and operating systems distinguish between sequential-access data files and random-access data files, allowing you to choose between the two types. Sequential-access files are faster if you always access records in the same order. Random-access files are faster if you need to read or write records in a random order.

Devices can also be classified as sequential access or random access. For example, a tape drive is a sequential-access device because to get to point *q* on the tape, the drive needs to pass through points *a* through *p*. A disk drive, on the other hand, is a random-access device because the drive can access any point on the disk without passing through all intervening points.

➡ See also *random access.*

serial: Refers to transmitting data one bit at a time. The opposite of serial is *parallel,* in which several bits are transmitted concurrently.

➡ See also *communications; modem; mouse; parallel; port; RS-232C; serial port.*

serial interface: Same as *serial port.*

serial mouse: A mouse that connects to a computer via a serial port. The other type of mouse is a *bus mouse,* which attaches to a computer via an expansion board. Serial mice are easier to install, but they require an unused serial port.

➡ See also *mouse; port; serial; serial port.*

serial port: A port, or *interface,* that can be used for serial communication, in which only 1 bit is transmitted at a time. Most serial ports on personal computers conform to the RS-232C or RS-422 standards. A serial port is a general-purpose interface that can be used for almost any type of device, including modems, mice, and printers (although most printers are connected to a parallel port).

➭ See also *communications; interface; parallel port; port; RS-232C; RS-422 and 423.*

serif: A small decorative line added as embellishment to the basic form of a character. Typefaces are often described as being *serif* or *sans serif* (without serifs). The most common serif typeface is Times Roman. A common sans serif typeface is Helvetica (see Figure 73 at *typeface*).

➭ See also *font; sans serif; typeface.*

server: A computer or device on a network that manages network resources. For example, a *file server* is a computer and storage device dedicated to storing files. Any user on the network can store files on the server. A *print server* is a computer that manages one or more printers, and a *network server* is a computer that manages network traffic. A *database server* is a computer system that processes database queries.

Servers are often *dedicated,* meaning that they perform no other tasks besides their server tasks. On multiprocessing operating systems, however, a single computer can execute several programs at once. A server in this case could refer to the program that is managing resources rather than the entire computer.

➭ See also *client/server architecture; dedicated; device; multiprocessing; network.*

service: (1) See *customer support.*
　　　　(2) See *on-line service.*

shadowing: A technique used to increase a computer's speed by using high-speed RAM memory in place of slower ROM memory. On IBM PCs, for example, all code to control hardware devices, such as monitors, is normally executed in a special ROM chip called the *ROM-BIOS*. However, this chip is slower than the general-purpose RAM that comprises main memory. Many manufacturers of IBM PC clones, therefore, copy the BIOS code into RAM when the computer boots.

Although shadowing speeds up the computer, it also takes RAM memory away from programs. Some computers allow the user to decide whether RAM is to be used for shadowing.

➡ See also *boot; IBM PCs; main memory; RAM; ROM.*

shareware: Software distributed on the basis of an honor system. Most shareware is delivered free of charge, but the author usually requests that you pay a small fee if you like the program and use it regularly. By sending the small fee, you become registered with the producer so that you can receive service assistance and updates. You can copy shareware and pass it along to friends and colleagues, but they too are expected to pay a fee if they use the product.

Shareware is inexpensive because it is usually produced by a single programmer and is offered directly to customers. Thus, there are practically no packaging or advertising expenses.

Shareware is available from a number of sources. Many universities distribute shareware, and it is often available through electronic bulletin boards.

Note that shareware differs from public-domain software in that shareware is copyrighted. This means that you cannot sell a shareware product as your own.

➡ See also *bulletin board system; proprietary; public domain software; software piracy; software.*

sheet feeder: Also called *cut-sheet feeder*, a mechanism that feeds separate pieces of paper into a printer. Sheet feeders are built into laser printers and are optional components for dot-matrix printers. Some FAX machines also come with sheet feeders, as do some optical scanners.

➡ See also *dot-matrix printer; FAX machine; laser printer; optical scanner; printer.*

shell: (1) The outermost layer of a program. *Shell* is another term for *user interface.* Operating systems and applications sometimes provide an alternative shell to make interaction with the program easier. For example, if the application is usually command driven, the shell might be a menu-driven system that translates the user's selections into the appropriate commands.

➡ See also *command driven; menu driven; user interface.*

(2) Sometimes called *command shell*, a shell is the command processor interface. The command processor is the program that executes operating system commands. The shell, therefore, is the part of the command processor that accepts commands. After verifying that the commands are valid, the shell sends them to another part of the command processor to be executed.

Many applications allow you to open a shell within the application. This enables you to execute operating system commands without exiting the application. If, for example, you want to rename a file without exiting your word processor, you can open a shell and execute the RENAME command (in DOS).

There are a number of products available for the DOS system that provide an alternate DOS shell. Instead of the bland > command prompt, these shells offer multiple windows and menus from which you can select DOS commands. So-called intelligent shells actually extend the capabilities of DOS. For example, they are able to associate data files with the applications that created them so that you can execute an application simply by selecting a data file. In addition, some shells manage extended and expanded memory. These shells are often called *operating environments* or *control programs*.

UNIX systems offer a choice between several different shells, the most popular being the *C shell*, the *Bourne shell*, and the *Korn shell*. Each offers a somewhat different command language.

➠ See also *command language; command processor; DOS; interface; operating environment; operating system; UNIX.*

shift clicking: Clicking a mouse button while holding the Shift key down. In Microsoft Windows and Macintosh systems, shift clicking enables you to select multiple items. Normally, when you select an item, the system deselects the previously selected item. However, if you shift click an item, the previously selected item(s) remain selected.

➠ See also *click; graphical user interface; Macintosh computer; Microsoft Windows; mouse; select.*

shut down: (1) Same as *log out.*
(2) To turn the power off.

SIG: Acronym for *special interest group*, a group of users interested in a particular subject who discuss the subject via an on-line data service, such as CompuServe or Delphi. SIGs exist for almost every conceivable subject. They are sometimes called *forums*.

➠ See also *bulletin board system; network.*

sign: A symbol that identifies a number as being either positive or negative. A positive sign is $+$; a negative sign is $-$. These two signs are also used to indicate addition and subtraction, respectively.

➡ See also *operators*.

SIMM: Acronym for *single in-line memory module*, a small circuit board that can hold up to 9 dynamic RAM chips. Eight are for data and the ninth is for parity error checking. SIMMs are usually easier to install than individual memory chips.

Unlike memory chips, SIMMs are measured in bytes rather than bits. Common sizes include 256K and 1MB.

➡ See also *chip; dynamic RAM; nanosecond; parity checking*.

single-density disk: A low-density floppy disk. All modern floppies are *double-density* or *high-density* disks, which have greater storage capacities than single-density disks.

➡ See also *floppy disk*.

single in-line memory module: See *SIMM*.

single-sided disk: A floppy disk with only one side prepared for storing data. Single-sided disks have half as much storage capacity as double-sided disks. Most floppies are double-sided.

➡ See also *floppy disk*.

68000: Short for the *Motorola 68000 microprocessor*.

➡ See also *Motorola microprocessors*.

68010: Short for the *Motorola 68010 microprocessor*.

➡ See also *Motorola microprocessors*.

68020: Short for the *Motorola 68020 microprocessor*.

➠ See also *Motorola microprocessors.*

68030: Short for the *Motorola 68030 microprocessor.*

➠ See also *Motorola microprocessors.*

size: To make an object larger or smaller. The term is used most commonly in word-processing applications, in which pages and illustrations can be sized. When you size a page, the word processor automatically adjusts all margins to accord with the new page size.

In graphical user interfaces, you can size windows to make them larger or smaller.

Other terms for *size* are *resize* and *scale.*

➠ See also *graphical user interface; scale; window; word processing.*

slate PC: A class of notebook computers that accept input from an electronic pen rather than from a keyboard. Slate PCs are particularly useful in situations where keyboards are awkward or unnecessary. Typically, slate PCs can decipher clearly written block letters and translate them into their ASCII equivalents. To date, however, they cannot handle script, although the technology of handwriting recognition is progressing rapidly.

➠ See also *ASCII; keyboard; notebook computer.*

slot: An opening in a computer where you can insert printed circuit boards. Slots are often called *expansion slots* because they allow you to expand the capabilities of a computer. The boards you insert in expansion slots are called *expansion boards* or *add-on boards.*

Do not confuse slots with *bays.* Bays are sites within the computer where you can install disk drives.

➠ See also *bay; expansion board; expansion slot; printed circuit board.*

small computer system interface: See *SCSI*.

smart terminal: A terminal that has some processing capabilities, but not as many as an *intelligent terminal*. Smart terminals have built-in logic for performing simple display operations, such as blinking and boldface. In contrast, a *dumb* terminal has no processing capabilities at all.

➡ See also *dumb terminal; intelligent terminal; terminal.*

smoothing: A technique used by some laser printers to make curves look smoother (see Figure 4 at *antialiasing*). Most printers that support smoothing implement it by reducing the dot size of the dots that make up a curved line. In addition, some printers can alter the horizontal alignment of dots to minimize jaggies.

➡ See also *antialiasing; jaggies; laser printer.*

soft: In computer science, *soft* is used to describe things that are not tangible. For example, you cannot touch *software*. It's like music—you can see musical scores and touch CDs and tapes, but the music itself is intangible. Similarly, you can see software instructions (programs), and touch floppy disks on which the programs are stored, but the software itself is intangible.

Soft is also used to describe things that are easily changed or impermanent. In contrast, *hard* is used to describe things that are immutable.

➡ See also *hard; hardware; software.*

soft font: A font that has been downloaded into a printer's memory. Soft fonts can be erased, unlike *resident fonts* (fonts that are built into the printer) or *font cartridges*.

Soft fonts are generated by a font program in the computer. You can control the program to specify the font size and other characteristics. The disadvantages of soft fonts are that they require a lot of disk space and printer memory (from 10K to over 200K for a single font), and it takes time to download the fonts to the printer.

Soft fonts are also called *downloadable fonts*.

➡ See also *download; font; font cartridge; laser printer; resident font*.

soft hyphen: See under *hyphenation*.

soft return: The term *return* refers to moving to the beginning of the next line in a text document. Word processors utilize two types of returns: *hard* and *soft*. In both cases, the return consists of special codes (usually a line feed and carriage return) inserted into the document to cause the display screen, printer, or other output device to advance to the next line.

The difference between the two types of returns is that soft returns are inserted automatically by the word processor as part of its word-wrap capability. Whenever too little room remains on the current line for the next word, the word processor inserts a soft return. The position of soft returns automatically changes, however, if you change the length of a line by adding or deleting words, or if you change the margins.

A hard return, on the other hand, always stays in the same place unless you explicitly delete it. Whenever you press the Return or Enter key, the word processor inserts a hard return. Hard returns are used to create new paragraphs or to align items in a table.

➡ See also *carriage return; hard return; line feed; margins; word processing; word wrap*.

software: Computer instructions or data. Anything that can be stored electronically or displayed on paper is software. The storage devices and display devices are hardware.

The terms *software* and *hardware* are used as both nouns and adjectives. For example, you can say: "The problem lies in the software," meaning that there is a problem with the program or data, not with the computer itself. You can also say: "It's a software problem."

The distinction between software and hardware is sometimes confusing because they are so integrally linked. Clearly, when you purchase a program, you are buying software. But to buy the software, you need to buy the disk (hardware) on which the software is recorded.

Software is often divided into two categories:

systems software: Includes the operating system and all the utilities that enable the computer to function.

applications software: Includes programs that do real work for users—for example, word processors, spreadsheets, and database management systems.

➡ See also *application; data; hardware; program; systems software.*

software piracy: The unauthorized copying of software. Most retail programs are licensed for use at just one computer site or for use by only one user at any time. By buying the software, you become a *licensed user* rather than an owner. You are allowed to make copies of the program for backup purposes, but it is against the law to give copies to friends and colleagues.

Software piracy is all but impossible to stop, although software companies are launching more and more lawsuits against major infractors. Originally, software companies tried to stop software piracy by copy-protecting their software. This strategy failed, however, because it was inconvenient for users and was not 100 percent foolproof.

An entirely different approach to software piracy, called *shareware,* acknowledges the futility of trying to stop people from copying software and instead relies on people's honesty. Shareware publishers encourage users to give copies of programs to friends and colleagues but ask everyone who uses a program regularly to pay the program's author directly.

➡ See also *copy protection; shareware; software.*

source: Many computer commands involve moving data from one place to another. The place from which the data is moved is called the *source*, whereas the place it is moved to is called the *destination* or *target.* If you copy a file from one directory to another, for example, you copy it from the *source directory* to the *destination directory.* The source and destination can be files, directories, or devices (that is, printers or storage devices).

➡ See also *copy; destination.*

source code: Program instructions in their original form. The word *source* differentiates code from various other forms that it can have (for example, *object code* and *executable code*).

Initially, a programmer writes a program in a particular programming language. This form of the program is called the *source program,* or more generically, *source code.* To execute the program, however, the programmer must translate it into machine language, the language that the computer understands. The first step of this translation process is usually performed by a utility called a *compiler* (see Figure 15 at *compile*). The compiler translates the source code into a form called *object code.* Sometimes the object code is the same as machine code; sometimes it needs to be translated into machine language by a utility called an *assembler.*

Source code is the only format that is readable by humans. When you purchase programs, you usually receive them in their machine-language format. This means that you can execute them directly, but cannot read or modify them. Some software manufacturers provide source code, but this is useful only to an experienced programmer.

➡ See also *assembler; code; compiler; language; machine language; object code; program.*

special character: A character that is not a letter, number, symbol, or punctuation mark. Control characters, for example, are special characters.

➡ See also *control character.*

special interest group: See *SIG.*

speech recognition: Same as *voice recognition.*

spell checker: See *spelling checker.*

spelling checker: A program that checks the spelling of words in a text document. Spelling checkers are particularly valuable for catching typos, but they do not help when your misspelling creates another valid word; for example, you type *too* instead of *to.*

Many word processors come with a built-in spelling checker, but you can also purchase standalone utilities. Some of the features that differentiate spelling checkers include the following:

size of dictionary: Probably the single most important characteristic of a spelling checker. The more words in the dictionary, the less likely the spelling checker is to flag correctly spelled words. In addition, a large dictionary means that the spelling checker is more likely to offer the correct substitute for a misspelled word. A large dictionary contains about 100,000 words. Most dictionaries allow you to add words, which is an important feature.

glossary function: Some spelling checkers allow you to define abbreviations for long words or phrases. When you enter the abbreviation, the spelling checker automatically converts it to the full text. Note that you can do the same thing with macros.

statistics: Some spelling checkers give statistics. The most useful statistic is the *word count*; the number of words in a document.

double words: Some spelling checkers flag double words such as *and and*, and then automatically delete the second occurrence of the word.

hyphenation: Some spelling checkers flag words that are incorrectly hyphenated.

speed: This is difficult to judge, but some spelling checkers are much faster than others.

➡ See also *hyphenation; macro; stand-alone; utility; word processing.*

split screen: A two-part division of the display screen. This enables you to view two different documents at the same time. Split screens are a precursor of windows, which allow you to divide a display screen much more creatively. Many applications that do not support windows support split screens.

➡ See also *window.*

spooler: A program that controls spooling—putting jobs on a queue and taking them off one at a time. Most operating systems come with one or more spoolers, such as a print spooler for spooling documents. In addition, some applications include spoolers. Many word processors, for example, include their own print spooler.

A good print spooler should allow you to change the order of documents in the queue and to cancel specific print jobs.

➡ See also *queue; spooling.*

spooling: Acronym for **s**imultaneous **p**eripheral **o**perations **on**-line, *spooling* refers to putting jobs in a buffer, a special area in memory or on a disk where a device can access them when it is ready. Spooling is useful because devices access data at different rates. The buffer provides a waiting station where data can rest while the slower device catches up.

The most common spooling application is *print spooling*. In print spooling, documents are loaded into a buffer (usually an area on a disk), and then the printer pulls them off the buffer at its own rate. Because the documents are in a buffer where they can be accessed by the printer, you can perform other operations on the computer while the printing takes place in the background. Spooling also lets you place a number of print jobs on a queue instead of waiting for each one to finish before specifying the next one.

➡ See also *background; buffer; queue.*

spreadsheet: A table of values arranged in rows and columns. Each value can have a predefined relationship to the other values. If you change one value, therefore, you may need to change other values as well.

Spreadsheet applications (often referred to simply as *spreadsheets*) are computer programs that let you create and manipulate spreadsheets electronically (Figure 64). In a spreadsheet application, each value sits in a cell, and you can define what type of data is in each cell and how different cells depend on one another. The relationships between cells are called *formulas*, and the names of the cells are called *labels*.

Once you have defined the cells and the formulas for linking them together, you can enter your data. You can then modify selected values to see

Figure 64
Spreadsheet Application

how all the other values change accordingly. This enables you to study various what-if scenarios.

A simple example of a useful spreadsheet application is one that calculates mortgage payments for a house. You would define five cells:

1. total cost of the house
2. down payment
3. mortgage rate
4. mortgage term
5. monthly payment

Once you had defined how these cells depend on one another, you could enter numbers and play with various possibilities. For example, keeping all the other values the same, you could see how different mortgage rates would affect your monthly payments.

There are a number of spreadsheet applications on the market, Lotus 1-2-3 and Excel being among the most famous. Some of the more powerful spreadsheet applications support graphics features that enable you to produce charts and graphs from the data.

In addition, some spreadsheets are *multidimensional,* meaning that you can link one spreadsheet to another. A three-dimensional spreadsheet, for example, is like a stack of spreadsheets all connected by formulas. A change made in one spreadsheet automatically affects other spreadsheets. This is sometimes referred to as *dynamic linking*.

➡ See also *application; cell; data; Excel; formula; label; Lotus 1-2-3; three-dimensional spreadsheet*.

SQL: Abbreviation of *structured query language*. Often pronounced *sequel,* SQL is a query language for requesting information from a database. Originally designed by an IBM research center in 1974 and 1975, *SEQUEL* stood for *structured English query language*. SQL was first introduced as a commercial database system in 1979 by Oracle Corporation.

Historically, SQL has been the favorite database management system for minicomputers and mainframes. Increasingly, however, SQL is being supported by PC database systems because it supports *distributed databases* (databases that are spread out over several computer systems). This enables several users on a local-area network to access the same database simultaneously.

Although there are different dialects of SQL, it is nevertheless the closest thing to a standard query language that currently exists. In 1986, ANSI approved a rudimentary version of SQL as the official standard, but most versions of SQL include many extensions to the ANSI standard. ANSI is currently working on a new version of the SQL standard, expected to be published in 1991.

➠ See also *ANSI; database management system; distributed database; query; query language; standards.*

SRAM: Short for *static random-access memory.* Pronounced *ess-ram,* SRAM is a type of memory that is faster and more reliable than the more common DRAM (**d**ynamic **RAM**). The term *static* is derived from the fact that it needs to be refreshed less often than dynamic RAM.

While DRAM supports access times between 50 and 150 nanoseconds, SRAM can give access times as low as 15 nanoseconds. Due to its high speed, SRAM is often used as a memory cache.

➠ See also *access time; cache; dynamic RAM; nanosecond; RAM.*

stack: (1) In programming, a stack is a special type of data structure in which items are removed in the reverse order from that in which they are added, so the most recently added item is the first one removed. This is also called *last-in, first-out (LIFO).*

Adding an item to a stack is called *pushing.* Removing an item from a stack is called *popping.*

➠ See also *data structure; pop; push; queue.*

(2) In Apple Computer's HyperCard software system, a stack is a collection of cards.

➠ See also *HyperCard.*

stand-alone: Refers to a device that is self-contained, one that does not require any other devices to function. For example, a FAX machine is a stand-alone device because it does not require a computer, printer, modem, or other device. A printer, on the other hand, is not a stand-alone device because it requires a computer to feed it data.

➠ See also *FAX machine.*

standard: A definition or format that has been approved by a recognized standards organization or is accepted as a de facto standard by the industry. Standards exist for programming languages, operating systems, data formats, communications protocols, and electrical interfaces. For example, the ASCII codes for characters is one standard for representing data.

From a user's standpoint, standards are extremely important in the computer industry because they allow the combination of products from different manufacturers to create a customized system. Without standards, only hardware and software from the same company could be used together. In addition, standard user interfaces can make it much easier to learn how to use new applications.

Most official computer standards are set by one of the following organizations:

- IEEE (Institute of Electrical and Electronics Engineers)
- ANSI (American National Standards Institute)
- CCITT (Comité Consultatif Internationale Télégraphique et Téléphonique)
- ISO (International Standards Organization)

IEEE sets standards for most types of electrical interfaces. Its most famous standard is probably RS-232C, which defines an interface for serial communication. This is the interface used by most modems, and a number of other devices, including display screens and mice. IEEE is also responsible for designing floating-point data formats.

While IEEE is generally concerned with hardware, ANSI is primarily concerned with software. ANSI has defined standards for a number of programming languages, including C, COBOL, and FORTRAN.

CCITT defines international standards, particularly communications protocols. It has defined a number of standards, including V.22, V.32, and

V.42, that specify protocols for passing data over telephone lines.

In addition to standards approved by organizations, there are also *de facto standards*. These are formats that have become standard simply because a large number of companies have agreed to use them. They have not been formally approved as standards, but they are standards nonetheless.

➡ See also *ANSI; architecture; ASCII; CCITT; compatibility; de facto standard; IEEE; ISO; open architecture; proprietary; RS-232C.*

standard input: The place from which input comes unless you specify a different input device. The standard input device is usually the keyboard.

➡ See also *input.*

standard output: The place where output goes unless you specify a different output device. The standard output device is usually the display screen.

➡ See also *output.*

start bit: In asynchronous communications, every byte of data is preceded by a start bit and followed by a stop bit. The start bit signals the receiver that data is coming.

➡ See also *asynchronous; bit; byte.*

statement: An instruction written in a high-level language. A statement directs the computer to perform a specified action. A single statement in a high-level language can represent several machine-language instructions. Programs consist of statements and *expressions*. An expression is a group of symbols that represent a value.

➡ See also *expression; programming language.*

static RAM: See *SRAM.*

static variable: A variable that retains the same data throughout the execution of a program. In contrast, a *dynamic variable* can have different values during the course of a program.

➡ See also *dynamic variable; variable.*

ST-412 interface: Same as *ST-506 interface.*

ST-506 interface: The standard interface for connecting hard disk drives to IBM PCs and compatibles. Newer standards, such as ESDI and SCSI, support faster data transfer rates. ESDI, for example, has data transfer rates of about twice those of ST-506.

ST-506 is sometimes referred to as *MFM,* which is the most prevalent encoding scheme used on ST-506 disk drives. ST-506 also supports the RLL encoding format.

➡ See also *ESDI; hard disk; IDE interface; interface; MFM; RLL; SCSI; standard.*

stop bit: In asynchronous communications, every byte of data is preceded by a start bit and followed by a stop bit.

➡ See also *asynchronous; bit; byte.*

storage: Memory that exists on media (that is, disks and tapes).

➡ See also *mass storage.*

storage device: A device capable of storing data. Storage devices include disk drives and tape drives.

➡ See also *disk drive; mass storage; tape drive.*

store: To copy data from a CPU to memory, or from memory to a mass storage device.

string: See *character string.*

Structured Query Language: See *SQL.*

style sheet: In word processing and desktop publishing, a style sheet is a file or form that defines the layout of a document. When you fill in a style sheet, you specify such parameters as the page size, margins, and fonts. Style sheets are useful because you can use the same style sheet for many documents. For example, you could define one style sheet for personal letters, another for official letters, and a third for reports.

➡ See also *desktop publishing; font; layout; margins; word processing.*

subdirectory: A directory below another directory. Every directory except the *root directory* is a subdirectory (see Figure 24 at *directory*). On Macintosh computers, subdirectories are called *folders.*

➡ See also *directory; folder; root directory.*

subroutine: Same as *routine.*

subscript: (1) In programming, a subscript is a symbol or number used to identify an element in an array. Usually, the subscript is placed in brackets following the array name. For example, AR[5] identifies element number 5 in an array called AR. If the array is multidimensional, you must specify a subscript for each dimension. For example, MD[5][3][9] identifies an element in a three-dimensional array called MD.

Different programming languages have different rules for specifying subscripts. For example, the BASIC language uses parentheses in place of brackets.

➡ See also *array.*

(2) In word processing, a subscript is a character that appears slightly below the line. Unless you have a graphics display screen, your word processor will not be able to display a subscript. Most word processors, however, enable you to enter a

special subscript code so that the subscript will be printed correctly.

A *superscript* is a character that appears slightly above the line.

➧ See also *superscript; word processing*.

supercomputer: The fastest type of computer. Supercomputers are extremely expensive (the least expensive cost more than $1 million) and are employed for specialized applications that require immense amounts of mathematical calculations. For example, weather forecasting requires a supercomputer. Other uses of supercomputers include animated graphics, fluid dynamic calculations, nuclear energy research, and petroleum exploration.

The chief difference between a supercomputer and a mainframe is that a supercomputer channels all its power into executing a few programs as fast as possible, whereas a mainframe uses its power to execute many programs concurrently.

➧ See also *computer; mainframe*.

SuperDrive: The common name for the *FDHD (floppy disk, high density)* disk drive that comes with certain models of the Apple Macintosh computer. The SuperDrive can read Apple-formatted or DOS-formatted 3½-inch floppy disks. It can read and write to all three Macintosh disk sizes (400K, 800K, and 1.2MB) as well as the two IBM disk sizes (720K and 1.44MB).

➧ See also *FDHD; floppy disk; Macintosh computer*.

superscript: A symbol or character that appears slightly above a line. For example, footnote numbers appearing in text are superscripts. Your word processor may not be able to display a superscript, but most word processors let you enter a special superscript code so that the superscript will be printed correctly.

A symbol or character that appears slightly below a line is called a *subscript*.

➨ See also *subscript; word processing*.

supertwist: A technique for improving LCD display screens by twisting light waves. Supertwist displays are among the most readable display screens used in laptop computers.

A special type of supertwist LCD, known as *dual supertwist*, produces *page-white display* that provides the greatest contrasts between the foreground and background.

➨ See also *background; backlighting; flat-panel display; foreground; laptop computer; LCD; page-white display*.

Super VGA: See *SVGA*.

support: (v) To have a specific functionality. For example, a word processor that *supports* graphics is one that has a graphics component. The word *support,* however, is vague. It could mean that the word processor enables you to create graphics illustrations, that you can insert graphics created by another program, or something entirely different.

As another example, an operating system that supports multiple users is one that enables several users to run programs at the same time.

(n) Short for *customer support,* the assistance that a vendor offers to customers. Support can vary widely, from nothing at all to a phone hotline to house calls.

➨ See also *customer support*.

surge protector: A device that protects a power supply from electrical surges. All computers come with some surge protection built into the power supply, but it is a good idea to purchase a separate device. A more robust form of protection from electrical disturbances is called an **uninterruptible power supply** (UPS).

➡ See also *UPS*.

SVGA: Short for *Super VGA*, a graphics standard designed to offer greater resolution than VGA. There are two types of SVGA: one with a resolution of 800 by 600, giving it about 50 percent more pixels than VGA, and the other with a resolution of 1,024 by 768.

The SVGA standard is being pushed by a consortium of monitor and graphics manufacturers called VESA. SVGA is also called *extended VGA* (usually limited to the 800-by-600 resolution) and *VGA Plus*.

➡ See also *palette; pixel; resolution; VESA; VGA; video standards; XGA*.

swap: (1) To replace pages or segments of data in memory. Swapping is a useful technique that enables a computer to execute programs and manipulate data files larger than main memory. The operating system copies as much data as possible into main memory, and leaves the rest on the disk. When the operating system needs data from the disk, it exchanges a portion of data (called a *page* or *segment*) in main memory with a portion of data on the disk.

DOS does not perform swapping, but OS/2 does. Most operating systems for minicomputers, including UNIX, perform swapping.

Swapping is often called *paging*.

➡ See also *memory; operating system; page; segment; virtual memory*.

(2) In UNIX systems, *swapping* refers to moving entire processes in and out of main memory.

➡ See also *main memory; process; UNIX*.

switch: (1) A small lever or button. The switches on the back of printers and on expansion boards are called *DIP switches*. A switch that has just two positions is called a *toggle switch*.

➠ See also *DIP switch; toggle*.

(2) Another word for *option* or *parameter*—a symbol that you add to a command to modify the command's behavior.

➠ See also *option; parameter*.

synchronous: Occurring at regular intervals. The opposite of *synchronous* is *asynchronous*. Most communication between computers and devices is asynchronous—it can occur at any time and at irregular intervals. Communication within a computer, however, is usually synchronous and is governed by the microprocessor clock. Signals along the bus, for example, can occur only at specific points in the clock cycle (see Figure 6 at *asynchronous*).

➠ See also *asynchronous; bus; clock speed*.

syntax: Refers to the spelling and grammar of a programming language. Computers are inflexible machines that understand what you type only if you type it in the exact form that the computer expects. The expected form is called the syntax.

Each program defines its own syntactical rules that control which words the computer understands, which combinations of words are meaningful, and what punctuation is necessary.

➠ See also *language; semantics*.

sysop: Short for *system operator*, a sysop is an individual who manages a *bulletin board system (BBS)* or *special interest group (SIG)* on a public network.

➡ See also *bulletin board system; network; SIG*.

system: (1) A somewhat vague term that usually refers to a combination of components working together. For example, a *computer system* includes both hardware and software.

(2) Short for *computer system*.

System: On Macintoshes, *System* is short for *System file*, an essential program that runs whenever you start up a Macintosh. The System provides information to all other applications that run on a Macintosh. The System and Finder programs together make up the Macintosh operating system.

➡ See also *Finder; Macintosh; operating system*.

system board: Same as *motherboard*.

system call: The invocation of an operating system routine. Operating systems contain sets of routines for performing various low-level operations. For example, all operating systems have a routine for creating a directory. Usually you execute operating system routines by entering a shell command (MKDIR in DOS). This only works, however, if you are at the shell command level. If you want to execute an operating system routine from a program, you must make a system call.

➡ See also *invoke; operating system; routine; shell*.

system folder: A standard folder on Macintoshes that contains the System and Finder programs.

➡ See also *System; Finder; folder; Macintosh*.

systems analyst: A programmer or consultant who designs and manages the development of business applications. Typically, systems analysts are more involved in design issues than in day-to-day coding. However, *systems analyst* is a somewhat arbitrary title, so different companies define the role differently.

➧ See also *programmer*.

systems software: Refers to the operating system and all utility programs that manage computer resources at a low level. Software is generally divided into systems software and *applications software*. Applications software comprises programs designed for an end user, such as word processors, database systems, and spreadsheet programs. Systems software includes compilers, loaders, linkers, and debuggers (see Figure 5 at *application*).

➧ See also *application; end user; software; utility*.

system unit: The main part of a personal computer. The system unit includes the chassis, microprocessor, main memory, bus, and ports, but does not include the keyboard or display screen.

—— T ——

tab character: A special character that can be inserted into a text document. Tab characters have an ASCII value of 9.

Different programs react to tab characters in different ways. Most word processors, for example, move the cursor or insertion point to the next *tab stop*, and most printers move the print head to the next tab stop as well. Some programs, however, simply ignore tabs.

➧ See also *cursor; insertion point; Tab key; tab stop*.

Tab key: In word processing, the Tab key moves the cursor or insertion point to the next tab stop. Tab stops generally occur at regular intervals, for example, every five spaces. However, most word processors allow you to specify where tab stops are to occur.

Pressing the Tab key on your keyboard does not necessarily enter a tab character. Some word processors respond to the tab key by inserting spaces up to the next tab stop. This is often called a *soft tab*, whereas a real tab character is called a *hard tab*.

Spreadsheet and database management applications usually respond to the Tab key by moving the cursor to the next field or cell.

➡ See also *cell; cursor; field; insertion point; tab character; tab stop.*

table: Refers to data arranged in rows and columns. A *spreadsheet,* for example, is a table. In relational database management systems, all information is stored in the form of tables.

➡ See also *database management system; relational database; spreadsheet.*

tablet: Short for *graphics tablet, digitizing tablet,* or *electronic tablet.*

➡ See also *digitizer.*

tab stop: A stop point for tabbing. In word processing, each line contains a number of tab stops placed at regular intervals (for example, every five spaces). They can be changed, however, as most word processors allow you to set tab stops wherever you want. When you press the Tab key, the cursor or insertion point jumps to the next tab stop, which itself is invisible. Although tab stops do not exist in the text file, the word processor keeps track of them so that it can react correctly to the Tab key.

➡ See also *cursor; insertion point; tab character; Tab key.*

tagged image file format: See *TIFF.*

tape: A magnetically coated strip of plastic on which data can be encoded. Tapes for computers are similar to tapes used to store music. Some personal computers, in fact, enable you to use normal cassette tapes.

Storing data on tapes is considerably cheaper than storing data on disks. They also have large storage capacities, from a few hundred kilobytes to several gigabytes. Accessing data on tapes, however, is much slower than accessing data on disks. Tapes are *sequential-access* media, which means that to get to a particular point on the tape, the tape must go through all the preceding points. In contrast, disks are *random-access* media because a disk drive can access any point at random without passing through intervening points.

Because tapes are so slow, they are generally used only for long-term storage and backup. Data to be used regularly is almost always kept on a disk. Tapes are also used for transporting large amounts of data.

Tapes come in a variety of sizes and formats. The most common are listed in Table 28.

Table 28: Tapes

TYPE	CAPACITY	NOTES
Half-inch	60MB to 400MB	Half-inch tapes come both as 9-track reels and as cartridges. The tapes themselves are relatively cheap, but they require expensive tape drives.

Table 28: *(continued)*

TYPE	CAPACITY	NOTES
Quarter-inch	40MB to 5GB	Quarter-inch cartridges (QIC tapes) are relatively inexpensive and support fast data transfer rates. Quarter-inch minicartridges are even less expensive, but their data capacities are smaller and their transfer rates are slower.
8-mm Helical-scan	1GB to 5GB	8-mm helical-scan cartridges use the same technology as VCR tapes and have the greatest capacity (along with DAT cartridges), but they require relatively expensive tape drives. They also have relatively slow data transfer rates.
4-mm DAT	1.3GB	DAT (Digital Audio Tape) cartridges have the greatest capacity (along with 8-mm helical-scan cartridges), but they require relatively expensive tape drives. They also have relatively slow data transfer rates.

➡ See also *backup; DAT; disk drive; mass storage; QIC; random access; sequential access.*

tape drive: A device, like a tape recorder, that reads data from and writes it onto a tape. Tape drives have data capacities of anywhere from a few hundred kilobytes to several gigabytes. Their transfer speeds also vary considerably. Fast tape drives can transfer as much as 20MB per minute.

The disadvantage of tape drives is that they are *sequential-access* devices, which means that to read any particular block of data, you need to read all the preceding blocks. This makes them much too slow for general-purpose storage operations. However, they are the fastest and most effective media for making backups.

➡ See also *backup; drive; gigabyte; K; megabyte; sequential access; tape.*

target: Synonymous with *destination,* a target is a file or device to which data is moved or copied. Many computer commands involve copying data from one place to another. One says that the computer copies from the source to the target (or destination).

➡ See also *source.*

task: Loosely speaking, a task is any job or operation that a computer performs. More specifically, a task is a programming unit. *Task* is often used as a synonym for *process,* but some operating systems make a distinction between the two.

Another term for *task* is *job.*

➡ See also *job; multitasking; process.*

task switching: Refers to operating systems or operating environments that enable you to switch from one application to another without losing your spot in the first application. Many programs are available (for example, DESQview) that add task switching to DOS systems.

Note that task switching is not the same as *multitasking.* In multitasking, the CPU switches back and forth quickly between programs, giving the appearance that all programs are running simultaneously. In task switching, the CPU does not switch back and forth, but executes only one program at a time. Task switching does allow you to switch smoothly from one program to another.

Task switching is sometimes called *context switching.*

➧ See also *CPU; DESQview; DOS; multitasking; operating environment; operating system.*

tear-off menu: A pop-up menu that you can move around the screen like a window. Regular pop-up windows are attached to the menu selection that caused them to pop up.

➧ See also *menu.*

technical support: See *support.*

telecommunications: Refers to all types of data transmission, from voice to video.

➧ See also *communications.*

telecommuting: A term coined by Jack Nilles in the early 1970s to describe a geographically dispersed office where workers can work at home on a computer and transmit data and documents to a central office via telephone line. One of the major arguments in favor of telecommuting over vehicular commuting is that it does not produce air pollution. In addition, many people are more productive working at home than in an office.

➧ See also *network; telecommunications.*

telecopy: To send a document from one place to another via a FAX machine.

➧ See also *FAX machine.*

Telenet: One of the largest public data networks (PDNs) in the United States. Telenet is owned by U.S. Sprint Communications Corporation. A competing network, called *Tymnet*, is owned by McDonnell Douglas.

➧ See also *network.*

template: (1) A plastic or paper diagram that you can

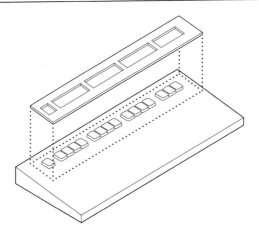

Figure 65
Template

put on your keyboard to indicate the meanings of
different keys for a particular program (Figure 65).

(2) A sheet of plastic with menus and command
boxes drawn on it that you place on top of a digitizing tablet. You can select commands by pressing
the digitizer's pen against a command box or by
positioning the cursor over a box and pressing one
of the cursor keys.

➥ See also *cursor; digitizer.*

(3) In spreadsheet and database applications, a
template is a blank form that shows which fields
exist, their locations, and their length. In spreadsheet applications, for example, a template is a
spreadsheet in which all the cells have been defined
but no data has yet been entered.

(4) DOS uses the term *template* to mean *command buffer.*

➥ See also *command buffer.*

terabyte: 2 to the 40th power (1,099,511,627,776) bytes. This is approximately 1 trillion bytes.

➡ See also *gigabyte; MB.*

terminal: (1) A device that enables you to communicate with a computer. Generally, a terminal is a combination of keyboard and display screen.

Terminals are sometimes divided into three classes based on how much processing power they contain:

> **intelligent terminal:** A stand-alone device that contains main memory and a CPU.

> **smart terminal:** Contains some processing power, but not as much as an intelligent terminal.

> **dumb terminal:** Has no processing capabilities. It relies entirely on the computer's processor.

➡ See also *display screen; dumb terminal; intelligent terminal; keyboard; monitor; smart terminal.*

(2) In networking, a terminal is a PC or workstation connected to a mainframe. The PC or workstation usually runs terminal emulation software that makes the mainframe think the terminal is like any other mainframe terminal.

➡ See also *emulation; network; personal computer; workstation.*

terminal emulation: Refers to making a computer respond like a particular type of terminal. Terminal emulation programs allow you to access a mainframe computer or bulletin board service with a personal computer.

➡ See also *bulletin board service; emulation; mainframe; terminal.*

terminate and stay resident: See *TSR.*

Texas Instruments Graphics Architecture (TIGA):
A high-resolution graphics specification designed by Texas Instruments. Unlike other graphics standards, TIGA does not specify a particular resolution or number of colors. Instead, it defines an interface between software and graphics processors. Programs written for TIGA, therefore, should be able to run on future systems that conform to the TIGA standard, regardless of resolution and color specifics.

Currently, the only graphics standard that conforms to TIGA is TI 34010, which defines a resolution of 1,024 by 768. Two competing standards with the same resolution are 8514/A from IBM and Super VGA from VESA.

➡ See also *8514/A; graphics; resolution; SVGA; TI 34010; VESA; video standards; XGA.*

text: Words, sentences, paragraphs. This book, for example, consists of text. *Text processing* refers to the ability to manipulate words, lines, and pages. The term *text* is useful in distinguishing different types of data. For example, the following are NOT text:

- tables of numbers
- illustrations
- graphs
- anything that is not in a *text format* (that is, not in ASCII)

Note that numbers can be considered text if they are stored in a text format and are not part of a table. By the same token, characters that appear as part of a table are generally not considered to be text.

➡ See also *ASCII.*

text editor: See *editor.*

text file: A file that holds text. The term *text file* is often used as a synonym for *ASCII file*, a file in which characters are represented by their ASCII codes.

➡ See also *ASCII; file; text*.

text flow: Same as *text wrap*.

text mode: A video mode in which a display screen is divided into rows and columns of boxes. Each box can contain one character. Text mode is also called *character mode*.

All video standards for the IBM PC—MDA, CGA, EGA, VGA, and XGA—support a text mode that divides the screen into 25 rows and 80 columns. In addition to text mode, most video adapters (with the exception of MDA) support a *graphics mode*, in which the display screen is divided into an array of *pixels*.

Whereas *character-based* programs run in text mode, all graphics-based programs run in graphics mode.

➡ See also *character based; display screen; graphics based; graphics mode; pixel; video mode; video standards*.

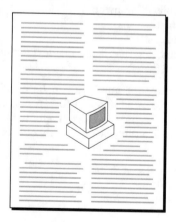

Figure 66
Text Wrap

text wrap: A feature supported by some word processors that enables you to surround a picture or diagram with text (Figure 66).

➡ See also *word processing.*

TFT: Abbreviation of ***thin film transistor***, a type of LCD flat-panel display screen, in which each pixel is controlled by from one to four transistors. The TFT technology provides the best resolution of all the flat-panel techniques, but it is also the most expensive. TFT screens are sometimes called *active-matrix LCDs.*

➡ See also *flat-panel display; LCD; pixel.*

thermal printer: A type of printer that produces images by pushing electrically heated pins against special heat-sensitive paper. Thermal printers are inexpensive and are used in most calculators and FAX machines. They produce low-quality print, and the paper tends to curl and fade after a few weeks.

➡ See also *FAX machine; printer.*

thin film transistor: See *TFT.*

three-dimensional spreadsheet: Spreadsheet programs that allow you to view more than one spreadsheet at a time. The three-dimension feature lets you link two or more spreadsheets together, making it easier to organize spreadsheets (because each one can be smaller) and giving you more perspectives on the data.

➡ See also *spreadsheet.*

3-D spreadsheet: See *three-dimensional spreadsheet.*

386: Short for the *Intel 80386 microprocessor.*

➡ See also *bus; Intel microprocessors; main memory; register; virtual memory.*

386SX: Short for the *Intel 80386SX microprocessor.*

➡ See also *Intel microprocessors.*

throughput: The amount of data transferred from one place to another or processed in a specified amount of time. For example, data transfer rates for disk drives and networks are measured in terms of throughput. Typically, throughputs are measured in *bits per second (bps).* For example, ESDI disk drives can support throughputs of up to 15 Mbps (megabits per second).

➡ See also *disk drive; ESDI; network.*

thumbnail: In desktop publishing systems, a thumbnail is a miniature display of text pages. Thumbnails enable you to see the layout of many pages on the screen at once. Generally, thumbnails are too small to show the actual text, so *greeking* is used to indicate how the text will look (see Figure 32 at *greeking*).

➡ See also *desktop publishing; greeking; layout.*

TIFF: Acronym for *tagged image file format,* the most widely supported file format for storing bit-mapped images on personal computers (both IBM PCs and Macintosh computers). Another popular format is *PCX.*

TIFF graphics can be black-and-white, gray scaled, or color.

➡ See also *bit map; graphics; graphics file formats; gray scaling; PCX.*

TIGA: See *Texas Instruments Graphics Architecture.*

tiled windows: Windows arranged so that they do not overlap each other. Overlapping windows are often called *overlaid* or *cascading* windows (see Figure 52 at *overlaid windows*).

➼ See also *cascading windows; overlaid windows; window.*

time-out: An interrupt signal generated by a program that has waited a certain length of time for some input but has not received it. Many programs perform time-outs so that the program does not sit idle waiting for input that may never come. For example, automatic bank-teller machines perform a time-out if you do not enter your password quickly enough.

➼ See also *interrupt.*

time sharing: Refers to the concurrent use of a computer by more than one user—users *share* the computer's time. *Time sharing* is synonymous with *multi-user.* Amost all mainframes and minicomputers are time-sharing systems, but most personal computers and workstations are not.

➼ See also *mainframe; minicomputer.*

TI 34010: A video standard from Texas Instruments that supports a resolution of 1,024 by 768. TI 34010 conforms to TI's Graphics Architecture (TIGA). Unlike IBM's 8514/A, which supports the same resolution, TI 34010 is noninterlaced.

➼ See also *8514/A; interlacing; TIGA; video standards.*

title bar: A bar on top of a window. The title bar contains the name of the file or application. In many graphical user interfaces, including the Macintosh and Microsoft Windows interfaces, you move (*drag*) a window by selecting the title bar.

➼ See also *drag; window.*

toggle: To switch from one setting to another. The term *toggle* implies that there are only two possible settings and that you are switching from the current setting to the other setting.

A *toggle switch* is a switch that has just two positions. For example, light switches that turn a light on or off are toggle switches. On computer keyboards, the Caps Lock key is a toggle switch because pressing it can have two meanings depending on what the current setting is. If Caps Lock is already on, then pressing the Caps Lock key turns it off. If Caps Lock is off, pressing the Caps Lock key turns it on.

➧ See also *switch, keyboard.*

token: (1) In programming languages, a token is a single element of a programming language. For example, a token could be a keyword, an operator, or a punctuation mark.

➧ See also *keyword; operator; programming language.*

(2) In networking, a token is a special series of bits that travels around a token-ring network. As the token circulates, computers attached to the network can capture it. The token acts like a ticket, enabling its owner to send a message across the network. There is only one token for each network, so there is no possibility that two computers will attempt to transmit messages at the same time (see Figure 67 at *token-ring network*).

➧ See also *token-ring network.*

token-ring network: (1) A type of computer network in which all the computers are arranged (schematically) in a circle (Figure 67). A *token,* which is a special bit pattern, travels around the circle. To send a message, a computer catches the token, attaches a message to it, and then lets it continue to travel around the network.

➧ See also *local-area network; network; token.*

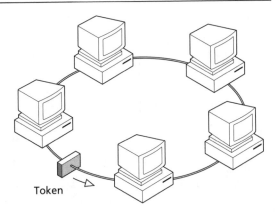

Token

Figure 67
Token-ring Network

(2) When capitalized, *Token Ring* refers to the PC network protocol developed by IBM. The IBM Token-Ring specification has been standardized by the IEEE as the IEEE 802.5 standard.

➠ See also *IEEE; local-area network.*

toner: A special type of ink used by copy machines and laser printers. Toner consists of a dry, powdery substance that is electrically charged so that it adheres to a drum, plate, or piece of paper charged with the opposite polarity.

For most laser printers, the toner comes in a cartridge that you insert into the printer. When the cartridge is empty, you can replace it or have it refilled. Typically, you can print thousands of pages with a single cartridge.

➠ See also *laser printer.*

topology: The shape of a local-area network (LAN). There are three principal topologies used in LANs (Figure 68):

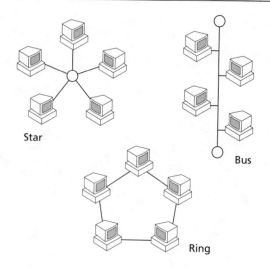

Figure 68
Topologies

bus topology: All devices are connected to a central cable, the *bus* or *backbone*. Bus networks are relatively inexpensive and easy to install. Ethernet systems use a bus topology.

ring topology: All devices are connected to one another in the shape of a closed loop, so that each device is connected directly to two other devices, one on either side of it. Ring topologies are relatively expensive and difficult to install, but they are robust (one failed device does not usually make the entire network fail).

star topology: All devices are connected to a central *hub*. Star networks are relatively easy to install and manage, but bottlenecks can occur because all data must pass through the hub.

➠ See also *Ethernet; local-area network.*

TOPS: Acronym for *transparent operating system*, a

type of local-area network designed by Sun Microsystems that can combine Apple Macintosh computers, IBM PCs, and Sun workstations on the same network. A particular strength of TOPS is that the networking software is *transparent,* meaning that users do not need to adjust to a new operating environment.

TOPS uses the Macintosh computer's built-in AppleTalk protocol. It is a peer-to-peer network, which means that it does not require any computers to be set aside as file servers. Authorized users can access files from any disk drive connected to the network.

➾ See also *AppleTalk; local-area network; peer-to-peer architecture; protocol; server.*

touch screen: A type of display screen that has a touch-sensitive transparent panel covering the screen. Instead of using a pointing device such as a mouse or light pen, you can use your finger to point directly to objects on the screen.

➾ See also *display screen; light pen; mouse; point.*

touch tablet: Same as *digitizer*.

tower configuration: Refers to a computer in which the power supply, motherboard, and mass storage devices are stacked on top of each other in a cabinet (Figure 69). This is in contrast to *desktop configurations,* in which these components are housed in a more compact box.

One advantage of tower configurations is that you can move the noisy devices away from your working area. Also, there are fewer space constraints in tower configurations, making installation of additional storage devices easier.

➾ See also *chassis; configuration; mass storage; motherboard; power supply.*

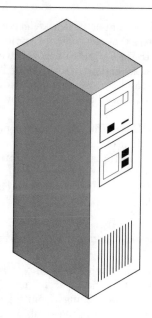

Figure 69
Tower Configuration

TPI: Short for *tracks per inch*. Refers to the density of tracks on a disk. For example, double-density floppies have a TPI of 48, while high-density floppies record 96 TPI.

➡ See also *disk; track*.

track: A circle on a disk where data can be written. When you purchase a new disk, it comes completely blank. Before you can store data on it, you must format it, which involves dividing it into *tracks,* concentric circles around the disk. A typical floppy disk has 40 (single-density) or 80 (double-density) tracks. For hard disks, each *platter* is divided into tracks, and a single track location that cuts through all platters is called a *cylinder*. A typical hard disk has more than 600 cylinders.

Each track is further divided into a number of *sectors*. The operating system and disk drive remember where information is stored by noting its track and sector numbers (see Figure 34 at *interleaving*).

The density of tracks (how close together they are) is measured in terms of tracks per inch (TPI).

➡ See also *cylinder; format; sector*.

trackball: An input device (Figure 70). Essentially, a trackball is a mouse lying on its back. To move the pointer, you rotate the ball with your fingers or the palm of your hand. There are usually one to three buttons next to the ball, which you use just like mouse buttons.

The advantage of trackballs over mice is that the trackball is stationary and does not require much space to use it. In addition, you can place a trackball on any type of surface, including your lap.

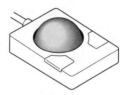

Figure 70
Trackball

➡ See also *input device; mouse; pointer*.

tracks per inch: See *TPI*.

tractor feed: A method of feeding paper through a printer. Tractor-feed printers have two sprocketed wheels on either side of the printer that fit into holes in the paper (Figure 71). As the wheels revolve, the paper is pulled through the printer. Tractor feed is also called *pin feed*.

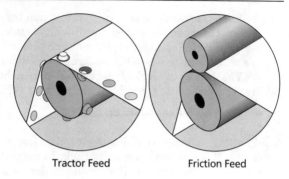

Tractor Feed   Friction Feed

Figure 71
Tractor Feed vs. Friction Feed

The other principal form of feeding paper into a printer is *friction feed,* which utilizes plastic or rubber rollers to squeeze a sheet of paper and pull it through the printer.

Tractor-feed printers require special paper (with holes), whereas friction feed printers can handle most types of cut-sheet paper, including envelopes. Many printers support both types of feeding mechanisms.

➡ See also *friction feed; printer.*

transaction processing: A type of computer processing in which the computer responds immediately to user requests. Each request is considered to be a *transaction.* Automatic teller machines for banks are an example of transaction processing.

The opposite of transaction processing is *batch processing,* in which a batch of requests is stored and then executed all at one time. Transaction processing requires interaction with a user, whereas batch processing can take place without a user being present.

➡ See also *batch processing.*

transparent: Invisible. In computer software, an action is transparent if it takes place without any visible effect. Transparency is usually considered to be a good characteristic of a system because it shields the user from the system's complexity.

transportable: This is the new term for portable computers. The term *transportable* distinguishes heavyweight portables (over 15 pounds) from true lightweight portable computers, called *laptop* or *notebook* computers.

Another term for *transportable* is *luggable*.

➡ See also *laptop computer; notebook computer; portable.*

tree structure: A type of data structure in which each element is attached to one or more elements directly *beneath* it. The connections between elements are called *branches*. Trees are often called *inverted trees* because they are normally drawn with the *root* at the top (Figure 72).

The elements at the very bottom of an inverted tree (that is, those that have no elements below them) are called *leaves*. Inverted trees are the data

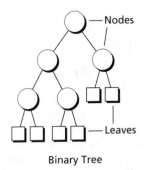

Binary Tree

Figure 72
Tree Structure

structures used to represent hierarchical file structures. In this case, the leaves are files and the other elements above the leaves are directories.

A *binary tree* is a special type of inverted tree in which each element has only two branches below it.

➡ See also *data structure; directory; hierarchical; leaf.*

truncate: To cut off the end of something. Usually the term is used to describe a type of rounding of floating-point numbers. For example, if there are too few spaces for a long floating-point number, a program may truncate the number by lopping off the decimal digits that do not fit. For example, 3.14126 might be truncated to 3.14. Note that truncation always rounds the number down. For example, if the number 1.19999 is truncated to one decimal digit, it becomes 1.1, not 1.2.

➡ See also *floating-point number.*

TSR: Abbreviation of *terminate and stay resident.* Refers to DOS programs that can be *memory resident* (remaining in memory at all times once they are loaded). Calendars, calculators, spell checkers, thesauruses, and notepads are often set up as TSRs so that you can instantly access them from within another program. TSRs are sometimes called *pop-up programs* because they can pop up in applications.

When you install a TSR, you define a special key sequence (usually a control character) that will invoke the TSR program. You can then press this *hot key* from within any application to run the TSR program. Many programs can be installed as a TSR, but TSRs reduce the amount of memory available to other programs. In addition, not all TSRs interact well with each other. You may have difficulties, therefore, if you try to keep too many TSRs in main memory at once.

TSRs are unnecessary with multitasking operating systems such as OS/2 and UNIX.

➡ See also *hot key; memory resident; multitasking; operating system.*

TTL monitor: TTL stands for *transistor-transistor logic* and refers to a special type of digital circuit. More commonly, however, *TTL* is used to designate any type of digital input or device. A TTL monitor, therefore, is a monitor that accepts digital input. TTL monitors are consistent with the MDA, CGA, and EGA graphics standards, but VGA graphics requires analog signals. Some monitors can accept both types of signal.

➡ See also *analog monitor; digital; digital monitor; monitor; VGA; video adapter.*

turnkey system: A computer system that has been customized for a particular application. The term derives from the idea that the end user can just turn a key and the system is ready to go. Turnkey systems include all the hardware and software necessary for the particular application. They are usually developed by *OEMs (original equipment manufacturers)* who buy a computer from another company and then add software and devices themselves.

➡ See also *application; OEM.*

286: Short for the Intel 80286 microprocessor.

➡ See also *Intel microprocessors.*

Tymnet: One of the largest public data networks (PDNs) in the United States. Tymnet is owned by McDonnell Douglas Corporation. A competing network, called *Telenet*, is owned by U.S. Sprint Communications Corporation.

➡ See also *network.*

type: (v) (1) To enter characters by pressing keys on the keyboard.

(2) In DOS, OS/2, and many other operating systems, the TYPE command causes a file to appear on the display screen.

(n) Short for *data type*.

typeface: A design for a set of characters (Figure 73). Popular examples of typefaces include Times Roman, Helvetica, and Courier. The typeface represents one aspect of a *font*. The font also includes such characteristics as size, boldness, and italics.

There are two general categories of typefaces: *serif* and *sans serif*. Sans serif typefaces are composed of simple lines, whereas serif typefaces use small decorative marks to embellish characters. Helvetica is a sans serif type and Times Roman is a serif type.

Serif   Sans Serif

Figure 73
Typefaces

 See also *font*.

U

underflow: Refers to the condition that occurs when a computer attempts to represent a number that is too small. Programs respond to underflow conditions in different ways. Some report an error, while others approximate as best they can and continue processing.

➧ See also *overflow error*.

undo: To return to a previous state by *undoing* the effects of one or more commands. The undo command is a valuable feature supported by many software products. It lets you try unknown commands with less risk, because you can always return to the previous state. Also, if you accidentally press the wrong function key, you can undo your mistake.

Note, however, that not all commands are undoable. For example, if you delete a file, you cannot generally bring it back.

Programs that support the undo feature usually designate a function key as the *Undo key*. Many programs allow you to undo an unlimited number of commands. Each time you press the undo key, the previous command is undone. You can roll back an entire editing session this way. Other programs impose a limit on the number of commands you can undo.

➧ See also *command; function keys*.

undocumented: Refers to features that are not described in the official documentation of a product. This lack of documentation can occur for a variety of reasons, including oversight. More often, though, undocumented features are features that were included because they were useful to the programmers developing the product but were deemed either unnecessary or potentially dangerous to end users. Undocumented features can also include untested features that will be officially supported in a future release of the product.

➧ See also *documentation*.

uninterruptible power supply: See *UPS*.

UNIX: A popular *multi-user, multiprocessing* operating system developed at Bell Labs in the early 1970s. Created by just a handful of programmers, UNIX was designed to be a small, flexible system used exclusively by programmers. Although it has matured considerably over the years, UNIX still betrays its origins by its cryptic command names and its general lack of user-friendliness. This is changing, however, with graphical user interfaces such as MOTIF.

UNIX was one of the first operating systems to be written in a high-level programming language, namely C. This meant that it could run on virtually any computer that had a C compiler. This natural portability combined with its low price made it a popular choice among universities. (It was inexpensive because antitrust regulations prohibited Bell Labs from marketing it as a full-scale product.)

Bell Labs distributed the operating system in its source language form, so anyone who obtained a copy could modify and customize it for his own purposes. By the end of the 1970s, dozens of different versions of UNIX were running at various sites.

After its breakup in 1982, AT&T began to market UNIX in earnest. It also began the long and difficult process of defining a standard version of UNIX. To date, there are two main dialects of UNIX; one produced by AT&T known as *System V* and one developed at Berkeley University and known as *BSD4.x,* x being a number from 1 to 3.

There are at least two competing efforts to produce a standard UNIX. One is being pursued by AT&T in collaboration with Sun Computer, the largest manufacturer of workstations. The other has been undertaken by the Open Systems Foundation (OSF), an organization composed of most of the large computer manufacturers, including IBM, DEC, and Hewlett-Packard. It is still too early to say which standard will find a greater market acceptance or whether the two standards will eventually merge into one.

Due to its portability, flexibility, and power, UNIX has become the leading operating system for workstations. It is less popular in the personal computer market, where it is known as *Xenix* or *AIX* (for IBM PCs) and *A/UX* operating system (for Macintosh computers). Until recently, most personal computers did not have enough power to take advantage of UNIX. Now UNIX must compete with OS/2, which offers many of the same features as UNIX while remaining compatible with DOS.

➡ See also *C; multiprocessing; operating system; OS/2; portable; source code; user-friendly; workstation.*

unpack: To convert a packed file into its original form. A packed file is a file that has been compressed to take up less storage area.

➡ See also *data compression; packed file.*

upload: To transmit data from a computer to a bulletin board service, mainframe, or network. For example, if you use a personal computer to log on to a network and you want to send files across the network, you must upload the files from your PC to the network.

➡ See also *bulletin board service; mainframe; network; download.*

uppercase: Uppercase characters are capital letters; *lowercase characters* are small letters. For example, *box* is in lowercase, while *BOX* is in uppercase. A program that distinguishes between uppercase and lowercase is said to be *case sensitive.*

➡ See also *case sensitive; lowercase.*

UPS: Abbreviation of *uninterruptible power supply*, a power supply that includes a battery to maintain power in the event of a power outage. Typically, a UPS keeps a computer running for several minutes

479

after a power outage, enabling you to save data that is in RAM and shut down the computer gracefully.

There are two basic types of UPS systems: *standby power systems (SPSs)* and *on-line* UPS systems. An SPS monitors the power line and switches to battery power as soon as it detects a problem. The switch to battery, however, can require several milliseconds, during which time the computer is not receiving any power.

An on-line UPS avoids these momentary power lapses by constantly providing power from its own inverter, even when the power line is functioning properly. In general, on-line UPSs are much more expensive than SPSs.

➧ See also *power supply*.

upward compatible: Refers to software that runs not only on the computer for which it was designed, but also on newer and more powerful models. For example, a program designed to run under MS-DOS 3.0 that also runs under MS-DOS 4.0 is upward compatible. Upward compatibility is important because it means you can move to a newer, larger, and more sophisticated computer without converting your data.

In contrast to upward compatibility, *downward (backward) compatible* means that a program runs not only on the computer for which it was designed, but also on smaller and older models. For example, a program designed to run under MS-DOS 4.0, which also works under MS-DOS 3.0, is downward compatible.

➧ See also *compatible; DOS; downward compatible*.

USENET: An enormous wide-area network that links many UNIX computer systems.

➧ See also *wide-area network*.

user: An individual who uses a computer. This includes expert programmers as well as novices. An *end user* is any individual who runs an application program.

➧ See also *application; end user.*

user-friendly: Refers to anything that makes it easier for novices to use a computer. Menu-driven programs, for example, are considered more user-friendly than command-driven systems. Graphical user interfaces, such as the one provided on Apple Macintosh computers, are also considered user-friendly. On-line help systems are another feature of user-friendly programs.

Although the term *user-friendly* represents an important concept, it has been so overused that it has become something of a cliché.

➧ See also *command driven; graphical user interface; help; menu driven.*

user interface: The junction between a user and a computer program. An interface is a set of commands or menus through which a user communicates with a program. A *command-driven* interface is one in which you enter commands. A *menu-driven* interface is one in which you select command choices from various menus displayed on the screen.

The user interface is one of the most important parts of any program because it determines how easily you can make the program do what you want. A powerful program with a poorly designed user interface has little value. Graphical user interfaces that use windows, icons, and pop-up menus are becoming increasingly popular. Many users, however, find that they are more effective with older-style command-driven interfaces.

➧ See also *command driven; graphical user interface; icon; menu; menu driven; window.*

user memory: The portion of main memory available to users. The amount of user memory is usually less than the amount of main memory because a piece of main memory is reserved by the operating system. In addition, many systems use part of main memory for *shadowing,* a technique used to increase execution speed.

On DOS systems, user memory is called *conventional memory*. The maximum amount of conventional memory is 640K. An additional 384K is reserved for system use. All memory above 1MB is either *extended memory* or *expanded memory*.

➡ See also *conventional memory; DOS; expanded memory; extended memory; main memory; operating system; shadowing.*

username: A name used to gain access to a computer system. Usernames, and often passwords, are required in multi-user systems. In most such systems, users can choose their own usernames and passwords.

Usernames are also required to access some bulletin board and on-line services.

➡ see also *bulletin board service; multi-user; on-line service; password.*

utility: A program that performs a very specific task, usually related to managing system resources. Operating systems contain a number of utilities for managing disk drives, printers, and other devices.

Utilities differ from *applications* mostly in terms of size and complexity. For example, word processors, spreadsheet programs, and database applications are considered applications because they are large programs that perform a variety of functions not directly related to managing computer resources.

Utilities are often installed as *memory-resident* programs. On DOS systems, such utilities are called

TSRs. On Apple Macintosh computers, they are called *desk accessories.*

➡ See also *application; desk accessory; memory resident; operating system; TSR.*

───── V ─────

V.22: Pronounced *V-dot-22*, V.22 is short for the *CCITT V.22* communications standard.

➡ See also *CCITT.*

V.22bis: Pronounced *V-dot-22-biss*, V.22 is short for the *CCITT V.22bis* communications standard.

➡ See also *CCITT.*

V.32: Pronounced *V-dot-32*, V.32 is short for the *CCITT V.32* communications standard.

➡ See also *CCITT.*

V.42: Pronounced *V-dot-42*, V.42 is short for the *CCITT V.42* communications standard.

➡ See also *CCITT.*

value-added reseller: See *VAR.*

vaporware: A sarcastic term used to designate software products that have been announced but are not yet publicly available.

VAR: Acronym for *value-added reseller.* Same as *OEM (original equipment manufacturer).*

variable: A symbol or name that stands for a value. For example, in the expression

$$x + y$$

x and *y* are variables. Variables can represent numeric values, characters, character strings, or memory addresses.

Variables play an important role in computer programming because they enable programmers to write flexible programs. Rather than entering data directly into a program, a programmer can use variables to represent the data. Then, when the program is executed, the variables are replaced with real data. This makes it possible for the same program to process different sets of data.

Every variable has a name, called the *variable name,* and a data type. A variable's data type indicates what sort of value the variable represents, as whether it is an integer, a floating-point number, or a character.

The opposite of a *variable* is a *constant.* Constants are values that never change. Because of their inflexibility, constants are used less often than variables in programming.

➡ See also *character string; constant; data; data type; expression.*

variable acceleration: Same as *dynamic acceleration.*

variable length: Refers to anything whose length can vary. For example, in databases, a *variable-length field* is a field that does not have a fixed length. Instead, the field length varies depending on what data is stored in it.

Variable-length fields are useful because they save space. Suppose, for example, that you want to define a NAME field. The length of each NAME field will vary according to the data placed in it. For example, *John Smith* is 10 characters long, but *Thomas Horatio Jefferson* is 24 characters long.

With fixed-length fields, you would need to define each field to be long enough to hold the longest name. This would be a waste of space for records that had short names. With variable-length fields, the NAME field in each record would be just long enough to hold its data.

The opposite of *variable length* is *fixed length*.

➡ See also *database management system; field; fixed length; record.*

variable-length record: A record that has at least one variable-length field. The length of the entire record, therefore, varies according to what data is placed in the variable-length field.

➡ See also *field; fixed length; record; variable length.*

VDT: Short for *video display terminal*. See under *monitor.*

VDT radiation: The radiation emitted by video display terminals. Like televisions, computer monitors emit various types of radiation. Since the late 1980s, there has been a public debate about whether this radiation poses a health problem. To date, however, there is no conclusive evidence to settle the question once and for all.

➡ See also *monitor.*

vector: A one-dimensional array.

➡ See also *array.*

vector graphics: Same as *object-oriented graphics, vector graphics* refers to software and hardware that use geometrical formulas to represent images. The other method for representing graphical images is through bit maps, in which the image is composed of a pattern of dots. This is sometimes called *raster graphics.*

Vector-oriented images are more flexible than bit maps because they can be resized, twisted, and rotated. In addition, images stored as vectors look better on devices (monitors and printers) with higher resolution, whereas bit-mapped images always appear the same regardless of a device's resolution. Another advantage of vector graphics is that representations of images require less memory than bit-mapped images do.

Almost all sophisticated graphics systems, including CADD systems and animation software, use vector graphics. In addition, some printers (PostScript printers, for example) use vector graphics. Fonts represented as vectors are called *vector fonts, scalable fonts, object-oriented fonts,* and *outline fonts*.

Note that most output devices, including dot-matrix printers, laser printers, and display monitors, are raster devices (plotters are the notable exception). This means that all objects, even vector objects, must be translated into bit maps before being output. The difference between vector graphics and raster graphics, therefore, is that vector graphics are not translated into bit maps until the last possible moment, after all sizes and resolutions have been specified. PostScript printers, for example, perform the translation within the printer. In their vector form, therefore, graphics representations can potentially be output on any device, with any resolution, and at any size.

➡ See also *autotracing; bit map; CADD; graphics; graphics file formats; object oriented; page description language; plotter; PostScript; raster graphics; scalable font*.

vertical justification: A feature supported by some word processors in which the system automatically adjusts the vertical space between lines (the *leading*) so that columns and pages have an even bottom margin.

➡ See also *justification; leading; word processing.*

vertical scrolling: See *scroll.*

very large-scale integration: See *VLSI.*

VESA: Short for *video electronics standards association,* a consortium of video adapter and monitor manufacturers led by NEC whose goal is to standardize video protocols. VESA's current projects include *Super VGA,* a video standard that provides greater resolution than VGA.

➡ See also *resolution; standard; SVGA; VGA; video adapter.*

VGA: Abbreviation of *video graphics array,* a graphics display system for IBM PCs. It is built into many computers and is available on others as an add-on board. In text mode, VGA systems provide a resolution of 720 by 400 pixels. In graphics mode, the resolution is either 640 by 480 (with 16 colors) or 320 by 200 (with 256 colors). The total palette of colors is 262,144. This is significantly better than the resolution and colors provided by EGA systems, the predecessor of VGA.

Unlike previous graphics standards for IBM PCs—MDA, CGA, and EGA—VGA uses analog signals rather than digital signals. Consequently, a monitor designed for one of the older standards will not be able to use VGA.

The majority of VGA add-on boards contain just one 15-pin port designed to connect to an analog monitor. Some boards, however, have an additional 9-pin port that enables you to attach them to a digital monitor.

➡ See also *add-on; analog monitor; digital monitor; EGA; graphics; port; resolution; SVGA; video adapter.*

VGA Plus: See under *SVGA.*

video adapter: An expansion board that plugs into a personal computer to give it enhanced display capabilities. The display capabilities of a computer, however, depend on both the logical circuitry (provided in the video adapter) and the display monitor. A monochrome monitor, for example, cannot display colors no matter how powerful the video adapter. Also, the maximum resolution and number of colors is determined by the monitor, not by the video card.

Many different types of video adapters are available for IBM personal computers and compatibles. Most conform to one of the video standards defined by IBM. There is, however, some confusion in the terminology on this point. For example, a *VGA adapter* is a video card that supports the VGA video standard. But frequently, the adapter is spoken of as if *it* were the standard.

Each adapter offers several different video modes. The two basic categories of video modes are *text* and *graphics*. In text mode, a monitor can display only ASCII characters. In graphics mode, a monitor can display any bit-mapped image. Within the text and graphics modes, some monitors also offer a choice of resolutions. At lower resolutions a monitor can display more colors.

Some of the more expensive video adapters contain memory, so that the computer's RAM is not used for storing displays. In addition, some adapters have their own graphics coprocessor for performing graphics calculations. These adapters are often called *graphics adapters*.

➡ See also *bit map; coprocessor; display screen; graphics; graphics mode; gray scaling; monitor; pixel; RAM; resolution; video mode; video standards.*

video display board: Same as *video adapter*.

Video Electronics Standards Association: See *VESA*.

video graphics array: See *VGA*.

video mode: The setting of a video adapter. Most video adapters can run in either *text mode* or *graphics mode*. In text mode, a monitor can display only ASCII characters. In graphics mode, a monitor can display any bit-mapped image. In addition to the text and graphics modes, some video adapters offer different resolution modes.

➠ See also *ASCII; bit map; graphics mode; resolution; text mode; video adapter.*

video standards: There are a variety of video standards that define the resolution and colors for displays (Table 29). Support for a graphics standard is determined both by the monitor and by the video adapter. The monitor must be able to show the resolution and colors defined by the standard, and the video adapter must be capable of transmitting the appropriate signals to the monitor.

Table 29: Popular Video Standards for IBM PCs

Listed here, in order of increasing power and sophistication, are the more popular video standards for IBM PCs.

VIDEO STANDARD	RESOLUTION	MODE	SIMULTANEOUS COLORS
MDA (monochrome display adapter)	720 by 350	text	1
CGA (color graphics adapter)	640 by 200	text	16
	160 by 200	graphics	16
	320 by 200	graphics	4
	640 by 200	graphics	2

Table 29: *(continued)*

VIDEO STANDARD	RESOLU-TION	MODE	SIMULTA-NEOUS COLORS
EGA (enhanced graphics adapter)	640 x 350	text	16
	720 by 350	text	4
	640 by 350	graphics	16
	320 by 200	graphics	16
	640 by 200	graphics	16
	640 by 350	graphics	16
PGA (professional graphics adapter)	640 by 480	graphics	256
Hercules monochrome graphics adapter	720 by 348	graphics	1
MCGA (memory controller gate array)	320 by 400	text	4
	640 by 200	text	2
	640 by 400	graphics	2
	320 by 200	graphics	256
VGA (video graphics array)	720 by 400	text	16
	360 by 400	text	16
	640 by 480	graphics	16
	320 by 200	graphics	256
SVGA	800 by 600	graphics	16
	1,024 by 768	graphics	256
8514/A	1,024 by 768	graphics	256
XGA (extended graphics array)	640 by 480	graphics	65,536
	1,024 by 768	graphics	256
	1,056 by 400	text	16
TI 34010	1,024 by 768	graphics	256

Table 29: *(continued)*

Note that many of these numbers represent only what is specified in the standards. Many suppliers of add-on boards provide
greater resolution and more colors. For more information,
refer to the entries for the specific graphics systems.

➡ See also *CGA; EGA; 8514/A; graphics; Hercules
graphics; MCGA; MDA; monitor; resolution;
SVGA; TI 34010; VGA; video adapter.*

view: In relational database management systems, a
view is a particular way of looking at a database. A
single database can support numerous different
views. Typically, a view arranges the records in
some order and makes only certain fields visible.
Note that different views do not affect the physical
organization of the database.

➡ See also *database; database management system; field; relational database.*

viewer: A utility program that enables you to read a
file in its *native format.* A Lotus 1-2-3 viewer, for
example, enables you to read Lotus 1-2-3 files. Many
shell utilities and file managers include viewers so
that you can display different types of files.

➡ See also *file management; format; shell.*

virtual: Not real. The term *virtual* is popular among
computer scientists and is used in a wide variety of
situations. In general, it is used to distinguish something that is merely conceptual from something
that has physical reality. For example, *virtual memory* refers to an imaginary set of locations, or addresses, where you can store data. It is imaginary in
the sense that the memory area is not the same as
the real physical memory composed of transistors.
The difference is a bit like the difference between
an architect's plans for a house and the actual

house. A computer scientist might call the plans a *virtual house.*

Another analogy is the difference between the brain and the mind. The mind is a *virtual brain.* It exists conceptually, but the actual physical matter is the brain.

The opposite of virtual is *real, absolute,* or *physical.*

➻ See also *virtual memory.*

virtual disk: Same as *RAM disk.*

virtual 8086 mode: A mode supported by Intel 80386 and 80486 microprocessors. In virtual 8086 mode, the microprocessor can divide memory into 1MB sections that can be accessed by programs designed for 8086 machines. This means that a computer equipped with one of these microprocessors can execute several DOS and OS/2 programs at once. In contrast, the 80286 microprocessor can execute programs in either real mode or protected mode, but not both at the same time.

➻ See also *DOS; Intel microprocessors; OS/2; protected mode; real mode.*

virtual memory: An imaginary memory area supported by some operating systems (for example, UNIX but not DOS) in conjunction with the hardware (Figure 74). You can think of virtual memory as an alternate set of memory addresses. Programs use these *virtual addresses* rather than real addresses to store instructions and data. When the program is actually executed, the virtual addresses are converted into real memory addresses.

The purpose of virtual memory is to enlarge the *address space,* the set of addresses a program can utilize. For example, virtual memory might contain twice as many addresses as main memory. A program using all of virtual memory, therefore, would not be able to fit in main memory all at once. Never-

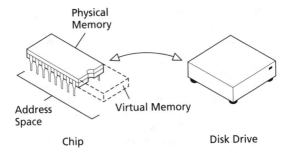

Figure 74
Virtual Memory

theless, the computer could execute such a program by copying into main memory those portions of the program needed at any given point during execution.

To facilitate copying virtual memory into real memory, the operating system divides virtual memory into *pages,* each of which contains a fixed number of addresses. Typically, a page is 256 bytes long, so it contains 256 addresses. Each page is stored on a disk until it is needed. When the page is needed, the operating system copies it from disk to main memory, translating the virtual addresses into real addresses.

The process of translating virtual addresses into real addresses is called *mapping.* The copying of virtual pages from disk to main memory is known as *paging* or *swapping.*

➡ See also *address space; main memory; operating system; page; paging; swap; virtual.*

virus: A piece of code that can replicate itself. All computer viruses are manmade. A simple virus that can make a copy of itself over and over again is relatively easy to produce. Even such a simple virus is dangerous because it will quickly use all available memory and bring the system to a halt. An even more dangerous type of virus is one capable of transmitting itself across networks and bypassing security systems.

Since 1987, when a virus infected ARPANET, a large network used by the Defense Department and many universities, many antivirus programs have become available. These programs periodically check your computer system for the best-known types of viruses. However, if you receive your software from reliable sources and you are not attached to a network, there is little chance that your system will be infected.

Some people distinguish between general viruses and *worms*. A worm is a special type of virus that can replicate itself and use memory, but cannot attach itself to other programs.

➡ See also *ARPANET; hacker; network*.

VLSI: Abbreviation of *very large-scale integration*, the process of placing thousands (or hundreds of thousands) of electronic components on a single chip.

➡ See also *chip; integrated circuit*.

voice mail: Refers to electronic mail systems that support audio. Users can leave spoken messages for one another and listen to the messages by executing the appropriate command in the electronic mail system.

➡ See also *electronic mail*.

voice recognition: The field of computer science that deals with designing computer systems that can recognize spoken words. Note that voice recognition implies only that the computer can take dictation, not that it *understands* what is being said. Comprehending human languages falls under a different field of computer science called *natural-language processing*.

A number of voice recognition systems are available on the market. The most powerful can recognize thousands of words. However, they require an extended training session during which the computer system becomes accustomed to a particular voice and accent. Such systems are said to be *speaker dependent*.

Most systems also require that the speaker speak slowly and distinctly and separate each word with a short pause. These systems are called *discrete speech* systems. It will be many years before voice recognition systems support *continuous speech* so that users can speak naturally.

Because of their limitations and high cost, voice recognition systems are used only in a few specialized situations. For example, such systems are useful in instances when the user is unable to use a keyboard to enter data because his or her hands are occupied or disabled. Instead of typing commands, the user can simply speak into a headset.

➭ See also *artificial intelligence; natural language*.

volatile memory: Memory that loses its contents when the power is turned off. All RAM, for example, is volatile. ROM, on the other hand, is *nonvolatile*.

➭ See also *memory; RAM; ROM*.

volume: A fixed amount of storage on a disk or tape. The term *volume* is often used as a synonym for the storage medium itself, but it is possible for a single disk to contain more than one volume or for a volume to span more than one disk.

➭ See also *disk; mass storage*.

volume label: The name of a volume (that is, the name of a disk or tape). Specifying a volume label makes it easier to keep track of what data is stored on each medium.

➭ See also *disk; label; volume*.

VRAM: Short for *video **RAM***, special-purpose memory used by video adapters. Unlike conventional RAM, VRAM can be accessed by two different devices simultaneously. This enables a monitor to access the VRAM for screen updates at the same time that a graphics processor provides new data. VRAM yields better graphics performance but is more expensive than normal RAM.

➡ See also *graphics; memory; monitor; processor; RAM.*

W

wait state: A time-out period during which a CPU or bus lies idle. Wait states are sometimes required because different components function at different clock speeds. For example, if the CPU is much faster than the memory chips, it may need to sit idle during some clock cycles so that the memory chips can catch up. Likewise, buses sometimes require wait states if expansion boards run slower than the bus.

A *zero wait state* microprocessor is one that runs at the maximum speed without any time-outs to compensate for slow memory. Typically, a zero wait state microprocessor runs 10 to 20 percent faster than the same microprocessor with wait states.

➡ See also *access time; bus; clock speed; CPU; interleaving; microprocessor.*

WAN: See *wide-area network.*

warm boot: Refers to resetting a computer that is already turned on. Resetting it returns the computer to its initial state, and any data or programs in main memory are erased. A warm boot is sometimes necessary when a program encounters an error from which it cannot recover. On IBM PCs, you can perform a warm boot by pressing the Control, Alt, and Delete keys simultaneously.

A *cold boot* refers to turning a computer on from the off position.

➡ See also *boot; cold boot.*

whitespace: Refers to all characters that appear as blanks on a display screen or printer. This includes the space character, the tab character, and sometimes other special characters that do not have a visual form (for example, the bell character and null character).

➡ See also *null character.*

wide-area network (WAN): A computer network that spans a relatively large geographical area. Computers connected to a wide-area network are connected through telephone lines or radio waves. Four of the largest wide-area networks are *ARPANET, BITNET, NSFnet,* and *USENET.*

➡ See also *ARPANET; BITNET; network; NSFnet; USENET.*

widow: In word processing, a widow is the last line of a paragraph that appears as the first line of a page. Widows are considered bad form in page layout, so many word processors allow you to avoid them. When the word processor detects a widow, it can end the page one or more lines early so that at least the last two lines from the paragraph start the next page. Some word processors avoid widows by moving all the lines on the page closer together so that the last line can fit on the same page.

The converse of a widow is an *orphan,* the first line of a paragraph appearing as the last line of a page.

➠ See also *orphan; word processing*.

wild card: A special symbol that stands for one or more characters. Many operating systems support wild cards for identifying files and directories. This enables you to select multiple files with a single specification. For example, in DOS and OS/2, the asterisk (*) is a wild card that stands for any combination of letters. The file specification

m*

therefore, refers to all files that begin with *m*. Similarly, the specification

m*.doc

refers to all files that start with *m* and end with *.doc*.

The UNIX operating system supports an even richer set of wild cards than DOS and OS/2. Many word processors also support wildcards for performing text searches.

➠ See also *filename; operating system; pathname; search*.

Winchester disk drive: Another term for *hard disk drive*. The term *Winchester* comes from a particular type of disk drive developed by IBM. The Winchester technology is used in most hard drives today, so *Winchester* has become synonymous with *hard*.

➠ See also *disk drive; hard disk*.

window: (1) An enclosed, rectangular area on a display screen. Many operating systems and applications have graphical user interfaces that let you divide your display into several windows. Within each window, you can run a different program or display a different file.

Windows are particularly valuable in *multitasking environments*, which allow you to execute several programs at once. By dividing your display into windows, you can see the output from all the programs at the same time. To enter input into a program, you simply click on the desired window to make it the foreground process. Windows are also useful with word processors because they allow you to edit two or more files at once.

Graphical user interfaces, such as the one supported by the Apple Macintosh or MS-Windows, enable you to set the dimensions and position of each window by moving the mouse and clicking appropriate buttons. Windows can be arranged so that they do not overlap (*tiled windows*) or so they do overlap (*overlaid windows*). Overlaid windows (also called *cascading windows*) resemble a stack of pieces of paper lying on top of one another; only the topmost window is displayed in full. You can move a window to the top of the stack by positioning the pointer in the portion of the window that is visible and clicking the mouse buttons. This is known as *popping*. You can expand a window to fill the entire screen by selecting the window's *zoom box*.

In addition to moving windows, changing their size, popping, and zooming them, you can also replace an entire window with an icon (this is sometimes called *minimizing*). An icon is a small picture that represents the program running in the window. By converting a window into an icon, you can free up space on the display screen without erasing the window entirely. It is always possible to reconvert the icon into a window whenever you want.

The Apple Macintosh computer and OS/2-based systems have windows built into their operating systems. You can add windows to DOS systems through a variety of operating environment products such as MS-Windows and DESQview.

➡ See also *DESQview; graphical user interface; icon; Macintosh computer; Microsoft Windows; mouse; multitasking; operating environment; OS/2; pointer; pop; push; zoom.*

(2) A window can also be a logical view of a file. By moving the window, you can view different portions of the file.

Windows: When spelled with a capital W, Windows is short for *Microsoft Windows*.

.WK1 file: Files that end with a .WK1 extension are Lotus 1-2-3 data files. Many programs, including other spreadsheet systems and database management systems, are capable of *importing* .WK1 files. Note that .WK1 is the extension used by all versions of Lotus since Release 2.0. Prior versions of Lotus generate files with a *.WKS* extension.

➡ See also *extension; filename; import; Lotus 1-2-3; spreadsheet.*

.WKS file: Files that end with a .WKS extension are Lotus 1-2-3 data files. Many programs, including other spreadsheet systems and database management systems, are capable of *importing* .WKS files. Note that .WKS is the extension used by all versions of Lotus prior to Release 2.0. Subsequent versions of Lotus generate files with a *.WK1* extension.

➡ See also *extension; filename; import; Lotus 1-2-3; spreadsheet.*

WMF (Windows Metafile Format): The graphics file format used to exchange graphics information between Microsoft Windows applications.

➡ See also *graphics; graphics file formats; Microsoft Windows.*

word: (1) In word processing, a word is any group of characters separated by spaces or punctuation on both sides. (Whether it is a real word or not is unimportant to the word processor.)

(2) In programming, a word is the natural data size of a computer. The size of a word varies from

one computer to another, depending on the CPU. For computers with a 16-bit CPU, a word is 16 bits (2 bytes). On large mainframes, a word can be as long as 64 bits (8 bytes).

Some computers and programming languages distinguish between *shortwords* and *longwords*. A shortword is usually 2 bytes long, while a longword is 4 bytes.

➠ See also *bit; byte; CPU.*

Word: When spelled with a capital *W*, Word refers to *Microsoft Word*, a powerful word processor.

WordPerfect: One of the most popular word processors for IBM PCs and compatibles. WordPerfect also runs on Apple Macintosh computers.

➠ See also *IBM PC; Macintosh computer; word processing.*

word processing: Refers to using a computer to create, edit, and print documents. Of all computer applications, word processing is the most common. To perform word processing, you need a computer, a special program called a *word processor,* and a printer. A word processor enables you to create a document, store it electronically on a disk, display it on a screen, modify it by entering commands and characters from the keyboard, and print it on a printer.

The great advantage of word processing over using a typewriter is that you can make changes without retyping the entire document. If you make a typing mistake, you simply back up the cursor and correct your mistake. If you want to delete a paragraph, you simply remove it, without leaving a trace. It is equally easy to insert a word, sentence, or paragraph in the middle of a document. Word processors also make it easy to move sections of text from one place to another within a document, or between documents. When you have made all the changes you want, you can send the file to a printer to get a hardcopy.

Word processors vary considerably, but all word processors support the following basic features:

insert text: Allows you to insert text anywhere in the document.

delete text: Allows you to erase characters, words, lines, or pages as easily as you can cross them out on paper.

cut and paste: Allows you to remove (*cut*) a section of text from one place in a document and insert (*paste*) it somewhere else.

copy: Allows you to duplicate a section of text instantaneously.

page size and margins: Allows you to define various page sizes and margins. The word processor will automatically readjust the text to fit.

search and replace: Allows you to direct the word processor to search for a particular word or phrase. You can also direct the word processor to replace one group of characters with another everywhere that the first group appears.

word wrap: The word processor will automatically move to the next line when you have filled one line with text, and it will readjust text if you change the margins.

print: Allows you to send a document to a printer to get hardcopy.

Word processors that support only these features (and maybe a few others) are called *text editors* or *executive* word processors. Many word processors, however, support additional features that enable you to manipulate and format documents in more sophisticated ways. These more advanced word processors are sometimes called *full-featured word processors.* Full-featured word processors usually support the following features:

layout: Allows you to specify different margins within a single document and to specify various methods for indenting paragraphs.

font specifications: Allows you to change fonts within a document. For example, you can usually specify bold, italics, and underlining. Some word processors let you change the font size and even the typeface.

spell checker: A utility that allows you to check the spelling of words. It will highlight any words that it does not recognize.

thesaurus: A built-in thesaurus that allows you to search for synonyms without leaving the word processor.

headers, footers, and page numbering: Allows you to specify customized headers and footers that the program will put at the top and bottom of every page. The program automatically keeps track of page numbers so that the correct number appears on each page.

macros: A *macro* is a character or word that represents a series of keystrokes. The keystrokes can represent text or commands. The ability to define macros allows you to save time by replacing common combinations of keystrokes.

merges: Allows you to merge text from one file into another file. This is particularly useful for generating many files that have the same format but different data. Generating mailing labels is the classic example of using merges.

file management: Many word processors contain file management capabilities that allow you to create, delete, move, and search for files.

The following features are supported by more-advanced word processors:

graphics: Allows you to embed illustrations and graphs into a document. Some word processors let you create the illustrations within the word processor; others let you insert an illustration produced by a different program.

windows: Allows you to edit two or more documents at the same time. Each document appears in a separate *window*. This is particularly valuable when working on a large project that consists of several different files.

tables of contents and indexes: Allows you to automatically create a table of contents and index based on special codes that you insert in the document.

One of the most sophisticated types of word processors is called a *WYSIWYG (what you see is what you get)*. In a WYSIWYG, a document appears on the display screen exactly as it will look when printed. The display screen must be capable of displaying different fonts and graphics, however. WYSIWYGs are used for desktop publishing.

➡ See also *copy; cut; delete; desktop publishing; editor; file management; font; footer; graphics; header; hyphenation; insert; justify; layout; macro; margins; merge; paste; spelling checker; window; word wrap; WYSIWYG.*

word processor: A program or computer that enables you to perform word-processing functions.

➡ See also *word processing.*

word wrap: In word processing, *word wrap* refers to a feature that causes the word processor to force all text to fit within the defined margins. When you fill one line with text, the word processor automatically jumps to the next line so that you are not required to keep track of line lengths and to press the Return key after each line. The word processor divides lines in such a way that a word is never split between two lines (unless the word processor supports *hyphenation*).

Word wrap also occurs if you change the margins. In this case, the word processor readjusts all the text so that it fits within the new margins.

Note that word wrap inserts a *soft return* at the end of each line, not a *hard return*. Soft returns are invisible codes that the word processor utilizes. Hard returns are real characters inserted into the document.

Some word processors allow you to turn off the word-wrap feature. This is useful for writing programs and other types of formatted text where you want complete control over new lines.

➡ See also *hard return; hyphenation; margins; soft return; word processing.*

workgroup computing: A *workgroup* is a collection of individuals working together on a task. Workgroup computing occurs when all the individuals have computers connected to a network that allows them to send electronic mail to one another, share data files, and schedule meetings.

Workgroup productivity packages are software packages that include electronic mail, calendar programs, scheduling programs, and other utilities that promote communication between users on a local-area network.

➡ See also *calendar; electronic mail; local-area network; scheduler.*

working directory: The directory in which you are currently working. Pathnames that do not start with the root directory are assumed by the operating system to start from the working directory.

➡ See also *directory; pathname; root directory.*

worksheet: Same as *spreadsheet.*

workstation: (1) A type of computer used for engineering applications (CAD/CAM), desktop publishing, software development, and other types of applications that require a moderate amount of computing power and relatively high quality graphics capabilities.

Workstations generally come with a large, high-resolution graphics screen, at least 2MB of RAM, built-in network support, and a graphical user interface. Most workstations also have a mass storage device such as a disk drive, but a special type of workstation, called a *diskless workstation,* comes without a disk drive. The most common operating system for workstations is UNIX.

In terms of computing power, workstations lie between personal computers and minicomputers, although the line is fuzzy on both ends. High-end personal computers such as the Macintosh II are equivalent to low-end workstations. And high-end workstations are equivalent to minicomputers.

Like personal computers, most workstations are single-user computers. However, workstations are typically linked together to form a local-area network, although they can also be used as stand-alone systems.

The leading manufacturers of workstations are Sun Computer, Hewlett-Packard Corporation, and Digital Electronics Corporation.

➡ See also *CAD/CAM; computer; desktop publishing; diskless workstation; graphics; local-area network; minicomputer; personal computer; stand-alone; UNIX.*

(2) In networking, *workstation* refers to any computer connected to a local-area network. It could be a workstation or a personal computer.

➡ See also *local-area network; network; personal computer.*

WORM (write-once, read-many): Refers to an optical disk technology that allows you to write data onto a disk just once. After that, the data is permanent and can be read any number of times. A single WORM disk can store from 600MB to 1,000MB of data.

Most WORMs use a recording technique known as *ablative pit,* in which a laser burns holes through the outer surface of the disk to mark bits of data. To read the data, the laser shines a low-power beam onto the disk, and a photosensor measures the reflected light to detect the presence or absence of pits.

WORM disks are becoming increasingly popular for archiving data. However, since there is currently no standard format for them, it is impossible to share data between different models.

Two other types of optical disks are *CD-ROMs,* which can only be read, and *erasable optical (EO)* disks, which can be read and written to just like magnetic disks.

➧ See also *CD-ROM; disk; erasable optical disk; mass storage; optical disk.*

write: To copy data from main memory to a storage device, such as a disk.

write once, read many: See *WORM.*

write-protect: To mark a file or disk so that its contents cannot be modified or deleted. When you want to make sure that neither you nor another user can destroy data, you can write-protect it. Many operating systems (though not DOS) include a command to write-protect files. You can also write-protect floppy disks by covering the *write-protect notch* with tape. Microfloppy disks have a small switch that you can set to turn on write-protection (see Figure 29 at *floppy disk*).

Write-protected files and media can only be

read; you cannot write to them, edit them, append data to them, or delete them.

➡ See also *floppy disk; microfloppy disk.*

WYSIWYG: Pronounced *wizzy-wig,* WYSIWYG stands for *what you see is what you get.* A WYSIWYG is a word processor that enables you to see on the display screen exactly what the text will look like when printed. This differs from other word processors, which are incapable of displaying different fonts and graphics on the display screen even though these formatting codes have been inserted into the file. WYSIWYGs are especially popular for desktop publishing.

Note that the WYSIWYGness of an application is relative. Originally, WYSIWYG referred to any word processor that could accurately show line breaks on the display screen. Later WYSIWYGs had to be able to show different font sizes, even if the screen display was limited to one typeface. Now, a word processor must be able to display many different typefaces to be considered a WYSIWYG.

Still, some WYSIWYGs are more WYSIWYG than others. For example, many desktop publishing systems print text using outline fonts (PostScript fonts, for example). Most of these systems, however, use corresponding bit-mapped fonts to display documents on a monitor. What you see on the display screen, therefore, is not exactly what you see when you print out the document. In addition, standard laser printers have a resolution of at least 300 dpi, whereas even the best graphics monitors have resolutions of only 100 dpi. Graphics and text, therefore, always look sharper when printed than they do on the display screen.

➡ See also *bit map; CPU; desktop publishing; font; main memory; monitor; outline font; PostScript; resolution; word processing; workstation.*

X

X.25: See under *CCITT*.

X.400: See under *CCITT*.

X.500: See under *CCITT*.

Xenix: A version of UNIX that runs on IBM-compatible personal computers. Xenix was developed by Microsoft Corporation and is compatible with AT&T's System V definition.

> ➡ See also *operating system; UNIX*.

XGA: Short for *extended graphics array*, a high-resolution graphics standard from IBM. XGA is fully compatible with VGA, but supports higher resolutions and more colors: 25,536 colors in its 640-by-480 mode and 256 colors in its 1,024-by-768 mode. Although the architecture supports both interlaced and noninterlaced modes, the initial version supports only interlaced mode at its higher resolution.

> ➡ See also *8514/A; interlacing; resolution; VGA; video standards*.

Xmodem: Originally developed by Ward Christiansen, Xmodem is one of the most popular file-transfer protocols. Although Xmodem is a relatively simple protocol, it is fairly effective at detecting errors. It works by sending blocks of data and then waiting for acknowledgment of the block's receipt. The waiting slows down the rate of data transmission considerably, but it ensures accurate transmission.

Xmodem can be implemented either in software or in hardware. Many modems, and almost all communications software packages, support Xmodem. However, it is only useful at relatively slow data transmission speeds (less than 4,800 bps).

Enhanced versions of Xmodem that work at higher transmission speeds are known as *Ymodem* and *Zmodem*. Another popular file-transfer protocol is *Kermit*.

➡ See also *communications protocol; communications software; Kermit; MNP; modem; protocol; Ymodem; Zmodem.*

XMS: Stands for *Extended Memory Specification*, a procedure developed jointly by AST Research, Intel, Lotus Development, and Microsoft for using extended memory and DOS's *high memory area*, a 64K block just above 1MB.

➡ See also *expanded memory; extended memory; high memory.*

XOR operator: Known as the *exclusive OR* operator, XOR is a Boolean operator that returns a value of TRUE only if its two operands have different values.

➡ See also *Boolean operator.*

X-Windows: A windowing and graphics system developed at the Massachusetts Institute of Technology. MIT has placed the X-Windows source code in the public domain, making it a particularly attractive system for UNIX vendors. Almost all UNIX graphical interfaces, including Motif and OpenLook, are based on X-Windows.

➡ See also *graphical user interface; public-domain software; UNIX.*

— Y —

Ymodem: An asynchronous communications protocol designed by Chuck Forsberg that extends Xmodem by increasing the transfer block size and by supporting batch file transfers. This enables you to specify a list of files and send them all at one time. With Xmodem, you can send only one file at a time.

➡ See also *batch processing; communications protocol; Xmodem; Zmodem.*

— Z —

zero wait state: Refers to microprocessors that have no *wait states*; that is, they run at their maximum speed without waiting for slower memory chips.

➡ See also *wait state.*

ZIP: A popular data compression format. The actual utilities for compressing and expanding files according to the ZIP format are called *PKZIP* and *PKUNZIP*, respectively. Files that have been compressed with PKZIP end with a *.ZIP* extension.

Another popular data compression format for PCs is *ARC*. For Macintoshes, a popular compression utility is *Stuffit*.

➡ See also *ARC; data compression.*

Zmodem: An asynchronous communications protocol that provides faster data transfer rates and better error detection than Xmodem.

⇒ See also *communications protocol; Xmodem; Ymodem*.

zoom: In graphical user interfaces, *zoom* means to make a window larger or smaller. Typically, there is a *zoom box* in one corner of the window. When you select the zoom box the first time, the system expands the window to fill the entire screen. (This is sometimes called *maximizing*.) When you select it again, the window shrinks to its original size. (This is sometimes called *restoring*.)

⇒ See also *box; maximize; graphical user interface; window*.